DOING EXERCISE PSYCHOLOGY

MARK B. ANDERSEN, PhD
Halmstad University, Sweden

STEPHANIE J. HANRAHAN, PhD
The University of Queensland, Australia

Editors

Human Kinetics

Library of Congress Cataloging-in-Publication Data

Doing exercise psychology / Mark B. Andersen, Stephanie J. Hanrahan, editors.
   p. ; cm.
Includes bibliographical references and index.
ISBN 978-1-4504-3184-2
I. Andersen, Mark B., 1951- editor. II. Hanrahan, Stephanie J., 1961- editor.
[DNLM: 1. Exercise--psychology. 2. Exercise Therapy--psychology. 3. Physical Fitness--psychology. QT 255]
RA781
613.7'1--dc23

2014013589

ISBN: 978-1-4504-3184-2 (print)

Acquisitions Editor: Myles Schrag; **Developmental Editor:** Christine M. Drews; **Associate Managing Editor:** B. Rego; **Copyeditor:** Joy Wotherspoon; **Indexer:** Laurel Plotzke; **Permissions Manager:** Dalene Reeder; **Cover Designer:** Keith Blomberg; **Photographer (cover):** Jason Allen; **Art Manager:** Kelly Hendren; **Associate Art Manager:** Alan L. Wilborn; **Printer:** Sheridan Books

Printed in the United States of America 10 9 8 7 6 5 4 3 2 1

The paper in this book is certified under a sustainable forestry program.

Human Kinetics
Website: www.HumanKinetics.com

United States: Human Kinetics
P.O. Box 5076
Champaign, IL 61825-5076
800-747-4457
e-mail: humank@hkusa.com

Canada: Human Kinetics
475 Devonshire Road Unit 100
Windsor, ON N8Y 2L5
800-465-7301 (in Canada only)
e-mail: info@hkcanada.com

Europe: Human Kinetics
107 Bradford Road
Stanningley
Leeds LS28 6AT, United Kingdom
+44 (0) 113 255 5665
e-mail: hk@hkeurope.com

Australia: Human Kinetics
57A Price Avenue
Lower Mitcham, South Australia 5062
08 8372 0999
e-mail: info@hkaustralia.com

New Zealand: Human Kinetics
P.O. Box 80
Torrens Park, South Australia 5062
0800 222 062
e-mail: info@hknewzealand.com

E5734

For my siblings, Sally Izora Andersen and Brittony Andersen Thomas. I chose my sisters well.

Mark

Let's hear it for sisters! For my sister, Sharon Hanrahan Clough.

Stephanie

Contents

Foreword

Enjoying a long and healthy life is an important goal for most people. We often assume that the way to achieve long life is to make the best use of medical care. Nevertheless, medical care has limited effects on the length of life and on health-related quality of life (Kaplan, 2009). The authors of at least 50 studies have explored this issue. In most cases, only about 10% of the variability in life expectancy is related to medical care (Woolf, 2006). In contrast, it has been estimated that between 40% and 55% of the variability in life expectancy is attributable to behavioral factors such as diet and physical activity (Schroeder, 2007). The Oxford Health Alliance (n.d.) estimates that nearly 60% of deaths in the world today result from four major categories of chronic diseases: diabetes, cardiovascular diseases, chronic lung diseases, and some cancers. Each of these four disease categories is associated with three major risk factors: tobacco consumption, poor diet, and physical inactivity. The epidemic of conditions associated with poor health habits is worldwide. An estimated 80% of deaths from the major chronic diseases occur in developing countries (Oxford Health Alliance, n.d.). Achieving a healthy world requires that we devote more attention to the behaviors associated with early mortality.

In contrast to our desires for healthy societies, most countries are now facing epidemics of obesity. Excess body weight typically results from an imbalance between calories consumed and calories expended. Exercise and other forms of physical activity are typically the most important sources of energy expenditure. Most often, increases in obesity are associated with declines in physical activity, including reduced participation in leisure-time sports and increased television time. Physical activity in schools has also declined dramatically. In many developed countries, more than half of the adult population failed to meet recommended levels of physical activity (Ferdinand, Sen, Rahurkar, Engler, & Menachemi, 2012). Clearly, we need fresh approaches to helping people become more active.

Doing Exercise Psychology is based on two propositions: (a) exercise and physical activity are good for us, and (b) we need help to get the optimum benefits from physical activity and sport. Systematic evidence supports each of these propositions.

Exercise Is Healthy

A mountain of evidence demonstrates that physical inactivity (sedentary living) is a risk factor for nearly all the major chronic diseases. In other words, exercise prevents disease. Further, exercise and other physical activities have the potential to improve health outcomes for a wide range of conditions, including diabetes mellitus, cancer, obesity, hypertension, musculoskeletal diseases, chronic lung diseases, and a range of mental health conditions (Warburton, Nicol, & Bredin, 2006). Exercise reduces the chances of death, not only from specific causes, but from all causes. The benefits for all-cause mortality are often unappreciated. For example, it is common for medical treatments to reduce deaths from specific causes, such as breast cancer, while having little or no impact on extending the life expectancy (Kaplan, 2009). Ultimately, we want to live longer and healthier lives, and exercise is one of the best-known pathways for achieving this objective. Recent meta-analyses suggest that increased levels of physical activity and fitness can reduce premature deaths by 20% to 35% (Haskell et al., 2007; Macera & Powell, 2001). Some studies indicate that the level of risk reduction can be as high as 50% (Myers et al., 2004).

For the most common causes of death, including hypertension, chronic obstructive pulmonary disease, diabetes, smoking, and overweight, there is a systematic relationship between level of physical activity and relative risk of death. Physical fitness is an important contributor to longer life expectancy, but even levels of physical activity below national recommendations are important contributors to survival and wellness (Kaminsky et al., 2013).

Although there are extensive debates about why exercise and other forms of physical activity are related to better long-term health outcomes, we may not need to understand the mechanism to take action. Even if we don't know the exact mechanism, there is ample support for engaging in programs to help people become more active. But, how well are we doing in assuring that physical activity and exercise programs will gain widespread implementation?

Behavior Can Be Changed

The second question raised in *Doing Exercise Psychology* is perhaps the most challenging. How do we assure that physical activity and exercise programs will be used? *Doing Exercise Psychology* offers a wealth of practitioner experiences in helping people remain active. Some of the chapters consider physical activity and exercise for people who are changing habits such as tobacco use and alcohol consumption. Much of the book is devoted to clinical application of exercise for people with a wide range of chronic conditions, including multiple sclerosis, cancer, chronic pain, disability, anxiety, and depression.

Doing Exercise Psychology makes the basic assumption that health habits can be changed. For years, we battled skepticism about our ability to change complex behaviors such as exercise. Further, there were questions about the sustainability of these behavioral changes. In recent years, however, a number of systematic clinical trials have reinforced the value of behavioral interventions. For example, one review for the United States Preventive Services Task Force examined high-quality clinical trials designed to promote a healthy diet, physical activity, or both among people who were at risk for heart disease (Lin, O'Connor, Whitlock, & Bell, 2010). The comprehensive review showed that behavioral counseling consistently resulted in improvements in a wide variety of outcomes. High-intensity lifestyle interventions were able to reduce the incidence of diabetes with three to four years of follow-up. The review documented positive outcomes for a number of important cardiovascular risk factors. Many of the studies included long-term follow-up, in some cases out to 10 years. So, the concern that behavior cannot be changed has been addressed.

We now need to move forward with better dissemination of proven exercise interventions. In contrast to the large amount of medical literature providing guidance for clinicians in treating particular diseases, exercise psychologists are often left with little direction. *Doing Exercise Psychology* addresses this need by combining clinical methods with clinical stories and instruction.

Many of the chapters suggest the need to be attuned to influences outside of the consultation room. To be effective, we need to go beyond the one-on-one clinical relationship and consider the effects of environmental influences. *Doing Exercise Psychology* is primarily about one-on-one treatment in the real world of practice, and that intimate environment is where we start the change process. The effectiveness of such treatments can be undermined when the clients return to social environments where the contingencies of reinforcement for sedentary living, substance use, and unhealthy eating remain in place. Such "enabling" environments (e.g., family life, workplaces) need attention as much as work at the individual level—for example, helping family members become part of the therapy and reinforcing changes initiated at the one-on-one level.

In addition to considering the social environment, effective programs must engage with physical environments. For example, restructuring of communities can have a profound effect on physical activity. Exercise-promoting environments include parks, trails, sidewalks, and other community features that are used for recreation and activity. One recent review showed that 89.2% of 169 published articles found a positive relationship between walkable environments and physical activity (Ferdinand et al., 2012). Psychologists are now working with urban planners, architects, and policy makers to create environments that will enhance exercise and activity (Kerr et al., 2013).

In conclusion, we have substantial evidence that exercise and physical activity has a profound effect on the health of human populations. We know much less about how to motivate people so that they can have continuing and sustained benefits from exercise and physical activity. *Doing Exercise Psychology* offers a wealth of information for practitioners in many exercise-related fields, not just psychologists. I hope it will improve clinical practice and also stimulate continuing thinking about how to address worldwide problems associated with sedentary living, obesity, chronic diseases, and poor diet.

Robert M. Kaplan

References

Ferdinand, A.O., Sen, B., Rahurkar, S., Engler, S., & Menachemi, N. (2012). The relationship between built environments and physical activity: A systematic review. *American Journal of Public Health, 102*(10), e7–e13.

Haskell, W.L., Lee, I.M., Pate, R.R., Powell, K.E., Blair, S.N., Franklin, B.A., . . . Bauman, A. (2007). Physical activity and public health: Updated recommendation for adults from the American College of Sports Medicine and the American Heart Association. *Medicine & Science in Sports & Exercise, 39,* 1423–1434.

Kaminsky, L.A., Arena, R., Beckie, T.M., Brubaker, P.H., Church, T.S., Forman, D.E., . . . Myers, J. (2013). The importance of cardiorespiratory fitness in the United States: The need for a National Registry. A policy statement from the American Heart Association. *Circulation, 127,* 652–662.

Kaplan, R.M. (2009). *Diseases, diagnoses, and dollars.* New York, NY: Copernicus Books.

Kerr, J., Sallis, J.F., Owen, N., De Bourdeaudhuij, I., Cerin, E., Sugiyama, T., . . . Bracy, N. (2013). Advancing science and policy through a coordinated international study of physical activity and built environments: IPEN adult methods. *Journal of Physical Activity and Health, 10,* 581–601.

Lin, J.S., O'Connor, E., Whitlock, E.P., & Bell, T.L. (2010). *Behavioral counseling to promote physical activity and a healthful diet to prevent cardiovascular disease in adults: A systematic review for the U.S. Preventive Services Task Force.* Available from www.uspreventiveservicestaskforce.org/uspstf11/physactivity/physart.htm

Macera, C.A., & Powell, K.E. (2001). Population attributable risk: Implications of physical activity dose. *Medicine & Science in Sports & Exercise, 33*(Suppl. 6), S635–S641.

Myers, J., Kaykha, A., George, S., Abella, J., Zaheer, N., Lear, S., . . . Froelicher, V. (2004). Fitness versus physical activity patterns in predicting mortality in men. *American Journal of Medicine, 117,* 912–918.

Oxford Health Alliance. (n.d.). Retrieved from www.oxha.org/about-us/who-we-are

Schroeder, S.A. (2007). Shattuck Lecture. We can do better: Improving the health of the American people. *New England Journal of Medicine, 357,* 1221–1228.

Warburton, D.E., Nicol, C.W., & Bredin, S.S. (2006). Health benefits of physical activity: The evidence. *Canadian Medical Association Journal, 174,* 801–809.

Woolf, S.H. (2006). The big answer: Rediscovering prevention at a time of crisis in health care. *Harvard Health Policy Review, 7*(2), 5–20.

Preface

There are at least two quasipanaceas in the world: exercise (and physical activity in general) and the experience of a warm, unconditional, and loving relationship. This book is about those two nearly universal remedies for the healing and the flourishing of human bodies, hearts, and minds. The title of this book is in keeping with Mark's first major work, *Doing Sport Psychology,* and it implies that this text is for psychologists working in exercise settings, but that professional group is only one part of a much larger audience that includes anyone working in exercise areas who have short-, medium-, and long-term relationships with people who are engaging (or attempting to engage) in some form of exercise or physical activity—for example, personal trainers, fitness facility directors, strength and conditioning coaches, physical therapists, activity directors for the elderly, sport coaches, corporate health directors, athletic trainers, biomechanists, life coaches, exercise physiologists, and nutritionists. Maybe the title should have been *Doing Exercise **and** Psychology.*

Discussions, examinations, and examples of what actually happens in applied exercise-focused service delivery are relatively rare in the literature. Although many journals (e.g., *Journal of Sport & Exercise Psychology, Psychology of Sport & Exercise, International Journal of Sport & Exercise Psychology*), organizations (e.g., College of Sport & Exercise Psychologists in Australia), and graduate degrees (e.g., master of sport and exercise psychology, master of applied psychology [sport and exercise]) include *exercise psychology* as a primary part of the journal or university program, there is little information about applied practice in this service area. Existing texts and journal articles tend to focus on theories and data related to the effects of exercise on psychological factors or exercise motivation and adherence. Aside from a few examples of using goal setting with want-to-be exercisers, there are no primers, or handbooks, or in-depth accounts on the actual practice of exercise psychology. With this book, we aim to (partially) fill that gap. As long-term members of the sport and exercise psychology community, we have found it difficult to obtain examples of the processes involved in dealing with the psychological components of exercise-related interventions or programs. If we find it difficult, what chance do exercise physiologists, strength and conditioning coaches, and other nonpsychologists who regularly work with people (and all their associated issues) in the area of exercise have?

The authors in this book explore a wide range of models of service, of diverse clients with medical and psychological difficulties, and of changes in unhealthy  behavioral patterns. For example, what happens when psychology practitioners either use exercise as a component of their therapies or help individuals with specific illnesses or issues start taking up exercise to enhance well-being? How can practitioners help clients with impaired movement abilities (e.g., arthritis) embrace physical activity as part of their therapy (or their lives)? What can psychologists do to assist individuals with limited cardiac or pulmonary function deal with fears they may associate with physical activity? What reactions might clients have if their psychologists suggest running as part of therapy? Why do people find dance helpful in decreasing anxiety and improving quality of life? These and other questions are addressed in this book. When we use the term *exercise psychology*, what we really mean is all those psychosocial, intra- and interpersonal, and cultural variables that come into play when people get together and exercise is on the agenda, no matter whether the practitioner is a psychologist, exercise physiologist, physical therapist, coach, or personal trainer.

We (the editors) have modeled this book on Mark's *Doing Sport Psychology* (2000) and *Sport Psychology in Practice* (2005), and we started this project to provide readers with real-world case studies of practitioner–client interactions, relationships, and interventions. In many chapters, we have followed the style of the previous two books. At least half of the chapters contain dialogue between exercise professionals and their clients. Interspersed in the dialogues are commentaries, interpretations, and the practitioners' internal affective and cognitive experiences. We believe that next to actually working with real clients or doing role plays at seminars or in classrooms, this form of presenting case studies is one of the best ways to make service come alive. Nevertheless, as the chapters came rolling in on the different topics, we began to notice that the dialogues in the chapters were becoming somewhat redundant with each other. For example, dialogues centered on motivational interviewing and the transtheoretical model of behavior change (e.g., matching interventions to the client's stage of change) cropped up repeatedly. At some point, we decided that we would open up the book to different forms of storytelling besides dialogue and interpretation. So, in this volume, readers will also find tales told in a narrative style (e.g., Martin and Peterson in chapter 2 from an exercise physiologist's viewpoint), autobiographical accounts (e.g., in Morris, chapter 4), and even conversations stemming from in-depth interviews on a major exercise problem (sport cultural imperatives to overexercise, chapter 15), as well as analyses of what all these approaches to storytelling have to say to practitioners working with individuals within different exercise environments.

In *Doing Exercise Psychology,* many of the examples are not the clean, ideal illustrations that models of practice might suggest; rather, they are sometimes the messy, problematic, warts-and-all experiences that occur in real life. Readers will be able to learn from the authors' mistakes as well as their successes. We are not presenting formulas regarding *how to be* an exercise professional, but instead we are bringing together a variety of viewpoints and experiences in exercise-focused work.

In all the case studies, narrative tales, and interviews, care has been taken to ensure the confidentiality of the clients. In many cases, the client–practitioner stories are based on single individuals, but there are also tales that are aggregates of two or more clients the authors have treated. These accounts, although they are "fictional," are still based in the professionals' experiences, and they represent real-world possibilities.

The Centrality of Relationships

In the two previous books in this series of applied sport and exercise practice (Andersen, 2000; 2005), the development, quality, and maintenance of relationships between practitioners and clients were threads that were woven throughout most of the chapters. In *Doing Exercise Psychology,* those threads have now become a rope, and that rope will feature prominently throughout the book. The more we both study and practice, the more we are convinced from research and real-world encounters in service that relationships, inter-relatedness, and attunement to others are the main vehicles for healthy change in whatever kind of therapy is being done. Or maybe a more apt metaphor is that relationships are the gasoline (petrol) that fuels the vehicle of change. Humans tend to be comfortable with homeostasis; some sort of energy is needed to shake things up. Change is often scary. Perhaps it is that rope (i.e., the relationship) that provides the anchor for people to be able to explore alternatives and consider or plan for change. It is the relationships developed in professional encounters that allow psychologists, physiologists, physiotherapists, and other exercise practitioners to be effective. If the interactions between the clients and the therapists were not potent, then people would have little need for professional help and could rely on self-help books (or Internet sites).

Who Will Read This Book?

The most obvious answer to this question is exercise (and sport) psychology academics, advanced undergraduate and graduate students in this field, and practitioners. There is also a rapidly growing profession in North America, Europe, and Australia of applied clinical exercise physiologists (professionals who work along with physicians and physiotherapists to help people, usually those in rehabilitation, exercise to regain strength and function). We see this book as being useful in advanced undergraduate and graduate courses in this field. There is also the potential for this book to be used in the education of personal trainers and fitness instructors. Another potentially large group of readers is clinical and counseling psychologists and psychotherapists (and graduate students in these fields) who wish to expand their services into the exercise, sport, and health psychology areas. As mentioned at the start of this preface, almost anyone involved in helping people exercise could benefit from studying this book.

Organization of the Book

We have divided the book into four sections. In part I, Beginnings and Basics in Exercise (and Sport) Psychology, we set some foundations for the practice of exercise psychology. Much of the content of the five chapters in this section of the book apply, generally across the board, to nearly all of applied exercise-focused practices, regardless of the model of service or the interventions employed. The authors explore the variety of interpersonal and intrapersonal relationships people have in exercise settings. The chapters in part II, Changing Habits, all involve changing relatively long-standing behavioral patterns (poor nutrition, smoking, alcohol abuse, and repeated failures when attempting weight loss). When exercise is added to the mix, individuals are attempting changes across two (or more) behaviors simultaneously. Part III, Exercise and People With Chronic Conditions, covers working with clients who have medical, physical, and psychological conditions (e.g., multiple sclerosis, cardiac disease, cancer, chronic pain, disabilities, depression) that often make it difficult to engage in exercise. In the final section of the book (part IV, The Dark Side of Exercise), the authors explore the issues of how exercise can become problematic, even seriously damaging, in people's lives

(e.g., in overtraining, as part of the behavioral pathology in some cases of eating disorders).

Reading This Book

Metaphorically, this book is a smörgåsbord, and readers can start with the first chapter that whets their appetites. If we were asked to make a suggestion of where to start, we would say, "Read part I first, and then dive in anywhere you want." But that is only a suggestion. For professionals who teach exercise psychology in universities and other settings, we would make one more suggestion, and that is to take notes on the case studies, especially in instances where the reader sees something else in the dialogue, narratives, and interviews that the author may have missed, or disagrees with the author on an interpretation or on a plan of action taken. Such notes will probably prove valuable when the chapters are assigned for class discussion or used in workshops. As Shane Murphy said in the afterword in *Doing Sport Psychology*:

> The author[s of the chapters] may propose various interpretations of the encounter, but when the actual words of the athlete and sport psychologist are set down in print, I am free to make up my own mind concerning the nature of what happened during the consultation experience. I had this experience on many occasions while reading these chapters: Yes, I see what the author is saying, but that's not what I think is happening here; or I would have done something quite different in that situation. (p. 275)

We (Mark and Steph) hope that readers of this text will also find all sorts of ways to agree and disagree with author interpretations or processes and to appreciate and take something from the stories the authors have shared. We can't thank them enough for their hard work, and we think that hard work has really paid off well.

PART I

Beginnings and Basics in Exercise (and Sport) Psychology

Here, at the start of the book, the chapters are, in a word, diverse. Part I is a bit of a mash-up, but there is a thread through all this diversity, and that is *relationships*. The chapters cover the wide variety of relationships that one might find in exercise and physical activity settings. There are therapeutic relationships between practitioners and clients, relationships between professionals in elite sport settings, relationships people have to culture and cultural differences, relationships we have to our own health, and relationships people have to their social bodies in physical activities such as dance. Part I is a mixed bag, but it is one with a purpose. To start things off, Joe Mannion and Mark Andersen begin at the beginning with a discussion of mindfulness and the neuroscience of therapeutic relationships not so much as interventions per se, but rather as a transtheoretical stance, or way of being, for exercise psychologists when they sit down with their clients. Joe and Mark show how research into mindfulness and interper-

sonal neurobiology can be translated into almost any therapeutic applied exercise psychology setting. In the second chapter, David Martin and Kirsten Peterson move away from a psychologist's perspective into the area of applied exercise physiology and how, here too, relationships (physiologist–coach) around the exercise and training of athletes can grow, blossom, and then rupture. It is a cautionary tale. In the third chapter in this section Stephanie Hanrahan discusses the multicultural sensitivities exercise practitioners should strive to acquire regardless of which allied health or applied science field one calls home. In chapter 4, Tony Morris presents an autobiographical account of his own struggles with health and exercise that echo the nearly universal tension of knowing what is good to do for one's health but then not engaging in those healthy activities. In the final chapter in this section, Stephanie makes an encore presentation with a discussion of the social and personal benefits of dancing.

CHAPTER 1

Mindfulness, Therapeutic Relationships, and Neuroscience in Applied Exercise Psychology

Joe Mannion and Mark B. Andersen

As an editor of this book, and the two other books in this series, I (Mark) thought it would be good to start out just like I did in *Doing Sport Psychology* (2000) with the first chapter being about the beginnings of exercise practitioner–client relationships and what happens in the first intake sessions. As I was writing that chapter for this book, I found myself wobbling on the line between overparaphrasing and self-plagiarism, and a fall on either side of that line would be distinctly uncomfortable. So I tossed out the original first chapter for this book. I think what I wrote about intakes back in 2000 is still good enough for sport psychologists and exercise practitioners, and readers can go back to chapter 1 in that first book for discussion and dialogue about first meetings. Reading *Doing Sport Psychology*, however, is not a prerequisite for understanding the content in this book. In this chapter, there will be lots of attention to the central topics in the title, but unlike many other chapters in this book, there will be no extended case studies with dialogue, only short excerpts from long conversations to illustrate some points briefly.

We (Joe and Mark) wanted to write a chapter on *starting out* in exercise psychology, and we thought that maybe a discussion of where we stand, even before we begin a new relationship with a client, would be a type of prologue, a *before the beginning*. We are both deeply interested in the various theoretical foundations psychologists and other exercise practitioners use to guide their encounters with clients. Models of therapy have a strong influence on what we do with clients, how we construe (and, eventually, help them coconstruct and reconstruct) their narratives, and what interventions we use. Models directly inform the doing of exercise psychology. Over the years, we have come to find our interests moving from the *doing* to the *being*, or how we *are* when we are doing those things we do with clients. And that brings us to the topics of this chapter, beginning with an examination of what mindfulness is and tracing its Nepalese origins through its contemporary Western scientific appeal. We then explore the latest conceptualization of *interpersonal mindfulness*, its correlates in interpersonal neurobiology, and the dynamics of each in therapeutic relationships and positive change, in dialogue with past research and counseling theory. We conclude by illustrating how these various facets may inform practice in two brief exercise psychology vignettes and by considering future directions for the area and the field.

The core business of exercise (and sport) psychologists is helping people change their brains through changes in their behaviors, thoughts, perceptions, and their relationships with themselves and others. We know from the fields of interpersonal neurobiology and the neuroscience of psychotherapy (Cozolino, 2010) that one of the central territories for effecting such changes is the landscape of forming a therapeutic relationship.

One of the best ways to form such relationships is for exercise psychologists (or any other helping professional) to be mindfully present when sitting down with clients (Hicks & Bien, 2008; Siegel, 2010). Before we delve into the neuroscience and interpersonal neurobiology of therapeutic relationships, we need to take one step back to our own intrapersonal mindfulness. This mindfulness is where we start from even before we sit down with a new client.

Diving Into Mindfulness: Definitions, Misconceptions, and Nuances

Definitions of *mindfulness* in Western psychological literature commonly describe it as a purposeful and nonjudgmental type of curiosity and attention directed at one's present-moment thoughts, feelings, and sensations as they rise and fall away in an ongoing stream (Epstein, 1995). Bishop et al. (2004) also described mindful attention as *non-elaborative* in that one does not expound on what one discovers; one continues to observe. Mindful awareness is evenly suspended in the present moment. Practitioners remain open, curious, and accepting rather than suppressing, avoiding, or intellectualizing what they observe (Kabat-Zinn, 1994).

In many Western exercise settings, the concept of mindfulness has already been introduced through a surge in popularity of yoga and yoga-like (e.g., Pilates) fitness classes. In our experiences in such settings, we have occasionally noticed mindfulness being discussed rather synonymously with relaxation. Nowhere, however, do we find relaxation within the aforementioned definitions. Although relaxation frequently results from mindfulness practice, they are not interchangeable constructs. Being mindful means being nonjudgmentally present with whatever is happening within, including anxiety, sadness, and other difficult emotions. As we will see in a later section, many of the qualities of staying nonjudgmentally in the present also have neurobiological underpinnings that may be influenced through the intentional use of mindfulness.

Many of the interventions in the canon of psychological skills training (PST) in sport psychology (e.g., relaxation, self-talk, imagery, concentration) are, at heart, mindful practices. When instructing exercisers and athletes in progressive muscle relaxation, we encourage them to take a passive attitude (e.g., "don't try to relax; just go with whatever happens," "when your mind wanders, just come back to focusing on your muscles") and intentionally and nonjudgmentally pay attention to what is happening when they tense and relax muscles, right now, in the present moment. Sport and exercise psychologists have been involved in mindful practices for decades, and mindfulness is not something new and foreign, but rather, something that sits at the heart of what many practitioners use in PST.

Siegel (2010) has developed a nuanced definition of mindfulness that is central to his neurobiological correlates of *mindful presence*, a noteworthy intrapersonal precursor to interpersonal mindfulness, reflected in our experiences of approaching new possibilities and not closing off, prematurely categorizing, or constraining our perceptions of ourselves, our environments, and others. This avoidance of closing off possibilities is important in intra- as well as interpersonal mindfulness.

Finally, distinctions may also be made between *state* experiences of mindfulness, *trait* (or dispositional) *mindfulness*, and the *mindfulness practices* used to intentionally cultivate state and trait mindfulness (Birrer, Rothlin, & Morgan, 2012). The aforementioned definitions of mindfulness describe qualities of mindful awareness, which may be state- and trait-like. Mindfulness practices used to cultivate these qualities aren't restricted to still, seated meditation. Common practices also include mindful walking meditation, mindful stretching, and mindful eating, as well as labeling, bare attention, and mindfulness education programs. Any activity may be done mindfully.

Mindfulness Then and Now, Here and There

Mindfulness has both a long history and a relatively short period of integration into modern medical and psychological practice. Let's start by turning the clock back to the Indian subcontinent at a time that roughly corresponds to the period of the pre-Socratic philosophers (e.g., Heraclitus, probably the most "Buddhist" of ancient Greek philosophers).

Eastern Origins of Mindfulness

Mindfulness research has begun to proliferate in contemporary Western psychological, medical, educational, and business literature, but the origins of mindfulness come from far away and long ago. Siddhartha Gautama, or Buddha, lived over 2,500 years ago in the area now known as Nepal. He is arguably the original thought leader and proponent of mindful living. Similarities and differences between Western and Eastern conceptualizations of mindfulness in context, process, and content have been noted in clinical psychology literature (Keng, Smoski, & Robins, 2011) and in sport and exercise psychology literature (Andersen & Mannion, 2011).

In Buddhism, mindfulness is part of a broader philosophical system (i.e., one of the Eightfold Paths in the Fourth Noble Truth) aimed at self-awakening and the reduction or elimination of human suffering. The Four Noble Truths make up a Buddhist formulation for understanding and alleviating this suffering. Tomes have been written about them, and the following descriptions should be regarded as basic summaries at best. The First Noble Truth states "life means suffering." On the surface, it may appear to suggest a rather absolute negative perspective on life, especially for Westerners. The English word *suffering*, however, is a translation of the original Pāli word *dukkha*, which may, more accurately than *suffering*, be defined as "pervasive unsatisfactoriness" or "disquietude." According to Buddhist philosophy, this pervasive sense of unsatisfactoriness results from the transience and impermanence of experience. Satisfaction does not last forever. Extended pleasure gives way to monotony. In Buddhism, which advocates a dispassionate observation of reality, transience is not considered negative (or positive). These concepts may seem abstract or foreign to some of us, but concrete examples of impermanence abound in Western exercise settings. The euphoria of a good workout, for example, dissipates within a relatively short amount time. The satisfaction of a healthy meal gives way to hunger. On a broader timescale, our ever-aging bodies may develop wrinkles, increased body fat percentage, and aches and pains.

The Second Noble Truth is commonly translated as "the origin of suffering is desire." Again, we encounter another translation problem. A lack of desire would be apathy, and apathy is not the cure for suffering in Buddhist philosophy. The subtle meaning of the original Pāli word for *desire* more closely resembles *clinging* or *craving*. Clinging to what we have and craving what we do not have represent the intense versions of desire or interest here. One could also say that our relationships with such strong desires are more emblematic of the problem than desire itself, as we become slave-like to this clinging and craving (Epstein, 2005). Further complicating matters is the "me" (or ego) that becomes slave-like to this clinging and craving, but this ego is not inherently real. The ego, or felt sense of "I," is reified, and we, subsequently, become attached to and defensive of it. Exercise settings offer many examples of this clinging, craving, and ego-defense. We may cling to the fitness of our youth, crave to have the body of the person on the machine next to us, or feel threatened as we enter a new gym for the first time. We may be tempted to overdo it or underdo it to protect or bolster our fragile egos.

The Third Noble Truth states that the cessation of *dukkha* is possible. When we release our grip on our attachments and desires for permanence and recognize the nebulosity of our egos and identities, our experiences of unsatisfactoriness and disquietude are transformed. We are liberated from impossible goals and set free to pursue and experience what may be within reach. We can shed the real psychological armor we've built to protect this unreal ego illusion and become present, open, accepting, and compassionate. The Fourth Noble Truth consists of an Eightfold Path, or Middle Way, which is part of the prescription for the cessation of *dukkha* and the beginning of liberation. Mindfulness is one of the paths and the means to accurately perceive these realities.

Westward Expansion: Mindfulness in Clinical and Counseling Psychology

Some of the earliest Western psychology interests in Buddhist philosophy and meditation seem to have started in psychoanalytic circles. Fromm (see Fromm, Suzuki, & Demartino, 1970), for example, participated in a conference on Zen Buddhism and psychoanalysis in Mexico in 1957. Jung (1964) compared and contrasted Zen Buddhist thought and exercises with Western psychology and religion and detailed challenges Westerners may face when attempting to understand Zen Buddhist concepts. Fingarette (1963) examined psychoanalytic thought and Eastern philosophy, including Buddhism.

Additional academic interest in meditation and, more specifically, mindfulness began to emerge in the United States in the 1970s. Harvard cardiologist Benson (1975/2000) published his classic text, *The Relaxation Response*, detailing physiological and psychological health benefits of a form of transcendental meditation, with particular attention to the parasympathetic nervous system. Shortly thereafter, Kabat-Zinn (1982) pioneered interest in mindfulness meditation as an intervention for individuals experiencing a variety of medical and psychological conditions. This system became formally known as *mindfulness-based stress reduction* (MBSR; Kabat-Zinn, 1990). It was followed in the clinical and counseling psychology literature by three other dominant mindfulness-based psychotherapies: (a) dialectical behavior therapy (DBT; Linehan, 1993), (b) acceptance and commitment therapy (ACT; Hayes, Strosahl, & Wilson, 1999), and (c) mindfulness-based cognitive therapy (MBCT; Segal, Williams, & Teasdale, 2002). They form part of a development that has been described as a third wave of behavioral and cognitive therapies (Hayes, 2004). Whereas traditional cognitive behavioral therapy (CBT) practitioners frequently seek to challenge, reframe, or replace the *content* of thoughts, the third wave is characterized by a *process* focus on the relationship between individuals and their thoughts, emotions, and sensations. In this perspective, the problem is not the content as much as it is our tendency to fuse with the content, viewing thoughts and emotions as literal facts and letting them guide our behaviors and choices, rather than accepting them as subjective mental activity that comes and goes (Hayes, Wilson, Gifford, Follette, & Strosahl, 1996).

Additionally, Kristeller and Hallett (1999) developed mindfulness-based eating awareness training (MB-EAT) by integrating principles of MBSR and CBT to help individuals with binge eating disorder. In this treatment protocol, mindfulness is used for, among other purposes, cultivating awareness of thoughts, emotions, and sensations related to hunger, binge eating, and satiety. MB-EAT may have potential relevance in exercise settings because it encourages healthy eating through improved self-regulation, and it may complement other uses of mindfulness in exercise-related endeavors outlined in this chapter.

These psychotherapies, like many other Western psychological, medical, educational, and business conceptualizations and uses of mindfulness, are generally devoid of the broader philosophical and ethical framework that encapsulates mindfulness in Buddhism. Instead, there is a specific focus on practices to cultivate mindfulness for the purposes of alleviating psychopathology, managing pain and other medical conditions, and enhancing other subclinical health and well-being concerns. Additionally, MBSR, MBCT, and MB-EAT are meditation-oriented in their treatment modalities, whereas DBT and ACT are not (see Keng et al., 2011, for a review of approximately 55 studies using these therapies with primarily positive outcomes).

In *Mindfulness* (1990), Langer explored mindfulness in contrast with *mindlessness*, which she defined as a type of automation that is prone to errors, pain, and a predetermined course of life. Langer's focus is nonmeditative and is also explicitly distinguished from the broader context of Buddhist philosophy (e.g., the "self" as an illusion, reincarnation). A noteworthy exception to the recent separation of mindfulness from its Buddhist origins in contemporary clinical psychology literature is Epstein's (1995) work. In *Thoughts Without a Thinker*, Epstein described, among other things, the psychology of Buddhism, its complementary role with psychoanalysis, and psychoanalytic conceptualizations of meditation.

Studies over the past decade have correlated trait (or dispositional) mindfulness with a variety of health outcomes, including many benefits with potential relevance to exercise psychology interventions. Brown and Ryan (2003), for example, found mindfulness to be positively associated with vitality, self-esteem, optimism, competence, sense of autonomy, and life satisfaction. Evans, Baer, and Segerstrom (2009) reported that mindfulness is positively correlated with persistence. Relevant inverse relationships have also been discovered between trait mindfulness and depression (Brown

& Ryan, 2003), reactivity (Raes, Dewulf, Van Heeringen, & Williams, 2009), social anxiety (Dekeyser, Raes, Leijssen, Leysen, & Dewulf, 2008), and experiential avoidance (Baer, Smith, & Allen, 2004). Optimism, persistence, social anxiety, and experiential avoidance are obviously relevant in exercise settings.

Researchers have proposed a multitude of potential mechanisms to account for the direct, moderating, and disaggregated benefits of mindfulness practice and dispositional mindfulness in clinical and counseling psychology literature. In their review, Keng et al. (2011) identified eight such psychological processes, some of which may overlap: (a) increases in mindful awareness, (b) reperceiving (also referred to as decentering, metacognitive awareness, or cognitive defusion), (c) exposure, (d) acceptance, (e) attentional control, (f) memory, (g) values clarification, and (h) behavioral self-regulation.

Additionally, Epstein (1995) has offered a psychoanalytic explanation, drawing upon Winnicott's (1971) object-relations concept of transitional objects. He likened the transformative mechanisms of meditation to the transitional experiences of children learning to tolerate separation anxiety from their parents or caregivers. In these early childhood experiences, transitional objects (e.g., blankets, dolls, stuffed animals) enable children to hold and tolerate their *separateness* and the associated affect until they are able to do so without the objects. Epstein proposed mindfulness meditation similarly creates a transitional space in which individuals may learn to hold and tolerate otherwise intolerable states (e.g., anxiety, self-loathing). In this transitional meditative space, difficult thoughts and feelings "lose their charge and come to be seen as 'just thoughts' or 'just feelings'" (Epstein, 1995, p. 124).

Mindfulness in Sport and Exercise Psychology

The integration of Buddhist philosophy, mindfulness, and sport and exercise appeared in Western popular and philosophical literature decades before it appeared in the sport and exercise psychology literature. We found this absence to be rather unusual given most applied sport psychology texts, for example, include key sections on staying in present time, which is both a component of flow (Csikszentmihalyi, 1990) and a central tenet of mindfulness and Buddhist philosophy. Notable Western popular and philosophical works include *Zen in the Art of Archery* (Herrigel, 1948/1999), *Zen, Yoga, and Sports* (Wertz, 1977), and *Zen in the Martial Arts* (Hyams, 1982).

One anomaly in the sport and exercise psychology literature is the 1985 conference paper in which Kabat-Zinn, Beall, and Rippe examined a systematic mental training program based on mindfulness meditation for collegiate and Olympic rowers. Athletes in the intervention group exceeded their coaches' expectations, and several athletes who medaled reported that mindfulness training helped them perform at their full potential. The next reference doesn't seem to occur until Maddux's (1997) article on Eastern philosophy and health and happiness in sport.

Interest in mindfulness in sport and exercise psychology literature, however, began to germinate and flourish in the 2000s. Traditional CBT-derived psychological skills training (PST) interventions in sport frequently emphasize active attempts to generate intrapersonal characteristics (e.g., positive thoughts, optimal arousal, feelings of confidence) that have been previously correlated with high performance, based on an assumption such changes will lead to improved performance. Correlation, of course, does not imply causation. Gardner and Moore (2004) called into question the efficacy of such interventions, citing equivocal findings in the literature, and reexamined the self-regulatory characteristics of elite performance in light of new discoveries in this third wave of behavioral and cognitive therapies. They suggested that a preoccupation with changing intrapersonal characteristics through, for example, modifications of self-talk, is often task-irrelevant and, thus, disruptive to performance. Alternatively, they proposed a mindfulness-acceptance-commitment (MAC) approach for enhancing sport performance, based on MBCT (Segal et al., 2002) and ACT (Hayes et al., 1999). MAC protocols, for example, encourage athletes to accept—rather than actively change, suppress, or control—cognitions and affect, while attending to task-relevant cues and maintaining behaviors necessary to reach valued goals (see also Gardner & Moore, 2007).

Birrer et al. (2012) expounded upon this work, further considering possible limitations of traditional PST in sports, and they identified eight empirical studies in English on mindfulness in sport (since 2008) that had promising results. They proposed that mindfulness practices and dispositional mindfulness may enhance several psychological skills and the efficacy of PST interventions on performance enhancement. Likewise, Vealey (2007) has suggested a hierarchy of psychological skill categories in which *performance skills* are predicated on *foundational skills* such as self-awareness. Previous clinical psychology literature (e.g., Keng et al., 2011) has also shown dispositional mindfulness to have moderating effects. Birrer et al. then examined how nine mechanisms of mindfulness may affect nine categories of psychological skills in a PST model (Birrer & Morgan, 2010) designed to be sensitive to sport-specific demands.

Interpersonal Mindfulness and Interpersonal Neurobiology

The aforementioned literature and definitions of mindfulness primarily concern *intrapersonal* psychological processes. Additionally, sport psychology researchers have primarily focused on these processes as they relate to potential enhanced performance (see also Gardner, 2009). Recently, researchers and practitioners have turned their attention to *interpersonal* psychological processes (Hicks & Bien, 2008) and neurobiological correlates of mindfulness in the clinical literature (Siegel, 2010) and in clinical sport psychology (Marks, 2008). We (Andersen & Mannion, 2011) have also sought to broaden the performance focus of previous sport and exercise psychology mindfulness literature to include the well-being of the athletes and exercisers in our care. The separation of a performance focus from well-being seems peculiar given that performance and well-being are, in many cases, intimately connected.

In *The Mindful Therapist*, Siegel (2010) has synthesized mindfulness research into practical and sequential elements for practitioners, which integrate the objective (i.e., neurobiological), subjective (i.e., cognitive-affective), and relational bases for harnessing mindfulness' potential for positive outcomes. Based on how we're hardwired to connect with others (from infancy to adulthood) and on attachment theory, the first three core elements, *presence*, *attunement*, and *resonance*, begin with the practitioner's (e.g., exercise psychologist, social worker, medical doctor) intrapersonal mindfulness and examine how it is the foundation for interpersonal mindfulness with clients. The basics of these three qualities are covered in the following sections. In much of the following, discussion of neurobiological correlates of presence, attunement, and resonance have been somewhat simplified. These processes are substantially more complex than represented here. We have pared the information down to basics because a full explanation would take the length of a couple chapters to complete.

Presence

Presence is the starting place for helpful and healing alliances with our clients. Freud (1912/1958) described this stance a century ago, well before the advent of mindfulness approaches in psychotherapy: "It rejects the use of any special expedient (even that of taking notes). It consists simply in not directing one's notice to anything in particular and in maintaining the same 'evenly suspended attention' in the face of all that one hears" (p. 111).

When we are mindful, we are in this receptive, evenly suspended, and present state, as opposed to a protective state. Subjectively, we are open, accepting, nonjudgmental, and curious as we alternately observe our endless streams of thoughts, feelings, sensations, and perceptions and our clients' verbal and nonverbal communications. Neurologically, this receptivity correlates with an approach state of cortical activity (see figure 1.1, e.g., increase in activity in the left and medial prefrontal cortex), moving toward, rather than away from, difficult situations (Siegel, 2010). If we encounter internal or external stimuli we find threatening (e.g., a well-being concern with which we aren't comfortable, a story that triggers memories of our own imperfect pasts), our prefrontal, limbic, and brain-stem processes may coordinate a protective fight-flight-freeze response. Subjectively, we may experience this response as noticeable discomfort in our minds and bodies. In the case of

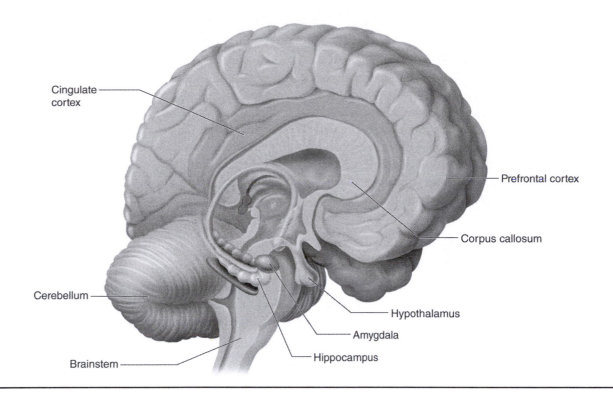

Figure 1.1   The limbic and cortical structures of the brain.

fight or flight, our sympathetic nervous systems (e.g., increased heart rate and muscle tension, shallower breathing) are activated. In a freeze stress response, the dorsal branch of our parasympathetic nervous systems is activated, frequently resulting in a sense of deflation, dissociation, and reduced functioning. The avoidance response may also be subtle (e.g., impatience, boredom, fatigue, inattention) and even outside of our awareness.

Clients may experience our shifts from receptivity to protection (or absence) in a variety of deleterious ways. The pathways for such transmissions may be objective as well as subjective. Iacoboni (2008) has suggested that recently discovered *mirror neurons* may contribute to our abilities to connect with others. Initial research (Iacoboni et al., 1999) found they function to detect and imitate others' behaviors, but Iacoboni has since suggested that mirror neurons may also translate detected behaviors in others as outward signs of inner states, contributing to the neurobiological reproduction of those states in the observer. Often primed by past hurts and disappointments to be socially and neurobiologically vigilant for signs of impending hurt and disappointment, clients may

interpret our vigilance or absence to mean we, too, cannot handle their difficulties. And if we, the professional healers, cannot handle their difficulties, then where does that leave our clients?

Thus, it would be helpful that we (continuously) learn to mindfully uncover, expand our tolerances for, and work through our own histories of hurt, triggers, and perceptual biases and filters to increase our presence. As we expand our windows of tolerance, we regain the receptive ability to consciously and fluidly shift through arising difficult thoughts, feelings, and sensations without our mindful awareness collapsing in neurobiological or cognitive-affective preoccupation, avoidance, and other protective strategies (Siegel, 2010). With such presence, we are well positioned for the next element.

Attunement

We can be mindfully present even when we're alone. Attunement, however, is an interpersonal process. When we are present with another person, undistracted by extraneous internal and external stimuli, we are open to making internal representations of their internal states. Neurologically, our clients' outward signs innervate beyond our cortical perceptions, beyond our five basic senses, to subcortical limbic, brain-stem, and bodily regions (Gallese, Eagle, & Migone, 2007). Corresponding subcortical shifts in our muscle tension, heart rates, breathing, and intestinal processes are then relayed up a layer of our spinal cords called Lamina I. En route back up to conscious prefrontal cortical areas, neural transmissions pass back through our brain stems and hypothalami, altering hormonal levels and further shaping our states of receptivity or protection.

These signals eventually (and rapidly) reach our posterior insula, where a cortical sense or map of the body's state is created and sent to the anterior insula to form a second representation. The anterior insula is where we gain a conscious awareness of these inner bodily sensations, also referred to as *interoception*. (Note: The insula is not represented in figure 1.1; it lies underneath the intersection of the frontal, parietal, and temporal lobes.) This area is also correlated with a metacognitive awareness (a key feature of mindfulness) of these sensations. These neural signals are finally pushed to the anterior cingulate cortex in the medial prefrontal cortex, which is correlated with self-regulation and, in social situations, works with the anterior insula to create a sense of self (Siegel, 2010). A recent neuroimaging study (Tang, Lu, Fan, Yang, & Posner, 2012) found a form of mindfulness meditation to increase axonal density and myelinization in the anterior cingulate cortex after just 4 weeks of practice. Iacoboni (2008) has further proposed super mirror neurons that help us to differentiate the source of these sensations as originating in our experience or in the other's experience.

Subjectively, if we are closed to our subcortical shifts, we are cut off from these internal representations of our clients' inner experiences. Even though our internal representations are not perfect re-creations, they are data that contribute to our empathic understanding. We must be mindfully self-attuned, though, to benefit from this insight. Yalom (2002) spoke of the importance of this self- and other-attunement when he described Fromm teaching students about empathy:

Erich Fromm often cited Terence's statement from two thousand years ago —["I am a man and reckon nothing human alien to me"]—and urged us to be open to that part of ourselves that corresponds to any deed or fantasy offered by patients, no matter how heinous, violent, lustful, masochistic, or sadistic. If we didn't, he suggested we investigate why we have chosen to close that part of ourselves. (p. 21)

Being mindfully self-attuned includes understanding our histories and our perceptual biases and how they may contribute to or restrict our cognitive, affective, behavioral, and interoceptive experiences, lest we confuse our issues with our clients' concerns. Supervision, mindfulness, and psychotherapy are fantastic ways for us to better understand these dynamics, expand our windows of tolerance (the edges of which trigger protective responses), and increase our effectiveness. Trait mindfulness has also been positively correlated with empathy (Dekeyser et al., 2008). As Rogers (1992) stated, "To sense the client's private world as if it were your own, but without ever losing the 'as if' quality—this is empathy, and this seems essential to therapy" (p. 832).

Resonance

As we stated at the beginning of this chapter, mindfulness, both intrapersonal (presence) and interpersonal (attunement with others), is not easy to maintain. We may be able, however, to hold a *good-enough* mindful stance. Winnicott (1971) described the *good-enough mother* as one who creates a holding environment in which a child may experience healthy psychological development. Congruent with Siegel's (2010) descriptions of interpersonal mindfulness in therapy, the good-enough mother's task was not to be perfect but, rather, to neither fight nor flee (nor freeze) in response to a distressed and inconsolable child. Instead, the mother's loving presence, neither intrusive nor neglectful, functions to help the child self-regulate—an attunement whereby the child, subjectively and objectively no doubt, takes in the mother's ability to cope and makes that internal representation her own (Gallese et al., 2007). In such exchanges, children form salubrious attachment styles.

In a similar way, our presence may be able to offer our clients healthy models of coping (e.g., moderation in exercise and eating) and love (e.g., one that isn't contingent on performance, weight, or percent body fat). As we take in our clients and help them learn to be mindfully present and attuned to us, they begin to take us in, subjectively and objectively, as well (Gallese et al., 2007). Resonance emerges as each takes in the other without losing themselves. As Siegel (2010) stated:

> In many ways we feel "close" or "heard" or "seen" by another person when we can detect that he has attuned to us and has taken us inside of his own mind. When we ourselves register this attunement, either consciously or not, our own state can change. . . . Beginning with a genuine sense of care and interest by the focus of the other's careful attention, resonance extends this positive interaction into a fuller dimension of the other being changed because of who we are . . . this is how two individuals become a "we." (pp. 54-55)

Not to be confused with boundary blurring or romantic love, this influence is ethically skewed in the direction of our clients, as we provide corrective cognitive-affective-neurobiological experiences, which they may make their own as we work our way out of a job. A central and compass-like question to ask throughout complex interpersonal exchanges in therapy is, "Whose needs are being met?" The answer must include the client. Again, our needs, like our triggers, subcortical shifts, and perceptual biases and filters, may not be conscious to us. They may be effectively uncovered in supervision, mindfulness, and psychotherapy.

That we can effect positive changes in neural pathways—subjective experience affecting objective—should be no surprise to most students of sport psychology, who are quite familiar with the use of imagery for performance enhancement. That we can effect positive interpersonal neurobiological change may be novel for many of us, but

these processes are not unsubstantiated. Reviews (e.g., Norcross, Beutler, & Levant, 2005; Sexton & Whiston, 1994) have previously and strongly suggested the quality of therapist–client relationships to be a key determinant of outcomes in clinical and counseling interventions. The quality of sport psychologist–athlete relationships has also been suggested to be a key influence on sport psychology intervention outcomes (e.g., Petitpas, Giges, & Danish, 1999). Furthermore, the utility and importance of interpersonal mindfulness has been explored in supervisor–supervisee relationships in applied sport psychology as well (Andersen, 2012).

Mindfulness as an Overarching, Transtheoretical Stance

As we have seen, there is converging evidence in mindfulness, interpersonal neurobiology, and clinical and counseling outcome meta-analytic research on a few points: (a) the pivotal importance of the therapeutic relationship underpinning, subjectively and objectively, positive outcomes in therapy, performance, and supervision, regardless of the theoretical framework of the intervention; (b) the key qualities of these relationships are identifiable and can be developed; and (c) intra- and interpersonal mindfulness may be highly efficacious at creating and cultivating these qualities (e.g., Rogerian attributes). Even a recent mindfulness study (Bowen & Kurz, 2012) found participant-rated quality of the *therapeutic alliance* to be a significant predictor of mindfulness levels 2 months after an 8-week mindfulness course, whereas between-session practice during the course was a significant predictor of levels at the end of the course but not at 2 months.

We have also seen convergence on these points by a variety of significant historical figures of different psychological orientations including Rogers, Freud, Yalom, Fromm, and Winnicott, using their respective languages. Although we do not believe mindfulness is a panacea, there is considerable evidence that using intra- and interpersonal mindfulness in practice may have a variety of direct, moderating, and disaggregated (e.g., type of mindfulness practice) positive effects on the therapeutic relationship and on the efficacy of interventions aimed at improving well-being, performance, and health behaviors. We, therefore, propose it as an effective overarching stance that may be adopted and integrated by practitioners of any theoretical orientation.

Mindfulness and Neuroscience: Exercise Analogies and Relationships

The plasticity of our neural networks is not homogenous throughout our brains. Neuroplasticity is contingent, among other things, on learning and epigenetic influences, and parts of our brains are more dependent on learning and experience for development than others (Cozolino, 2010). The cerebral cortex, for example, is involved in a variety of executive functions (e.g., language, motor behavior, reasoning, memory, self-regulation) and is shaped by experience throughout our lifetimes. In contrast, the brain stem, for example, is responsible for a variety of bodily processes necessary for survival (e.g., breathing, heart rate, reflexes) and is fully functional at birth. Likewise, the expression of our genotype (i.e., inherited DNA) to phenotype (e.g., stress sensitivity) results from nature and environmental influences and is, thus, both experience independent and dependent, like various neural networks (Cozolino, 2010).

These neurobiological processes have important implications in applied work, from the telling of stories to the teaching of skills, whether motor or psychological. Clients tell us stories based on the accessibility of a variety of neural networks, from episodic memories in the hippocampus to associated (or dissociated) affective memories in the limbic system and somatic memories in the parietal and frontal lobes. When we reflect on those stories with mindful presence and attunement, situated in Rogerian qualities, we help coconstruct rich and well-understood stories. Eventually, we co-reconstruct these stories in ways that serve the needs of our clients. In this process, we also help co-reconstruct the experience-dependent neural networks of our clients as we integrate dissociated networks (Cozolino, 2010).

Our psychological orientations offer maps in the building process, helping us know where we are, the direction we may want to head, and what may be missing. Cozolino (2010) has offered some

seminal considerations on how various orientations, from CBT to psychoanalysis (PST would also fit comfortably here), may affect various neural networks by examining their processes and neurobiological correlates. He also identified common factors of a variety of treatments, many of which (e.g., empathic attunement) underscore parts of the therapeutic relationship found to determine outcomes in aforementioned reviews.

These processes are also relevant to learning psychological skills in exercise settings. I (Joe) worked with a motivated and competitive exercising client (Jack) who was keen to learn mindfulness. We began the first few weeks by discussing and practicing basic mindful breathing and body awareness. Jack recorded my prompts using his smartphone during our seated meditations and reported listening to it and practicing every day. He was so determined he bought and read all of Siegel's (2010) *The Mindful Therapist* within 2 weeks of my first mention of it. Even though we talked about how our mindful awareness will invariably drift away from the objects of attention (e.g., breathing) again and again, Jack reported great frustration, perceiving this loss of focus as a failure.

Regular mindfulness practice is associated with a shift of dominance from the brain's right hemisphere, which is associated with avoidant, anxious, and protective reactions, to the left hemisphere, which is associated with an openness and curiosity toward novelty and an approach response to challenge (Cozolino, 2010; Siegel, 2010). Jack's subjective verbal reports and his rigid body language (observed as part of my mindful attunement) offered evidence that his limbic system was on red alert. In the exchange, I also noted that I was feeling some anxiety and frustration within my own psychological and somatic experience. A sarcastic voice in my head arose exclaiming, "Doing a great job teaching this guy mindfulness for exercise and performance, Joe—not! And you're trying to write a chapter on this stuff?" I noticed muscle tension in a number of places in my body, from an increasingly hunched posture to flexion in my hands and stomach, which constricted my breathing. Recognizing and embracing my internal set of responses with openness, acceptance, and nonjudgment and without fusing (identifying) with them, I was able to mindfully separate my internal representation of Jack's experience from its interplay with my own self-critical voices and use it as a basis of empathy and understanding. I took a deep breath, straightened up, and let the inner sarcastic voice fade without getting into an argument with it, and that's exactly what I needed to help Jack do.

It seemed to me his narrative of competitiveness (possibly stored in deep, unconscious neural networks) primed his limbic system for signs of threat, not to his life but to his woundedness, perhaps from internalized experiences that conditioned him to believe his worthiness was contingent on engaging in (probably excessive) exercise and executing perfect performances. This hypothesis was plausible but subject to further scrutiny. I made a judgment call that such an inquiry would be better explored when our therapeutic relationship became more developed than it currently was. In the interim, perhaps an analogy would work better than a premature interpretation. Jack was an enthusiastic exerciser, and I recalled Siegel's (2010) analogy of mindful focus and mindless loss of focus to the concentric and eccentric phases of lifting weights.

I asked him, "Jack, when you do a set of bicep curls, do you get pissed off and consider it a 'failure' every time you lower the dumbbell before the next rep?" He laughed and said, "No, of course not." I responded, "Well, mindfulness practice is a lot like lifting weights. When we're mindfully aware of the part of our experience we wish to pay attention to, such as the breath, it's like the contraction phase of the bicep curl. And when our mindful awareness inevitably drifts, it's like the relaxation phase. When we realize we've mindlessly drifted, we become mindful again and begin the next rep. When we're mindful, we activate our 'mindful neurons.' And when we drift, we deactivate our mindful neurons. Like doing a set of bicep curls, it's all part of the exercise." Jack got a big smile on his face and said, "I get it!" From that point forward, he was able to coach himself through this set of frustrations in his practice using the exercise analogy.

Structures such as the hippocampus and prefrontal cortex also serve to inhibit, not just activate, the limbic system. It's possible that the ex-

ercise analogy, while consciously processed in Jack's prefrontal cortex and recruiting the strength of previously stored procedural memory (i.e., bicep curl motor patterns) in areas such as the cerebellum, formed a declarative memory in his hippocampus. In subsequent practice, his ability to consciously recall this declarative memory may have recruited neural networks involved in inhibition of the limbic area's activation of sympathetic nervous system responses. Each time Jack used this analogy for restructuring his experience, he helped reconfigure, integrate, and strengthen the associated neural networks in his brain. Also, I purposely used the words "we" and "our" when telling the exercise-analogy story to help normalize the experience and to further contribute to the development of our therapeutic alliance.

To mine the exercise analogy, in some exercises and lifts for weight training, the moves are complex and even risky. For example, the clean and jerk is a complicated movement. It takes loads of practice with low weights to get the movement right and to avoid injury. Part of the process may be overcoming anxiety about potentially damaging stress and strain, which may actually inhibit learning the proper technique. Learning mindful attention may, in some ways, be similar to complex weight training. It takes practice, practice, practice.

Over the course of approximately 20 more sessions, the early hypothesis that Jack's sense of worth was dependent on high performance gained considerable evidence and support. Our therapeutic relationship had developed in such a way that it offered a mindful "no-judgment zone" (which I explicitly referenced at various times) and a sense of safety for him to explore previously off-limit emotions. In this mindful holding environment, Jack was able to reduce his self-judgment and explore how those inner critical voices were active in many areas of his life, especially in relationships. It turned out his mother was a "mega-aerobics and spinning instructor" throughout his childhood. He reported that she would often make him drink "green slimy" smoothies and other health foods, which he detested. Occasionally, Jack's father would bring home ice cream or other treats, and his mom would consistently scold both him and his father for it, telling Jack that he would end up "chubby and soft" like his dad and telling his dad to stop "babying" him. To regain her approval, Jack would often go for a jog around his neighborhood or join one of her fitness classes. Pleasing her and avoiding her scorn through exercise became a mode of gaining the attention and love that he craved. He eventually increased his capacity to look at these thoughts, feelings, and memories without fighting, fleeing, or dissociating from them. Using interpersonal mindfulness in our relationship, we were able to examine the discomfort and mini-sabotages that occurred when he began to make progress and feel (noncontingently) comforted by me. The unconditional positive regard within the therapeutic relationship may act as a kind of re-parenting with noncontingent love and care for the client that is free of judgment. This new relationship in a client's life may help rewire connections in attachment centers in the brain and move the client from anxious or avoidant styles to secure attachment circuits. Also, the exercise therapist may become an internalized neurological representation of how *to be* in the world (e.g., curious, approach oriented, left prefrontal cortex dominant) that the client can internally consult with during trying times to help change old maladaptive patterns of thoughts, feelings, and behaviors. The downside of this internalization process is when the exercise professional is demanding and judgmental or contingently praises clients. In Jack's case, such a practitioner would contribute to reinforcing old, established neural circuits representing his insecure attachment to his mom.

Jack and I were able to reconnect his mysterious shame and sabotaging behaviors during these seemingly positive periods with dissociated and repressed memories, allowing him to work through them at a conscious level. At a neurobiological level, we may have rewired and reconnected the neural correlates of these subjective experiences, bringing repressed memory in, among other places, the hippocampus into conscious processing in the prefrontal cortex, where it could be integrated with the affect and sabotaging behavior drives in the limbic system. In time, Jack came to see that he was using "success" to earn what he really wanted: love. Even though we had

barely discussed his romantic relationship, he subsequently reported a growing sense of well-being with his girlfriend and disclosed his intent to marry her. In his words, Jack was no longer projecting what he thought she wanted; he was able to be present, attuned, and resonant with the love she actually had for him. The dissociation (and subsequent reintegration) of neural networks may also be moderated by the lessons learned in the therapeutic relationship, transferring the client's experiences in treatment to a variety of domains in life. By remaining open and paying attention to what's happening in their therapeutic relationships, exercise professionals may discover new and effective ways to serve their clients. Within a few months, I worked my way out of a job as these neurobiological changes began to take hold deeply within Jack, who no longer needed the support of our relationship.

Using Neuroscience Storytelling as Part of Exercise Psychology Service

Most exercise professionals have some practical knowledge of how central and peripheral nervous systems work (e.g., reaction time, exercise and brain chemistry, fast-twitch versus slow-twitch muscle fibers, and innervation). Explaining to clients what is happening in their brains and peripheral nervous systems when they are anxious, depressed, cared for, or loved may go a fair way in helping them overcome, to use an acceptance and commitment therapy term, some of their *fusion* with their thoughts and emotions (e.g., "I am my anxiety," "I am worthless"). For example, overweight clients may avoid going to a gym because being in that environment brings about social physique anxiety that may be coupled to histories of being bullied about their weight, nasty things others have said to them, parental disappointment, and feelings of being unworthy of love because of their size. Many overweight people's histories provide plenty of aversive experiences to keep them avoiding exercise in public places. Stepping into a gym may bring about an anxious response, worries about what others think of them, and then a whole cascade of past trauma may start to roll. Fusion begins with self-statements such as "I am fat," "I am unattractive," "that person over there is looking at me with disgust; I am disgusting" and the one that sits at the heart of a lot of human suffering, "I am unworthy of love." Fusion complete. Why would they ever want to go to the gym?

All such painful thoughts and emotions have correlates in the structures and functions of the brain, and some compassionate, didactic approaches explaining to clients what is happening for them in anxious or depressed conditions may begin to take the sting out of their fusions with their internal states. Let's take an example of an overweight client who has had bad experiences in attempting to exercise in a gym. He has tried, but he becomes so self-conscious and anxious that he soon leaves. The exercise professional may sit down with him and say, "It sounds so difficult for you to go to a gym, and that environment brings up all sorts of painful reactions that make you just want to run out of the building. I would like to talk for a little while about what is probably happening in your brain when all this crap is flying about. We can think of the brain as having three layers that are all interconnected. The oldest part of the brain sits at the base and takes care of basic survival such as keeping you breathing, making your heart pump, and regulating things like sleep. The middle part of the brain takes care of, among other things, emotions and perceptions of threats to survival. One part of this middle brain is fully functioning at birth, and it is called the amygdala, which is Latin for *almond*, so let's just call it 'your almond.' Well, your almond is set to look out for and record anything that may threaten your survival. It is intimately involved in the flight, fight, or freeze response when you are in a dangerous situation. It is great at recording threats to you from birth until you die. It is also a pattern recognition device. It looks out at the world and searches for current patterns that look similar to past threats, and if it finds one then it fires up, and you start to experience all sorts of anxiety and dread. It's how our brains are wired. Evolution favored those who remembered threats and could respond fast to similar future threats. Those folks survived, so we ended up with brains biased to pay attention to threats and to activate us. So, when you walk into a gym, your almond pattern recognizer may be detecting a bunch of patterns that look similar to past threatening experiences, as if the fit jocks who teased or bullied you in high school are in there lifting weights. Or someone may look at you, and you interpret that look as disapproval, and then feel bad about yourself. And pretty soon you are all activated and anxious. But that activation is based on past experiences, not necessarily current realities. And that is where the top part of your brain can come in handy. It's the last part of the brain to develop, and it comes into the world at birth, unlike your fully formed almond, with a lot of growing to do. Your top part of the brain, your cortex, keeps growing into your 20s. It is the part of your brain that has to do with many things such as language and rational thought, and one of its great functions is to tell the almond when it is firing up that 'No, this is not a high school bully. This is just a gym, and no one is really looking at me; they all have their own thoughts, and worries, and (imperfect) histories, and dreams.'" Such storytelling may help clients recognize that their current anxious activations are really old patterns left over from a relatively distant past, and that they can defuse from those reactions and let their cortical activity begin to downregulate unmoderated subcortical responses so that with repeated exposure they change their brains from avoidance reactions to approach and curiosity modes.

The Future of Mindfulness, Relationships, and Neuroscience in Exercise Psychology

We are both students with mindful practices but do not consider ourselves more than novices. Our mindful stances with therapy clients, of sitting with them in the present moment, in curious and nonjudgmental loving kindness (unconditional positive regard), in empathy, and in compassion, evaporate all the time. Judgment comes marching in with a full brass band, or the story a client is telling us plants hooks in our own anxieties and past traumas and reels us out of the room and into our own internal landscapes of unhappiness. But we know that getting hooked into our own stuff will happen, because it happens all the time, and then we gently and lovingly take the hook out and come back to *be* with the persons in our care.

We hope that mindfulness and attention to therapeutic relationships will spread through the exercise professions, and not just exercise psychology, but we are also realists. The field of sport psychology seems to lag substantially behind mainstream clinical and counseling psychology in the attention paid to central features of service (e.g., supervision, therapeutic relationships), and we can't expect exercise psychology and exercise practitioners to leap over sport psychology and travel through these territories of service. So we need to be patient.

The neuroscience of psychotherapy (e.g., Cozolino, 2010) and interpersonal neurobiology (e.g., Siegel, 2010) are making great strides toward Freud's ultimate goal of explaining human thoughts, emotions, behaviors, and relationships through unveiling the secrets of the central and peripheral nervous systems, but these fields are still in their infancy (or maybe early childhood). We have a long way to go. But maybe we can take what is known from these fields and help people move from being trapped by maladaptive subcortical patterns of responses to integrating their brains in ways that lead to happier lives and less suffering. This hope applies to most all exercise professionals, because what we are all doing when we assist people in changing exercise behaviors, using PST interventions (e.g., relaxation, imagery, self-talk), or doing psychotherapy is helping clients integrate their brains.

A Final Story About Exercise

During the time of writing this chapter, I (Joe) have been in long-term psychodynamic psychotherapy. During the seemingly interminable process of trying to tell our story of exercise, mindfulness, relationships, and neuroscience, this chapter has occasionally been the subject of conversations with my therapist (Mark's and my joys, frustrations, procrastinations, and aha moments).

One day, regarding my own exercise, I told my therapist that I hadn't been working out the past month, but I had started doing cardio the past few days for my anxiety (I had been relying on Xanax too much). She asked, "What does cardio do?" I said, "It helps the neurobiology of my brain." She asked again, "What else does cardio do?"

I paused and smiled and said, "It's good for the heart."

References

Andersen, M.B. (Ed.). (2000). *Doing sport psychology*. Champaign, IL: Human Kinetics.

Andersen, M.B. (2012). Supervision and mindfulness in sport and performance psychology. In S.M. Murphy (Ed.), *Oxford handbook of sport and performance psychology* (pp. 725–737). New York, NY: Oxford University Press.

Andersen, M.B., & Mannion, J. (2011). If you meet the Buddha on the football field, tackle him! In D. Gilbourne & M.B. Andersen (Eds.), *Critical essays in applied sport psychology* (pp. 173–192). Champaign, IL: Human Kinetics.

Baer, R.A., Smith, G.T., & Allen, K.B. (2004). Assessment of mindfulness by self-report: The Kentucky Inventory of Mindfulness Skills. *Assessment, 11,* 191–206.

Benson, H. (with Klipper, M.Z.). (2000). *The relaxation response*. New York, NY: Avon Books. (Original work published 1975)

Birrer, D., & Morgan, G. (2010). Psychological skills training as a way to enhance an athlete's performance in high-intensity sports. *Scandinavian Journal of Medicine & Science in Sports, 20,* 78–87.

Birrer, D., Rothlin, P., & Morgan, G. (2012). Mindfulness to enhance athletic performance: Theoretical considerations and possible impact mechanisms. *Mindfulness, 3,* 235–246.

Bishop, S.R., Lau, M., Shapiro, S., Carlson, L., Anderson, N.D., Carmody, J., . . . Devins, G. (2004). Mindfulness: A proposed operational definition. *Clinical Psychology: Science and Practice, 11,* 230–241.

Bowen, S., & Kurz, A.S. (2012). Between-session practice and therapeutic alliance as predictors of mindfulness after mindfulness-based relapse prevention. *Journal of Clinical Psychology, 68,* 236–245.

Brown, K.W., & Ryan, R.M. (2003). The benefits of being present: Mindfulness and its role in psychological well-being. *Journal of Personality and Social Psychology, 84,* 822–848.

Cozolino, L. (2010). *The neuroscience of psychotherapy: Healing the social brain* (2nd ed.). New York, NY: Norton.

Csikszentmihalyi, M. (1990). *Flow: The psychology of optimal experience*. New York, NY: HarperCollins.

Dekeyser, M., Raes, F., Leijssen, M., Leysen, S., & Dewulf, D. (2008). Mindfulness skills and interpersonal behavior. *Personality and Individual Differences, 44,* 1235–1245.

Epstein, M. (1995). *Thoughts without a thinker: Psychotherapy from a Buddhist perspective*. New York, NY: Basic Books.

Epstein, M. (2005). *Open to desire, embracing a lust for life: Insights from Buddhism and psychotherapy*. New York, NY: Gotham Books.

Evans, D.R., Baer, R.A., & Segerstrom, S.C. (2009). The effects of mindfulness and self-consciousness on persistence. *Personality and Individual Differences, 47,* 379–382.

Fingarette, H. (1963). *The self in transformation: Psychoanalysis, philosophy, and the life of the spirit*. New York, NY: Basic Books.

Freud, S. (1958). Recommendations to physicians practicing psychoanalysis. In J. Stachey (Ed. & Trans.), *The standard edition of the complete psychological works of Sigmund Freud* (Vol. 12, pp. 111–112). London, England: Hogarth. (Original work published 1912)

Fromm, E., Suzuki, D.T., & Demartino, R. (1970). *Zen Buddhism and psychoanalysis*. New York, NY: HarperCollins.

Gallese, V., Eagle, M.N., and Migone, P. (2007). Intentional attunement: Mirror neurons and the neural underpinnings of interpersonal relations. *Journal of the American Psychoanalytic Association, 55,* 131–175.

Gardner, F.E. (Ed.) (2009). Mindfulness- and acceptance-based approaches to sport performance and well-being [Special issue]. *Journal of Clinical Sport Psychology, 3*(4).

Gardner, F.E., & Moore, Z.E. (2004). A mindfulness-acceptance-commitment-based approach to athletic performance enhancement: Theoretical considerations. *Behavior Therapy, 35,* 707–723.

Gardner, F.E., & Moore, Z.E. (2007). *The psychology of enhancing human performance: The mindfulness-acceptance-commitment-based approach*. New York, NY: Springer.

Hayes, S.C. (2004). Acceptance and commitment therapy, relational frame theory, and the third wave of behavioral and cognitive therapies. *Behavior Therapy, 35,* 639–665.

Hayes, S.C., Strosahl, K.D., & Wilson, K.G. (1999). *Acceptance and commitment therapy*. New York, NY: Guilford Press.

Hayes, S.C., Wilson, K.G., Gifford, E.V., Follette, V.M., & Strosahl, K. (1996). Experiential avoidance and behavioral disorders: A functional dimensional approach to diagnosis and treatment. *Journal of Consulting and Clinical Psychology, 64,* 1152–1168.

Herrigel, E. (with Suzuki, D.T.). (1999). *Zen in the art of archery* (R.F.C. Hull, Trans.). New York, NY: Vintage Books. (Original work published 1948)

Hicks, S.F., & Bien, T. (Eds.). (2008). *Mindfulness and the therapeutic relationship*. New York, NY: Guilford Press.

Hyams, J. (1982). *Zen in the martial arts*. New York, NY: Bantam Books.

Iacoboni, M. (2008). *Mirroring people*. New York, NY: Farrar, Straus, & Giroux.

Iacoboni, M., Woods, R.P., Brass, M., Bekkering, H., Mazziotta, J.C., & Rizzolatti, G. (1999). Cortical mechanisms of human imitation. *Science, 286,* 2526–2528.

Jung, C.G. (1964). Foreword. In D.T. Suzuki, *An introduction to Zen Buddhism* (pp. ix–xxix). New York, NY: Grover Press.

Kabat-Zinn, J. (1982). An outpatient program in behavioral medicine for chronic pain patients based on the practice of mindfulness meditation: Theoretical considerations and preliminary results. *General Hospital Psychiatry, 4,* 33–47.

Kabat-Zinn, J. (1990). *Full catastrophe living: How to cope with stress, pain, and illness using mindfulness meditation*. New York, NY: Bantam Dell.

Kabat-Zinn, J. (1994). *Wherever you go, there you are: Mindfulness meditation in everyday life*. New York, NY: Hyperion.

Kabat-Zinn, J., Beall, B., & Rippe, J. (1985, June). *A systematic mental training program based on mindfulness meditation to optimize performance in collegiate and Olympic rowers*. Paper presented at the World Congress of Sport Psychology, Copenhagen, Denmark.

Kristeller, J.L., & Hallett, C.B. (1999). An exploratory study of a meditation-based intervention for binge eating disorder. *Journal of Health Psychology, 4,* 357–363.

Keng, S.L., Smoski, M.J., & Robins, C.J. (2011). Effects of mindfulness on psychological health: A review of empirical studies. *Clinical Psychology Review, 31,* 1041–1056.

Langer, E.J. (1990). *Mindfulness*. Cambridge, MA: Da Capo Press.

Linehan, M. (1993). *Cognitive-behavioral treatment of borderline personality disorder*. New York, NY: Guilford Press.

Maddux, J.E. (1997). Habit, health, and happiness. *Journal of Sport & Exercise Psychology, 19,* 331–346.

Marks, D.R. (2008). The Buddha's extra scoop: Neural correlates of mindfulness and clinical sport psychology. *Journal of Clinical Sport Psychology, 2,* 216–241.

Norcross, J., Beutler, L., & Levant, R. (2005). *Evidence-based practices in mental health: Debate and dialogue on the fundamental questions*. Oxford, England: Oxford University Press.

Petitpas, A.J., Giges, B., & Danish, S. (1999). The sport psychologist-athlete relationship: Implications for training. *The Sport Psychologist, 13,* 344–357.

Raes, F., Dewulf, D., Van Heeringen, C., & Williams, J.M.G. (2009). Mindfulness and reduced cognitive reactivity to sad mood: Evidence from a correlational study and a non-randomized waiting list controlled study. *Behaviour Research and Therapy, 47,* 623–627.

Rogers, C.R. (1992). The necessary and sufficient conditions of therapeutic personality change. *Journal of Consulting and Clinical Psychology, 60,* 827–832.

Segal, Z.V., Williams, J.M.G., & Teasdale, J.D. (2002). *Mindfulness-based cognitive behavioral therapy for depression: A new approach for preventing relapse.* New York, NY: Guilford Press.

Sexton, T.L., & Whiston, S.C. (1994). The status of the counseling relationship: An empirical review, theoretical implications, and research directions. *The Counseling Psychologist, 22,* 6–78.

Siegel, D.J. (2010). *The mindful therapist: A clinician's guide to mindsight and neural integration.* New York, NY: Norton.

Tang, Y., Lu, Q., Fan, M., Yang, Y., & Posner, M.I. (2012). Mechanisms of white matter changes induced by meditation. *Proceedings of the National Academy of Sciences, 109,* 10570–10574.

Vealey, S.R. (2007). Mental skills training in sport. In G. Tenenbaum & R. Eklund (Eds.), *Handbook of sport psychology* (3rd ed., pp. 287–309). Hoboken, NJ: Wiley.

Wertz, S.K. (1977). Zen, yoga, and sports: Eastern philosophy for Western athletes. *Journal of the Philosophy of Sport, IV,* 68–82.

Winnicott, D.W. (1971). *Playing and reality.* London, England: Routledge.

Yalom, I.D. (2002). *The gift of therapy: An open letter to a new generation of therapists and their patients.* New York, NY: Harper Perennial.

CHAPTER 2

Relationships Between Coaches, Athletes, and Sport and Exercise Scientists

David T. Martin and Kirsten Peterson

As foreshadowed in the preface, this chapter might seem a bit odd for inclusion in an exercise psychology text (rather than in a sport psychology text). The setting of this chapter is the elite sport environment. Nevertheless, the focus of the chapter is on the interactions among professionals (and clients), which is a logical extension of the discussion of therapeutic relationships in chapter 1. Many exercise scientists work in sport settings, and most sport and exercise scientists can benefit from reminders that they operate in complex social, interpersonal, and often hierarchical milieus.

We have each worked as sport and exercise scientists with Olympic athletes and coaches for more than 20 years. Both of us began our sport science careers at the same time, working as research assistants for the U.S. Olympic Committee (USOC) in the late 1980s. Both of us then pursued our doctoral studies and began careers in the sport and exercise science industry, David as a sport and exercise physiologist at the Australian Institute of Sport (AIS) and Kirsten as a sport psychologist at the USOC and more recently at the AIS.

Over the past two decades, we have both been part of high-performance teams involved in preparing athletes for competition at the Olympic Games (1996–2012). During this time we have experienced the many highs and lows associated with working with exceptional and, in some cases, not so exceptional teams. As we have attempted to "do sport and exercise science," we have often found ourselves making mistakes, but over time our perspectives on the topic of how to help elite coaches and athletes have matured and become more refined.

Not all that long ago, the world of elite sport was a simpler place. Athletes participated in competitive sport primarily because they loved it (e.g., Mallet & Hanrahan, 2004). Sportsmen and women generally enjoyed the challenges sport presented; they were excited by the opportunities that being good at sport provided, and the coaches and support staff who assisted athletes were essentially altruistic volunteers who helped because they enjoyed the adventure, the challenge, and the relationships.

Today, competitive sport is a different place. Athletes can enjoy fame, fortune, and power, and professionals who support elite athletes may both make a good income and, in some cases, become famous in their own right. This rapidly growing profession provides some high-profile scientists with unique opportunities to engage in practices that, although highly lucrative, are considered unethical (e.g., doping). High-performance sport has grown and matured. For many teams, support staff who are formally trained in exercise science have now specialized. They are known as "sport and exercise scientists" and are employed full-time to help athletes gain a winning edge. The introduction of academically trained specialists who focus on a wide range of performance-related factors may sound like a highly desirable secret weapon, but in the rapidly growing professions within sport and exercise science, this new expansion introduces novel social dynamics to professional and Olympic sport that can, at times, be problematic.

Although the topic of psychological stress experienced by coaches or athletes and the topics of communication and group dynamics in sport have been formally examined and scientifically reviewed (e.g., Eccles & Tenenbaum, 2004), far less attention has been focused on the effect of these factors on practitioners such as psychologists, physiologists, physiotherapists, or athletic trainers who work in sport and exercise environments. Nor is this topic typically addressed in most sport and exercise science or coaching curriculums. This chapter addresses this deficiency by focusing on the "how" of effective exercise and sport science service delivery as opposed to the "what." In so doing, we provide the reader with an understanding of important interactions and dynamics that occur among scientists, coaches, and athletes. These relationships underpin and often determine the effectiveness of sport and exercise science support for high-performance athletes and coaches and more often than not provide the answer to the question of why some sport and exercise scientists become highly sought after, whereas others, unfortunately, become perceived as liabilities. Although the focus of this chapter is these relationships in the context of elite sport, there are certainly parallels with regard to practitioners working in exercise contexts as well with regard to professionals seeking to effectively understand and manage the dynamics of their sometimes conflicting work relationships.

Lions, Cheetahs, and Monkeys

The business of coaching involves asking many questions and then making difficult decisions, sometimes under high-pressure situations and with tight time constraints. In these situations, coaches learn to make decisions based on their gut feelings as well as evidence. Unlike scientists, coaches often don't need, or have the time, to provide evidence to justify their decisions. They can often just tell everyone to trust them—they have won before, and they know what they are doing. Coaches usually come through a highly competitive industry, and their rise to power as head coaches is complicated with many challenges and confrontations (Stebbings, Taylor, Spray, & Ntoumanis,

2012). Head coaches, in particular, are faced with the tasks of earning respect, winning over the hearts and minds of athletes, and being well connected and even admired within their sports. Many highly paid coaches could be compared to Fortune 500 CEOs in their need for simultaneous focus on threats to their authority and job security as well as performance.

To be successful, elite athletes must consistently demonstrate that they know how to win within the rules of their sports. To succeed at this level, they must have great talent, be physically well suited for their sports, and commit to their goals. Although many internationally competitive athletes take on advice when prudent, it is also true that they rely on their own expertise and look to themselves for answers. Our experiences in the field suggest that it is almost a developmental rite of passage in elite sport for athletes to reach a point in their careers when they start to question the wisdom and advice their coaches offer. When it comes to winning, truly elite athletes know that the final results are up to them.

Sport and exercise scientists can be thought of as a different kind of animal when compared to coaches and athletes. Scientists are trained to be skeptics, and most spend years learning techniques that will allow them to contribute toward knowledge discovery. They are interested in learning and curious about how things work, and they have trained to explore and question how and why. When it comes to sport and exercise, it is possible to imagine why it would be useful to have a scientist involved or why it would be nice to think, at times, like a scientist. It becomes apparent that people in these three different, and sometimes conflicting, roles within elite sport — coach, athlete, and scientist—might experience unique challenges when they are required to work together effectively. In hopes of better relating to the complexities associated with this intrateam communication, it may be helpful to think of the coach as a lion, the athlete as a cheetah, and the scientist as a monkey.

The head coach can be likened to the alpha male lion of the pride. The alpha male is the patriarch of the pride. At his peak, he is typically stronger, older, and wiser than the other males. The pride enjoys the comfort and stability of being driven by a powerful leader, but they also display subservience and caution. The alpha male defends the pride and its territory, gets first choice of the pride's kills, and determines the order of eating for the pride. Moreover, to ensure that his line of descendants is primary in the pride, a new alpha male will kill all cubs born of his predecessor. In short, all major decisions are made in a manner that reinforces the alpha male's authority. The primary similarities between an alpha male lion and a head coach center on leadership, respect, and authority.

The cheetah is a wonderful animal—blindingly fast, incredibly capable, and solitary by nature. When it comes to hunting, a cheetah doesn't need any help to succeed. In between predatory efforts, the cheetah passes time in a singularly relaxed state. Like the cheetah, elite athletes are confident in their abilities, which are underpinned by success. They don't like to put in a top effort if success is unlikely, and they are quite happy to hang out and look after themselves as they prepare for their next big event.

Monkeys are well recognized for their intelligence. Curious and capable, they enjoy investigating, learning, and socializing. When monkeys explore together in a group, things can get animated and quite noisy rather quickly. Spontaneous exclamations of delight emerge, and the volume of the discussion can escalate as all members of the group compete to express how they think things should work. Researchers have been investigating ideal environments that promote innovation and problem solving (Kitchen, 2012), and it is likely that conditions that favor scientific interaction may be relatively unfamiliar to some head coaches. For those unfamiliar with the profession of science, the enthusiastic exploration of different ideas can often appear to reflect something akin to a bunch of monkey business.

How do these three distinctly different species interact? When it comes to new and novel ideas, coaches come at their decision making from perspectives of authority and control. Athletes want to maximize their successes and make sure they don't look stupid or waste energy. Scientists are full of energy; they love the complexities of novel ideas and want to forever explore the many issues and resulting options that emerge. When times get tough, the lion, the cheetah, and the monkey will likely regress back to their respective comfort zones. The lion will roar, the cheetah will withdraw to wait for a better time to hunt, and the monkey will want to explore the situation even further to discover new and potentially helpful options. Sport administrators watching the emotional fireworks will wonder why everyone doesn't just get on with the job.

Add to this mix the stress associated with the looming threat that everyone could lose their jobs if the athletes don't win, and you have the potential for conflict as fatigued or distressed coaches and athletes who strive for perfection watch their expectations become more and more distant. Sport science practitioners who lack the skills of emotional intelligence needed to maneuver effectively in times of stress tend to undermine their own value as a member of the sport's support team (Rapisarda, 2002).

This chapter differs somewhat from the other chapters in this book. In telling our story and presenting case examples, we have opted for a narrative account, rather than dialogue and commentary, because we focus primarily on the internal states and professional understandings of a sport and exercise scientist as he developed over time.

Evolution of a Sport and Exercise Scientist: Part 1

In part 1 of this story, I (Dave) relate the early stages of my role within high-level sport. Although the coach–athlete relationship has received considerable attention in the research literature (e.g., Kristiansen, Tomten, Hanstad, & Roberts, 2012), this story focuses on the far less discussed relationships between the sport scientist and coaches and athletes.

My first relationship with an Olympic coach was very one sided. The coach had come to Australia from Europe, and he had an amazing background as an elite cycling coach. He played the alpha male role to a tee, telling me what to do and when to do it, and it was up to me to work as hard as I could to complete the tasks I had been assigned. I would spend hours in the laboratory and then hours working on my spreadsheets in an attempt to quantify fitness characteristics for each of the cyclists on the team. I still remember the first data sets I collected on elite cyclists. It was so exciting; I was documenting the fitness of Australia's most talented cyclists, and I took great pleasure in providing feedback to the coaches and athletes. It was a real buzz, not just because of the novelty but because I was starting to feel like I was part of a very exciting team pursuing a very important goal. After a few years, however, the work became a little bit routine, and I began to hope that there was more to the job than just conducting fitness tests. I had started to become aware of what I wasn't able to do, and that there were elements of my expertise not being used. This realization became more and more frustrating, yet I felt powerless to change my role.

When a new women's road cycling coach was hired, I immediately connected with him. This new coach was young, motivated, and incredibly ambitious. He not only told me what to do but also asked me what I thought (a first for me), and he seemed to value my opinions. This was the kind of relationship I had been hoping for. Together we would dream about a better high-performance cycling program—wouldn't it be cool if Australia had the number one ranked women's road cycling team in the world? When he asked me, "Dave, what would it take to make this dream a reality?" I felt connected, empowered, and important. My job moved from merely assessing fitness in the lab to actually traveling with the team and sharing in some of the important decision making. The coach sought my advice, and I thought that I was making a real difference. I was also starting to really get to know the elite cyclists. They would ask me questions, tell me about their frustrations, celebrate their wins with me, and rely on my feedback as they contemplated how they could improve. What a wonderful feeling it was. I felt like I belonged, that I mattered professionally, and that I was part of something important and special.

Roles of Sport and Exercise Scientists

To the uninitiated, the role of a sport and exercise scientist might seem easy to define. Scientists apply their knowledge in their areas of expertise to ensure that preparation and competition strategies are evidence based and cutting-edge. For example,

it would be straightforward to assume that sport and exercise physiologists would design interval training programs that strategically overload energy systems to enhance physical development, whereas psychologists would deliver mental training programs that help athletes to reach the starting line at an optimal state of focus and arousal. Large teams of sport scientists would work around the clock to make sure that no stone was left unturned and that their athletes were prepared to perform at their full potentials. The reality, as illustrated in the previous example, is that sport and exercise scientists often take on a number of roles that are not outlined, or even formally recognized, in most job descriptions. Moreover, sport and exercise science can be likened to a pharmacy—a repository of treatments to manage and even cure the common ailments of athletes and coaches. This pharmacy cannot be put to good use, however, unless people are available to play the roles of doctor and pharmacist—someone to diagnose the ailments and someone else to review and carry out the initiatives required to ensure that outcomes are being met.

A sport and exercise scientist who is well integrated into a team will often discover that the traditional boundaries that define and separate science disciplines don't exist. Over time, effective sport and exercise scientists soak up knowledge in many areas, and they may find themselves pressed into reflecting this acquired knowledge back for the good of the sport. Experienced physiologists can find themselves discussing sport nutrition issues, biomechanists can become involved in giving training advice, dieticians can help out with wound care management, and many of the sport and exercise scientists and medical professionals can find themselves, at times, managing team dynamics and relationships. For this reason, qualities and characteristics linked with successful and highly sought after sport and exercise scientists include openness, emotional intelligence, resilience, compassion, altruism, and a caring nature. Earning the respect and trust to interact effectively at this level is not easy, but once the scientist achieves that higher level of acceptance, new opportunities to support the team through a variety of different roles emerge.

Sport and exercise scientists can find themselves working in many different roles when they attempt to help an elite sporting program. The following list describes some of these wide-ranging roles:

• *Scientist.* Use scientific methods to reveal a better understanding about important aspects of improving an athlete's performance. Make careful, detailed observations and use the scientific method to promote knowledge discovery and to guide the process of selecting and preparing athletes for competition.

• *Advisor.* Based on prior experiences, interactions with other sport science experts, and a critical review of the scientific literature, form an evidence-based opinion. In some cases, opinions may be no more than educated guesses, which can be useful as long as the recommendations are not guided by selfish or self-fulfilling motives.

• *Counselor.* Give coaches and key athletes opportunities to talk freely about their concerns and worries. Use reflective-listening techniques and provide leaders with a chance to explore issues and options. Bring facts to the table and guide discussions so that coaches and athletes learn and grow. As described so well by the authors Bornstein and Languirand (2003), create an environment where athletes can depend upon the scientists but not become dependent upon them.

• *Consultant.* There are many opportunities for special projects where a sport and exercise scientist may take on a leadership role and focus on an issue such as (a) rehabilitation of an injured athlete, (b) a weight management plan for helping an athlete train optimally and make weight for competitions, or (c) development of technology that can be used to improve athletes' timing during interval training. For these projects, the scientist acts as the project officer and leads a small team of technical staff and external scientists. Important in this role is communication with the head coaches and key athletes to increase role clarity and eliminate perceptions of threats to the coach as leader.

• *Innovator or strategic direction driver.* Coaches and athletes, often by necessity, focus narrowly on immediate concerns and short-term goals, but sustained success requires attention to longer-term initiatives as well. Sport and exercise scientists are often well placed to increase

awareness of and maintain attention to this broader perspective, including the athlete-development pipeline, succession planning with staff, equipment upgrades, and emerging techniques and methodology for preparing for competition.

• *"BS" detector.* In the world of elite sport, competitive advantage is highly sought after. For many sports, there is also quite a bit of money available. This potent mix of need for achievement and ample resources can create vulnerabilities that enterprising salespeople, pushing the latest devices or supplements, will try to exploit. It is useful for a team to have a sport scientist or medical expert on board who can sort out truth from snake oil when salespeople come knocking.

• *Director.* The director of a Broadway play ensures that rehearsals (practice sessions) conform to a high standard and replicate the activities that will ultimately be used in the final performance. Similarly, sport scientists often find themselves focusing on identifying and then replicating critical mental, physical, and environmental aspects of competition during training sessions. Supervising competition-specific sessions and providing feedback on whether the objectives of the training session were achieved can be highly valuable for fitness, competitive readiness, team morale, and confidence.

• *Police.* For many training sessions, it can be difficult for coaches and athletes to know if they have conformed to the expectations of the session. For instance, were target heart rates reached? Was the training session technically executed as intended? Was the optimal mind-set achieved? Sport and exercise scientists will use equipment such as heart rate monitors, power meters, video feedback, and debriefs to discriminate between athletes who are achieving desired training objectives and those who are not, and they often offer suggestions on how to adjust athletes' approaches accordingly.

• *Meteorologist.* Professional weather forecasters make a living by using science and technology in an attempt to predict the future. Similarly, sport and exercise scientists can monitor trends and forecast developments in physical form, skill acquisition, motivation, and mind-set. Sometimes it is less important to get one's predictions right than to simply allay unnecessary in-the-moment worries on the part of the coach, which can in and of itself enhance performance—both for the coach and the athlete.

• *Friend.* As Ralph Waldo Emerson wrote, "A friend is a person with whom I may be sincere. Before him I may think aloud" (Cohen & Cohen, 1998, p. 158). As a profession, coaching can be exciting and enriching, but it can also be demanding, challenging, and in some cases isolating. Having a friend who shares the coach's interests and honestly wishes the best for the coach and team, yet also gives honest feedback, can enrich the coaching environment and lead to many desirable outcomes. With a good friend, the burden of defeat and disappointment is lightened. In great coach–scientist relationships, it is often easy to recognize many elements of friendship that can enhance resiliency to perceived failures.

At any given moment, a sport or exercise scientist will not be fulfilling all of these roles. The sport science job requirements are dynamic, and they will change over time depending on the phase of the program and the current logistical demands and priorities faced by coaches. For a variety of reasons, including personality and expertise, sport and exercise scientists will likely find that they gravitate to a few roles where they excel. A good team environment allows scientists to provide the program with extensive coverage across several roles.

Interplay of Experience Levels

One approach to understanding the relationship between coaches and scientists is based on categorizing magnitudes of experience. There are new coaches who are full of enthusiasm but just beginning to establish themselves, and then there are the senior coaches with decades in the business. There are the young sport and exercise scientists who may act confident but can rely only upon textbooks and internship experiences versus the experienced scientists who have knowledge and intuition honed by many years of experience working within elite sport (Ericsson, Krampe, & Tesch-Romer, 1993). Although no two relationships between coaches and sport and exercise scientists are the same, the following categorizations may be helpful for illustrating differing levels of experience that can influence how scientists and coaches work together.

• *Inexperienced coach and inexperienced scientist.* The young sport scientist combined with the young coach can result in an exciting relationship. When both coach and scientist are ambitious, confident, easily excitable, and resourceful, much learning can happen. This relationship tends to be full of action. It moves quickly and can have a chaotic and jumbled feel to it. It can sometimes be difficult for the sport scientist to set limits if the coach's appetite for new and novel approaches is insatiable. The potential for mistakes is high.

• *Experienced coach and experienced scientist.* This partnership can have stability on its side. The veteran coach has often had many opportunities to learn how sport science can best be applied. A seasoned sport and exercise scientist knows that the big picture of success is as much about solid relationships, energy, belief, and commitment as it is about technical expertise. For this reason, both the coach and the scientist tend to see beyond the problems and logistical frustrations that can derail enthusiasm. They seek value in the process of doing versus an obsession with outcome. The experienced coach–scientist combination can rely on their respective past successes and challenges to guide implementation of initiatives with less experimentation. Both sides have to be open when it comes to beginning these relationships, but neither can claim the high ground as the unchallenged expert.

• *Experienced coach and inexperienced scientist.* During the time when sport science programs were being developed, this combination may have been one of the most common due to the limited number of sport and exercise scientists. Even now, however, the ranks of truly experienced sport and exercise scientists are still small. Experienced coaches can find themselves with a team of scientists who are short on experience but full of motivation and ambition. Here, the coach typically takes on the role of an army general, giving orders that the scientists attempt to carry out. Primary goals for the scientist in this scenario are to demonstrate commitment (often achieved by working long hours), build credibility and integrity by following through on tasks, and demonstrate respect for the coach's leadership. A potential development area for the new scientist is overcoming fear and learning how and when to stand up to or confront the coach when necessary.

• *Inexperienced coach and experienced scientist.* Currently, with the recent growth of the sport and exercise science profession, there are opportunities for relatively inexperienced coaches to partner with experienced, and in some cases even famous, scientists. In this scenario, the experienced scientist will take on the role of a teacher, whereas the coach will often adopt the role of a talented student. Although inexperienced coaches are in charge of their programs, they will often seek advice from their scientific advisors, who can sometimes act as mentors. In this relationship, scientists must show respect toward inexperienced coaches with regard to their leadership because if coaches begin to feel inadequate or threatened by scientists, relationships can quickly break down.

By reviewing the different types of relationships between scientists and coaches based on experience, we do not mean to ignore the many different personalities of coaches and sport and exercise scientists. Rather, knowing that these different types of relationships exist can be comforting and helpful for scientists, especially for those who know that the relationship with the coach is important but are not sure what the relationship should look like. By understanding the different types of relationships, it is possible for both coaches and scientists to better understand and become aware of the different perspectives possessed by different members of the team.

How a Well-Intentioned Sport and Exercise Scientist Can Go Wrong

Years of academic training in one's specialty are often only the beginning of the learning process for sport and exercise scientists aspiring to be effective in the high-performance sphere. Scientists must also learn the art of timing and diplomacy when skating between athletes and coaches on the thin ice often inherent in highly charged performance cultures. This section details some actual scenarios where well-intentioned and clever sport and exercise scientists have had their messages derail due to errors of timing and differences in beliefs.

Timing

Imagine the young scientist who, based on extensive reading of the latest research, comes to the opinion that the pregame warm-up for a rugby team is suboptimal and, therefore, needs to be changed. After a series of losses, the team gathers together for a Tuesday morning training session. The game tapes have been reviewed, and the coach passionately addresses his team in the locker room, revealing his frustration. "We are obviously going to have to improve the way we play if we are going to start winning. Can any of you tell me what we can do to be better?"

After a long awkward silence where the majority of the team's players look for comfort by staring at their shoelaces, a sport and exercise scientist decides to boldly offer some advice and says, "Perhaps we could change our warm-up. Some of the latest research would suggest that we could cut our warm-up time down by half and increase the game-specific intensity we use for the drills." This advice may be good and evidence based, but the timing is most likely wrong. The coach is upset, the players are dejected, and now the scientist draws everyone's attention to a part of the game that may not be that important in the big scheme of things and addresses the topic as if he knows the solution to the team's problem.

Actually, the team needs to gain confidence, bond together, and prepare for the next challenges with a logical and tactical approach that they can embrace. There is a time and a place for the scientist to discuss pregame routines and warm-ups with the team. Taking the opportunity to raise some issues in front of the players when the mood is dark is likely not that time. To make a positive impact, the scientist should consider that coaches are constantly looking for buy-in and belief (regardless of whether they verbalize this feeling or not).

Differences in Beliefs

In this scenario, the sport and exercise scientist discovers research that suggests a particular supplement has the potential to improve performance of the athletes in her team. She presses her case with the coach, who (after some persuasion) sells the athletes on the need for the supplementation. Several months pass, and the anticipated benefits do not materialize. Athletes are disillusioned, and the coach is disappointed. The scientist's excitement about this discovery should have been tempered by the reality that sport and exercise science research is often conducted in ways to control for variables that could confound results, which is not the same as demonstrating effectiveness. One scientific study that highlights the benefits of a unique ergogenic aid does not ensure that use of this supplement will positively influence athletes' performances. For this reason, it is often not worth a prolonged, emotional, and relationship-damaging argument with a coach about whether supplement X should be administered to the team if, for a variety of reasons, the coach doesn't want her players taking supplement X. Believing that a supplement will work (or won't work, in this instance), in many cases, may be as important as the effect the supplement has. What was a minor ingredient in the performance mix can become, at the least, a distraction, but it could also lead to problems with team harmony and belief and create a breach in the relationship between the head coach and the scientist.

An equally worrisome scenario can occur when the coach gets excited about a new recovery practice and decides that he wants the entire team to adopt the new approach. The scientist thinks that the latest research does not support this new recovery plan. As the nonbeliever, the sport scientist now struggles with how to interact with the coach, who is committed to the new protocol. What happens when a team does something they believe in even though there is no evidence that the new procedure or supplement will make a difference? There are a few studies documenting that it may be better to believe in a placebo than to doubt a treatment that has scientifically been proven to be effective (e.g., Clark, Hopkins, Hawley, & Burke, 2000; Foad, Beedle, & Coleman, 2008). The informed and experienced sport scientist understands that it can be smarter to leave some battles unwaged if they have little effect on the program at large.

What Motivates Sport and Exercise Scientists?

Why would a sport and exercise scientist want a professional position in elite sport? In the early days of sport and exercise science support for elite athletes, it was less about gaining money, power, or fame and more about wanting to help, giving back to a favored sport, and valuing the relationship with the coach and the adventure associated with pursuing extraordinary goals. Now the profession of sport and exercise science does pay money; in some situations, there are career paths and opportunities for individuals to progress in their professional roles. The following list identifies our top six reasons why someone would want to become a sport and exercise scientist:

• *Money.* As with many professions, some individuals feel that money, or the making of it, is the most important thing. There are, however, differences in how one is employed. Sport and exercise scientists who work for organizations that pay regular salaries, no matter the hours worked, could act differently than the professional hired and paid for by the hour. Scientists who have their eyes on maximizing working hours to increase their paychecks tend to look (or worse, are perceived by others to look) at every decision as a potential moneymaker.

• *Professional recognition.* Ambitious sport and exercise scientists seeking to climb their respective professional ladders may start to think about their work from the perspective of whether it allows them to publish peer-reviewed articles, give keynote addresses at conferences, or promote themselves in the media. Coaches and athletes can take a jaundiced view if they perceive that sport scientists are taking undue credit for their hard-won outcomes or associating themselves with winning teams for self-promotion.

• *Lifestyle.* Work at home when you want, mingle with famous athletes on a weekly basis, and have free access to fully equipped gyms, swimming pools, and tennis courts. Travel the world and go to the Olympic Games. What a job . . . what a life! Unfortunately, when the importance of lifestyle takes priority over the work, scientists can fall prey to making decisions to suit personal preferences over optimal outcomes, and, just as damaging, can appear to others to be doing so. Scientists who are, or who are perceived to be, more concerned with themselves than the program they are supporting quickly lose credibility.

• *Power.* Being in charge of people, money, and projects can feel good. Because most head coaches are quite focused on maintaining their own leadership roles, it can become problematic if scientists try to take too much control because they can quickly be perceived as threats to coaches. The other problem that can arise is when scientists spend all their time trying to achieve or maintain positions of power compared with trying to help the athletes.

• *Need to be needed.* Many sport and exercise scientists are motivated to help athletes across the spectrum and enjoy the sense of being needed and useful. These scientists need to be wary of encouraging elite athletes or coaches to enter into unhealthy codependent relationships (e.g., "you can't win without me"). It can also be painful for such an individual when things are going well, and there is no identified need. In such situations, a well-meaning professional can derail a good situation by trying too hard to be helpful when little, if any, help is required.

• *Job security.* Good timing or personal connections can enable some scientists to land jobs for which they are ill suited or underqualified. Over time, in these bad-fit situations, it is quite easy for scientists to feel ambivalent with regard to sporting outcomes because they are most concerned with not wanting to lose a job they know many other skillful professionals would like to have. Equally damaging is the long-term sport scientist who is competent but satisfied with being comfortable in the role. When key coaches and fellow staff move on, new staff and coaches can take over and evaluate the scientist with an increased level of scrutiny. Change becomes a threat when the possible outcome is having one's incompetence or limited commitment or interest revealed.

• *Genuine interest.* These professionals want to be exceptional at their jobs. They are motivated by their desire to learn and to contribute to the overall competitiveness of the team. Excellence is at the top of their favorite-attributes list, and they are prepared to work long and hard to be excellent in their areas of sport and exercise science. When this genuine interest is combined with solid appreciation for coaches and athletes (plus a high level of emotional intelligence), then scientists will rarely be disappointed because they can take pride in the quality of their work and their approaches, even when the team is not winning.

The major motivators for sport and exercise scientists are useful to recognize because they may noticeably contribute to how major decisions and conflicts are addressed. When the motivation to be a sport and exercise scientist drifts away from genuine interest and the desire to help others, there is a risk that the scientist may act in ways that undermine work quality and erode trust in key relationships (Brummelhuis, ter Hoeven, Bakker, & Peper, 2011).

Evolution of a Sport and Exercise Scientist: Part 2

Here, I (Dave) continue the tale of my involvement with the cycling team and how my own motivations and need to succeed in my role almost derailed the relationship I had with the team, as well as how I recognized and ultimately rectified my mistakes.

After finishing a difficult training session, Jane (not her real name) approached me while I was unpacking the car. She greeted me with, "Hey, Dave, it's great having you out here with us at training! I wondered if you were free this afternoon, maybe after my massage session, to talk a bit about how the training session went?" I thought to myself, "Could it get any better?" Not only was the coach inviting me to be part of the team during a training camp in Germany, but one of the most competitive female cyclists in the world was asking me for my advice on how to train in the lead-up to some important competitions.

I tried to act calm, saying, "Yeah, I am pretty sure I can fit in a meeting with you later this afternoon," but I was secretly thinking, "Yes, yes, yes—one of the best cyclists in the world wants my advice and support. Isn't this exciting? How good am I?"

I ate lunch with the national team coach (John, not his real name) that afternoon, and as we discussed our plans for the day, I casually mentioned my big news. "Jane asked me to meet with her this afternoon to talk about her training." I immediately noticed a change in John's demeanor, but with my self-absorbed focus on Jane and what she might want to talk about, I didn't think it was any big deal. Even if I had wanted to learn more about the coach's behavior, I certainly didn't feel that I had the kind of relationship with John that would allow me to explore his feelings.

We finished lunch, and I started to prepare for the meeting with Jane. I buried myself into facts and figures associated with the current training plan and the demands of Jane's upcoming races. By the time Jane arrived at my room, I was prepared and ready to go.

Upon arriving, Jane said, "Hello, thanks so much for seeing me, Dave. I have been watching you work and really appreciate your insights and contributions to the team. I was wondering if you could take a look at my training program and tell me if you think that scientifically we are doing the best thing to promote my fitness."

These comments were music to my ears. I was feeling confident and excited as I asked Jane to outline what she wanted to talk about. Jane's smile faded to a serious expression, and with some worry in her voice, she told me about her concerns with fatigue and her recent form. "I have been really struggling on some of the training rides, and so when I saw the program that John handed out yesterday, I got a little worried about whether it will really work for me. It seems like he writes the same thing for everyone—usually dishing out a bit too much—without taking my specific situation into account."

It didn't even occur to me that Jane might be trying to manipulate me; I was hooked and engaged in the moment. Her message came through loud and clear: the coach had given her an average, generic, and unscientific training program, and she wanted me, the expert, to prepare a plan that was exceptional! She had me at "hello."

I responded, "Well, we know that John is a good guy and an incredibly knowledgeable coach. However, I can also imagine, with all the demands on his time, that he might not have the time to be able to get to really individualizing his programs." Jane was in total agreement and pressed me by saying, "Just take a look—any feedback would be great!" I reviewed the training program prepared for Jane and came to the conclusion that a little less volume would be the best plan of attack. When I suggested that Jane reduce her total training volume with a greater emphasis on race-specific intervals and recovery, her face lit up. I was thinking that we were now unified in thought, connecting philosophically and trusting one another completely. For me, it was another successful day in the office.

After planning out a couple of training weeks for Jane with this changed focus, I started to think about how I would address this topic with John, the head coach. I assumed that when John heard about the time I invested into one of his top athletes, he was going to tell me how much he appreciated my support. In my mind, the conversation would end with John giving me a congratulatory pat on the back and buying me a beer. Was I wrong! The next day, after some preliminary discussions about the day's logistics, I brought up the situation with Jane and how I modified her training. John's anger quickly became evident. He exclaimed, "So you have decided to start coaching Jane! How many other athletes on my team have you decided to coach?" I was startled and a bit shocked at the question. I answered, "John, I know that there is only one head coach, and that's you!" even as I realized full well that my interaction with Jane suggested otherwise. John shot back, "Well, I am just letting you know that Jane told me that after 'a very long and extensive review of her training with Dr. Martin,' she would not be participating in the long ride scheduled for tomorrow, but instead would get some much-needed sleep and prepare for her next hard session. Not only that, Jane tells me that you provided her with great insight into a far more appropriate and individualized training program." As John described this conversation to me, his disappointment and frustration were clear. He asked me again, "How many cyclists on my team are you coaching? It's important for me to know because I'm really busy running the show, and if you're taking over the job of writing training programs, it would save me a hell of a lot of time."

I was just starting to become aware of what was happening, and the realization brought a sense of dread and guilt. I tried to explain. "Coach, she came to me, I did not approach her. In any event, I want you to know that I supported you and was only trying to help! I had been planning on talking to you to see what you thought about the training option I had outlined—that's why I came to you today!" None of my apologies, rationales, or excuses was working. John was outraged, and his anger (justifiably) was directed at me. How could I have been so stupid and naïve? I was completely unsettled. Was it possible that my little meeting with Jane had actually made things worse, not better? Perhaps Jane and I could get together with John in a three-way face-to-face meeting and talk through our emotions and perceptions. I tried to offer this option to John, but he wouldn't even consider it. He brushed aside my plea for forgiveness and walked out while muttering something about me not knowing the first thing about coaching.

The next week was agonizing for me. John gave me the silent treatment and wouldn't acknowledge my presence. The comments that did come my way were laced with resentment. He would inform the training squad that "Dr. Martin and Jane will be doing 'their own thing,' so there will be a few extra seats in the bus on the way home." Bottom line, Jane got her special treatment, the coach repositioned his relationship with me to ensure he maintained power and respect, and I was left out in the cold. I felt used, abused, unappreciated, guilty, and hopeless. To make matters worse, when the coach was not around and I had a chance to link up with other members of the support team (soft-tissue therapist and mechanic), I would vent and let the others know that the coach was being a real jerk. I told the other uninformed support staff that I thought the coach was emotionally unintelligent and had completely lost the plot, and I retold the story in a way that favored my virtues. I spent the week feeling like "poor me." For a while, I was able to convince myself that for no reason at all, an irrational coach was treating me like crap.

After a couple of weeks and after a lot of reflection, I had a chance in a team meeting to announce to the group that I had made a terrible mistake, and I wanted to let everyone know that I was going to adopt some new rules of engagement with athletes. I mentioned that John was an amazing coach and that I had long wanted to work with someone of his caliber and with his great insight. Although I was very excited by the talent of the cyclists on the team, and as much as I wanted to help everyone out, I could see now that John was the one with the big picture. Therefore, I would talk to athletes about their training programs only with him in the room. Over time, perhaps because of what I said, but maybe due only to time, the head coach softened his anger. Without any formal resolution, our relationship got back on track, and we started to work together again.

In retrospect, this was a painful but wonderful learning experience that taught me how important the higher order of "the pride" is for ultimate balance and performance. I learned that I was not just attached to the team but was truly part of the team; therefore, every one of my actions could have profound reactions, sometimes bad but also sometimes good. The experience also left me with a new appreciation for the many difficulties head coaches face and an understanding of how complex the social interactions among a team of passionate experts can become. I learned how critical it was to be aware of the big picture, as well as how my actions could be perceived by both leadership staff and the athletes on the team. Although I had been honestly trying to help out an elite athlete, my ego had become involved, and my actions reflected my desire to be liked and feel approval. I was not purely contributing to the higher ideals of a winning team.

Other Sport Scientist Mistakes

There are so many ways to contribute to conflict when working within the intense environments associated with elite sport. In many cases, the kinds of personalities that thrive in this dog-eat-dog world—supremely confident, brash, outgoing, and arrogant are common descriptors—can be a scientist's undoing when negotiating outcomes for others' benefit in the white-hot stress of a competitive season.

Different forms of undoing can happen to those scientists who, usually unwittingly, overstep a healthy sense of self-esteem and allow narcissistic needs to dominate their actions. Narcissism is an aspect of self we all share in varying degrees when we consider ourselves as important, expect others to treat us as such, and see criticisms as attacks (Twenge & Campbell, 2009). It is the job of sport and exercise scientists to manage their narcissistic needs in a healthy way and to not allow those needs to confuse their motives or prompt them to put themselves ahead of the coaches and athletes they are serving. Despite our best intentions, however, elite sport culture, with its high-profile status, excitement, unpredictability, and in many cases significant rewards to the victor, can sometimes seduce even the well-intentioned scientist. Here is a list of the more frequent mistakes made by ambitious, yet usually well-meaning, sport and exercise scientists.

• *"You are nothing without me."* It is a wonderful feeling to be needed, respected, admired, and important. Unfortunately, for the majority of sport and exercise scientists, time spent researching, analyzing, and educating elite athletes does not directly transfer to improved performances. Often, some scientists can find themselves seeking external validation of their worth by twisting the truth and creating elaborate rationales, erroneously linking their work to performance outcomes to convince the athletes and the coaches that they cannot be world class without the scientist's expertise.

• *"You will win if you buy this."* Money is a major motivator for so many professionals, and sport and exercise scientists are no different. Dieticians selling supplements, strength and conditioning specialists selling resistance training devices, and recovery scientists selling portable hydrotherapy units are all at risk of putting their business interests first and the actual needs of athletes second. When these sorts of scenarios play out, the coach and athlete can end up feeling used and manipulated, which can have negative lingering effects that taint ongoing relationships.

• *"I am the (best) expert."* It is easy for a sport and exercise scientist to pretend to be great and wise to help sell a message with conviction. Even more dangerous are those scientists who actually believe what they are saying, even when what they are saying is not research based or widely supported. All too often, ambitious scientists, even smart ones, forget that for many questions that pertain to elite sport, it is OK and preferable to say, "I don't know." The scientist can then collaborate with other experts to come up with a reasonable solution after discussing the matter with the coach (often the true expert) and the athletes.

• *"Don't trust the coach."* Coaches who recognize that winning takes a lot of hard work often make decisions that don't sit well with athletes. Match such a situation with a sport and exercise scientist who needs to be liked by the athletes, and you have a perfect recipe for a scientist who will (perhaps even unwittingly) undermine the leadership of the coach. All sport psychologists or physiotherapists need to say when they find themselves alone with an exhausted athlete who is performing poorly is, "I can't believe how much the coach is making you do. I reckon they need to back off if you are ever going to start performing well again." One statement like this one, and the scientist has undermined the coach. Be clear about your own need to be liked and how you are meeting it, and be crystal clear about who it is you are working for by respecting the person in that position with both word and action.

• *"What's in it for me?"* Life as a sport and exercise scientist is hard work, and it requires the scientist to be available and giving. This stance doesn't come naturally to many scientists, who have been primarily focused on proving to the world how smart they are. This servant mentality can be tested when it is party time for everyone else but the scientist, who still has to pack up equipment or review the technical aspects of a performance. For a variety of reasons—a blurring of roles, the resentment emanating from unmet narcissistic needs, or simple complacency—over time, the scientist can feel like he has earned some privileges and, consequently, can turn lazy, selfish, and choosy about the type of work he wants to do. Supporting a track cycling race in Moscow in the middle of the winter becomes "impossible to schedule in," but there seems to be plenty of time to fit in a trip to Hawaii to help out some Ironman triathletes. Coaches and athletes can quickly discriminate between those professionals who go the hard yards and earn respect through their willingness to dig in and learn and those who don't.

• *"Everyone loves a winner."* When athletes are winning, everyone wants to be associated with them. The media call and the fans want autographs. It can be seductive for the scientist to want to bask in the glory and maybe along the way take ownership of a little piece of the pie as well. Healthy scientists have a realistic sense of the value of their own contributions to outcomes and can freely give credit where it is due, to the athletes who achieved the results and to the coaches who coached them. They also recognize the fallacy of taking credit for outcomes they may or may not have influenced and are not theirs to own. On the other hand, even talented athletes can have a bad day in the office, and when that happens, it is often a starkly different story. The "losers" are often left on their own—sad, frustrated, sometimes angry, and disappointed. Savvy scientists will recognize an athlete's struggles as a great opportunity. In the vacuum of support that can follow a perceived failure, gestures of support are often the most appreciated. It is also true that in the humble aftermath of deep disappointment, some athletes will finally be receptive to exploring new preparation strategies for competition. If the scientist makes it a habit to hang out only with the winners, it can cause resentment in those athletes who start to sense they are working with a fair-weather sailor, someone more concerned with being associated with winners than with actually helping everyone get better.

• *"You'll never make it."* For the scientist harboring a sense of inflated superiority, thoughts of "I should be spending my time with the best athletes!" can easily justify the dismissal of athletes perceived as less valuable. If sport and exercise scientists start to form opinions that particular athletes will never become successful, they may be doing a disservice to the profession. There are many examples of athletes, such as Michael Jordan, who failed repeatedly early in their careers but later developed capabilities and approaches that allowed them to dominate their sports. Athletes need people who believe in them if they are going to grow and achieve sporting goals. It may do little good, and possibly great harm, when sport scientists, who are perceived by some as experts, give up on athletes based on some preliminary test results or performances.

• *"The glass is half empty."* Having fun, remaining optimistic, selling hope, and being motivational are all prerequisites for people working in elite sport. True, there are highly successful coaches who don't tick all these boxes, but for sport and exercise scientists who want to be catalysts for success, being positive and optimistic around the coaches and athletes is probably the best professional stance to take.

Final Thoughts

When it comes to elite sport and exercise science, it is our experience that the relationships we develop are a large part of what drives our potential successes or failures as we work in this dynamic and challenging environment. If awareness of relationships contributes to understanding, and understanding contributes to improvements in practice, then we are hopeful that this chapter will assist many sport and exercise scientists who are wrestling with emotional and relationship issues that can interrupt and derail the real value that scientists can bring to elite sport. Engaging in regular self-reflection can help sport and exercise scientists monitor their emotions and motives so that their intentions remain genuine and unclouded by ego and personal gain.

References

Bornstein, R.F., & Languirand, M.A. (2003). *Healthy dependency: Leaning on others without losing yourself.* New York, NY: New Market Press.

Brummelhuis, L.L., ter Hoeven, C.L., Bakker, A.B., & Peper, B. (2011). Breaking through the loss cycle of burnout: The role of motivation. *Journal of Occupational and Organizational Psychology, 84,* 268–287.

Clark, V.R., Hopkins W.G., Hawley, J.A,. & Burke, L.M. (2000). Placebo effect of carbohydrate feedings during a 40-km cycling time trial. *Medicine & Science in Sports & Exercise, 32,* 1642–1647.

Cohen, J.M., & Cohen, J. (Eds.). (1998). *The new Penguin dictionary of quotations* (Rev. ed.). London, England: Penguin Books.

Eccles, D.W., & Tenenbaum, G. (2004). Why an expert team is more than a team of experts: A social-cognitive conceptualization of team coordination and communication in sport. *Journal of Sport & Exercise Psychology, 26,* 542–560.

Ericsson, K.A., Krampe, R.T., & Tesch-Romer, C. (1993). The role of deliberate practice in the acquisition of expert performance. *Psychological Review, 100,* 363–406.

Foad, A.J., Beedie, C.J., & Coleman, D.A. (2008). Pharmacological and psychological effects of caffeine ingestion in 40-km cycling performance. *Medicine & Science in Sports & Exercise, 30,* 158–165.

Kitchen, M. (2012). Facilitating small groups: How to encourage student learning. *The Clinical Teacher, 9,* 3–8.

Kristiansen, E., Tomten, S.E., Hanstad, D.V., & Roberts, G.C. (2012). Coaching communication issues with elite female athletes: Two Norwegian case studies. *Scandinavian Journal of Medicine and Science in Sports, 22,* 156–167.

Mallett, C.J., & Hanrahan, S.J. (2004). Elite athletes: Why does the 'fire' burn so brightly? *Psychology of Sport and Exercise, 5,* 183–200.

Rapisarda, B.A. (2002). The impact of emotional intelligence on work team cohesiveness and performance. *International Journal of Organizational Analysis, 10,* 363–379.

Stebbings, J., Taylor, I.M., Spray, C.M., & Ntoumanis, N. (2012). Antecedents of perceived coach interpersonal behaviors: The coaching environment and coach psychological well- and ill-being. *Journal of Sport & Exercise Psychology, 34,* 481–502.

Twenge, J.M., & Campbell, W.K. (2009). *The narcissism epidemic: Living in the age of entitlement.* New York, NY: Simon & Schuster.

CHAPTER 3

Running Across Borders
Cross-Cultural Exercise Psychology

Stephanie J. Hanrahan

The anatomy and physiology of people is fairly consistent across cultures, and physical activity generally has a protective effect for all people. The direction of the association between physical activity and health outcomes is the same across racial and ethnic groups (Physical Activity Guidelines Advisory Committee, 2008). Similarly, sedentary living is a problem across cultures. Physical inactivity is the fourth leading risk factor for global mortality (World Health Organization, 2010). Inactivity is not just an issue in developed countries. Physical inactivity levels are rising in many countries, a trend that has major implications for the prevalence of noncommunicable diseases and the general health of the world's population (World Health Organization, 2010).

Although it would be possible to write an entire book on the relationships between culture, psychology, and exercise (perhaps similar to Schinke and Hanrahan's [2009] *Cultural Sport Psychology*, but for exercise), this chapter serves as only an introduction to the topic. The issues considered include culturally sensitive measurement of physical activity; the effects of immigration, religion, and ethnicity on physical activity; practical examples of cultural competency; and a model of cultural competence development.

Culturally Sensitive Measurement of Physical Activity

Many studies have investigated the rates of physical activity in various countries. For example, in a survey of 11,033 Brazilian adults (20 years of age or older), only 13% reported performing a minimum of 30 minutes of leisure-time physical activity on one or more days of the week,

and only 3.3% reported doing the recommended 30 minutes on five or more days per week (Monteiro et al., 2003). In another study, over 57,000 individuals from 22 African countries completed the Global Physical Activity Questionnaire (Armstrong & Bull, 2006) to assess physical activity in a typical week. When physical activity for work, transport, and leisure time was included, 83.8% of men and 75.7% of women were moderately active at least 150 minutes per week. The percentages differed by country and ranged from 46.8% to 96%. Most of the activity was related to work or transport; leisure-time physical activity was rare (Guthold et al., 2011).

What is evident from looking at these two studies is that how physical activity is measured will definitely influence results. On the surface, Brazilians appear to be less active than Africans, but the African study included activity related to work and transport, whereas the Brazilian study did not. Many of the questionnaires used to measure physical activity have been constructed for use in developed countries, so the transfer to use in other settings may be questionable. Even if surveys include activities that are relevant to multiple cultures, the energy expenditures may vary widely across cultures. For example, some questionnaires include the work activity of light farming, but the energy cost of light farming is probably different in sub-Saharan Africa than in the United States (Wareham, 2001). Not including culture-specific activities may underestimate physical activities in that culture, but including culture-specific activities may make it difficult to compare physical activity across cultures. Measurement of physical activity is not the focus of this chapter, but nevertheless there is a need to be able to demonstrate the equivalency, or lack thereof, of cross-cultural activity questionnaires (Mâsse, 2000).

One aspect of physical activity engagement (or disengagement) that appears to be true across many cultures is age-related decline in physical activity. Even within relatively small age ranges, there is evidence of declines in physical activity in Turkey (ages 11–14; Kin-Isler, Asci, Altintas, & Guven-Karahan, 2009), Finland (ages 12–15; Telama & Yang, 2000), and the United States (ages 12–18; Caspersen, Pereira, & Curran, 2000).

Effects of Immigration

Immigration can have an effect on physical activity. Sometimes that immigration can have a positive effect. For example, the percentage of Israelis who engaged in physical activity more than doubled (to almost 56%) between 1992 and 2008, with the most dominant form of exercise being walking (Galily, Tamir, Meckel, & Eliakim, 2012). One possible explanation of this increase in activity is the demographic changes that took place during that time. There had been mass immigration from the former Soviet Union (now 20% of the Israeli population), which had a strong sporting culture. Levin, Ainsworth, Kwok, Addy, and Popkin (1999) found that almost 70% of Russian youth (14–18 years) engage in 30 minutes or more of physical activity five or more days per week. Immigration may not have been the only factor influencing the increase in Israeli physical activity. In the same time period, there was a decrease in working hours (resulting in more time for leisure), media campaigns that likely increased public awareness of health issues, and improved urban infrastructure (e.g., bike paths, sports fields, fitness apparatus in parks). There may also have been a perceived gain in social prestige through engagement in physical activity (i.e., physical activity had become fashionable), and increased recognition of women's rights and abilities that may have strengthened the legitimacy of female engagement in physical activity (Galily et al., 2012).

Immigration, however, may not have a positive effect. Migration from non-English-speaking countries to Western, English-speaking societies can have detrimental effects on health behaviors and health status as the migrants explore new cultures and customs and assimilate to their new surroundings. At the same time, these migrants are unlikely to be proactive in accessing health care or undertaking preventative measures. Physical inactivity is common in these migrants, and is a key contributing risk factor to chronic diseases (Caperchione, Kolt, & Mummery, 2009).

Even without major immigration influences, cultural norms regarding exercise change over time. Hu et al. (2002) found that people in Tiankin, China, engage in a high level of physical activity when commuting (i.e., 96% of females and 91% of males reported about 30 minutes of daily walking or cycling to and from work, school, and shops). Even so, the marked increase in the acquisition of motor vehicles has resulted in a growing prevalence of obesity in men and women in China (Bell & Popkin, 2002). The low level of leisure-time physical activity in Tiankin (Hu et al., 2002) may therefore become problematic with a decrease in physical activity for travel.

During this discussion of different cultures, I want to stress what should be an obvious point: people from one country are not culturally homogenous. For example, Hong Kong Chinese people (60–91 years) who had migrated to Australia were interviewed about their views on aging and their experience of participation in physical activity (Koo, 2011). Some participants defined age as number of years alive. These individuals tended to have fatalistic attitudes, low levels of physical activity, and the belief that it is their children's responsibility to take care of them in the future. Other Hong Kong Chinese immigrants to Australia defined age as a state of one's physical health, appearance, and ability to continue to fulfill one's social roles. These individuals tended to focus on quality of life, lead active lives, and believe in the importance of having physical independence.

For many migrants, language can be a barrier to physical activity. If individuals are not able to follow activity instructions from instructors or program manuals, they will find it difficult to take part and may drop out in frustration. For some individuals (e.g., some Latin and South Asian migrants), a sense of religious fatalism can get in the way of regular exercise. Examples of this, sometimes subtle, fatalism are that prayer alone can help them stay healthy; their health is in God's hands; and health, illness, and death are pre-ordained by Allah or God (Caperchione et al., 2009). A third frequently reported barrier is the effect of migration on social relationships. Separation from family and friends can result in social isolation. In turn, loss of social connectedness can have a negative effect on physical activity participation.

Migrants and refugees who move to Western countries because of economic hardships, war, or displacement are frequently dealing with poverty, limited access to facilities or transportation, and low education and literacy levels. These socioeconomic challenges can result in environmental barriers. Low socioeconomic status (SES) often means living in areas of high crime and violence, which can lead to fears for safety that will limit outdoor activity. Changes in climate may also be a barrier to physical activity. For example, those migrants from warm climates have reported finding it difficult to breathe in cold weather (Caperchione et al., 2009). Another potential barrier is the perception of health and injury. Some individuals of Pakistani and Indian origin who had recently migrated to the UK perceived sweating, increased heart rate, and breathlessness during exercise to be illness states and something to be avoided (Caperchione et al., 2009). Some migrants also have reported having a fear of injury from falling or overexertion (Caperchione et al., 2009).

Even when people do not leave their countries of origin, they (and their physical activity patterns) can be influenced through colonialization. In Africa, physical education is considered to have gone through four historic phases (Amusa & Toriola, 2010). Initially, physical education was rooted in traditional practices such as food gathering and hunting, as well as in intertribal conflicts. During this time, physical prowess was highly revered. The second phase involved colonial and missionary models of education that considered indigenous physical activities to be primitive and immoral. Western and colonial influences placed emphasis on military drills and physical training, both of which had limited relevance to indigenous African populations. During the third phase, when the African countries attained independence, physical education was redefined with the emergence of the continent as a

sport power. In the fourth and current phase, several physical education and sport programs have collapsed due to limited funding. What remains is still a replica of the colonial and postindependence model—not truly African and, therefore, probably not sustainable (Amusa & Toriola, 2010).

Effects of Religion

Religion can also influence physical activity. In a study with Jewish adolescents from two large U.S. cities with significant Jewish populations, the less religious adolescents perceived greater paternal support of physical activity, but the more religious adolescents perceived stronger environmental support of physical activity (Kahan, 2005). Another example is Muslims who traditionally pray five times per day, something that might be perceived by non-Muslims as disruptive to planned activity programs. Also, many Muslims interpret scriptures of the Quran as prohibiting women from participating in many types of physical activity (e.g., those not centered on household, familial, and wifely duties; Caperchione et al., 2009).

Walseth and Fasting (2003) investigated Egyptian university student women's views on the relationship between Islam and physical activity and sport. Egypt is a country where 46% of women aged 15 to 24 are illiterate compared to 29% of men in the same age group and where a feature of Sharia law (i.e., the testimony from one man is equal to the testimonies of two women) is applied in family court (but not criminal proceedings). The women in the study generally thought that Islam is positive toward physical activity and sport in three ways: (a) physical activity is good for health, and Muslims are to take care of their bodies because the body is a gift from Allah; (b) life should contain both seriousness and play, and physical activity or sport can be a form of play; and (c) Islam emphasizes the importance of being in good physical condition in case of war (Walseth & Fasting, 2003).

In terms of women participating in sport and physical activity, however, the views were less positive. Some followers of the various subgroups within Islam prefer that Muslim women wear the veil, and many participants felt it was impossible to do sport with the veil on. They felt that they could be physically active only at home or in sex-segregated studios. Generally, they thought it was okay to be physically active in front of men if their bodies were covered, and they were not doing moves that might excite the men who watch them (such as gymnastics and dance). The more fundamental Muslim women, however, thought that all kinds of physical activity by women were dangerous because of the excitement it creates if done in front of men. Regardless of their personal views, most of the women in the study felt that their patriarchal society meant that men in their families decided whether they were allowed to participate in sport and physical activity (Walseth & Fasting, 2003). Some of the Muslim women in the study described a nonsecular relationship between sport and religion—people may participate in sport to get closer to God (rather than athletes using religion or God to perform better in sport; Walseth & Fasting, 2003).

Another view of issues related to Muslim females participating in physical activity comes from Dagkas and Benn's (2006) interviews with Muslim girls living in Greece (ages 13–15) and England (ages 18–21) about their experience in physical education (PE). Most of the girls had enjoyed PE, and recognized the health benefits of the activity. Enjoyment of PE was linked to being successful, doing interesting things in a comfortable environment, and having understanding teachers. The Muslim girls needed private spaces to change clothes and needed to participate in same-sex groupings that were not in public spaces. Some of the girls had experienced problems with strict policies about what they should wear (they wanted to cover their legs). The month of Ramadan was also an issue. During Ramadan, many Muslims do not eat or drink during the day. Culturally sensitive teachers allowed the girls to perform less strenuous and demanding activities during Ramadan and wear tracksuit bottoms or leggings. Meeting religious requirements was seen to be more problematic in England than Greece. British teachers seemed to be less aware of Muslim religious requirements than their Greek counterparts. In addition, British students had higher consciousness and more anxiety about meeting religious requirements than the Greek students. Greek Muslims appeared to have more closely assimi-

lated into the dominant culture (Dagkas & Benn, 2006).

A third perspective of Muslim girls and physical activity comes from East African (Somali and Ethiopian) adolescent girls who were first- or second-generation immigrants to the United States (i.e., Muslims who were migrants to a country where Muslims are a minority; Thul & LaVoi, 2011). These East African Muslim girls perceived swimming (in a guaranteed female-only space), jump rope, biking, dance, and nonorganized recreational sports (e.g., soccer and basketball) as the most culturally relevant physical activities. After-school obligations (e.g., cooking, cleaning, babysitting, homework) meant that many did not have enough time for physical activity. The girls suggested that having physical activity programs before and during school might help them deal with this barrier. These girls also felt they had low perceived competence about physical activity in relation to their non-Muslim peers. They felt that a possible solution to this issue would be to have culturally relevant activities with instruction from female coaches who were culturally respectful and understanding. Two additional deterrents to physical activity were their male peers' gender stereotypes (i.e., girls are weak and incapable of being physically active) and their parents' limited understanding (and support) of the importance of physical activity and the belief that physical activity may detract from normative gender roles that girls are expected to uphold in East African families. The girls felt that educating parents about the importance of physical activity was central to increasing their activity levels (Thul & LaVoi, 2011).

Effects of Ethnicity

To group people by religion (e.g., Muslim) is also a kind of cultural myopia. For example, followers of Islam represent a huge variety of ethnic groups from around the world, and within any one country (e.g., United States), there may be folks from literally hundreds of different cultures. In a qualitative study, Eyler and colleagues (1998) gathered information from focus groups of minority women in the United States who were over 40 years of age. Most of the participants, who were Chinese Americans, Filipino Americans,

Blacks, Hispanics, and Native Americans, believed themselves to be adequately physically active, but many stated that *exercise* had greater mental health benefits than physical activity. Housework and workday activities involved physical activity but were not considered to be exercise. Dancing was described as a favorite activity, and many did lots of walking because they did not drive. Several stated that women of their ethnicity were naturally physically active due to gender roles within their culture. Many indicated they cared for extended family (e.g., grandchildren). Being a single parent was a reason some gave for not exercising or participating in more physical activities. Some of the women considered mainstream forms of exercise such as aerobics to be a waste of time because nothing is being accomplished. Fear of a heart attack was a common reason for not beginning an exercise program. Safety concerns (e.g., traffic, people, dogs) were mentioned by all groups as a deterrent to exercise, and a limited number of age and culturally appropriate programs in their communities and the associated costs of activity programs were perceived to be environmental barriers. Facilitating factors for physical activity were social support (e.g., help with caregiving responsibilities), programs at community centers with culturally similar people, and having scenic places to exercise (mentioned only by Native American groups; Eyler et al., 1998).

Belza et al. (2004) also investigated the motivations and barriers of physical activity with focus groups, each of a different minority in the United States (Native Americans, African Americans, Vietnamese, Filipinos, Chinese, Latinos, and Koreans), but with an older age group (mean age = 71). All groups considered exercise to be a component of health promotion, preferred walking as the main form of exercise, reported that chronic conditions and environmental barriers (e.g., weather, safety, and cost) hindered their involvement in physical activity, and considered family to be encouraging of exercise. There were, however, ethnic-specific themes. The Chinese, Korean, and Vietnamese participants all mentioned the importance of having a daily physical activity routine. Nevertheless, there were also differences between the various Asian groups. The Cantonese-speaking Chinese tended to believe exercise was

critical for maintaining health in older adults, but felt that social obligations might get in the way of exercise. The Koreans (of all ages) expressed feelings of being isolated from other Koreans (even among other Asians). The Vietnamese generally agreed with the Koreans that geographic isolation was a main barrier to physical activity, but also believed that physical activity helps with longevity and the avoidance of medication use. They also mentioned that determination and willpower were important for regular participation in physical activity. Native Americans in the study reported that low self-esteem was associated with low motivation for self-care (including physical activity), and tended to feel uncomfortable exercising around people from other cultures. Within the Filipino cohort, exercise was perceived to be important to counteract the high-fat diet in the United States. Community, laughter, and socializing were also identified as important contributors to physical activity, although many of the participants were involved in paid or volunteer work that kept them physically active. Older Filipinos also noted the effect of the age of participants. They felt out of place when physical activities predominantly involved young people. The Latinos in the study emphasized music, singing, and dancing as ways to remain physically active. They perceived the primary barrier to physical activity to be not having a friend with whom to be active. The strongest theme for African Americans was the importance of friends encouraging them to exercise. They favored group activities and, similar to the Vietnamese respondents, they considered determination to be of high importance (Belza et al., 2004).

Qualitative studies about physical activity have been done with Hispanic women living in the United States and African American men and women. In a study with eight middle-aged immigrant Hispanic women whose primary motive for moving to the United States was to make money for their families, D'Alonzo and Sharma (2010) found that six of the eight had not worked outside the home in their native countries. All eight women unanimously agreed that they had no time for themselves. They had multiple jobs, most of which entailed heavy physical work, yet the women were still responsible for domestic duties at home (even though none still had young children). For them it was an economic necessity that work came first. This norm of placing family needs above their own, a form of female self-sacrifice, is known as *marianismo*, the female counterpart of *machismo*. Marianismo has a negative effect on health-promoting behaviors such as exercise among Hispanic women. Physical activity is often perceived to be self-indulgent rather than health promoting (D'Alonzo & Sharma, 2010). Hispanic women living in the United States may experience cultural conflict between marianismo and mainstream American culture, even though they may feel that working hard and getting ahead is part of the American way.

Day-to-day cultural conflict can lead to depressed moods and low exercise self-efficacy (when the cultural mismatch relates to physical activity). Having an individualistic perspective about self-care (the North American norm) may ignore perceived responsibilities toward others. It is worth noting here that the majority of health recommendations for physical activity (e.g., Centers for Disease Control and Prevention, American Council on Exercise, and the President's Council on Fitness, Sports & Nutrition) are based on leisure-time physical activity, which is an elitist viewpoint. All eight women in D'Alonzo and Sharma's (2010) study acknowledged that their lives were unhealthy, but they believed they did not have leisure time in which to engage in physical activity. Short-term strategies to contribute to family incomes had grown into long-term strategies that were draining them physically and emotionally. As one participant stated, "We know this is no good for us. We are killing ourselves" (D'Alonzo & Sharma, 2010, p. 245).

Similar to Hispanic women perceiving a relationship between their gender roles and barriers to physical activity, some urban African American men perceive barriers to physical activity related to male gender-role strain (Griffith, Gunter, & Allen, 2011). Many African American men perceive work, family, and community commitments to be more important than engaging in physical activity. Their social and cultural norms prioritize work and other responsibilities ahead of physical activity, either individually or as a social activity. Many also feel that the effort they are exerting to try to fulfill the provider role limits their energy to engage in physical activity (Griffith et al., 2011).

Airhihenbuwa, Kumanyika, Agurs, and Lowe (1995) explored the motives and attitudes toward exercise of urban African Americans ($N = 53$) using focus groups that were stratified by age (13–17, 18–35, 36–64, 65+). The majority of respondents had incomes of less than $20,000 (USD) per year, so it is possible that the results could be attributed as much to low SES as to ethnicity. The researchers defined exercise as leisure-time physical activity for the purpose of improving cardiorespiratory fitness and general well-being. Most of the participants considered exercise, on top of their work or daily activities, not to be needed. They generally considered rest to be more important than exercise. There was a wide perception that the only jobs available to [low-income] African Americans involved physical labor. Multiple age groups acknowledged that young African American males might exercise for better physiques, which were believed to be sought after for three reasons; (a) they like to have nice bodies, (b) they have to be tough to survive in low-income areas, and (c) they have nothing other than their bodies with which to attract young women (Airhihenbuwa et al., 1995). One focus group explained that young White males focus on studying to find a job and young African American males focus on physical goals. Older African American men reported that they did not exercise because they were happy to retire to rest after lifetimes of hard physical labor, or they could not exercise because of physical problems (e.g., heart disease, injuries). This age group acknowledged that many health problems can be alleviated by exercise, but participants also reported that African American men are more accepting of death than White men, and therefore they don't try to use exercise to delay death (Airhihenbuwa et al., 1995). Their perceptions were that Whites exercise because of a greater fear of death. Among professional African American women, exercising during lunch hour was not considered to be an option because they dislike public showers and don't want to mess up their hair. Respondents across ages reported preferring group-related activities (e.g., social dancing, playing ball), and thought that Whites preferred individual activities such as jogging (Airhihenbuwa et al., 1995).

Yan and McCullagh (2004) determined that cultural differences appear to affect children's physical activity motivation more than gender or age. Children (ages 12–16) from China ($n = 155$), American-born Chinese ($n = 122$), and American children (at least one Caucasian parent; $n = 147$) responded to a questionnaire about physical activity motivation. Regardless of gender or age, the American children tended to be motivated by competition and improving skills, $\chi^2 (421) = 4.88, p < .05$; the Chinese children indicated socializing and getting-fit motives, $\chi^2 (421) = 6.28, p < .01$; and the American-born Chinese children appeared to be motivated by travel, equipment use, and having fun, $\chi^2 (421) = 3.55, p < .05$ (Yan & McCullagh, 2004).

Madanat and Merrill (2006) found Jordanian college students to be similar to the Chinese children in that staying in shape was the strongest motivational factor for physical activity. But, unlike the Chinese children, the Jordanians' weakest motivation factors were socializing and recreation. These results were the same regardless of the stage of change of the individual (i.e., precontemplation, contemplation, preparation, action, or maintenance; Madanat & Merrill, 2006).

Some of the international differences in motives might be related to different construals of self (Markus & Kitayama, 1991). People with independent construals of self (individualistic cultures) strive to be unique and direct, and to express themselves, realize internal attributes, and promote their own goals. Others are used for social comparison and reflected appraisal to evaluate the self. People with interdependent construals of self (collectivistic cultures) endeavor to be indirect, and to belong, fit in, occupy their proper places, engage in appropriate actions, promote others' goals. The role of others is to define the self; relationships with others in specific contexts define the self. These different construals of self influence cognitions, emotions, and motivations (Markus & Kitayama, 1991), and in turn may affect why, where, and how individuals engage in exercise.

Practical Applications and Developing Cultural Competence

Given all of these cultural differences in terms of motives and attitudes toward physical activity and exercise, what practical tactics might emanate from this knowledge? Some of the considerations for health professionals include acknowledging cultural diversity, being culturally sensitive, and delivering programs and interventions that place individuals at the center and respond to their specific needs. Examples for working with some Muslim girls and women could include structuring activity times to work around prayer and Ramadan and blocking windows so men cannot see women engaging in exercise. For people from other cultures, activity interventions might need to involve bringing programs to the geographic areas where they live or providing child care, transportation, and activities that involve culture-specific traditions and customs (Caperchione et al., 2009).

Henwood (2007) provided an example of using local cultural knowledge as a vehicle to promote health within a Maori (New Zealand) community. Using Maori customs and traditions as vehicles for improving physical activity (and nutrition) validated the Maori way of doing things. Maori traditional games, activities, and weaponry were repackaged as forms of entertainment and exercise (e.g., performing traditional and contemporary dance, rebuilding and restoring a traditional sailing canoe, walking to historic places of local significance, training with weapons). Doing the activities at a Maori meeting place was perceived to be spiritually uplifting and more conducive to the community members' overall well-being than attending a gym (it also avoided the costs associated with gyms; Henwood, 2007). This Maori physical activity program is a demonstration of cultural competence.

Some people tend to perceive cultural competence as a dichotomized variable; one is either culturally competent or culturally incompetent. Wells (2000), however, offered a six-stage model of cultural development, with three cognitive and three affective stages. The cognitive stages come first and involve gaining knowledge about culture and its manifestations. The affective stages emphasize attitudinal and behavioral change through the application of knowledge gained in the cognitive phases. Wells (2000) noted that the affective phase requires actual engagement with people from diverse cultures. The first stage is cultural incompetence, where there is no awareness of the cultural implications of health behavior. The second stage is cultural knowledge, which involves the process of learning the elements of cultures and their roles that shape and define health behavior. The final cognitive stage is cultural awareness, where there is recognition and understanding of the cultural implications of behavior. The first affective stage is cultural sensitivity, which involves the integration of cultural knowledge and awareness into individual and institutional behaviors. The second affective stage is cultural competence, where there is routine application of culturally appropriate health care interventions and practices. The final stage is cultural proficiency, which involves integrating cultural competence into practice, teaching, and research as well as extending cultural competence into the organizational culture. Wells (2000) noted two guiding principles for cultural development: (a) maintaining a broad, objective, and open attitude toward individuals and their cultures (avoiding the use of one's own culture as a yardstick against which other cultural practices are judged), and (b) avoiding seeing individuals as alike because stereotyping does not allow for individual differences.

One could argue that many researchers in the area of exercise psychology have been culturally incompetent, at least in terms of their research. Many of the theories used within exercise psychology have been largely developed in studies that used White, English-speaking, middle- or high-SES participants and operated on an unvoiced assumption that these theories apply to everyone. Edmunds, Duda, and Ntoumanis (2010) studied the applicability of self-determination theory (SDT) and optimal distinctiveness theory (ODT) to White British, Black British, and Asian British exercise class participants. According to SDT (Deci & Ryan, 1985), individuals have three psychological needs: autonomy, competence, and relatedness. ODT (Brewer, 1991) outlines two motivational principles for individuals in groups: assimilation, which is the desire to feel included within a larger collective, and differentiation, which is the desire to distinguish oneself from others in the social context. Relatedness and group distinctiveness significantly predicted self-determined forms of motivation among White and Black exercise class participants. For White and Black exercise participants, more self-determined forms of motivational regulation positively predicted adaptive affective and cognitive outcomes. These results, however, did not hold true for Asian participants. Personal distinctiveness and group inclusion predicted commitment to exercise classes for Blacks and Asians, but not Whites. These results underscore that conceptualizations of motivation may be applicable only to North American and Western cultures (Edmunds et al., 2010).

How Might Practitioners Develop a Multicultural Exercise Program?

Most of the chapters in this book include single case studies to demonstrate the application (or misapplication) of some of the concepts introduced in the literature reviews. In a chapter where I am attempting to address multicultural issues, it is pretty much impossible to come up with a single case example. If I presented a story of an exercise program for people in one particular culture, it might cover some of the issues relevant to working with people from that culture, but it could be mostly irrelevant to people from other cultures. I then thought that I might present an exercise intervention program that had worked well in one culture, and was subsequently used in other locations with people from various cultures, and then get feedback from people from different cultures about what did and did not work for them. I think that this course of action would unfairly suggest that practitioners would blindly apply a program developed for one culture to another culture. As Mark Andersen would say, I would be attacking a straw man (person?). I am hopeful that few professionals would blindly apply a program developed for one culture to a different culture.

Because a case study seemed virtually impossible to present as representative of cross-cultural exercise psychology, I decided to speak to some personal trainers, exercise physiologists, and exercise and physical activity promotion professionals to find out what they might do to address the needs of participants in a multicultural environment. This book is designed to reflect what is happening in the real world, so finding out what practitioners at the coal face have done or would do to address multicultural needs within a physical activity program fits in nicely (after all, the book is about doing). All of the people approached were White and members of the mainstream culture. Many of the professionals I spoke to made comments such as, "Wow, I've never thought about that," which is indicative of the need for greater cultural awareness within the field. Once they did think about the issues, they came up with a variety of responses.

It was interesting to note differences in how they would approach the issue. A few individuals said they would Google the particular culture or cultures that were to be involved and then adapt their program accordingly. After some discussion (and one Google attempt), they tended to come to the realization that Google might not actually provide much help (although Googling for the phonetic pronunciation in different languages of simple words and phrases such as *hello* and *how are you* can demonstrate to participants who speak those languages that an effort has been made to learn something about their cultures). Only a couple of respondents indicated that they would build the program from the bottom up, going out into the relative communities, holding focus groups, and gaining feedback and endorsement from advocacy groups and cultural leaders. The remaining respondents jumped straight in with ideas about what they would do in delivering a multicultural exercise program.

A few practitioners indicated, from their experience, that communication would be the primary issue, because many of the participants may not have English as a first language. To deal with this issue, they would explain exercises through diagrams and demonstrations rather than relying on their standard verbal explanations. One person mentioned the possibility of using multiple languages for promotional materials and perhaps for evaluations of the exercise program, but also commented that she was not sure if this action would be a demonstration of cultural sensitivity or cultural exclusion (because not all languages could be included). One respondent also noted that language (and culture) might influence the sort of encouragement provided to participants.

A number of the practitioners were aware that gender might be an issue and that they would probably need to offer single-sex classes with instructors of the same gender. One practitioner (female) stated that it would be important to have both males and females on staff. In her work with Muslim men, she felt that they were not open to taking instructions from her, but that they readily complied when a male student who was on practicum helped out. Another exercise physiologist emphasized the need to match client and practitioner gender in many cultures when fitness testing (e.g., measuring girths, taking skin folds).

A few experienced practitioners pointed out that it would be important to have a neutral setting for the program. If the aim was to get people from multiple cultures involved, then a park or a community hall with no religious or cultural affiliations would need to be used. One person commented that the location would need to be central with good public transportation connections.

In addition to location, the timing of programs or classes was mentioned as a consideration. Examples of those who might have timing issues included cultural groups who may have specific days and times for prayer as well as religious observances that involve fasting. Another practicality mentioned was clothing. Although participants would likely wear clothing that was appropriate for their culture, program coordinators may want to consider having their staff wear clothing that is culturally considerate (e.g., covering shoulders or knees).

A couple of people commented that exercise options other than traditional adult classes or one-on-one training sessions would need to be considered. Family activities were mentioned as a possibility. One respondent indicated that it might be useful to begin by getting the kids involved, who could in turn bring in their parents and grandparents. Another mentioned that child care would need to be incorporated into the program; alternatively, exercise classes could be done with children and parents together.

A health promotion specialist (who also happens to be a psychologist) mentioned that knowing the values of the participants would be imperative. How one would promote the program would vary depending on if the participants believed that the main purpose of exercise was to help them look good and live longer, or to be together as a family. She believed that values are culturally determined, and that participants would attend and adhere only to programs that addressed their values. An exercise physiologist (who used to teach dance) felt that music would be an important consideration for any multicultural program. When she taught dance, she was surprised by the cultural variety of dance students, so in addition to music, she felt that dance should be offered as an option. Along the same lines of having wide appeal, a couple of respondents stated that including football (i.e., soccer) could be advantageous because of the relevance of the sport to so many different cultures. One person stated that if she were working only with people from a particular nationality, it might be worth investigating the relevant national sporting activities for ideas for a fitness program.

One health promotion specialist stated point blank that it would not be possible to create a single exercise or physical activity program that would be effective across multiple cultures, "something general will not work for specific groups." He acknowledged that a walking program might work for women across multiple cultures, but that it would probably not catch on with young men. This comment really points out the inade-

quacy of considering culture only in terms of nationality, religion, or ethnicity.

In Gilbourne and Andersen's *Critical Essays in Applied Sport Psychology*, I argued that whenever a sport psychologist sits down with an athlete, there is a multicultural encounter (Hanrahan, 2011). The same principle holds true any time any two individuals meet. Culture affects interactions. In addition to nationality, religion, and ethnicity, however, culture also involves gender, sexual orientation, [dis]ability, socioeconomic status, and age. Generally, people who are creating and delivering exercise programs need to be open to others having different ways of being and doing that are influenced by the macro- and microcultures in which they have lived. The usually well-intended actions of some practitioners may backfire because of limited cultural awareness. See table 3.1 for a list of some cultural issues that may influence the effectiveness of exercise practitioners when working with individuals from different cultures. Considering these issues may help those involved in the delivery of exercise programs increase their cultural awareness and effectively develop rapport with clients from other cultures. The challenge is that people are different—what works with one person may not work with another. This variability, however, is what makes life interesting!

Table 3.1   Cultural Issues in Exercise Program Delivery

Issue	Examples or possible effects
Norms: standards, models, or patterns regarded as typical	Walking versus driving Community dances
Values: ideals, customs, standards, or qualities toward which there is affective regard	Family Looking good Living a long life
Beliefs: mental acceptance of and conviction in what is the truth	Lifting weights is for people who want to be bodybuilders Regular physical activity is a necessity
Behaviors: objective elements of culture	Dress Language Gender-appropriate behavior
Clock-based time	Annoyed when others are late Easily allows for planning to meet with different people

Issue	Examples or possible effects
Event-based time	Exchanges can be less hurried Exchanging ideas and the process of the meeting are prioritized over time
Interpersonal space (e.g., zone of personal distance)	18 inches to 4 feet in mainstream North America Considerably less within some Latin American countries Considerably more in some North African and Asian countries
Eye contact	Aggression, seduction, or attention Lack of eye contact can mean disinterest or be a sign of respect
Invitations (e.g., to participate in an exercise program)	Opportunity, request, or obligation
"Yes" (as a response)	"I hear you." "I'm obliging and want to be thought well of." "I agree."
Reluctance to state a firm opinion	Not in a position to make comment Do not want to disagree with others Have no opinion
Silence	Indifference Genuine interest

Final Thoughts

Although measuring physical activity across cultures is challenging, evidence indicates that physical inactivity is an issue in many countries. Although inactivity may be a universal problem, it is doubtful there is a universal solution. Major cultural markers such as religion and ethnicity influence exercise behaviors. Subtler cultural issues such as norms, values, beliefs, perceptions of time, and nuances of language also play a role in the adoption and maintenance of regular physical activity. The challenge for practitioners is to routinely apply culturally appropriate health care interventions and practices, ideally integrating cultural competence not only into practice, teaching, and research, but also into organizational cultures.

References

Airhihenbuwa, C.O., Kumanyika, S., Agurs, T.D., & Lowe, A. (1995). Perceptions and beliefs about exercise, rest, and health among African-Americans. *American Journal of Health Promotion, 9,* 426–429.

Amusa, L.O., & Toriola, A.L. (2010). The changing phases of physical education and sport in Africa: Can a uniquely African model emerge? *African Journal for Physical, Health Education, Recreation & Dance, 16,* 666–680.

Armstrong, T., & Bull, F. (2006). Development of the World Health Organization Global Health Questionnaire (GPAQ). *Journal of Public Health, 14,* 66–70.

Bell, A.C., & Popkin, B.M. (2002). The road to obesity or the path to prevention: Motorized transportation and obesity in China. *Obesity Research, 10,* 277–283.

Belza, B., Walwick, J., Shiu-Thornton, S., Schwartz, S., Taylor, M., & LoGerfo, J. (2004). Older adult perspectives on physical activity and exercise: Voices from multiple cultures. *Preventing Chronic Disease: Public Health Research, Practice, and Policy 1*(4), 1–12.

Brewer, M. (1991). The social self: On being the same and different at the same time. *Personality and Social Psychology Bulletin, 17,* 475–482.

Caperchione, C.M., Kolt, G.S., & Mummery, W.K. (2009). Physical activity in culturally and linguistically diverse migrant groups to Western society: A review of barriers, enablers and experiences. *Sports Medicine, 39,* 167–177.

Caspersen, C.J., Pereira, M.A., & Curran, K.M. (2000). Changes in physical activity patterns in the United States, by sex and cross-sectional age. *Medicine & Science in Sports & Exercise, 32,* 1601–1609.

Dagkas, S., & Benn, T. (2006). Young Muslim women's experiences of Islam and physical education in Greece and Britain: A comparative study. *Sport, Education and Society, 11,* 21–38.

D'Alonzo, K.T., & Sharma, M. (2010). The influence of marianismo beliefs on physical activity of mid-life immigrant Latinas: A Photovoice study. *Qualitative Research in Sport and Exercise, 2,* 229–249.

Deci, E.L., & Ryan, R.M. (1985). *Intrinsic motivation and self-determination in human behavior.* New York, NY: Plenum Press.

Edmunds, J.A., Duda, J.L., & Ntoumanis, N. (2010). Psychological needs and the prediction of exercise-related cognitions and affect among an ethnically diverse cohort of adult women. *Journal of Sport & Exercise Psychology, 8,* 446–463.

Eyler, A.A., Baker, E., Cromer, L., King, A.C., Brownson, R.C., & Donatelle, R.J. (1998). Physical activity and minority women: A qualitative study. *Health Education & Behavior, 25,* 640–652.

Galily, Y., Tamir, I., Meckel, Y., & Eliakim, A. (2012). Socio-cultural characteristics of physical activity habits in Israel (1992–2008). *International Journal of Sociology and Social Policy, 32,* 461–479.

Griffith, D.M., Gunter, K., & Allen, J.O. (2011). Male gender role strain as a barrier to African American men's physical activity. *Health Education & Behavior, 38,* 482–491.

Guthold, R., Louazani, S.A., Riley, R.M., Cowan, M.J., Bovet, P., Damasceno, A., . . . Armstrong, T.P. (2011). Physical activity in 22 African countries: Results from the World Health Organization STEPwise approach to chronic disease risk factor surveillance. *American Journal of Preventive Medicine, 41,* 52–60.

Hanrahan, S.J. (2011). Sport psychology services are multicultural encounters: Differences as strengths in therapeutic relationships. In D. Gilbourne & M. B. Andersen (Eds.), *Critical essays in applied sport psychology* (pp. 145–156). Champaign, IL: Human Kinetics.

Henwood, W. (2007). Maori knowledge: A key ingredient in nutrition and physical exercise health promotion programmes for Maori. *Social Policy Journal of New Zealand, 32,* 155–164.

Hu, G., Pekkarinen, H., Hanninen, O., Yu, Z., Tian, H., Guo, Z., & Nissinen, A. (2002). Physical activity during leisure and commuting in Tianjin, China. *Bulletin of the World Health Organization, 80,* 933–938.

Kahan, D. (2005). Jewish day-schooled adolescents' perceptions of parental and environmental support of physical activity. *Research Quarterly for Exercise and Sport, 76,* 243–250.

Kin-Isler, A., Asci, F.H., Altintas, A., & Guven-Karahan, B. (2009). Physical activity levels and patterns of 11-14 year-old Turkish adolescents. *Adolescence, 44,* 1005–1015.

Koo, F.K. (2011). A case study on the perception of aging and participation in physical activities of older Chinese immigrants in Australia. *Journal of Aging and Physical Activity, 19,* 388–417.

Levin, S., Ainsworth, B.E., Kwok, C.W., Addy, C.L., & Popkin, B.M. (1999). Patterns of physical activity among Russian youth. *European Journal of Public Health, 9,* 166–173.

Madanat, H., & Merrill, R.M. (2006). Motivational factors and stages of change for physical activity among college students in Amman, Jordan. *Promotion and Education, 13,* 185–190.

Markus, H.R., & Kitayama, S. (1991). Culture and the self: Implications for cognition, emotion, and motivation. *Psychological Review, 98,* 224–253.

Mâsse, L.C. (2000). Reliability, validity, and methodological issues in assessing physical activity in a cross-cultural setting. *Research Quarterly for Exercise and Sport, 71*(Suppl. 2), S54–S58.

Monteiro, C.A., Conde, W.L., Matsudo, S.M., Matsudo, V.R., Bonseñor, I.M., & Lutufo, P.A. (2003). A descriptive epidemiology of leisure-time physical activity in Brazil, 1996–1997. *Pan American Journal of Public Health, 14,* 246–254.

Physical Activity Guidelines Advisory Committee. (2008). *Physical Activity Guidelines Advisory Committee report, 2008.* Washington, DC: US Department of Health and Human Services.

Schinke, R., & Hanrahan, S.J. (Eds.) (2009). *Cultural sport psychology.* Champaign, IL: Human Kinetics.

Telama, R., & Yang, X. (2000). Decline of physical activity from youth to young adulthood in Finland. *Medicine & Science in Sports & Exercise, 32,* 1617–1622.

Thul, C.M., & LaVoi, N.M. (2011). Reducing physical inactivity and promoting active living: From the voices of East African immigrant adolescent girls. *Qualitative Research in Sport, Exercise and Health, 3,* 211–237.

Walseth, K., & Fasting, K. (2003). Islam's view on physical activity and sport: Egyptian women interpreting Islam. *International Review for the Sociology of Sport, 38,* 45–60.

Wareham, N.J. (2001). Commentary: Measuring physical activity in Sub-Saharan Africa. *International Journal of Epidemiology, 30,* 1369–1370.

Wells, M.I. (2000). Beyond cultural competence: A model for individual and institutional cultural development. *Journal of Community Health Nursing, 17,* 189–199.

World Health Organization. (2010). *Global recommendations on physical activity for health.* Geneva, Switzerland: Author.

Yan, J.H., & McCullagh, P. (2004). Cultural influence on youth's motivation of participation in physical activity. *Journal of Sport Behavior, 27,* 378–390.

CHAPTER 4

Should I Consult a Psychologist?

An Autobiographical Account of Physical Inactivity in an Exercise and Sport Psychologist

Tony Morris

"Physician, heal thyself" is an overused statement, but if the shoe fits! The message about the benefits of physical activity for health is spreading widely in the general community, yet in many countries less than 50% of the population undertakes physical activity sufficient for obtaining health benefits on a regular basis, according to the World Health Organization (WHO, 2011). In the study of a number of chronic illnesses, researchers have acknowledged the important role of physical activity in treatment. These conditions represent some of the major sources of global morbidity and mortality, including cardiovascular disease (CVD), type 2 diabetes mellitus (T2DM), obesity, and some forms of cancer (WHO, 2012). Medical and health practitioners repeatedly present information about the importance of physical activity for people who live with these conditions. Physical activity is also promoted in leaflets and online advisory software, and in the media generally.

As an adjunct to the "physician, heal thyself" adage, it appears that medical practitioners' own physical activity plays a role in the advice they give to patients (e.g., Frank, Tong, Lobelo, Carrera, & Duperly, 2008; Joy, Blair, McBride, & Sallis, 2013). Physicians who are physically active are more likely to counsel patients to be active. Further, researchers have shown that patient perceptions of medical practitioners' levels of physical activity affect the likelihood that they will follow their physicians' medical advice. Frank, Breyan, and Elon (2000) gave patients in the waiting room a video in which the physician disclosed personal healthy diet and physical activity or a control video. Patients rated the physician who disclosed to be healthier and considered that practitioner more motivating than the same practitioner in the control video. Puhl, Gold, Luedicke, and DePierre (2013) found that patients expressed greater mistrust of obese physicians than nonobese ones and reported that they were less inclined to follow the medical advice of the overweight practitioner. Despite the evidence that medical practitioners have greater influence with their patients if they are physically active and look healthy themselves than if they are inactive and overweight, many do not undertake sufficient exercise (e.g., Joy et al., 2013). Gupta and Fan (2008) found that only 21% of physicians undertaking an advanced training program met the UK Department of Health exercise recommendations. Of the 79% who did not meet the recommendations, 58% claimed they had no time, 29% said they lacked motivation, and 13% stated that they had no exercise facilities. Ironically, Gupta and Fan found that those practitioners who worked at hospitals with gym facilities were less likely to be active than those who did not have facilities at their workplaces. Regarding their training and professional education, 64% of the sample indicated that they had been active as students, but only 23% of those were still active when surveyed later in their careers. Thus, although medical practitioners know that physical activity is an important aspect of health and understand that they are role models for their patients, many are not physically active themselves.

A similar pattern is evident in the psychology profession, with its focus on the necessity of self-care for mental health professionals, along with recognizing the role of physical activity in promoting well-being for both clients and practitioners. Barnett (2007) argued the case to professional psychologists in a paper on the pursuit of wellness that emphasized the "self-care imperative" (p. 603). Barnett raised the ethical requirement of the American Psychological Association (APA) for psychologists to be aware of the effects of their own physical and mental health on their abilities to help the clients with whom they work. Barnett argued that the demands of psychological practice, especially with demanding clients, can lead to distress, burnout, or maladaptive coping. He also observed that some psychologists choose the profession because they are unconsciously seeking help for themselves. Baker (2007) echoed this concern, citing "masked narcissism" (Grosch & Olsen, 1994) as caretaking that is reflexive, based on an unacknowledged need in the psychologist to be taken care of. Yet many psychologists do not seek the support of their peers by undertaking therapy and adopting other self-care strategies such as healthy diet and exercise. Elman (2007) also argued for the need to promote self-care, stating that training and professional education programs should emphasize the point that all psychologists need to practice self-care. Schoener (2007) used the epithet "do as I say, not as I do" (p. 610).

In a study of psychotherapists who abstain from personal therapy, Norcross, Bike, Evans, and Schatz (2008) stated that many practitioners do not practice what they preach by seeking therapy when they experience stress. Norcross et al. reported that the main reasons therapists gave for not undertaking therapy were dealing with stress in other ways, getting sufficient support from friends and family, having beliefs that they possessed effective coping strategies, and holding convictions that they could resolve problems before therapy was needed. They found that cognitive behavioral therapists were less likely to seek therapy than humanistic psychotherapists, and almost all psychodynamic therapists had experienced therapy. Norcross et al. stated that academic psychologists were the least likely to undergo therapy. When they asked psychotherapists who had not sought therapy the one reason they "probably would" seek therapy, the main reasons were associated with loss, namely loss of adequate functioning, loss of a loved one, loss of necessary coping capacity, or loss of a close relationship, usually marriage by divorce.

Wise, Hersh, and Gibson (2012) put the case for psychologist self-care in a positive light. They observed that the APA expressed concerns about the dangers of stress leading to a downward spiral of distress, impairment, and improper behavior among practicing psychologists. This negative perspective can be perceived by practitioners as indicating that there is a stigma associated with self-care. Wise et al. argued that the psychology profession should promote a positive self-care spiral based on four foundational principles: flourishing rather than surviving as a psychologist; intentionally choosing an appropriate self-care plan; acknowledging that psychologists are not different from their clients, so if therapy and other forms of self-care work for their clients they also work for the psychologist; and embracing the principle that self-care should be integrated into psychologists' lives, not perceived as an "add-on." Wise et al. proposed that the positive side of self-care could be reflected in mindfulness-based positive principles and practices (MPPPs) based on mindfulness-based stress reduction (MBSR; Kabat-Zinn, 1990), acceptance and commitment therapy (ACT; Hayes, Strosahl, & Wilson, 1999), and positive psychology (Seligman, Steen, Park, & Petersen, 2005).

In their discussions of self-care among psychologists, writers such as Barnett (2007), Baker (2007), and Wise et al. (2012) included healthy life choices, particularly diet and exercise, alongside other mental health practices, especially seeking peer support whenever it is needed. These themes have also been promoted within the medical and related health professions (e.g., Blake & Harrison, 2013; Joy et al., 2013). It is worth reflecting whether a similar view should be promulgated among exercise psychologists. This question raises the issue of whether exercise psychologists are more diligent in "practicing what they preach" than their colleagues in psychology and medicine. On this issue, my reading of the literature suggests there is silence. I am not aware of research that has examined the physical activity practices of exercise (or sport) psychologists or whether this behavior varies throughout their careers or, concomitantly, with age. Perhaps asking this question hits a bit too close to home?

Do I Practice What I Preach?

As a person who researches and writes about the importance of increasing physical activity among the whole population and especially among those with chronic conditions, I live with this message and promulgate it every day. So the question arises, why don't I do sufficient physical activity myself?

In this chapter, I do not answer this question. If I knew the answer, surely I would be active and there would be no chapter to write. My aim here is to describe my life and medical history, current health status, and physical activity experience dispassionately to highlight the disjunction between knowledge and behavior in one person who might be considered to represent rather an extreme case of such a disconnection. I hope that reflecting on this single case might lead those interested in addressing the issue of physical inactivity to generate new hypotheses to examine in the broader sedentary population. To paint the picture on as wide a canvas as possible, I first summarize my life history, and then I consider the role of physical activity and sport in my life before reporting on my medical history. Next, I comment on my personal experience of the impact of diet and physical activity on my health. Then I reflect on the conundrum of the knowledge–behavior disconnection based on a number of psychological factors, before drawing the chapter to an inconclusive end.

Life History

I was born in 1950 in the north of England. I was a "late child." My mother was 41 and my father was 53 when I was born. They had only recently married. It was his second time. She had married later in life, staying at home to look after her aging mother when all her brothers and sisters married. I was the first and only child, and I was delivered by Caesarian section; precious, but not to be repeated! I have long thought of myself like the new car that came off the assembly line on Friday afternoon when everybody was thinking about the weekend. Things seem to go wrong when they are still in warranty! At the same time, my early years were lived during the period when the UK Prime Minister, Harold Macmillan, said we had "never had it so good." My parents had lived through two world wars and the Great Depression, so although we were not well off financially, they gave me everything they had often been denied, including chips for dinner on most evenings, always plenty of chocolate afterwards, and fresh cream cakes whenever my mother passed a pastry shop. Remember that this was the 1950s, and they believed they were giving me all the best things they had missed.

Although I always perceived myself to be a little chubby, I cannot remember a time during childhood when I was not active whenever the opportunity arose. I was always in the woods at the bottom of our street, climbing trees, jumping the stream, and following its path, such that I wandered well away from home. Occasionally, when I was just 5 or 6 years old, this wandering led to search parties being sent out, although I had no idea I was "missing"! From as far back as I can remember, I loved sport. I'd play anything, anywhere, any time. Usually it was football (i.e., soccer) in the street and cricket in the driveway during summer, but it could just as easily be a made-up game such as alternating with an opponent to kick a tennis ball against a wall, where scoring was a point every time one of us missed the target. This combination between squash and football was a useful competitive way to develop ball control skills. We also played a hand version in the summer. If I didn't have anybody to play with, I would often compete against myself, trying to beat my best number of shots against the wall without a miss. Our nearest shops were a 10-minute walk away, and the bus to school was a little beyond that, so I did plenty of walking. I often ran back home from the shops, which was downhill. Obviously, I was highly active, but there was always a purpose, even if it was just exploring. It would never have occurred to me to do physical activity just for its own sake.

In 1961, when I was 10 years old, my father died after a heart attack. He was 64. He'd had angina for some years. I recall little about him, which is not surprising because he left for work before I got up in the morning for school and arrived home not long before I went to bed (or while I was still out roaming the woods or playing sport in the street!). I was fortunate to go to a good grammar school, although I hated school and survived only because I considered classes to be fillers between games of football at morning break and lunchtime. When I got a little older, we also played for an hour after school before heading home. During this time, my mother was working full time to help us survive, so there was nobody waiting at home. I stumbled through secondary school, my academic performance fluctuating wildly. Nobody told me about studying for examinations until I was 15, so in the early years of secondary education I answered June exam questions in physics and chemistry on material I had been taught the previous September based simply on what I could remember. Given that my thoughts had been focused on the football game we had just played or the match that was coming up after that class, I did not recall much science, or history and geography come to that. I also did minimal homework. That would have interfered with the important activities, sport in the street and then in organized settings as time progressed. I have dwelt on life during this period because it seems to me to be important to note that I was very physically active from a young age, exercising most often with a competitive goal in mind.

In my later years at school, my physical activity was largely in organized, competitive sport, which I describe in the next section. Having studied little, I more or less fell into psychology at university. I was aiming to do medicine, but when I attended interviews, I realized it was not a fitting career choice for me. Fortunately, I switched to psy-

chology, which was the first discipline I studied that had meaning for me. With newfound interest, I gradually increased my attention to study. As an undergraduate, I continued to play competitive sport, but without serious intent. I went home to do my PhD and slipped back into my previous club and team, where I continued at the same level of competitive sport.

I started my academic career with several short-term positions. I was busy with all the new preparation because one position involved teaching psychology of education at the graduate level, and the next focused on undergraduate psychology for science students, so the content was substantially different. I did little physical activity during this period. My next position was a research fellowship, and I started playing competitive sport again and undertook some exercise. Then I moved to a substantive position for 8 years in a sport science program, where I taught some practical sport classes and continued to play competitive sport and exercise regularly. During this time period, I married and started a family. When my daughter was 20 months old and my son was 5 months old, we moved from England to Australia.

This move combined several changes. In addition to my new academic role, which increasingly involved managing and conducting research and research supervision, I had to devote time to the family and home. Also, Melbourne is a large city, and we lived the best part of an hour from the university. As my work days expanded, with travel at either end, I felt I had little time left for involvement in organized sport. I continued to undertake informal physical activity only, and this involvement continued to reduce in frequency. In 1991, a year after arriving in Australia, I found out I had type 2 diabetes (T2DM). I modified my diet and tried to maintain the physical activity, but competing demands usually won out. The intensity of work continued to increase as I became involved in national bodies, international organizations, and senior research management roles. Also, I diversified my research interests into exercise and physical activity, as did many of my sport psychology colleagues during the 1990s. The difference for me is that I had a personal interest in T2DM and then CVD and associated conditions, such as obesity. At the end of 2001, I had a heart episode, and then had two more over the next few years. After the first heart event, I started to walk, building up the duration gradually, but once again over a period of time, work demands interfered. For several years now, my physical activity has been quite limited. I curtailed my involvement in management roles, which I had always carried out alongside a substantial research and research supervision load. My passion is for doing research and guiding others in their research activity as mentor or supervisor, and those have been my foci in recent years, alongside continued work in exercise and sport psychology development at the international level, especially in Asia.

Physical Activity and Sport History

I described my childhood physical activity in the previous section, so I discuss my experiences since adolescence in this section. Like many children, I did a wide range of activities that varied from physically active play to informal sport to a little formal sport involvement. I had no parental support or encouragement beyond being provided with basic kit and equipment because there was little money, especially after my father died, and my mother had no interest in sport. From 12 or 13 years of age, I became increasingly involved in organized competitive sport. I never possessed the natural physical attributes of an athlete, but I always competed intensely. I also seemed to possess a capacity to read sport situations well; I made up, at least to some extent, for my physical limitations by superior tactics and strategies. In a quasi-public school environment, I played rugby and cricket and did track and field for my house (British public school practice of assigning students to groups with which they would identify, similar to the U.S. college fraternity system). I ran the 100 meters (or was it yards in those days?) and was a passable fourth in my age group among a group of skinny boys, none of whom also competed let alone made the top three in the shot put and discus, as I did. I had the key role of fly-half in the house rugby team (it was a rugby school in those days; no football was allowed), and both batted and bowled in the house cricket team. I was good enough to be invited to play both sports for the school, but was not keen to get involved in those days. My winter sport passion was football from around the age of 5 until I was about 15

years old. We played in plimsolls (what are now called training shoes) with a lightweight plastic ball and bags for goal posts two or three times a day. It was all about skills: tight control; mesmerizing dribbles; quick, short passing interchanges; long balls and crosses curled from the wing; and shots bent inside the goal post. I did try to play for a team in a league when I was 14 or 15, but we played with a heavy leather ball, in ankle-deep mud and cold rain. I played on the wing, a position that the rest of the team seemed to forget existed. On the other hand, the opposition's fullback seemed to think it was more important to kick me than the ball! I stopped playing football.

In the summer, I preferred to play tennis to cricket. Some of our predecessors had won the right for tennis to be an option to cricket by being rather good and earning ranks among the top juniors in England. The school, thus, began to play at the Boys' (Public) Schools Championship, which was played on the outside, hard courts at Wimbledon, until the finals, which moved onto the grass. This competition satisfied the school's quest for social status! I played with an 8-shilling (around 40 UK pence!) racket from Woolworths for several years, but bought a Dunlop racket for 10 pounds when I became school tennis captain and went to those Boys' Schools Championships at Wimbledon, as much to save myself from embarrassment as to benefit from the racket's technical qualities!

At around age 14, I was given a tiny table tennis table, about 4 feet long and 2 feet wide. I cannot recall who gave it to me or why. I learned tight control playing on that table. I heard about trials for the school table tennis club, attended, and got in. From then on, as my enthusiasm for football waned, I played table tennis pretty much every lunchtime and gradually gained ground on older boys who were quite highly ranked in the city juniors. After some time I was invited to the city junior coaching group, and with continued practice I became the number one junior in the city, a rank I held until age forced me out of the junior competition. This foray into organized sport was my only experience of sport coaching. Looking back on it, I was a poor student despite my commitment to table tennis. My coach told me fitness was important and gave me the Swedish circuit-training program, which was what English international players did then. I received permission to do it during gym, rather than have to climb ropes and do head springs. I could never really pull my weight up a rope, and head springs just seemed to defy gravity. Also, I didn't "bounce" like some boys, so if I went down, I stayed down! I fared little better with the circuit. The first time I did it I felt dizzy and nauseous, so I decided not to do it again. This aversive experience was unfortunate because fitness was what let me down in county ranking. This assessment was conducted on a Sunday at the start of the season. In the morning there was a round robin, and the winners went through to another round robin in the early afternoon. This paring-down process produced six players, who then played off for the top ranks. I made that final group in two successive years, but was so knackered by that time I could not give a decent account of myself. I ended up ranked number 5, although I beat all the boys above me when I played them individually in intercity matches (not all the time, but three of them played for England juniors). Sadly, I still did not get the message about the need for fitness or that getting fit and staying fit was going to hurt.

I continued playing table tennis at university, but I did not practice regularly, let alone do any fitness work. Nonetheless, the university table tennis team I was in as an undergraduate won the British Universities Table Tennis Championship. Back at home for my PhD, I played for the club I had represented since I was 14. I was still one of the top four or five players in the city, even though I did no training or practice, just played matches once a week. Once I started work, I was in new cities each year and had demanding teaching schedules, as often befalls junior staff, so I did not play any sport. Most of my time had to be devoted to preparation. I put on weight and felt rather uncomfortable.

By that time I had started my research fellowship in motor learning in a psychology department, and my office window had a direct view of the university swimming pool. I started a strict diet and began to swim. I could manage only one length of the pool at the start, but I was determined, and I saw the rewards as the weight dropped off. After a while I was doing more than

20 lengths a day, but I was bored silly, so I switched to jogging. I liked this little more than swimming, but at least the scenery changed. At that stage, I moved to my new position in sports science in a former teacher-training college, so it was fortunate that at 32, I was in the best physical shape of my life. I taught tennis and table tennis in the physical education teacher-training program and the sports science degree, alongside motor learning and sport psychology. I established a college table tennis team in the West Sussex league. Some students came to do sports science at the college specifically because they knew there was an enthusiast on staff there. They did undergraduate projects on table tennis, and our college team won the top division of the league. At around 38 years old, I still had the best winning record of any player in the league for my final competitive season.

When I moved to Melbourne in 1990, I was not in a position to continue playing table tennis. Work, travel, infants, and family life in general filled my time. I continued to jog for a while, but I had little motivation to sustain me. Gradually, the frequency of my runs declined. I was jolted into action somewhat by the news that I had diabetes. This health blow seemed to be ironic given that I had been watching my diet rigorously and doing more physical activity during the previous 10 years than at any stage in my life. Nevertheless, my mother had type 2 diabetes, and I knew there was a strong hereditary component. It just seemed to occur earlier in my life than I had expected (I was just over 40 years of age), especially considering all that mind-numbing exercise I'd done in the preceding years!

From the early 1990s, my physical activity dropped off. I took on extremely heavy workloads in my position in Australia, due to ambition and interest. I expanded the sport psychology units, so I had a massive teaching load. The institution became a university. As its leading academic unit, sports science was expected to build up its PhD student numbers. We advertised locally, and over 20 students applied to work in sport psychology. I was promised extra staff in my field if I supervised them, so I did. In 1994, Mark Andersen and Vance Tammen joined the staff. From 1992, I was also director of the new university research Centre for

Rehabilitation, Exercise, and Sport Science (CRESS), which was a notional half-time role. I say "notional" because my hours worked out to be more than what two full-time staff were supposed to do! Although the balance of teaching, research, and administration has shifted about somewhat since then, I have always been working way over the official workload. This situation limited the time I had for physical activity. After my first heart episode in December 2001, I started walking and built up to more than 30 minutes on several days of the week. As work expanded again, my walking reduced and then stopped. For several years, I have done no regular physical activity.

Medical History

I was never a fit person even as a child, but I was very active. When I played sport, I think my competitiveness and determination drove me on despite my lack of physical fitness. I was generally healthy, but I contracted the usual childhood illnesses. I had surgery when I was a preschooler to remove my adenoids. I think I was a noisy sleeper, and my parents followed the trend in the early 1950s for kids to have their adenoids removed if their breathing was suspect and their tonsils taken out if they were prone to get sore throats. When I was 11 years old, I had a problem with asthma. The doctor prescribed breathing exercises that involved blowing a table tennis ball across a woolly blanket—rather portentous in view of my future love of table tennis. Since training in psychology, I have wondered whether the asthma was actually a reaction to my father's death. I was rather stoic at the time he died. Anyway, I soon became bored with the blowing exercises and continued to do a lot of physical activity. When I took up jogging many years later I found that, despite training frequently, I did not seem to have the lung capacity to push beyond a couple of miles. Going back to the earlier analogy of the sloppily assembled Friday afternoon car, I have reflected whether my lungs were never quite right from the start, just not in such bad shape that they really broke down, but enough to limit my physical capacity. Interestingly, despite working in sports science departments for over 30 years, I have never done a $\dot{V}O_2$ max test. Perhaps unconsciously I knew what the answer would be.

I started having a problem with gastric reflux when I was around 30, after I lived in a small single room for a few months, eating take-away dinners while lying on the bed. Over a period of time the episodes reduced, but this condition has always been liable to spring up, and the discomfort in the chest became more problematic once I developed a heart condition because acid indigestion and heart pain are not easy to distinguish subjectively. Actually, my original heart episode was one occasion when I misdiagnosed chest pain as severe indigestion. I went to see the doctor to ask for stronger medication than the over-the-counter indigestion concoctions and was fortunate that the doctor, who was examining me for the first time, decided to check my heart, using ECG and blood tests. He phoned me after midnight to say the blood tests had come back, and I should go straight to the hospital. I had an angiogram a day or two later, and was then moved to another hospital for an angioplasty because my local hospital didn't have the facilities to do that procedure. I had my angioplasty on Christmas Eve 2001 and went home for Christmas dinner the next day, having already had the hospital Christmas lunch!

It is fair to say that the heart problems are probably related to my diabetes, which had been diagnosed 10 years earlier. During the course of those 10 years, I went through a number of phases when I made efforts to manage my diet and exercise as prescribed by the endocrinologist. These active phases, however, alternated with those when I took less care (largely because I like food and do not like exercising), and I could not see a great difference in the results of periodic medical tests depending on whether I did or did not adopt the recommended treatment strategies. Over a period of time, I moved from management by diet and exercise to oral medication and then to a mixture of oral medication and insulin injections. Once the heart condition was diagnosed, there were more pills, and gradually medication for blood pressure was increased because high blood pressure and diabetes are not a good combination for the kidneys. Presently, I take seven tablets and administer four insulin injections every day.

Diet, Physical Activity, and Subjective Perceptions of Health

For more than 20 years, my diet and exercise behaviors have fluctuated as I have experienced the onset of major chronic conditions, first diabetes in 1991 and then CVD in 2001, or when I have had poor periodic test results that prompted the endocrinologist or cardiologist to get tough. Before that, I spent 10 years on the strictest diet of my life, along with a regular schedule of exercise. Moderation was not an option for me. During that time period, aside from my birthday and Christmas Day perhaps, I just did not lapse from the diet. Also, I jogged pretty much every day. I consider myself to be naturally hedonistic and lazy. Thus, I felt that if I cut myself a bit of slack, I'd soon stop dieting or exercising altogether. Perhaps the capacity to discipline myself in that way was associated with my life stage. When I started this regimen, I was living on my own and had just turned 30 years of age. On the other hand, it did seem to me that I *could* stop or ease off at any time, and it is easier to maintain such discipline when there is the expectation of an end point.

Since I was diagnosed with diabetes 22 years ago and then the heart condition 12 years ago, I have no longer believed that there will be a point at which I can stop watching my diet, trying to exercise, or taking medication. It is a life sentence. This state of affairs is difficult to handle, and I have managed it by compromising between my desire to eat whatever I like and exercise only when it suits and interests me and the knowledge that I really should be on a strict diet at all times and exercising regularly. This compromise has been associated with a few occasions when my test results have deteriorated, making the endocrinologist, the cardiologist, or both unhappy, so I tighten up, and with other times when they are not too displeased, so I continue with the compromise or even slide back further in terms of diet and exercise practices.

My subjective experiences are also associated with mixed messages. On occasions when my diet changes to include less fat and sugar, such as when I visit a number of Asian countries, I can start to have hypoglycemic episodes if I don't reduce the amount of insulin I take. A similar outcome occurs when I am placed in a context where I have to do more physical activity, such as when I must walk considerable distances in locations where I do not have access to mechanized transport. These occurrences clearly send the message that diet and exercise do affect blood sugar level in an acute, as opposed to chronic, manner. I acknowledge them, but they do not persuade me to do more exercise and to watch my diet more carefully in the longer term.

The Conundrum

This personal and honest account of my life in relation to sport and physical activity reflects a passion for sport and other activities that I considered to be good fun during my childhood and adolescence. As my involvement in sports became a serious matter, although I was prepared to dedicate time to practicing the skills, I was unwilling to do the necessary physical conditioning work to achieve the success that was possible. This paradox occurred although I was told directly by my table tennis coach that I needed to increase my fitness and despite the experiences I had at key points in my performing career that my fitness levels were not adequate. As a young adult my overall physical activity levels reduced, leading me finally to undertake physical activity, in the form of swimming and then jogging, along with a dietary regimen. It was a chore that I always expected I would stop, but I maintained the exercise for several years by becoming obsessive about it. I never enjoyed doing any of that physical activity. As my health deteriorated, first with diabetes and then with a heart condition, I was informed by many credible sources that I needed to engage in more physical activity to manage my medical conditions, but as work and other activities increased, I did less physical activity, not more. Ironically, a substantial component of that increasing workload was teaching exercise psychology and conducting research on physical activity in people with chronic diseases and disabilities. Thus, not only was I hearing from medical experts that I needed to be more active, but in lectures, book chapters, and journal papers, I was telling others that physical activity is important for health and in the treatment of chronic illness.

The conundrum presented here appears to relate to this question: What psychological processes have reduced my physical activity levels as the personal and professional evidence has increased that physical activity enhances health and well-being and reduces the impact of chronic conditions like T2DM and CVD? There could be many answers to this question. One approach might be associated with stress and coping, as discussed in the introductory material, particularly that related to self-care among psychologists (e.g., Barnett, 2007; Wise et al., 2012). Another is surely associated with the issue of motivation. Researchers examining physical activity among medical practitioners have cited low motivation as a reason for not doing sufficient physical activity for health benefits (e.g., Gupta & Fan, 2008). Major time constraints was the most common reason for physicians not engaging in physical activity, but this explanation seems to be simplistic, and it does not consider the attraction of competing activities. One perspective that might seem unpromising at first, but which addresses issues of stress and coping as well as motivation and other relevant variables, is overtraining (OT).

The Overtraining Academic

In my dedication to the book *Overtraining Athletes: Personal Journeys in Sport* (Richardson, Andersen, & Morris, 2008), I thanked my family, "who have put up with my own extreme overtraining in sport psychology for way too long." Although this "confession" was a somewhat contrived attempt to link the dedication to the topic of the book, on reflection, perhaps there is more to it than even I thought when I wrote it. In the book, Richardson et al. described their research on OT, based on Sean Richardson's efforts to understand his own overtraining, leading to injury, when close to selection for the Canadian rowing team for the Olympic Games. Expanding on his PhD research with Mark and me, the first part of the book examined in-depth interviews about OT with experts and athletes. Based on that research, Richardson et al. proposed an OT risks and outcomes model. This model owed much to previous work, especially Meyers and Whelan's (1998) multisystemic model, which recognized the influence of society, culture, and even politics and economics on athlete behavior, and Kenttä and Hassmén's (1998; 2002) underrecovery model, which also recognized the roles of different systems. Kenttä and Hassmén

proposed that a key factor associated with OT is the balance between stress and recovery. They argued that underrecovery, that is, recovery that does not match the level of stress experienced, is as important to the occurrence of OT as actual management of the stress.

Although our work in this book owed much to the earlier models, we considered that the OT risks and outcomes model was novel in considering the risk factors that led to OT, as well as the experience of overtraining. The model also addressed the different outcomes that could result from OT, and we argued that outcomes such as injury and illness, as well as fatigue and burnout, could result from OT behaviors well before an athlete developed full-blown overtraining syndrome (OTS). Central to the model is the examination of risk factors for OT. A long list of these variables emerged from scrutiny of the literature, the analysis of experts' views, and from the accounts provided by elite athletes that were woven into four stories to illustrate some of the major themes. We emphasized that some of the risk factors may not be evident in individual cases of OT and that different risk factors are prominent in the OT experiences of each athlete, even varying across occasions for the same athlete.

Here, I am summarizing the complex OT risks and outcomes model (Richardson et al., 2008) we proposed in a way that cannot do justice to its subtleties. We proposed four stages in the OT risks and outcomes model: risk factors, early signs, behavioral responses, and outcomes. We identified four categories of risk factors: intrapersonal, interpersonal, situational, and sociocultural. We argued that risk factors should include intrapersonal (e.g., motivation, perfectionism) and interpersonal (e.g., parent and coach influences) factors that might originate in individuals' past experiences. Situational risk factors (e.g., competing for Olympic selection) and sociocultural risk factors originating in the culture of sport (e.g., "no pain, no gain," "more is better," "playing while injured is heroic") interact with the intra- and interpersonal risks to produce the potential for OT. Early signs of the risk of OT can be detected in current physical (e.g., fatigue, frequent infections) and psychological (e.g., heightened emotions, guilt about missing training) states. Behavioral responses relate to the different ways in which individuals handle the potential for OT, some responses being relatively adaptive, whereas other experiences of OT reflect mild to severe maladaptive reactions. Finally, outcomes differ depending on the responses. Adaptive responses result in return to balance, whereas maladaptive responses lead in a downward spiral to serious adverse outcomes, such as injuries, illness, distress, fatigue, and full-blown OTS.

It is interesting to reflect whether what I (almost flippantly) called my academic overtraining can be interpreted through the OT risks and outcomes model. First, there are the risk factors that might have driven my pattern of ever increasing my work. That pattern is exemplified by my recent experience of accepting several visiting professorships around the world. At home I work most of the time, giving only what time is needed to family and domestic needs. During those times when I am away from home, perhaps I could accept that the already heavy workload is enough. Compared with when I am at home, I do not need to spend as much time shopping for and cooking food, cleaning the house and washing clothes, and participating in family activities. I should be able to use the time I have overseas to enjoy some leisure. No, instead I fill the extra time with more work! Risk factors that might be associated with my overworking could be intrapersonal, including supermotivation, perfectionism, or the "need-to-please disease" to which Richardson et al. (2008) referred.

But what could be the origins of these traits? Richardson et al. suggested that parents can have a big influence. I hardly knew my father, and my mother was a kind person who doted on me. Yet when I dig deep into memory, I recall that she was also quite difficult to please, or at least she did not readily display pleasure and excitement at my achievements. One example that is still a vivid memory is when I came home from school and reported that I had passed all nine O levels—key examinations for academic progression—and one more subject than any other student in my school had taken. My mother just continued frying the liver! It was no more than she expected, or at least that was the message I received. Another recollection is my mother's great disappointment when,

at a stage just prior to university, I announced that I was not going to medical school, which had been my professed career for around 10 years. Medicine did not suit me. Even when I received my PhD, I don't think it made up for my mother's dashed expectation of introducing me as "my son, the doctor." Perhaps those kinds of experiences of parental expectations underpin my continued driving for greater achievements in the academic realm, the need to please my mother even though she now lives only in my mind, and the reflexive judgment that nothing I do is good enough. It is sometimes comforting to know I am not alone in my experiences. My fellow author, Mark, has written about still trying to distract and please his depressed mother through his accomplishments even though she has been dead for over 20 years (Andersen & Mannion, 2011). Sean Richardson, the first author of our overtraining book, also wrote about how his own overtraining was linked to trying to fix his father's unhappiness over perceived failures in rowing for Canada at the Mexico City Olympics. It seems we all float in similar boats.

Driven by the risk factors underpinned by early childhood and adolescent experiences, I continue to work long hours. Like the athlete who goes out to the basketball court in the dark to do an extra 30 minutes of free-throw shooting practice, I try to squeeze ever more time to work from each day. I know I should allocate some time for physical activity, yet I would have to give up 30 to 60 minutes of work time to do it. Thus, it could be argued that it is my academic OT that leads me to give the weak "I have no time" excuse for not exercising. Of course there is time, but I'd have to give up something else and that something would be work.

Perhaps the early manifest signs of academic OT are to be found in diabetes and the related problems of high cholesterol and other lipids. When I was first diagnosed, I did not feel ill. I was still relatively fit: My weight was lower than during my early adulthood, and my diet was generally careful. I did make temporary adjustments, but the big opportunities for work were just opening up, and I needed to grab them. Nearly a decade later, my first heart attack was like a big road works sign stating, "Overtraining in Progress." It was a shock that required me to make adjustments. I stopped working for a little while, but it was actually during a time period when I had already taken recreation leave, so I didn't feel so guilty about not working. I behaved like an invalid, but started to do some remedial activity, mainly short walks. As I realized I was still here, alive and kicking, work built up again. At first I did try to ensure there was adequate recovery time, but gradually recovery dwindled. At that time, I understood recovery as rest, rather than exercise. Thus, my behavioral responses were largely reflective of the maladaptive ones in the Richardson et al. (2008) model. I made temporary changes to my life, but in the long term, work became the priority again and soaked up my time.

The outcomes of my academic OT behaviors have been further medical problems, but in the view that I am still alive and busy with work 12 years after the first heart episode, perhaps I would be classified in the "mild" maladaptive category, not that heart attacks can be considered mild, of course. This classification as mildly maladaptive might be justified, because when I do start to feel unwell, I will stop work to rest, usually for a few hours. I do appreciate that at some times continuing to work is counterproductive because I know I am not functioning as I would hope or expect. Perhaps this realization is a benefit of my understanding as a psychologist. At least at one level, I seem to consider self-care to be necessary for me to do my work effectively. It is also consistent with the view in the OT model that some individuals can manage some degree of stress/recovery imbalance for a period of time by adopting temporary modifications to their training or competition schedules.

I think that interpreting my life of heavy work and little else, including scant physical activity, in terms of the OT risks and outcomes model has provided some insights for me. One is that, whether it is labeled supermotivation, perfectionism, or the need to please, my drive to do more and achieve more is probably rooted in parental experiences. Perhaps simply recognizing that historical root will help me manage my time more effectively than I have in the past. Another insight is that I have not been good at recognizing the early signs of stress/recovery imbalance. Further, I have long walked a tightrope of mild maladaptive re-

sponses, including occasional recovery activities and some physical activity. Illness has certainly been a significant outcome of underrecovery at some times. The insight that has greatest relevance for this chapter is that, in my case, academic overtraining has probably been a critical factor in habitual underrecovery, particularly in relation to physical activity. I hope that the reflections on my life in (and out of) sport and physical activity—which I know are not unique, but represent a cautionary tale—might stimulate some ideas for colleagues in exercise psychology. Perhaps this story of an exercise psychologist who struggles with health issues "in spite of himself" could inform research that will generate some therapeutic approaches that can be applied to academic or other occupational overtraining, particularly in the realm of using participation in physical activity as a healthy antidote to long-established patterns of overdoing it in relatively sedentary work settings.

Conclusions

In this chapter, I bared my soul, as it were, to reveal the puzzle of a life devoted to sport during childhood and adolescence that gradually shifted to dedication to academic work at the expense of physical activity, among other things, during mature adulthood. I have no explanation of this shift that satisfies me. At the same time, examination of the idea of academic overtraining that overwhelms all other activities seems to present some insights that could lead to interesting research directions. I look forward to other exercise psychology researchers reflecting on this account and, perhaps, identifying new research directions and interventions that will help the academic and occupational overtrainers of the world lead more balanced lives.

References

Andersen, M.B., & Mannion, J. (2011). If you meet the Buddha on the football field, tackle him! In D. Gilbourne & M.B. Andersen (Eds.), *Critical essays in applied sport psychology* (pp. 173–192). Champaign, IL: Human Kinetics.

Baker, E.K. (2007). Therapist self-care: Challenges within ourselves and within the profession. *Professional Psychology: Research & Practice, 38,* 607–608.

Barnett, J.E. (2007). In pursuit of wellness: The self-care imperative. *Professional Psychology: Research & Practice, 38,* 603–607.

Blake, H., & Harrison, C. (2013). Health behaviours and attitudes towards being role models. *British Journal of Nursing, 22,* 86–94.

Elman, N.S. (2007). Who needs self-care anyway? We all do! *Professional Psychology: Research & Practice, 38,* 608–610.

Frank, E., Breyan, J., & Elon, L. (2000). Physician disclosure of healthy personal behaviors improves credibility and ability to motivate. *Archives of Family Medicine, 9,* 287–290.

Frank, E., Tong, E., Lobelo, F., Carrera, J., & Duperly, J. (2008). Physical activity levels and counseling practices of U.S. medical students. *Medicine & Science in Sports & Exercise, 40,* 413–421.

Grosch, W.N., & Olsen, D.C. (1994). *When helping starts to hurt.* New York, NY: Norton.

Gupta, K., & Fan, L. (2008). Doctors: Fighting fit or couch potatoes. *British Journal of Sports Medicine, 43,* 153–154.

Hayes, S.C., Strosahl, K.D., & Wilson, K.G. (1999). *Acceptance and commitment therapy: An experiential approach to behavior change.* New York, NY: Guilford Press.

Joy, E., Blair, S.N., McBride, P., & Sallis, R. (2013). Physical activity counselling in sports medicine: A call to action. *British Journal of Sports Medicine, 47,* 49–53.

Kabat-Zinn, J. (1990). *Full catastrophe living: Using the wisdom of your body and mind to face stress, pain, and illness.* New York, NY: Bantam Dell.

Kenttä, G., & Hassmén, P. (1998). Overtraining and recovery: A conceptual model. *Sports Medicine, 26,* 1–16.

Kenttä, G., & Hassmén, P. (2002). Underrecovery and overtraining: A conceptual model. In M. Kellmann (Ed.), *Enhancing recovery: Preventing underper-*

formance in athletes (pp. 57–80). Champaign, IL: Human Kinetics.

Meyers, A.W., & Whelan, J.P. (1998). A systemic model for understanding psychological influences in overtraining. In R.B. Kreider, A.C. Fry, & M.L. O'Toole (Eds.), *Overtraining in sport* (pp. 335–372). Champaign, IL: Human Kinetics.

Norcross, J.C., Bike, D.H., Evans, K.L., & Schatz, D.M. (2008). Psychologists who abstain from personal therapy: Do they practice what they preach? *Journal of Clinical Psychology, 64,* 1368–1376.

Puhl, R.M., Gold, J.A., Luedicke, J., & DePierre, J.A. (2013). The effect of physicians' body weight on patient attitudes: Implications for physician selection, trust and adherence to medical advice. *International Journal of Obesity, 37,* 1–7.

Richardson, S.O., Andersen, M.B., & Morris, T. (2008). *Overtraining athletes: Personal journeys in sport.* Champaign, IL: Human Kinetics.

Schoener, G. (2007). Do as I say, not as I do. *Professional Psychology: Research & Practice, 38,* 610–612.

Seligman, M.E.P., Steen, T.A., Park, N., & Peterson, C. (2005). Positive psychology progress. *American Psychologist, 60,* 410–421.

Wise, E.H., Hersh, M.A., & Gibson, C.M. (2012). Ethics, self-care and well-being for psychologists: Reenvisioning the stress-distress continuum. *Professional Psychology: Research & Practice, 43,* 487–494.

World Health Organization. (2011). *Global status report on non-communicable diseases 2010.* Geneva, Switzerland: World Health Organization Press.

World Health Organization. (2012). *Assessing national capacity for the prevention and control of non-communicable diseases: Report of the 2010 global survey.* Geneva, Switzerland: World Health Organization Press.

CHAPTER 5

Dancing for Your Life
Movement, Health, and Well-Being

Stephanie J. Hanrahan

In many primitive societies, dance was as essential as eating and sleeping. It provided individuals with a means to express themselves, to communicate feelings to others, and to commune with nature.

Levy, 1988, p. 1

At the age of 7 or 8 years, I began ballet lessons. In the three or four years I took lessons, the highlight was probably being a gingersnap in the Laguna Beach Civic Ballet Company's annual production of *The Nutcracker*. I was pretty good at picking up and remembering steps, but probably not so good at executing the steps with any level of expertise. First, I was naturally extremely pigeon-toed—to the point where I had scuff marks on the inside heels of my shoes caused by the toes of the opposite foot. Ballet requires feet to be turned out. One of the reasons my knees are decrepit now is that with no natural turnout from the hips, I forced the turnout of my feet from the knees (i.e., my knees would be pointing forward and my feet would be turned out). Second, I had really bony elbows, which made it virtually impossible to create the nice, curved arms expected in ballet. Third, I was the tallest kid in the class. And ballerinas are usually small, dainty things. Fourth, my older sister was really good at ballet, and she made dance the focus of her life for many years. There wasn't any overt sibling rivalry, but at that age I definitely felt more comfortable and had greater skill when it came to swimming and

tennis. I didn't hate ballet, but I didn't look forward to going to class either.

So, with that introduction, readers may be wondering why I (of all people) am writing a chapter promoting the benefits of dance. For many years (about a quarter of a century) after quitting ballet, I focused on sport—tennis, where I won both the girl's and boy's trophies at an end of summer tournament (top three girls got to compete on the boy's ladder), figure skating (I lost my amateur standing, back when that meant something), and volleyball (I competed at nationals in three countries and competed internationally for one country). I was forced to retire from competitive sport when my seriously abused knees made it impossible to run or jump. For a year or two, I made myself go the gym or swim laps in the pool, but it was definitely a chore. After years of looking forward to going to tennis, figure skating, and later, volleyball training, it was strange not to be excited about being active. One day I was invited to go to a dinner dance to celebrate Colombian Independence Day. The music was a live salsa band. I loved the music, but really had no idea how to dance to it. The next week I saw an ad for a Latin dance school: "Try your first class for free." I attended the class, and have since danced salsa, merengue, forró, tango, lambada, zouk, bolero, bachata, gafieira, and cha-cha in more than 10 different countries and have even performed on stage in Cuba and at home in Australia. At the age of 53 with plates and screws in both legs (reminders of two of the five knee surgeries I've had), my latest weekly activity is West African dance. So, what is it about dance that turned a jock into a dance aficionado?

Positive Effects of Dance

Dance has obvious physical benefits, but it has also been associated with salubrious emotional, social, spiritual, and psychological outcomes. These positive results of participating in dance are found across age, ability levels, and styles of dance. Evidence of the physical benefits of dance includes improved balance and physical performance (e.g., walking, stair climbing) in a randomized control trial of healthy elderly females involved in Turkish folkloric dance (Eyigor, Karapolat, Durmaz, Ibisoglu, & Cakir, 2009), improved balance in healthy older women participating in jazz dance classes (Alpert et al., 2009), and greater flexibility and respiratory resistance in older Brazilians involved in ballroom dancing (Lima & Vieira, 2007).

The positive physical effects of dancing are not limited to older individuals. In a study of African American and Hispanic adolescents (7th graders), a dance for health curriculum resulted in significantly greater decreases in body mass index and resting heart rate compared to a standard physical activity class (Flores, 1995). Advantages of dance in a school curriculum are that all students can be successful (unlike competitive sports–based programs); minimal skills are necessary to take part; overweight students can participate; minimal equipment is needed; the class is perceived to be fun without being repetitive; and music that is popular with the students can be used.

In addition to physical benefits, dance also has emotional and psychological effects. It is easy to demonstrate how our bodies influence how we feel. Posture alone can influence emotions (Levy, 1988). Hunched shoulders and a droopy head produce different emotions than shoulders back, head up, and chest out. If stationary posture can affect feelings, just think how much greater the effect of bodily movement might be. Individuals can express emotions through dance, and emotional states can cause bodies to move differently. Dancers can develop insight into their internal worlds where feelings are accepted and welcome (instead of questioned or denied; Leseho & Maxwell, 2010). Through dance, people can let go of stress, release tension from the body, express emotions, replace darker emotions (e.g., melancholy, grief) with more pleasant emotions (e.g., joy), and cope with stress and unpleasant emotional states (Leseho & Maxwell, 2010).

Studies with university students have shown immediate positive emotional effects of dance. A study of university students attending a biology class, a Hatha yoga class, or an African dance class showed that participants experienced significant decreases in perceived stress and negative affect after the yoga and dance classes, and a significant increase in positive affect after a dance class (there was a significant decrease in positive affect after a biology class; West, Otte, Geher, Johnson, & Mohr, 2004). Similarly, McInman and Berger (1993) found that female university students who attended an aerobic dance class and completed questionnaires immediately before and after the class reported mood benefits (decreased anger, confusion, sadness, and tension, and increased vigor) and improved self-concept.

The emotional and psychological effects of dance are not only experienced immediately after individual classes. College students in a modern dance class showed a significant reduction in state anxiety over a 3-month period (Leste & Rust, 1984). It appears as though the benefits of dance are not due to just being physically active or just listening to music. Leste and Rust found no significant changes in anxiety for students in a physical education group (exercise) or a music group (aesthetic appreciation). These results suggest that dance has a unique combination of exercise and aesthetic appreciation that leads to the positive change. Nevertheless, the contribution of music to dance's positive effects should not be dismissed. Dance typically combines physical movement and expression with a musical component. Music speaks to people. It can be a form of communication in and of itself, and it can motivate people to move their bodies (Trevarthen & Malloch, 2000).

Dance may also have positive cognitive effects. In participants over 75 years of age, ballroom dancing resulted in a decreased risk of dementia (Verghese, Lipton, & Katz, 2003). Likewise, daily 30-minute waltz lessons for 12 days resulted in a significant effect on procedural learning in patients with moderate symptoms of Alzheimer's disease (Rosler et al., 2002). The waltz lessons improved smoothness of movements and rhythm, and the individuals with Alzheimer's explicitly learned dance steps.

Dance can also be a bridge between body, mind, and spirit. The connection to spirit through dance has been described by people from different countries and different styles of dance as experiencing the sacred within, discovering one's essence or core, connecting to The Divine (different for different religions), feeling a sense of wholeness, reestablishing personal links to spirituality, and accessing and appreciating the sacred both within and outside the dancers (Leseho & Maxwell, 2010). Dance can be both an expression of spirit and a connection to spirit, however people interpret the spiritual.

Dance also has social benefits. Although individuals can dance at home alone with the music blaring (e.g., Tom Cruise in the movie *Risky Business*), dance is usually a social activity. Dancing done with partners obviously involves direct physical contact, but even in genres that involve moving individually (e.g., hula, tap, belly dancing), dancing typically takes place in a social environment, allowing for (or encouraging) not just social contact but also social networking and friendship development.

Individuals can also learn to develop trust through dance (Leseho & Maxwell, 2010), particularly when dancing with a partner. Trust is clearly required in dance where lifts or tricks are involved, but even a sedate waltz involves trust—followers trusting leaders to keep them safe and not cause collisions with other couples, leaders trusting followers to pick up on subtle shifts in weight or direction, and everyone trusting themselves to move in a way that fits the type of dance.

These physical, emotional, psychological, spiritual, and social benefits of dance may, either individually or in combination, influence quality of life. For example, healthy elderly females in a randomized control trial with Turkish folkloric dance as an intervention demonstrated significant improvements in quality of life (Eyigor et al., 2009). Even when dance does not result in significant physiological changes, the perceptions of well-being can be heightened. In a study of women with chronic fatigue syndrome (aged 35–55 years), participating in dance movement therapy resulted in no significant changes in per-

formance on a maximal test to measure maximum oxygen consumption peak, but the participants perceived significant improvements in their physical and psychological well-being after each session as well as after the entire program (Blazquez, Guillamo, & Javierre, 2010).

In a study of 60 Brazilian seniors over 60 years of age (mostly women) who had attended ballroom dance classes for 1 year (1 hour, twice per week), five qualitative themes emerged (Lima & Vieira, 2007). The dancers mentioned benefits including self-esteem, capacity for leadership and creativity, and increased qualities of elegance and lightness. They also recognized that dance provides opportunities for socializing (although some acknowledged that it can be embarrassing when other people focus their attention on them when they are expressing themselves freely). The Brazilian seniors mentioned three other advantages of participating in ballroom dance: It brings back good dancing memories (music from their youth was used in the classes), it allows the establishment of cultural connections to the larger Brazilian dancing culture, and (possibly most important) it is fun (Lima & Vieira, 2007).

Leseho and Maxwell (2010) interviewed 29 women aged 16 to 67 from 12 countries and different religions. They practiced multiple types of dance. The purpose of the study was to understand the contribution of dance to women's lives. In addition to many of the themes already mentioned, the authors found that dance can be empowering, and it can provide a sense of freedom. "To dance tango you have to be on your axis, on your own centre, and grounded . . . . [And it] just kind of expands to the rest of your life" (Leseho & Maxwell, 2010, p. 22). Empowerment was also discussed in terms of some cultures and experiences leading people (women) to believe it is not okay to take up too much space in the world; dance can reverse this belief and make it acceptable to take up space (and not just on the dance floor). For example, "I'd become very small and I was shrinking. [Through dancing] I realize that there's so much bigness in me . . . energy and light" (Leseho & Maxwell, 2010, p. 23). Dance can lead to the realization that the dancer is not insignificant.

Leseho and Maxwell's (2010) interviews also indicated that dance can be transforming and healing. When dancing, the body and mind interact in a way that a change in movement can affect total functioning. Movement improvisation can allow dancers to experiment with new ways of being. The participants reported that dancing can provide a sense of presence or grounding. Dance combines movements, music, and breath, bringing the dancer into the present moment rather than thinking about the past or the future. Dance provides "an openness to simply experiencing life" (Leseho & Maxwell, 2010, p. 24).

But There Can Be Challenges

Even with the physical, social, emotional, spiritual, and psychological advantages of dancing, my involvement in dance as an adult has not been without its challenges. In the preceding review I acknowledged that some people find it embarrassing to dance when they think other people are watching (even though in many social dance scenarios, people are too involved in their own dancing to pay much attention to how others are dancing). Perhaps because of my background of competing in elite sport in front of spectators, embarrassment was not a big issue for me. My two biggest challenges were related to control and my identity as an athlete. I was comfortable with the world of competitive sport. The physicality and sweat of dance were no concern. In sport, however, shorts, T-shirts, and sports shoes were the norm. In the social Latin dance scene, there are suddenly skirts, makeup, and high heels. I've moved to somewhere between these two extremes. Additionally, in volleyball, being big and tall is an advantage. On the dance floor, many guys are not comfortable dancing with someone who is bigger than they are. In some dance styles (e.g., tango), leading someone who is notably taller can be challenging. On bad days I could look around at tiny girls in miniskirts and stilettos and question what I was doing there. Once I'd start dancing, though, I could get out of my head and enjoy all of the previously named benefits.

My second big challenge was related to control. As an athlete, I had been accustomed to making all decisions and determining what my body would do. When it came to Latin dancing, I was suddenly moving with somebody else. Although volleyball is a team sport that requires communication and teamwork, I still decided what I did, and I rarely touched other athletes while performing. Latin dancing was confronting—I was physically close to a lot of different men (with the space, or lack thereof, between partners differing by dance style), and I had to do what they wanted me to do. I was a strong, independent woman who needed to learn how to follow the leads of different partners, something that was particularly frustrating when they were out of time with the music. Once I learned to stop battling the lead, I discovered the euphoria of two people moving as one and the serenity of turning my brain off and just letting my body follow my partner's.

Case Study

Kevin is a 27-year-old Caucasian basketball player who comes to see me because he wants to want to dance. A colleague of mine who is a strength and conditioning coach working with Kevin's basketball team put him on to me. Kevin's partner (Kim) has been supportive of his athletic career by attending games as well as doing off-season fitness training with him. Basketball takes up most of Kevin's nonwork time (he works part time in a bank), and Kim's nonwork life revolves around dance. She does not compete in DanceSport (i.e., competitive ballroom dancing), but she takes classes and goes to workshops in different dance genres, attends social dances most weekends, and occasionally performs. After completing a basic intake interview, I explain to Kevin the model of therapy I envision for our sessions and check to see if he is okay with that plan.

> **Stephanie (S):** Kevin, the way I often work is to take an approach that focuses on the ways we think, and how our thinking influences how we feel in both positive and negative ways. So I will be asking a lot of questions about your thoughts and perceptions, both the rational and irrational ones. It will feel at times that I am really challenging your thinking. How does that approach sound to you?

> **Kevin (K):** I suppose. I mean I'm cool with you challenging my thinking, but

what do you mean by "irrational"? I don't think I'm an irrational person.

S: I did not in any way mean to suggest that you are an irrational person. Rather, the idea is that we all have a variety of thoughts, some of which are less rational than others. I don't mean irrational as in psychotic or insane, but thoughts that are not entirely based on the truth. For example, a swimmer might think, "I never perform well in lane 2." The swimmer can turn that thought into a self-fulfilling prophecy. When assigned lane 2, the swimmer loses confidence and motivation because of the irrational thought that lane 2 is in some way jinxed, resulting in a slow swim time that then reinforces the original belief. In this example, my role would be challenging the belief that the athlete never performs well in lane 2.

K: Okay, that makes sense.

S: So are you comfortable with that type of approach in our sessions?

K: Yes.

With the basic approach of the sessions agreed upon, we then get on to the topic of dance.

K: You probably expected me to come to you with issues related to basketball, but I really came to see you because I want to want to dance. That probably sounds weird, but things are going great with basketball, and I want to try to dance, but even saying that aloud it sounds stupid.

In my own mind, I acknowledge that I am surprised the topic is dance (even though I try not to have expectations when I enter relationships with clients—blank slate and all that). At the same time I can feel myself getting excited that an athletically competent (and tall) guy wants to dance. I consciously stop myself from saying how brilliant I think it is that he wants to dance and how won-derful the experience of dance can be. My decision now is whether to follow the idea of his wanting to dance or why he thinks it sounds stupid. Potentially my own pro-dance bias leads me to begin with the former.

S: What do you mean by wanting to want to dance?

K: Well, Kim, my partner, she dances a lot. She doesn't nag me about doing it myself or anything, but she loves it so much, and I just don't get it. I'd like to discover what she likes about it, but at the same time, you just don't see tall, White guys being brilliant dancers.

S: I've seen some fairly brilliant tall, White male dancers.

As soon as I say that, I wish I had said something else. Whether or not I have seen brilliant tall White male dancers is irrelevant. I've also blatantly stated that he is wrong. My positive pro-dance bias probably made me defensive. I passionately believe that anyone who can walk (and many who cannot) can dance. I therefore immediately jumped to the defense of dance and corrected what I perceived to be Kevin's misperception.

K: Well maybe so, but they probably started dancing when they were kids.

S: Are you thinking that you are too old to start dancing?

K: It might not be age so much, as it's just something totally foreign to me.

S: Is foreign bad?

K: Not bad, just scary.

S: Scary how?

K: I could make a complete fool of myself. I mean I probably have two left feet.

S: You might be selling yourself short. I'm guessing that you are fairly coordinated on the basketball court.

K: Yeah, but that's different. I've been playing basketball for years.

Something has been bugging me, and I decide to go back to it. What is the real reason he wants to learn to dance? It doesn't ring true that he just wants to find out what his partner likes about it. My question might disrupt the flow of the conversation, but I take the chance, thinking it is something better addressed sooner than later.

S: You've been playing basketball for years, yet now you suddenly want to try dancing so that you can figure out why your partner likes it so much. Have you asked her to explain to you what she loves about it?

K: I have, but she says she can't really put it into words. She says it is just like me and basketball. She gets that I like to demonstrate ability, thrive on challenge, and enjoy being with my teammates, but that that description doesn't thoroughly explain what I like about hoops.

S: You like basketball, she likes dance, and neither one of you can put into words specifically what it is about your respective activities that draw you to them.

K: Yes.

S: That then brings me back to my original question, why do you want to want to learn to dance? Do you think that your experience of dance will be the same as hers and that you will then suddenly understand what she likes about it? Might your experience with basketball be closer to her experience of dance than you being a beginner in dance—something that she has been doing for most of her life?

How many questions can I ask at once? I have not only inundated him with three questions at once, but also ended with my opinion phrased as a question. I don't normally tend to deluge clients with multiple questions in one breath. I'm really just dancing around the point (no pun intended) that I don't believe he has given me his real reason for wanting to want to dance. I probably could have just asked him if there were any other reasons he wanted to want to dance.

K: When you put it like that, I guess that isn't completely the reason why I want to want to dance. Yes, I think there is something about dance that is different to basketball—of course there is, but I also want to be able to share in an activity that Kim likes so much.

S (intentionally playing devil's advocate): I commend you for wanting to get closer to your partner, but couldn't you just find a third, neutral activity that you could both do together instead of you trying to get into her world?

K: That's partially it—I do want to get into her world. Almost every weekend she is off dancing with other guys. I know there is nothing sexual about it, but I'm jealous! I want to be the one moving with her, instead of some stranger, or perhaps worse, some guy she dances with regularly who shares her passion for dance. I feel I'm on the outer.

I think we are now getting to his main motive for wanting to want to dance. Here I could use basic counseling skills and empathize and reflect on his distress, but I decide to stick with what I perceive to be a significant change in his mind-set.

S: It sounds to me like you want to dance with Kim. Do you want to dance or are you still at wanting to want to dance?

K: Yes, I want to dance with Kim, but I'm worried I'll make a complete fool of myself. I may be coordinated on the basketball court, but the dance floor is something else.

Because of my focus on changing cognitions, I avoid offering empathy regarding his anxieties. It is possible (or even probable) that I would have focused more on his feelings if I did not already have familiarity with many novice dancers having successfully decreased their anxieties through changing thoughts and behavior.

S: Do you expect to be able to dance like someone who has been doing it for years your first time out?

K: No . . . but I'd like to be able to.

S: What is the worst thing that could happen if you went dancing and were less than brilliant?

K: People would laugh at me.

S: And if they did laugh at you, how would that affect you?

K: I'd feel stupid, and I'd want to leave.

S: Say for a moment that you couldn't leave. What would you do?

K: I'd probably get mad.

S: Mad at whom?

K: Mad at myself.

S: Why would you be mad at yourself?

K: Because I made a fool of myself.

S: How would you have made a fool of yourself?

K: I would have tried to do something I couldn't do, and looked stupid. Other people would have seen me.

S: I'm a bit confused. You said that you would not expect yourself to dance very well, seeing as you have never done it before, but at the same time you would be mad at yourself because you didn't dance well.

K: True. I don't expect myself to dance well, but I don't want to have other people judging me and seeing me fail.

S: Is having a go at something new and making mistakes failing?

K: Not really.

S: What would be failing?

K: Making the same mistakes over and over.

S: It would be okay if you went to a dance class, tried a few moves, made some mistakes, but learned something and didn't make the same mistake over and over.

K: Yeah, I suppose, but I still don't like making mistakes in front of other people.

S: Have you ever made a mistake on the basketball court?

K: Of course I have, but I make a lot more smart plays than I do mistakes.

S: What happens when you make a mistake during a game?

K: I usually shrug it off and focus on my next job—try even harder to make up for the mistake.

S: Do you worry about people laughing at you or making a fool of yourself?

K: No. I know that I'm a better basketball player than probably 98% of the audience.

S: Is your success on the court, how well you personally play, determined by how much better you are than the people in the audience?

K: No, it's just that I know that I can make up for any mistakes, and I doubt that any would be laughing at me.

S: What would be the worst thing that could happen if people did laugh at you?

K: Nothing would really happen. I'd just get on with what I had to do.

S: If you make a mistake on the basketball court, you shrug it off and get on with what you were doing, but you think that if you were to make a mistake in a beginner dance class that you would feel stupid and get mad at yourself.

K: Yeah, I see how that really isn't consistent. But I mean I'm a jock, and jocks don't dance.

S: Says who?

My pro-dance bias again causes me to immediately challenge Kevin. Perhaps my focus has temporarily shifted from the client to my own agenda.

K: Well, no one. I have heard of soccer players down in South America improve their agility through dance, but they're Latin—it is in their blood.

S: Have you ever heard of the movie *White Men Can't Jump*?

K: That was a bit before my time, but yeah, I've heard of it—what a crock!

S: So some White men can jump. Perhaps some White men can also dance?

K: Yeah, yeah—I'm just not comfortable doing it.

S: Have you ever done it? Have you ever danced?

K: Not proper dancing. Just mucking around at parties or clubs.

S: Is the fear of making a fool of yourself the only thing that is keeping you from trying a dance class?

K: Pretty much, although I'm not really sure where I'd start even if I didn't think I'd make a fool of myself.

S: What do you mean, "where you'd start"?

K: Where I'd go, what type of dancing, who I'd do it with.

S: There are lots of different dance styles. Have you given it any thought?

K: Not really, I just know I don't want to do ballet or anything else where I'd be expected to wear tights and prance around.

S: How would you feel about having a bit of a homework assignment before our next session?

K: That would depend on what it was.

That is a fair comment on Kevin's part. My previous question was too vague. He has no idea what I have in mind and could be thinking that the homework might be going to the ballet or signing up for dance classes.

S: Well, I can list some different styles of dance off the top of my head now, and your homework would be to find out a little bit about two or three of them, or maybe other styles of dance that you might come across by Googling or talking to Kim.

K: I'm not going to talk to Kim about it yet —not until I'm sure I'm actually going to be dancing, and maybe not even then. I might wait and surprise her after I've done a few classes and am not a complete motor moron on the dance floor. What do you mean by finding out a little bit about them?

S: Just finding and watching a few YouTube videos and seeing what dance styles might or might not interest you.

K: So I don't actually have to dance yet.

S: You can if you want to, but that isn't part of the homework.

K: Sure, I can spend a bit of time surfing the Internet. What are some dance styles I might look at?

We then brainstorm together and come up with the following list (although, granted, the majority of the styles on the list came from me: line dancing, ballroom, salsa, zouk, tango, bachata, contemporary, African, tap, hip-hop, hula, belly, Bollywood, and break. I want Kevin to see that the world of dance is wide and varied, and that some dance styles are done with a partner, some alone, and some in groups. I let him know that he does not need to look up all of the dance styles listed, but that it would be great if he came to the next session with a couple that he might be open to investigating further.

At our next session Kevin arrives with the list, but it now has some comments and descriptors that he has added:

- Line dancing: Need to remember steps and order of them; would stick out like a sore thumb if I stuffed up, but some of it does look pretty easy.
- Ballroom: No way I'm wearing that crap; half of them look orange!
- Salsa: Partnering, learn steps—but may not need to perform them in a particular order, I know Kim likes salsa.

- Zouk: Looks pretty cool, but looks hard; Kim might get jealous if she saw me dancing that with some other girl!
- Tango: I'm afraid I'd be kicked in the balls.
- Bachata: Cool, could potentially try it.
- Contemporary: No way, too much like ballet.
- African: Seems to be space for individual expression and creativity, couldn't tell if someone makes a mistake, wouldn't have to worry about leading, but not sure I have it in me.
- Tap: I get shin splints just looking at it, but it would be good for fitness.
- Hip-hop: Really athletic, am I gangsta enough?
- Hula: Only if I moved to Hawaii, and probably not even then.
- Belly: Some hot-looking girls, but I don't think guys do it.
- Bollywood: Seems a bit geeky; what they do with their hands looks almost impossible.
- Break: Athletic, but spinning on my head is never going to happen, I'm too gangly.

K: It was actually kind of fun watching those YouTube clips. I was originally only going to look at a couple, but they intrigued me. There is a hell of a lot of talent out there. I didn't actually look at the dance styles in the order they are on the list, but I really got sucked into surfing the net.

I might normally question a client's overcompliance with a homework assignment, but I perceive his actions to be the result of enjoying the task rather than a great need to please. I had never used YouTube videos before in homework for clients. Kevin is only one client, but it seems to have worked well with him. The success of this experiment suggests to me that I need to be open to trying techniques that did not exist when I was training as a psychologist. It reinforces that I need to keep up with the times!

S: Which of the dance styles intrigued you the most?

K: Do you mean intrigued as in "wow, I can't believe they can do that" or intrigued as in "I might want to try that"?

S: As in "I might want to try that."

K: Well, line dancing looked pretty easy, but it didn't look that fun. Definitely not ballroom. I guess it would be between salsa, bachata, or hip-hop, or maybe African.

S: Perhaps you might want to personally try a couple different ones before you make any decisions?

K: I suppose. I mean I don't want to pay for a bunch of classes and find out I hate it after the first one.

S: A lot of dance studios . . . instructors . . . whatever . . . offer free trial classes.

I stumble on my words a bit here because I'm thinking that my use of the term "studio" might freak him out, make him think of ballet studios. I'm basing this assumption entirely on my own previous history of entering the dance world after years in competitive sport. He doesn't even seem to notice.

K: Really? That would be great.

S: So where to from here?

K: What do you mean?

S: What is your next step?

K: Do you mean what class am I going to do first? That seems a bit quick. I'm still not sure; I mean I'm still not completely comfortable with the possibility, or probability of making a fool of myself.

I unintentionally rushed him with my question. I wasn't really thinking that he would go off and do a class the next day. I really wanted him to con-

sider what options he might have. In hindsight, his enthusiasm at the thought of free classes may have resulted in my being unclear in my question—perhaps subconsciously hoping that he would want to go straight off to a dance class. It is possibly unprofessional of me, but I must admit I'm excited by the idea of a coordinated, tall male thinking of taking up dance. Most adult social dances and dance studios in Australia have many more women than men, and nothing against short guys, but more than once I've had my head hit by the arm of a guy who doesn't raise his arm high enough when leading me to spin or turn. I refocus on the situation at hand.

S: Sorry, I meant that maybe you should consider your options. The way I see it, your options range from deciding to not dance at all to signing up for a whole bunch of different classes, but I do think there are some other, perhaps less obvious, options to consider.

K: Such as?

S: Well again—thinking of extremes within the option of choosing dance—taking a private lesson where there would be no spectators, getting some instructional DVDs where you could learn on your own. Or at the other extreme, going to a group class and intentionally making a fool of yourself.

K: Why would I want to intentionally make a fool of myself?

S: It is a technique referred to as a behavioral experiment. Often what we fear isn't as bad as the real thing. It can be scary to set yourself up, but once you've survived the worst, you realize that you can survive it, and that in reality it isn't really that bad.

Behavioral experiments are prearranged activities or assignments in which clients engage to undermine their beliefs that other people will be harsh and critical, that they will be humiliated, or that they won't know how to behave in a particular situation (Heimberg, 2002). Behavioral experiments are a technique within cognitive behavioral therapy that is often used with clients who are experiencing social anxiety.

K: I don't know, you mean go to a dance class and intentionally trip myself or something?

S: Yes, that is one option. Another, probably less scary, option would be to observe a couple of beginner dance classes and see if your expectations about how good you think you need to be are supported by what you actually see.

K: Have you ever intentionally screwed up or had other people you work with intentionally screw up?

To self-disclose or not to self-disclose, that is the question. Among other purposes, self-disclosure can enhance positive expectations and motivation, strengthen the therapeutic bond, normalize the client's reaction, or model effective ways of functioning (Goldfried, Burckell, & Eubanks-Carter, 2003). Nevertheless, self-disclosure should not be for the therapist's self-enhancement. As recommended by Goldfried et al. (2003), I ask myself (a) why I wanted to say what I was about say and (b) what impact it would likely have on Kevin. My answers are (a) to give a real example of how falling down in front of a bunch of people may result in decreased rather than increased anxiety, and (b) to have Kevin consider that whatever happened in a dance class might not be that bad, regardless of whether or not he decides to try a behavioral experiment. Therefore, I decide to self-disclose.

S: Years ago I was skating in my first-ever exhibition, and I was really nervous. Although I'd been involved in competitive sport, I'd never been in a situation where I was the only one performing, let alone in an ice arena where people are surrounding you on all sides, and you are

the entire focus of attention. Anyway, I hadn't planned it, but I skated to the middle to stop and wait for my music to start my program. Instead of stopping elegantly, however, I tripped myself and fell. There was muffled laughter. I could have totally freaked out, but instead I thought to myself that the audience would have virtually no expectations about my skating ability now, so anything at all would be an improvement. I ended up skating a clean program, but more importantly, I wasn't nervous anymore. The worst had happened.

K: So it wasn't intentional. Any examples of when it was intentional?

S: I had a client who was a soccer player who was afraid to attempt a new skill in competitions. He could perform the skill well in training, but was worried that he'd stuff up and make a fool of himself if he tried it in a game. He argued that in training no one was watching, and it didn't really matter, but that a game was different. On his own he had done some reading about behavioral experiments, and he decided to intentionally trip himself in a game in a situation when he could use the new skill. He told me that he was more nervous about being able to trip himself on purpose than he was about using the new skill, but he stuck to his guns, and he did trip himself. He was surprised that no one had really noticed and that the game just kept going. That experience gave him the confidence to try the new skill in the game, which he did successfully.

K: That makes sense, but I'm not sure if I could do that, I mean intentionally fall down.

S: Doing the full-on behavioral experiment is only one option. How about we make a list of possible courses of action, and then when you get home you

Table 5.1   Kevin's Pros and Cons of Different Dance Options

Option	Pros	Cons
Don't dance	• Won't make a fool of myself (at least not on a dance floor)	• Don't like to think of myself as a quitter • Won't ever dance with Kim
Get some dance lessons on DVD	• Won't make a fool of myself in public • Could go over the same moves as many times as I want	• No feedback from someone who knows what they're doing • Don't really have much space to move in front of the TV
Get Kim to teach me	• Wouldn't cost any $ • She might like telling me what to do • I'd be dancing with Kim	• I wouldn't be able to surprise her • If either of us gets frustrated, it could be bad for the relationship • She isn't a dance teacher
Get private lessons	• Would probably learn faster than in a group class • No one around to laugh at me	• Expensive • Wouldn't have any experience dancing with partners who aren't professional
Go to some come-and-try classes in a couple of dance styles and then decide	• Could try a couple of different styles (and instructors) that would allow me to make a more informed decision about future classes • Could probably do them for free • If I really make a total fool of myself I've not made any commitment to go back	• Potentially wider audience of people who could see me stuff up
Sign up for a regular block of classes	• Would commit me to attend	• If I didn't really like it, I'd be kicking myself for not trying a couple of dance styles first • Might make a fool of myself
Do a regular block of classes and intentionally make a fool of myself in the first class	• If I did it, the pressure would be off	• It would really stress me out beforehand • Not sure I could do it
Go observe one or two group classes	• Could get any idea of how classes work and the level of coordination/ability of students	• Might feel weird, like I'm perving • They may not want people they don't know watching classes

jot down your perceptions in terms of the possible pros and cons of the different possibilities?

K: Probably not as fun as checking out YouTube clips, but yeah, I can do that.

Before our next scheduled appointment, Kevin called to cancel. He said that he'd done the homework, which helped him to decide what to do. He had been to two come-and-try dance classes with a third scheduled, and so far, so good. He volunteered to send me a fax or a scan of his homework. I accepted his offer (see table 5.1). I must admit that I did so more out of curiosity than because of any potential therapeutic value, but justified the decision by indicating that having it on file might be helpful if he decided to see me again in the future. I don't know what type of dance styles he selected, but he did comment that the classes he had done so far were more fun than what he'd originally expected.

I'd like to know more about Kevin's experiences with dance and what effect, if any, it had on Kevin's relationship with Kim. In applied practice, however, abrupt endings of relationships between practitioners and clients happen. That is just how things can be. Clients may figure that they got what they came for, that the sessions were a waste of time or at least not meeting their perceived needs, or that they just are not yet ready to deal with the issues that have arisen during therapy. As a result, psychologists do not always achieve a sense of closure with their clients. Nevertheless, Kevin's story tells us that nondancers can change their view of dance and themselves and enter the world of dance. Although I don't know what happened with Kevin, I hope that he was able to experience at least some of the potential physical, social, emotional, spiritual, and psychological benefits of dance.

Final Thoughts

Dance is a wonderful form of physical activity that is sometimes overlooked because it does not neatly fit into the traditional dichotomy of sport (typically in the form of competitions) or exercise (usually considered in terms of running, swimming, cycling, gym, or fitness classes). Dance, sport, and exercise all tend to have physical, psychological, and social benefits. Dance may also offer emotional and spiritual benefits that may be less evident in sport and exercise programs. I don't want to sound too zealous, though; dance is not a panacea. Some individuals may have issues with dancing—feeling self-conscious, being rhythmically challenged, buying into gender stereotypes, fearing having to memorize set choreography, or feeling uncoordinated (the proverbial "two left feet syndrome"). Nevertheless, the variety of dance options (classes and social events) available in most communities allows people of any age from any background to at least consider dance as a form of physical activity.

References

Alpert, P.T., Miller, S.K., Wallmann, H., Havey, R., Cross, C., Chevalia, T., . . . Kodandapari, K. (2009). The effect of modified jazz dance on balance, cognition, and mood in older adults. *Journal of the American Academy of Nurse Practitioners, 21,* 108–115.

Blazquez, A., Guillamo, E., & Javierre, C. (2010). Preliminary experience with dance movement therapy in patients with chronic fatigue syndrome. *The Arts in Psychotherapy, 37,* 285–292.

Eyigor, S., Karapolat, H., Durmaz, B., Ibisoglu, U., & Cakir, S. (2009). A randomized controlled trial of Turkish folklore dance on the physical performance, balance, depression and quality of life in older women. *Archives of Gerontology and Geriatrics, 48,* 84–88.

Flores, R. (1995). Dance for health: Improving fitness in African American and Hispanic adolescents. *Public Health Reports, 110,* 189–193.

Goldfried, M.R., Burckell, L.A., & Eubanks-Carter, C. (2003). Therapist self-disclosure in cognitive-behavior therapy. *Journal of Clinical Psychology, 59,* 555–568.

Heimberg, R.G. (2002). Cognitive-behavioral therapy for social anxiety disorder: Current status and future directions. *Biological Psychiatry, 51,* 101–108.

Leseho, J., & Maxwell, L.R. (2010). Coming alive: Creative movement as a personal coping strategy on the path to healing and growth. *British Journal of Guidance & Counselling, 38,* 17–30.

Leste, A., & Rust, J. (1984). Effects of dance on anxiety. *Perceptual and Motor Skills, 58,* 767–772.

Levy, F.J. (1988). *Dance/movement therapy: A healing art.* Reston, VA: AAHPERD.

Lima, M.M.S., & Vieira, A.P (2007). Ballroom dance as therapy for the elderly in Brazil. *American Journal of Dance Therapy, 29,* 129–142.

McInman, A.D., & Berger, B.G. (1993). Self-concept and mood changes associated with aerobic dance. *Australian Journal of Psychology, 45,* 134–140.

Rosler, A., Seifritz, E., Krauchi, K., Spoerl, D., Brokuslaus, I., Proserpi, S., . . . Hofmann, M. (2002). Skill learning in patients with moderate Alzheimer's disease: A prospective pilot-study of waltz-lessons. *International Journal of Geriatric Psychiatry, 17,* 1155–1156.

Trevarthen, C., & Malloch, S.N. (2000). The dance of wellbeing: Defining the musical therapeutic effect. *Nordic Journal of Music Therapy, 9*(2), 3–17.

Verghese, J., Lipton, R.B., & Katz, M.J. (2003). Leisure activities and the risk of dementia in the elderly. *The New England Journal of Medicine, 348,* 2508–2516.

West, J., Otte, C., Geher, K., Johnson, J., & Mohr, D.C. (2004). Effects of Hatha yoga and African dance on perceived stress, affect, and salivary cortisol. *Annals of Behavioral Medicine, 28,* 114–118.

PART II

Changing Habits

The authors of the chapters in this section explore the challenges and benefits of attempting (and maintaining) behavior change on more than one front at the same time. In chapter 6, Jeff Breckon provides a detailed example of the subtleties, complexities, and effectiveness of motivational interviewing to help a client who is struggling with weight, poor eating habits, and low physical activity. In the following chapter, Adrian Taylor and Tom Thompson illustrate how exercise can become a part of a smoking cessation program and how just the simple act of *noticing* (being mindful of) one's smoking can be a large step in the process. In the last chapter in this section, Matthew Martens and Ashley Smith examine the role exercise may play in treating people with alcohol use issues. They illustrate the beginnings of this process with a consciousness-raising session with a university student who is moving down a substance abuse path.

CHAPTER 6

Motivational Interviewing, Exercise, and Nutrition Counseling

Jeff Breckon

If you are arguing for change and your client is arguing against it, you've got it exactly backward.

Miller & Rollnick, 2012

Traditional medical approaches to health behavior change, which entail advice giving, education, and information provision, have been shown to be largely ineffective, and they are slowly giving way to more person-centered and community-oriented interventions (Brodie, Inoue, & Shaw, 2008). Although evidence shows that the benefits of being active and eating healthily are clear, the general population's motivation to engage in these shifts in behavior appears to be a significant barrier to change. Research is increasingly illustrating that it is not the amount of information or advice we provide (with regard to health) that is effective, but rather the level of motivation that determines whether an individual will make a lifestyle change, and traditional advice giving can be counterproductive (Rollnick, Miller, & Butler, 2008). Individuals with sedentary lives rarely move toward government recommendations of regular, lifelong activity. For nutrition or dietary changes, the social nature of eating makes the behavior change challenging and often requires cognitive-behavioral adaptations and extensive maintenance strategies that can be adapted to changes over time.

To effect change, health professionals need to help their clients increase motivation for change, and this process will no doubt include the elicitation and strengthening of self-determined values and self-efficacy. I have worked clinically with clients since the early nineties, and I realized fairly early on that my approach of swamping the session with information and enthusiasm was both exhausting and, worryingly, not too effective. I therefore sought an approach to highlight a method of interaction that engages and challenges clients by using an empathetic approach to encourage them to take on responsibility for their own health behaviors. One such approach that I find to be effective in a number of health behavior change settings is motivational interviewing (MI). In this chapter, I aim to describe how I use MI in exploring the client's own motivations for physical activity, exercise, and diet change and the role of the relational (or *spirit,* which is described later) and technical facets of this approach to support behavior change. I describe the approach and its elements and then provide a context of its application with a case study drawn from real client interactions.

What Is Motivational Interviewing?

Miller and Rollnick (2009) described MI as "a collaborative, goal-oriented method of communication with particular attention to the language of change. It is intended to strengthen personal motivation for and commitment to a change goal by eliciting and exploring an individual's own arguments for change" (p. 137). Motivational interviewing was born out of Miller's clinical work in the addictions field, and since the early 1980s, it has become a popular and commonly researched, trained, and applied form of communicating. Its popularity is based on the appreciation of the role the client must take in the change process, and it supports a person-centered approach and partnership. Although it evolved from the early work of Rogers (1959), the direction, goal-orientation, and focus on change talk (Amrhein, Miller, Yahne, Palmer, & Fulcher, 2003) makes it distinct. The approach is becoming mature in regard to empirical support. Even though aspects seem similar to those of cognitive behavior therapy (CBT), it is distinct, and it can be clearly defined. When applied robustly with integrity and consistency, it is an effective form of counseling across an increasingly diverse range of settings.

Nevertheless, the integrity and robust nature of the intervention are often not clearly applied in research and community settings, which has often raised the question of treatment fidelity (Bellg et al., 2004; Breckon, Johnston, & Hutchison, 2008). Although reading books and watching video examples of MI can take you a certain distance, it is ultimately consistent practice with accurate reflective feedback and supervision that has repeatedly shown positive results in high-quality MI delivery (Madson, Loignon, & Lane, 2009). Practitioners who are considering using MI in their own settings should seek to understand the technical aspects and, perhaps more important, the spirit of the approach. In this chapter, I present examples from a practitioner perspective in a physical activity and nutrition context.

In many settings, clients raise concerns or objections and overt resistance to change that can raise a number of natural responses from us as practitioners. Do we convince them with evidence? Argue against them with statistics? Use our position as experts who have seen thousands of cases like theirs? Ignore their objections? Fall into the action-planning mode to "fix" things? Or, as Rosengren (2009) suggested, do we respond in a manner to try to understand their concerns? Understand their motives, values, and perspective? Attempt to empathize and use this momentum to change in a slightly different direction? Practitioners have choices in the ways they respond, and consideration of these choices begins to describe

the philosophy and principles of MI. To present an example of MI as concisely as possible (see figure 6.1), this section presents four elements of MI: the spirit of MI, the technical components of MI (OARS), principles of MI (R.U.L.E), and change talk.

The Spirit of MI

The spirit of MI (see Miller & Rollnick, 2012) can be described as a way of being with the client. It provides the underpinning style, philosophy, and approach by which the technical aspects (such as OARS, see later) can become effective. The spirit is a guiding principle of MI, and it can be predictive of practitioner effectiveness and, in turn, client behavior change and treatment efficacy. The spirit of MI is perhaps best described by four elements (figure 6.1). This way of being and thinking is common in the approach of many MI practitioners (Westra, 2012). It is this interpersonal process between the practitioner and client that often translates into the approach that I have defined here in terms of the spirit of MI. Later sections explain how to apply specific technical skills (OARS).

Collaboration

Collaboration is a guiding principle for me and for many others who use MI, and it guides my approach as a practitioner by ensuring that I do not take the expert role and make clients passive recipients of instructions for their own changes. As Miller and Rollnick (2012) described, "MI is done 'for' and 'with' a person" (p. 15). It is an active collaboration with an appreciation that clients are experts in their own knowledge about their changes. As clients rightly suggest, no one knows them better than they know themselves. With this principle in mind, I work with a genuine interest in the client and seek to create a positive interpersonal relationship that values the client's perspective and resources. I am still there to act as an active guide, not leading or coercing, but working in partnership. As an active part of this partnership, I bring expertise and knowledge about what the evidence suggests and typically what works for others in similar positions, but when it comes to clients' situations, I have to appreciate that I need their help in understanding what they

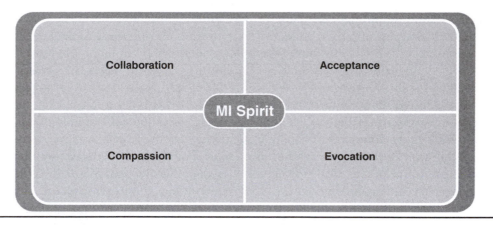

Figure 6.1   The underlying spirit of motivational interviewing.

Adapted, by permissions, from W.R. Miller and S. Rollnick, 2012, *Motivational interviewing: Helping people change,* 3rd ed. (London: Guilford Press), 22.

already know and feel and, more important, what the clients' goals and aspirations are (Rosengren, 2009).

Acceptance

To allay the fears of many practitioners, acceptance does not mean one necessarily agrees with or approves of clients' actions or attitudes toward change. Personal approval (or disapproval) is irrelevant here; rather, one appreciates the absolute worth of clients in what Carl Rogers described as unconditional positive regard (1980). This stance can be a challenge for many practitioners, and many health professionals whom I have trained are often fearful of too much client involvement in their own change. Practitioners may worry that the client might give them the wrong answer when asked about strategies or options, but respecting the clients' own potential for growth can be helpful in supporting their change. With this fear and lack of trust in the client, the default position of the *expert trap* can emerge, where the practitioner takes the lead in advising and problem solving in the change plan phase. Acceptance, however, in the context of MI, links closely to self-actualization (Maslow, 1970) and places trust and respect in the client.

Evocation

In health settings there is a tendency to fall into the trap of the *righting reflex,* which describes unsolicited advice giving and a tendency to fix problems and solve clients' barriers to change without really understanding clients' perspectives or the re-

sources they bring to managing their own change processes. This tendency can often translate into premature problem solving and can place the client in a passive role (Naar-King & Suarez, 2011). In MI, I try to evoke and elicit reasons, ideas, strategies, and motives for change from the client, which help me understand and appreciate the resources the client brings to the change situation. In the MI spirit, we try to avoid unsolicited advice giving, to engage clients by having them appreciate and demonstrate their worth, which helps them feel respected, and to affirm their knowledge, skills, and attitudes that will be helpful as we move forward together in partnership. The process of evocation and elicitation from the client moves beyond a person-centered approach and adds a dimension of autonomy and goal-orientation. As practitioners, we are aware of what the evidence suggests, and what seems to work (or not) for others, but with regard to the clients in front of us, we must appreciate that they are the experts of their experiences, challenges, and opportunities for change. With MI we recognize that clients are ultimately responsible for choosing their own paths, so we avoid arguing for change. Although we have opportunities to share concerns when paths that may do them harm appear, we have to respect their choices for autonomy in health behavior change contexts (Rosengren, 2009).

Compassion

The most recent addition to the description of the MI spirit, from the early iterations, reflects the need to cultivate a virtue of compassion and seek the value of well-being in others (Miller & Rollnick, 2012). Working with compassion does not mean taking a sympathetic stance—an emotional or associated feeling toward a client's change—but rather making a commitment toward the welfare and best interests of the clients with whom we are working. An important distinction has been made with the addition of compassion to the existing three elements of the MI spirit (i.e., evocation, collaboration, acceptance) because it is possible to practice the other three elements to achieve self-interest, which can sometimes be used to exploit the individual in sales and marketing.

The spirit of MI is perhaps the most fundamental part of MI and supports the clear attempt to gain empathy and engagement, which are consistently cited as essential in creating an effective therapeutic relationship (Miller & Rose, 2009). MI is a challenging approach for practitioners whose default position is one of advice giving and falling into the expert trap. There are, without doubt, challenges in our work settings, such as limited client contact time, client progression targets, and complex multiple health behavior factors. Practitioners often feel that these challenges inhibit their opportunities to work in person-centered ways. Nevertheless, as I have tried to illustrate, challenging the client to engage in change with an empathic stance can reduce resistance and time spent convincing and can create an environment of trust and acceptance that is conducive toward collaboration and progress.

Technical Skills of Motivational Interviewing: OARS

Often referred to as the technical components of MI, the OARS include open questions, affirmations, reflective listening, and summarizing. It is important to stress before I go any further that although the technical aspects of MI are clearly important, the use of these technical components without the spirit of MI is like lyrics without music and is not MI as we know it. MI is fundamentally a way of being with the client; it may often emerge from using the technical skills, but the use of these technical components alone does not represent MI. Here I describe what have become known as the technical aspects of MI.

Open Questions

Using open questions (OQs), rather than their closed alternatives, helps to elicit a deeper understanding, and it is often effective in engendering client engagement. As Miller and Rollnick (2012) stated, "an open question is like an open door," and it helps the asker understand deeper values and not just facts. As practitioners, we need to use tools that create an open environment that increases the likelihood of knowing and understanding our client's position.

It is tempting to fall into a closed-question trap where the practitioner may ask multiple health behavior questions such as "Do you exercise regularly?", "Would you like to be more active?", "Do you have a healthy diet?", all of which run the risk of having the practitioner fall into the expert trap and allow little opportunity for clients to unpack their understanding or stories. Expanding on the idea of remaining open, rather than closed, there is also the opportunity to use specific forms of OQs at specific times. These adaptations can include OQs that target intention to change, advantages of change, disadvantages of change, and optimism for change. Considering these forms of OQs, our alternatives to the previous examples would be "What would you like to do about your diet?" (intention to change), "How would it feel if you were to become more active?" (advantages of change), "If you didn't begin to make changes soon, how would that feel?" (disadvantages of not changing), and "What would it feel like if you were able to manage your diet better?" (optimism for change).

Affirmations

Affirmations are one of the most challenging communication skills to develop for those learning MI because they seem to require a cultural shift. It is easy to get caught in the *praise trap* because it seems so right to offer this form of feedback to our clients and patients when they describe how they have increased their activities, changed their diets, or reduced their levels of smoking. It seems so natural to offer a comment of "That's great, well done" or "I'm really pleased; that's excellent and will really help" when really all we are actually offering is our judgment on their performance based on our own values. Although subtle, we are at risk here of falling into the expert trap. Actually, what we want our clients to do is develop autonomy and self-reflection about the changes they have made.

In MI, one approach we can take is to offer an affirmation that is a nonjudgmental reflection on our clients' behaviors or attitudes toward change and to maintain a position of openness and future discussions around "where next?" As Naar-King and Suarez (2011) rightly suggested, honesty and specificity are key ingredients of an effective affirmation, where one targets a specific strength with genuineness. Like reflections, the affirmation is close to what the client has already said and generally accepted. For example, rather than the praise "It's great that you are now cycling to work," the affirmation alternative would be "So you've made a real life change" or "You've built strategies into your daily routine when it would have been easier to stay with the status quo." Avoiding "I" statements, such as "I'm really pleased with what you have achieved," is another key ingredient to effective affirmations and tends to reduce client resistance and increase genuineness.

A consideration for practitioners in using affirmations is not just the *what* but also the *when*. When working with a client, I'm listening for cues about readiness, at which point I might affirm (a form of reflection) that readiness ("You are willing to make a change to your daily routine"), whereas for the more ambivalent, or contemplative state, I might offer an affirmation reflection regarding the client's strengths and values ("You are willing to make a decision to change even though it is the more challenging route"). Note here that these are statements (reflections) rather than questions. This aspect of MI leads me on to the most important technical component of MI, reflective listening.

Reflective Listening

Eliciting and strengthening self-motivation is an important component in developing self-determined behaviors and autonomy, which is evident in research toward maintenance of long-term change (Johnston, Breckon, & Hutchinson, 2009). Perhaps reflective listening should appear first in the OARS mnemonic because it is fundamental when attempting to understand the meanings clients express (Miller & Rollnick, 2012) on the way to developing autonomy and resolving ambivalence toward change. In using reflective listening,

I am trying to both engage and empathize with my client; this is, without doubt, the most significant communication skill I have in MI to that end. The essence of high-quality reflective listening is to provide evidence to clients that I am trying to *come alongside* them in a nonjudgmental manner while still challenging their perspectives but in a respectful and supportive style to develop a partnership toward their change. This *accurate empathy* allows me to test my hypotheses about what I feel the client means or feels while simultaneously emphasizing or amplifying this meaning to move to an accurate shared understanding quickly.

Miller and Rollnick (2012) described clients who often do not say what they mean; therefore, our task as listeners is "to hear the words accurately and decode their meaning" (p. 52). This process can be described as three steps where communication can go wrong: encoding, hearing, and decoding. Figure 6.2 illustrates this process, whereby checking my hypothesis of what I think the speaker (client) means allows for a decoding of this meaning and a shared understanding (and increased empathy) as the session unfolds.

It is so much more common for practitioners to ask questions than to offer reflections of meaning, so why bother changing? Well, as Miller and Rollnick (2012) suggested, a question demands a response, which can be uncomfortable for the respondent, whereas a statement encourages continued exploration and allows me to challenge with empathy. The use of a well-formed reflection can sound similar, yet the inflection can be clearly differentiated in both simple and complex reflections.

Simple reflections. With a simple reflection I am repeating, or adapting minimally, what my client has said to express understanding. Whereas the words may be similar to those used in questions, the delivery style, and subsequent client response, is different. For example, the inflection upward can distinguish between a question and a simple reflection, such as "Being more active is what you want to achieve?" (question), as compared to the downward inflection of "Being more active is what you want to achieve" (reflection). The removal of "?" is subtle but significant in MI, and it leads to clarification by the speaker and increased exploration that cannot be achieved by

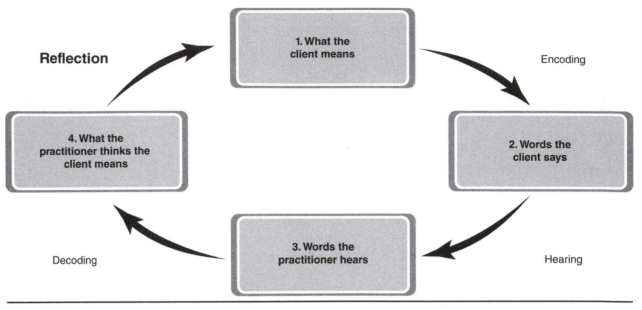

Figure 6.2   The process of communication.

Adapted, by permissions, from W.R. Miller and S. Rollnick, 2012, *Motivational interviewing: Helping people change,* 3rd ed. (London: Guilford Press), 26.

questioning alone (Rosengren, 2009). One may seem unsure of the value of simply offering back what the client has said in a reflection, and it may seem clumsy, but as Naar-King and Suarez (2011) suggested, getting past these early stages with practice and accurate self-reflection will help one to be proficient and fluent at allowing clients to take some control over the content of the sessions, and it will increase clients' engagement with the process and the practitioner.

Varying the depth of the reflection that one offers the client can allow for exploration of the client's meaning. This depth can range from communications close to the client's words (figure 6.2) to reflections significantly beyond what the client has said. The depth of reflection should be a response to the position of the conversation, with simple reflections early on and perhaps deeper, or more complex reflections, as the relationship develops.

Complex reflections.   Adding intensity of the content or feeling of the reflection back to clients can be a helpful way of unearthing the deep personal meaning of the clients' perspectives. When used well, complex reflections can help clarify and solidify the understanding of the clients' own thoughts and offer another perspective that they had not been necessarily considering. The use of

complex reflections alters the affective tone of the conversation (Rosengren, 2009), and although one complex reflection is not better than another, experienced MI practitioners will be able to choose from their toolboxes more effectively following supervision and reflective practice. To that end, a range of complex reflections are available, and table 6.1 provides examples of these together with examples of potential responses to a client's ambivalent statement of "Even though I know I should be more active, I'm not sure whether I can do it regularly." As can be seen in these examples, I am clearly hearing my client because my reflections directly relate to the statement, yet I am adding more than was explicitly stated, creating forward movement and client exploration. For example, with the *double-sided* reflection, I am making explicit the client's ambivalence toward behavior change and challenging (with empathy) the client to explore the issues and consider future movement. Ambivalence is common in most people considering a significant life or behavior change; therefore, this form of complex reflection is one that I seem to use in most client consultations. In the *amplified* complex reflection, I am turning up the volume on the emotional elements of the client statement. This reflection is often a truer representation of where the client is at than what has been verbalized so far, thus moving the

Table 6.1   Types and Examples of Complex Reflections

Type of complex reflection	Example of complex reflection from practitioner
Double-sided	"So you aren't sure you can stick to it, but you are clear that being more active would be better in the long run."
Amplified	"So being more active is particularly important to you."
Siding with the negative	"It would be easier to not bother and remain as you are."
Reframing	"You are starting to think about the long-term likelihood of this life change."
Emphasizing personal control	"Whether you do or do not change is completely under your control."

session forward relatively quickly. In *siding with the negative*, I am again offering back a hypothesis that the client would rather remain in the status quo, often resulting in the client defending the alternate position of change—defending the irrational and illogical position of the value of a sedentary life is not a position the ambivalent client will often take. Complex reflections add to the self-understanding of the client by presenting contrasting positions, and these reflective statements may also contain additional cognitive reframes and directions.

Some of the most commonly used complex reflections are illustrated in table 6.1, but others exist. For those early in learning MI, it can be helpful to consider simple and complex reflections when working with clients, or perhaps even considering them as *content* versus *feelings* reflections. Knowing what and when, in regard to complex reflections, is certainly challenging for a practitioner early in the learning of MI, but coding audio tapes of sessions can be extremely helpful in reflecting on the effectiveness and suitability of reflective listening by tagging both the practitioner use of OARS against the client responses and strength of change talk (Amrhein et al., 2003). When training practitioners in the use of reflective listening, it is common to hear concerns regarding the risk of putting words into the mouths of our clients. The two most important considerations that will help practitioners avoid speaking for clients are to (a) respond with genuineness and empathy using the spirit of MI, and (b) think critically about what clients mean and offer reflections that will challenge their perspectives while supporting them with respect and empathy. It is common to have this concern, but in skillful re-

flective listening, it is rare that a client responds in anything other than engagement and willingness to explore and come alongside.

Summarizing

Throughout this chapter, I emphasize the use of MI as an approach that helps practitioners attempt to clearly explore client ambivalence and to develop engagement and empathy while maintaining a clear direction toward client change. The final component of OARS draws together the conversation in such a way as to demonstrate, like no other component can, that the practitioner has engaged and heard the client. It is common when I work with trainee practitioners to ask them, "What have you just heard from the client?" More often than not, they can recite the content accurately. Nevertheless, when I ask them, "How did the client feel about that content?" they often have to guess because they haven't offered it back for clients to hear their own stories, process them, and respond. The challenge is retaining complex information from the client and presenting it back as the client's own story. *Summarizing* is an essential skill in demonstrating our involvement in the process. In essence, the summary is a form of reflection offering the chance to amplify, side with the negative result of the status quo, reflect both sides of the ambivalence, reframe, and blend content and feeling reflections as required. It helps the practitioner and the client pull out the relevant information from the conversation at regular points; clarify one's understanding of the client's position; provide an opportunity for the therapist to be corrected; offer the client the chance to correct, amplify, or reduce content the client has recently relayed; and, again, highlight that one is

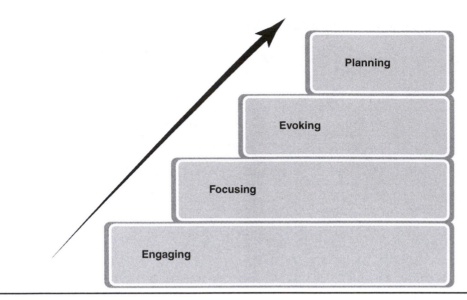

Figure 6.3   The four processes of motivational interviewing.

Adapted, by permissions, from W.R. Miller and S. Rollnick, 2012, *Motivational interviewing: Helping people change,* 3rd ed. (London: Guilford Press), 52.

willing to hear the client's story. There is no right and wrong as to how often a professional should offer a summary, although it is worthwhile to be ready to offer a reflective summary to provide a "base camp" from which to move next (e.g., movement from background to agenda setting, exploration of ambivalence to action planning, action planning to relapse prevention and maintenance).

The Four Processes of Motivational Interviewing

The first two editions of *Motivational Interviewing* (Miller & Rollnick, 1991; 2002) described two phases of practitioner–client interactions. Phase 1 includes the process of building motivation for change and exploring readiness and importance, whereas phase 2 focuses on eliciting commitment and planning toward change.

This linear approach has evolved into the useful (and heuristic) four processes in MI (Miller & Rollnick, 2012): engaging, focusing, evoking, and planning. They provide a clear structure and framework for sessions within which practitioners adapt their use of the technique depending on the readiness, motivation, and level of sustain or change talk emerging from the client (Rosengren, 2009). The processes can be seen in figure 6.3.

Engaging

Engaging is the process of establishing a connection and a therapeutic relationship. It forms the bedrock of my sessions. In MI, there are techniques I use that will increase the likelihood that the client will be willing to engage and work with me. The development of this connection can take seconds or weeks, and it is often influenced by external factors such as service settings, the client's emotional state, and the readiness for change. Nevertheless, I enter the interaction mindful that the spirit of MI—patience and respect—will form the core of my approach in this relationship and increase the likelihood that the client will engage in the change process with me. Specifically, I use the MI spirit and technical skills (OARS) to develop this empathetic and engaging approach, and it is clear from my experience of working in an MI style that developing this engagement is central. Engaging is pivotal for everything that follows, and it can help me and the client develop an effective and respectful relationship. It can be helpful throughout the process, but it is especially important in the early stages. The tools that help me in these early stages can be seen in table 6.2.

Focusing

Focusing is the process by which I am developing and maintaining a specific direction in the conversation about change. I have already mentioned the

Table 6.2 The Four Processes of Motivational Interviewing and Corresponding Content

MI process	MI content
Engaging	Opening exchange and agenda setting
Focusing	Decisional balance
Evoking	Importance of change [agreed target behavior]
	Readiness to change [agreed target behavior]
Planning	Action planning and relapse prevention

challenge that arises when a client experiences multiple health-related behaviors and risk factors. It is rare that clients present with a single issue; for example, the need for physical activity or behavior adoption is often the result of obesity or weight increase combined with alcohol and smoking. Moreover, practitioners often have to manage the conflict between their (or their agency's) agenda and that of the client (one hopes that the two overlap often). It is naïve to assume we enter a session without an agenda. Although preemptive approach happens, there can sometimes be a discrepancy between the agency's agenda (ultimately, my agenda) and that of the client.

Client ambivalence toward change can be explored using decisional balance tools (table 6.2). The process of focusing reduces discrepancy between the client and the practitioner, and will help maintain a specific direction in conversations about the client's change. As I work with the client, I often find that maintaining a broad focus in the early stages increases the chances that a change plan will emerge, but I am also aware that a range of change options are often possible, so flexibility is important. Change goals can be overt or covert, and can be linked to a behavioral (tangible) change or an adaptation of a thought process or attitude. It is this variety of possible changes that makes me appreciate the need for a flexible and dynamic approach that again collaborates and engages with the client as we progress.

Evoking

In this chapter, I describe the need to engage and collaborate, using the MI spirit. The process of *evoking* involves eliciting the client's own motivations for change using the MI spirit and technical skills and lies at the heart of the approach. Once

we have agreed on one or more change goals, it is important to capture the client's own motivation and evoke from them their desire, potential, willingness, and motivation for change rather than imposing my own attitudes and values. It is this latter exploration of *values matching* that will help clients clarify their own ideas about what to change and how they might effect change. In health behavior change settings, such as physical activity and nutrition change, a traditional expert-didactic approach of diagnosis and prescription, unlike clinical medical settings, is likely to be ineffective. An MI approach, however, helps me to engage clients and evoke their resources around their change processes. In simple terms, it is far more powerful and effective to have the client voice and argue for change than for the practitioner to do so, which is often counterproductive.

Planning

The *planning* process encompasses both developing commitment to change and formulating a concrete plan of action. Those practitioners early in learning MI can often find themselves going round in circles from using too many simple reflections or relying on open questions. The direction component of MI helps practitioners move toward a change goal by challenging the client (with empathy) and using directional complex reflections with a view toward a goal. In the planning phase, the practitioner needs to remain engaged and dynamic because challenges and high risks of client setbacks are always around the corner. As table 6.2 illustrates, practitioners should be aware of both change (goal setting) strategies and relapse prevention and maintenance, using active follow-ups, as opposed to passive information gathering, where possible.

Principles of MI

In 2008, Rollnick and colleagues updated the original principles of MI from those they had suggested previously (Miller & Rollnick, 2002) that act as a useful adjunct to the spirit (or relational) and technical components of the approach. The original principles included expressing empathy, supporting self-efficacy, developing discrepancy, and rolling with client resistance. Recently these principles have been described using the acronym RULE, which stands for the following:

- R: Resist the righting reflex.
- U: Understand your client's motivation.
- L: Listen to your client.
- E: Empower your client.

These principles can complement the technical and relational aspects and act as a framework or guide for choosing techniques, strategies, and skills within MI at any phase of the interaction (Rosengren, 2009). More extensive descriptions of these principles are available elsewhere (see Rosengren, 2009; Rollnick et al., 2008), but in the context of physical activity and nutrition change, a brief set of examples are provided here.

Traps to Avoid in Consultations

Before we consider the application of MI and its components, it is worth exploring some of the traps to avoid in consultations in order to support the development of an MI approach. Miller and Rollnick (2002) suggested that early in a consultation, avoiding these common pitfalls is important for creating an empathetic, respectful, and fruitful relationship that is a partnership toward change. Examples of these traps are provided in the following section, and alternatives are considered in a later section as we explore an MI approach.

Question–Answer Trap

It is easy to fall into a pattern of short questions and even shorter responses that is not dissimilar to typical short health consultations where the primary aim is diagnosis and prescription. This survey approach, where a long list of questions are presented with a view to gaining a short and concise, often numeric, response, tends to elicit no more than limited content, and client responses are not likely to provide any context, feeling, or perceived consequences. Typical "yes" or "no" responses tend to emerge that can have the client feeling restricted and submissive, and the practitioner satisfied but unaware of the larger picture of deeper context and meaning. As Miller and Rollnick (2012) pointed out, this approach can have a negative consequence in that the client is learning to give only short answers with no elaboration, and it subtly implies a mismatch in power between the (now passive) client and (expert) practitioner. In physical activity and nutrition settings, readers can imagine (and have perhaps even experienced) the impact of this approach.

> **Practitioner (P):** So, what have you come to the session for?
>
> **Client (C):** I need to lose some weight and become healthier.
>
> **P:** Have you tried to lose weight before?
>
> **C:** Yes, but it didn't go so well, and I soon put the weight back on.
>
> **P:** How much weight did you lose?
>
> **C:** About 20 kilograms.
>
> **P:** And is that the kind of amount you are looking at losing this time?
>
> **C:** Possibly, although I'm not sure I am going to be successful.
>
> **P:** Are you married?
>
> **C:** Yes, but we are separated.

In this exchange, we can begin to see the impact of asking a number of closed questions in a row, and the practitioner is not taking any of the opportunities to elaborate and understand what has happened, the context, emotion, feeling, or effect of previous experiences. If we are going to engage and understand the client, then being aware of the roadblocks that occur with the Q-and-A trap is important. As something to bear in mind as we move forward, consider the final question asked by the practitioner. What do you feel would be a more effective and helpful alternative to the question "Are you married?" Surely, a more effective alternative could be "Who in your life may help support this change?"

Expert Trap

Similar to the Q and A problem, this trap can subtly emerge and create an impression of the passive client and the expert practitioner who conveys a sense of knowledge and answers to all the questions being posed. Although the practitioner is being nothing more than enthusiastic and knowledgeable, this trap can present a sense of control and reduces the likelihood that clients will explore and resolve ambivalence for themselves. This trap can also sound like fixing and solving problems, which is fine, and positively encouraged at suitable times, but in the early stages of the interaction, it is important to avoid prescribing answers when the underlying position of the client is one of ambivalence. When practitioners fall into this problem-solving trap, their desperation to help the client actually limits their understanding of the extent of the client's concerns and issues.

> P: So, what activities have you tried?
>
> C: I used to cycle, but I struggled to find the time to fit it in after work.
>
> P: Why don't you cycle to work instead, then?
>
> C: I tried that once, but I had to take lots of spare clothes with me.
>
> P: Why don't you take some spares next time you drive and leave them there?
>
> C: I could, yes, but I don't really want to leave my clothes lying around at work. Anyway, the shower facilities aren't very good, and it takes time.

As we can see here, contrary to the aim of the interaction, trying to fix with expertise, enthusiasm, and ideas is actually increasing client resistance, and the typical "yes, but . . ." response is

emerging—a key indicator that it is time to shift approaches. Motivational interviewing highlights the need to use the client as the resource and to value that it is actually clients who are experts on what their situations, motives, or barriers to change actually are. Falling into this expert trap negates this opportunity and paradoxically reduces clients' likelihood to engage in the change process. This need for close collaboration is an important facet of MI.

Premature Focus Trap

Client resistance can often occur if the practitioner and client wish to focus on different aspects or topics in the change process. This conflict (or incongruence) can emerge when practitioners want to focus on (what they perceive to be) particular problems but clients have other priorities and concerns or place less importance on the practitioner-identified problems. Generally, the discrepancy can develop quickly if the importance and direction for change between the two parties differ and are not accounted for or appreciated by the practitioner. In the client's mind, focusing on what the practitioner sees as the problem is detracting from broader concerns. If pushed and not considered, this discrepancy can lead to resistance and the two becoming engaged in a struggle about the proper topic for early discussion (Miller & Rollnick, 2002). Therefore, focusing on the client's concerns in the early stages will help to avoid this dissonance happening, and often exploring what the client sees as the problem will eventually lead back to what the practitioner considers the main issue.

Spending time listening to the client can help build trust and engagement and the essential ingredients of rapport. For example, prematurely focusing on diet change for a client who is overweight and failing to address other life issues can lead to a superficial focus on food alone and not the broader aspects of family life, previous experiences, and emotional issues.

> C: My diet is OK, really, but I could do with being more active.
>
> P: But if we can reduce more harmful foods in your diet, it will really help.

C: Well, I've tried a whole load of different diets in the past, and it hasn't worked.

P: Well, maybe you've tried the wrong types or made too many changes all at once.

C: I know I wasn't all that active when I had tried, and my family would benefit as well from that.

P: Maybe your family would benefit from an improved diet plan as well?

C: The kids won't change their food for anything, I've tried that before. My partner is really picky about food as well, which doesn't help, although he is trying to cut down other things like smoking.

P: I could give you some diet plans that would suit the whole family, though.

C: I just don't see how that would work.

As we can see here, there are signs of desire and need for change of other life factors (including physical activity and smoking) that the practitioner misses, and maintaining the premature focus on diet alone is slowly increasing the client's resistance and, ultimately, preventing engagement and rapport. Adapting and shifting with clients' concerns can take confidence and a willingness to give up some control in the session, but this is a key aspect of a person-centered approach.

Labeling Trap

In many care pathways that promote physical activity and diet change, it is common for practitioners to have received diagnostic information from the referrer. Even in community-based settings, it is usual for baseline assessments to be taken in areas such as body fat, weight, health-related behaviors (e.g., smoking, alcohol consumption, physical activity), fitness levels, and self-report measures (e.g., diet diaries). Although such information can provide useful guides for the session in regard to the focus of change, it is also likely to increase the risk of *labeling* the client as obese or sedentary, and some clinicians seem to believe it is important for the client to accept such labels as part of the change process. In settings such as alcohol cessation, Miller and Rollnick (2002) suggested that there is little evidence of the benefit of a client accepting the label of being an alcoholic, for example, and those high in self-esteem are more likely to resist a label attached to them by a practitioner.

The labeling trap can represent an underlying power struggle between stakeholders, including clients, their family members, and health professionals, and this conflict can increase the dissonance between the clients and their change desires. Often, an attempt to identify the problem and attach the label is less likely to increase client change, and is something to avoid when using motivational interviewing. When we are not mindful of the labeling trap, the result can again be client resistance.

P: So, based on the BMI score, you are categorized as "obese."

C: Well, I'm surprised because I do eat well, and I have a really active work life.

P: But the results don't suggest that, and the measures are pretty accurate. So, you need to think about making some changes.

C: But I've tried changing my diet before, and it didn't work.

P: But for those in the obese category, the risks from a range of diseases are increased significantly, and you really need to do something about it.

C: I'm just surprised that I am in that obese range, and it feels really uncomfortable to be given that stigma.

Here, we see not just the use of labeling from the practitioner but also a defense and arguments for the need for change that amplify dissonance and client resistance. As mentioned previously, there is little evidence to suggest that using terms such as *addict* or *obese,* and clients accepting those labels, actually increases their likelihood to make sustained changes.

Blaming Trap

Finally, we need to consider a cause for client defensiveness in many settings that is closely aligned to the labeling and premature focus traps. In many health settings, clients are often likely to enter interactions feeling defensive because their ill health is likely to be the result of life choices and subsequent behaviors, and obesity, cardiac diseases, and other hypokinetic illnesses are no exception. It is important to disarm this feeling of blame so that the focus is toward change rather than the attribution of who is at fault. If this sense of blame is not managed and circumvented, a great deal of time and energy can be wasted by both parties on *defense* rather than *change* strategies. In motivational interviewing, the fault and blame issue is dealt with as irrelevant and not helpful in the movement toward change, and when this topic emerges in the client–practitioner interaction, the use of reflecting and reframing can be applied effectively to continue moving forward. If this blaming is not addressed, then the session can become stagnated and progression stunted.

> P: So, what have you done that has caused your increase in body weight?

> C: Well, I guess I haven't always eaten so well, and I don't really take too much exercise.

> P: So, all the things you have or haven't done have caused this.

> C: Well, I guess so, but it has been a gradual decline.

> P: But, nonetheless, something that you haven't managed and dealt with sooner.

This scenario might seem like an extreme response, but the philosophical approach and subtext behind each practitioner statement is seen in many health interactions in one form or another. If we are going to support a healthy and effective forward direction toward change, then this trap needs mindful attention.

Change Talk

Although the *psycholinguistics of change* might seem a complex term, it points to the issue that what we say often reflects what we are likely to do (or not do, as the case might be!). Amrhein and colleagues (2003) reported the relationship between client language and subsequent behaviors, in the context of health behavior change, which has led to effective changes in the way we manage language in MI settings. When we hear clients respond to our enthusiastic statements about change, we often hear "Yes, but . . ." statements where clients are subtly beginning to make the arguments against change. The ideal language should be that which indicates they are talking themselves into changing (Rollnick et al., 2008). With MI, our task is to elicit and strengthen change talk, which requires us to first be able to recognize when it occurs. As Rollnick and colleagues (2008) suggest, "Your task is to elicit 'change' from your patients rather than resistance" (p. 35). In everyday conversations, we can pick up the likelihood of someone changing from what they say. It is clear that "I wish I could" is far less likely to result in a subsequent behavior change than "I am going to . . ." or "I really need to . . ." While this language does not provide a perfect causal relationship, it is certainly extremely useful; it challenges practitioners to correlate client responses to their own and, in turn, adds clarity to the direction of the clinical session. Table 6.3 provides lists of the six categories of change talk together with examples from diet, or nutrition, and physical activity change settings. While these can be seen as hierarchical in regard to their predictability of behavior change, evidence suggests that the first set of four—desire, ability, reasons, and need—have a similar correlation to preparing to change, whereas the existence of language in the final two categories—commitment and taking steps—are far more likely to result in medium- and long-term change, and are therefore known as predictive change talk (Amrhein et al., 2003). This research has been seminal for MI researchers, trainers, and practitioners, and it has enhanced our applied practice by challenging us to pay close attention to

Table 6.3 The Six Categories of Client Change Talk

Category	Examples
Preparatory change talk	
Desire	Statements from clients regarding their preference for behavior change: "I would *like* to be more active." "I *want* to be able to control what I eat."
Ability	Statements about perceived capability to make these behavior changes: "I know I *could* be more active." "I *can* reduce my sugar intake."
Reasons	Client arguments for behavior change: "My health would probably improve if I did . . ." "My doctor and my family would be happy if I changed . . ."
Need	Statements about the general importance of change: "I *need* to watch less television and get more active." "I *must* do something about eating in between meals."
Predictive change talk	
Commitment	Statements about the likelihood of action: "I *will* walk to work instead of taking the car." "I am *going to* use a food diary for the next week."
Taking steps	Statements about having done something in the direction of change: "I walked to the shops yesterday rather than taking the car." "I started a food diary last week and have begun to cut down on . . ."

the level of motivation immersed within subtle language.

The challenge in MI is both to recognize change talk and to adapt accordingly using the microskills outlined previously. It is clear from the examples in table 6.3 how subtle language changes can shift the likelihood of change from our clients. When we hear the preparatory statements such as "I want...", "I can...", or "I need..." it is clear that more work is required to resolve ambivalence and increase our client's motivation for change. Conversely, predictive language such as "I am going to...", "I will...", or "I have started to..." indicates a time for the session to move forward, for the practitioner to strengthen this motivation and readiness and then move on. This is not to say it will be smooth sailing, and we can go into neutral expecting changes to occur naturally, but rather that it is time to move to a planning phase, which will include goal setting, relapse prevention, and maintenance strategies.

The Case of Carole

In this case study I demonstrate the application of MI and the phases within which the technical and relational aspects are applied, along with the emergence of and reaction to *change talk*. The session is a composite of real client interactions focusing on physical activity and nutrition change to demonstrate the approach and visual tools that I use throughout clinical sessions. I make reflections, as the session unfolds, to offer a practitioner perspective and how responses might be formulated. For brevity sake, this example does not include all aspects of the phases of MI, and some considerations, such as "typical day," can be found elsewhere (Miller & Rollnick, 2012). Nevertheless, the case provides an outline of the use of key skills and tools.

The client, Carole (C), is a 55-year-old woman who has struggled to maintain a healthy weight over the last 16 years, since being diagnosed with diabetes, and she was referred to me (J) by her family medicine physician (general practitioner in

the UK). There is a rea...
may have conti...
aim of the oper...
understanding...
issues and to u...
and curiosity. T...
shared understan...
of fault or a...
(Rosengren, 2009...

Opening (Expl...

J: Thanks f...
know more...
ferred to the...
know that w...
dential, and...
mation with...
sionals, if the...
your permissi...

C: That's fine...
my weight, ar...
my physician f...

J: A concern fo...

C: Hmm...

J: Tell me more a...

C: Well, I'm n...
moment, and it's...
for a while. A few years in fact, and, as
you know, I have been suffering with diabetes for years.

J: So this is an ongoing issue you've
been managing for some time, and it got
to a point of concern now for one of you.

C: I know my weight doesn't help, but
I've tried to diet so many times, and am
sick of failing.

I am using reflective listening skills here to explore the issue and to demonstrate empathy
without judgment. I have also reflected the need
for change, beginning to challenge Carole to consider a direction forward rather than maintaining

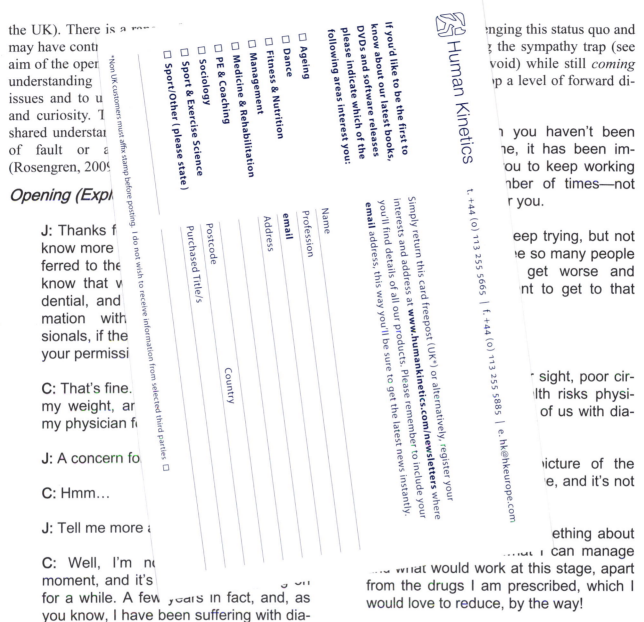

...nging this status quo and
...the sympathy trap (see
...void) while still *coming*
...p a level of forward di-

...n you haven't been
...e, it has been im-
...ou to keep working
...nber of times—not
...r you.

...eep trying, but not
...e so many people
...get worse and
...nt to get to that

...r sight, poor cir-
...lth risks physi-
...of us with dia-

...icture of the
...e, and it's not

...ething about
...at I can manage
...what would work at this stage, apart
from the drugs I am prescribed, which I
would love to reduce, by the way!

J: OK. Go on.

C: I'm on a load of drugs that are
probably helping, but I can probably do
things that will mean I need less of them.

J: So, if you were back in control of your
health, and not depending on drugs so
much, that would feel great compared to
where you are now.

C: Yep, and I have managed it before,
but this time I need to stick with the

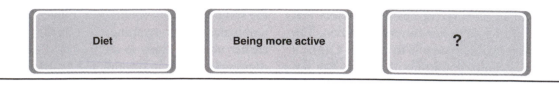

Figure 6.4   Agenda setting (identifying target behaviors).

changes I make; otherwise, it isn't looking good.

J: So you've managed your own health previously and that felt better than now. Tell me more about that.

In this last exchange, one can begin to see the impact of an *affirmation,* whereby I am using a complex reflection to highlight Carole's strengths, attitudes, and behaviors that emphasize her need for change rather than telling her how important it is to change (and thus avoiding the expert trap). One can also see how I use open questions to gain elaboration from Carole. In the next phase, I am keen to work with the *change talk* (her use of "I need") and collaboratively begin to set the agenda for the session with Carole.

Agenda Setting

J: In order that we make the best use of our time together today, is it OK if we start to identify what it is you feel is important and what will help you make and maintain health changes?

C: Yes, I'd be happy to do that, and I know it's something I need to think about.

J: So, tell me more about what you have tried in the past and what we might focus on today.

C: Well, I know it has to be diet, and I guess it should also be exercise, or at least that's what my physician has told me.

J: So, one thing you are thinking about is diet, and one thing your physician is

talking about is being more active. Can we add those two aspects to the boxes [. . .] and focus on at least one of them today?

We are now beginning to formulate the agenda (see figure 6.4), but Carol is still showing ambivalence with regard to her motives and areas of importance (diet) compared to those of her physician (exercise or being more active). This discrepancy is normal, but ambivalence can turn to resistance if I prematurely focus on what I feel is important as opposed to what Carole thinks. In opening interactions it is often worth exploring the importance of each potential change domain to clarify what the target behaviors might be. I am trying to understand Carole's position with interest and curiosity, avoiding prejudging the focus of the session, emphasizing her autonomy, and encouraging a sense of collaboration (the spirit of MI). I am asking permission and using a combination of OARS to explore the situation and the potential for change. This section also allows me to explore Carole's level of readiness and her likelihood to change, and I am ready to adapt my approach accordingly.

J: So tell me, using a scale of 0 being not important and 10 being essential, what value would you attach to these two behaviors in relation to you?

C: Well, I guess it has to be diet because that's the thing I've done before, and I know I can do again. I'm not so sure on the exercise, but maybe we look at that later. I would probably say 9 for diet and 4 for exercise, then.

J: So diet is something that is important for you to do something about, and for now exercise is less so, but perhaps something to consider later.

C: Yes, I would say that's it, and I know I need to probably do both, but let's look at diet first.

J: You can see the value of doing both things together, but for now it's diet that we should focus on.

C: It's what I need to do.

Preparatory change talk has emerged throughout these early exchanges (desire, ability, reasons, and need), so I continue with empathic challenges, using reflective listening, aimed at strengthening this change talk toward commitment. A shift to commitment is unlikely in the early exchanges with an ambivalent or resistant client, but when I do hear evidence of this shift, I need to be ready to act quickly. The next phase includes the use of E-P-E (elicit-provide-elicit) to understand what Carole has tried before, to allow me to provide (with permission) ideas to complement her input, and to explore what she thinks of the ideas I have proposed.

Decisional Balance (Pros and Cons of Change and No Change)

J: So tell me what aspect of diet we might focus on as we move forward.

C: It's got to be snacking [between meals], and I suppose changing some aspects of my life to walk more, but let's talk about cutting down on snacks first.

J: Eating between meals.

C: Yes, it's something I know I shouldn't do, but I don't think I can help myself. I just do it without even thinking about it most of the time.

J: You don't control when it happens.

C: Well, it's down to me. I know that, but I need to have more willpower for sure.

J: Let's look at what the benefits and drawbacks might be of you making changes or not, then. Quite often people in a similar position to you will try to make changes and will feel there are benefits and things they miss. I'd like to explore all aspects of this change, if that's OK.

C: That sounds OK.

J: Can we keep track of these pros and cons? And I will fill out this grid with you [see figure 6.5]. Tell me about the benefits of you cutting down or stopping completely the snacking between meals.

C: Well, it's going to cut down my weight, without doubt. I don't need to eat more food, but it just kind of happens. I think my family would also benefit because I probably wouldn't have as many snacks in the cupboard.

J: So, the benefits include your weight, and the reduced health risk from that, and also you being a role model for your kids and family; they are important in this.

C: I've always worried about what impact my weight and eating has had on the kids, but I've always tried to put my head in the sand on that one.

J: It's easier not to worry about it—if you did, you'd feel guilty.

C: I guess so. I know I have to be a better role model.

J: Being a good parent is really important to you.

C: Of course, but I'm not sure I have been so far, and as they get older, it would be good if they had a better diet.

J: And it is more than just diet that you could influence.

Target behavior: Reducing snacks between meals	Pros	Cons
Change	Weight loss. Positive effect on my family. Being a good role model. Feeling healthier. Looking better (and feeling more confident). Save money.	Snacking between proper meals is easy; stopping isn't. I'm not sure how to stick to the change.
No change	I won't have to change my habits (it will take no effort). The kids will be happy at not having to change.	I will just drift along and not be in control. The increase of ill-health. Being judged by people because of weight. Not comfortable and no choice of clothes.

Figure 6.5   Decisional balance for reducing snacks.

C: I suppose that, together with being more active, yes. For now, though, feeling and looking better would be a real change.

J: So, feeling healthier and having more confidence from the way you look would be benefits.

C: Absolutely, yes.

J: Any other pros of change?

C: I think that's about it, all I can think of at this point.

J: Tell me about the cons or downsides of cutting down snacks between meals.

C: Well, I don't think there are any, really, although it is something I am happy doing; it's easy.

J: Happy to have the snacks and unhappy with the impact it has.

C: Hmm, that's about it, and I need to do something about that. There's no real benefit to my weight.

J: While it's an easy habit to keep, it's more difficult to break, but something you need to change.

C: It will also save me money on snacks that we don't need.

J: Can I add that to the benefits of change box?

C: Yes.

J: What about staying as you are [still snacking], what are the benefits or pros?

C: Well, I won't have to make any changes, which won't require effort.

J: That would be the easy route for you.

C: And I suppose the kids might be happy, but I wouldn't be.

J: You can see how easy it might be and not having to change for those around you, and that contradicts your reasons and motives for change.

C: Yes, it's something that has to happen.

J: And what about the downside, or cons, of staying as you are? Tell me about that.

C: I'm not going anywhere, am I? I'm not in control, and I know the health risks are only going to get worse. People already look at me in a negative way, and I don't feel comfortable with that, as much as I try to ignore it. It's simple things like not having the choice when I go clothes shopping or even trying to get into my clothes as I used to be able to.

Here I am coming alongside Carole and challenging again with empathic reflective listening that challenges without judging or blaming. There is a reframe opportunity where I can affirm her values and intentions to be a good role model. Using decisional balance enables a clear picture to emerge between the two of us as to the many possibilities of changing or not changing. This tool (figure 6.5) enables ambivalence to be explored and a direction forward to emerge, based again on Carole's change talk. Figure 6.5 illustrates how this conversation expands to explore the positives (pros) and the downside (cons) of changing and not changing. If, as one can see in the grid, there is a clear weighting of pros of change and cons of not changing, that then signals a clear opportunity to move toward action planning. Before this next phase, it may be worth applying another tool (readiness to change ruler) to make explicit and affirm Carole's position. There remains a consistent attempt to challenge her with empathy and to use reflective listening statements, more than questions, to understate and overstate to explore her ambivalence and amplify any discrepancies. Issues can emerge at different points even as other areas are being examined, as can be seen when *saving money* emerges while exploring the cons of change. It is important to be willing to attend to these issues in a flexible manner.

Readiness (to Change) Ruler

J: So it looks like there are more benefits to changing than there are downsides.

C: It does look like that, doesn't it? I think that's pretty accurate, although I know it's not going to be easy.

J: Not easy, yet important, compared to the option of staying as you are. [I pause briefly.] Tell me how ready you are to begin to make this change and develop an action plan together [figure 6.6].

C: What do you mean?

J: Well, using the same 0 to 10 scale we used before, with 0 not being ready and 10 being extremely ready, where would you put yourself?

C: Probably about a 7.

J: More ready than the option of staying as you are.

C: Yes, I'm going to make a start. I'm not sure how well I will do at this point, but I know the benefits, and I know the risk of not making changes.

J: Why 7 and not, say, 4 or 5?

C: Well, because I need to do something now, and there are some clear reasons to make this change.

J: So you are at a crossroads, and change is important for you now.

C: It has to be.

Rulers and scaling seen here in figure 6.6 are being used together with complex reflections to elicit change talk, which is achieved by understating the value of change and challenging the client to defend the value of 7. By asking her "why 7 and not 4 or 5?" Carole is now justifying the im-

ideas you might have that we haven't talked about yet.

C: I like the idea of specific shopping so that I only get what I go in for, and it is planned.

J: That will really help you stay in control and manage the family's diet more than you do now.

C: Yes, and it would be difficult to convince the kids, but they will get used to it if I can be consistent.

J: Being consistent and communicating clearly the reasons with them might be useful ways of managing that situation as you see it.

C: And although I haven't really thought too much about it, I suppose being more active can't do any harm.

Even at this late stage, there may often be contemplation and the emergence of additional behavior change factors such as physical activity. This emergence of different motives (or perceived barriers) demands flexibility and innovation from me to adapt and accommodate these shifts. This can be recorded in a variety of forms, as illustrated in figure 6.7.

Arrive at a Plan

As Miller and Rollnick (2012) reiterated, planning is a process of negotiation and collaboration, and the process of this engagement can continue to build a strong therapeutic relationship that challenges the client with empathy. The relational spirit and technical aspects of MI help me to formulate an approach to increase the likelihood of engagement with Carole, still appreciating the need to challenge her while *coming alongside* her to support the often inevitable ambivalence and dip in motivation toward change as the session progresses.

J: What do you think you might try first?

C: I could start tonight when I shop, but that feels a bit sudden.

J: There's nothing actually stopping you starting today, it's just the thought of doing something different.

C: I suppose so, and it would be nice to actually know I've started at last.

J: Started?

C: Yes, you know, to get back on top of things and be in control of what happens to me and my family's health.

J: So, even though it seems scary to start taking that first step, today would be quite invigorating.

C: It would, yes. I'll try it when I shop and take a list with me.

J: And other aspects of the plan we discussed?

C: Well, I'm not going to go out and join a gym or anything, but if the weather is nice tomorrow, I will walk the kids to school.

J: A start to building activity into your daily routine. How would the kids benefit from that?

C: It's obvious, isn't it? If they get used to walking to school with me they might do it by themselves eventually.

J: You would be that good role model, and that is so important to you as a mother.

In this exchange I am clarifying the intent and motivation in Carole to start implementing the change plan and to strengthen change talk. There is still a high level of coming alongside and employing empathy while challenging with more reflections than questions, which has helped me maintain a high level of engagement and elicitation of change ideas from Carole rather than falling into the expert role. It is clear that there is still ambivalence toward change. Allowing this ambivalence to emerge, and then managing it, is part of a skillful application of MI. At the end, I have offered an affirmation in the form of the reflection "You would be a good role model, and that is so important to you as a mother" to underpin and reiterate Carole's value as a mother.

Reaffirm Commitment

Having worked together to negotiate one or two initial change strategies, it can be disconcerting for a practitioner to hear continued ambivalence or reluctance. This ambivalence is fairly typical because the client now has to make that step from consideration into commitment, and even though I have engaged, focused, and evoked, trying to implement a change plan before the client is ready can be problematic. By reaffirming commitment, I am doing two things: first, checking that the plan is owned by Carole and is clear, and second, that she is actually ready, willing, and confident to start. At this point, if she started to retract or move back to ambivalence (often via sustain language), I would switch back to evoking (or even re-engaging) and adapt accordingly rather than pushing prematurely for change (Miller & Rollnick, 2012).

> J: While there are some aspects that worry you about the two first changes, you seem clear as to the benefits. I wonder if you would think about those and maybe tell me the first things you would notice if you took that first step.
>
> C: If I changed my food shopping habits, it would cut down on the rubbish that the kids could choose from. They wouldn't be too happy at first . . .
>
> J: . . . but eventually it would be normal for them, different to the choices they have now.
>
> C: Definitely different, and probably better.
>
> J: So what will you do?

> C: I'm going to go home and think about the information I have already on good food. Not everything will change, but I can change small things tonight.
>
> J: You seem pretty positive about the benefits of doing that.
>
> C: I am.
>
> J: And being more active?
>
> C: Walking certainly, it's not far to school, and it would be good for the kids.
>
> J: Is that something you will do, even if the weather isn't too good?
>
> C: I'm more likely to if it's sunny, to be honest, but I'll definitely think about it either way.

Whereas the main change strategy included a behavioral change, in terms of shopping differently, over the duration of the session, Carole has moved (verbally) from not contemplating physical activity change to contemplating and even preparing for a change in diet. It is clear that where ambivalence or reluctance existed, pushing and convincing for change is likely to increase ambivalence and sustain talk (see previous sections on sustain to change talk). Skillful appreciation of the continuous movement of a client such as Carole during a session is an important aspect of MI, and continuous engagement, empathy, autonomy support (the spirit), and technical applications (OARS) can help to manage these fluctuations and work in collaboration to move toward change. Figure 6.8 provides a summary form that I would use with a client when moving through the action stages to help clarify what is involved in the change process, identify social support, and identify aspects for managing relapse and maintaining change.

ACTION PLANNING

The change I want to make is:

_____

The most important reasons why I want to make this change are:

_____

I plan to do these things to accomplish my goals:

Specific action _____

When? _____

Other people could help me with change in these ways:

Person _____

Possible ways to help _____

These are some of the obstacles to change, and how I could handle them:

Possible obstacles to change _____

What I will do _____

If I lapse, I will do the following:

_____

I will know that my plan is working when I see these results:

_____

How confident am I that I can make this change?

0	1	2	3	4	5	6	7	8	9	10

Not at all confident   Extremely confident

Figure 6.8   Action planning sheet and confidence ruler.

Summary

In this chapter, I describe my use of MI when working with clients who are considering the adoption of a behavior change such as modifying diet and nutrition or increasing levels of physical activity. I cite a case example where ambivalence is apparent, and this is a common phenomenon in most people considering a challenging and significant lifestyle change. My approach centers on the spirit of MI to increase client–practitioner engagement and empathy, increasing my clients' autonomy and evoking from them the need and potential for change, as opposed to imposing my beliefs using a directive and educational approach. This development of a shared resource is respectful, and it is more likely than a traditional expert-driven approach to increase their independence and movement toward change. The microskills (OARS) help me to operationalize the spirit and, subsequently, increase client engagement and evoke the client's values, attitudes, perceived benefits, resources, and barriers toward change. The applications of these technical skills are clearly recognizable in a high-quality MI interaction. The use of self-reflection, using coding instruments such as the Motivational Interviewing Treatment Integrity (MITI; Moyers, Martin, Manuel, Miller, & Ernst, 2007), is helpful in regard to skills development and supervision of those developing MI skills in clinical settings.

An important indicator of the effectiveness of the relationship, and the readiness and likelihood of the client to contemplate and engage in change, is the emergence of change talk. These psycholinguistic pointers are subtle, and using recognizing, eliciting, and strengthening skills takes practice. Along with sustain talk, these pointers can be helpful for me when deciding whether to move forward to action planning or remain in a position of exploration and develop a shared understanding of the motives and barriers toward change. The four processes of MI (Miller & Rollnick, 2012) are a useful meta-framework for me as a practitioner, and they help develop an understanding of the need to engage throughout, while embedding direction and planning toward change, to avoid encountering session fatigue and going round in circles. The combination of the spirit, microskills (OARS), four processes, and elicitation and strengthening of change talk are the foundations of MI. I continue to find this combined approach effective in developing the client–practitioner relationship and supporting clients in making challenging lifestyle behavior changes. Practitioners should feel able and willing to challenge clients in therapeutic sessions, and using MI can help them do this with empathy and a high level of engagement.

References

Amrhein, P.C., Miller, W.R., Yahne, C.E., Palmer, M., & Fulcher, L. (2003). Client commitment language during motivational interviewing predicts drug use outcomes. *Journal of Consulting and Clinical Psychology, 71,* 862–878.

Bellg, A.J., Borrelli, B., Resnick, B., Hecht, J., Minicucci, D.S., & Ory, M. (2004). Enhancing treatment fidelity in health behavior change studies: Best practices and recommendations from the NIH behavior change consortium. *Health Psychology, 23,* 443–451.

Breckon, J.D., Johnston, L.H., & Hutchison, A. (2008). Physical activity counseling content and competency: A systematic review. *Journal of Physical Activity and Health, 5,* 398–417.

Brodie, D.A., Inoue, A., & Shaw, D.G. (2008). Motivational interviewing to change quality of life for people with chronic heart failure: A randomised controlled trial. *International Journal of Nursing Studies, 45,* 489–500.

Gordon, T. (1970). *Parent effectiveness training.* New York, NY: Wyden.

Johnston, L.H., Breckon, J.D., & Hutchison, A. (2009). Influencing health behaviour: Applying theory to practice. In L. Dugdill, D. Crone, & R. Murphy (Eds.), *Physical activity and health promotion: Evidence-based approaches to practice* (pp. 21–38). London, England: Blackwell.

Madson, M.B., Loignon, A.C., & Lane, C. (2009). Training in motivational interviewing: A systematic review. *Journal of Substance Abuse Treatment, 36,* 101–109.

Maslow, A.H. (1970). *Motivation and personality.* New York, NY: Harper & Row.

Miller, W.R., & Rollnick, S. (1991). *Motivational interviewing: Preparing people for change.* London, England: Guilford Press.

Miller, W.R., & Rollnick, S. (2002). *Motivational interviewing: Preparing people for change* (2nd ed.). London, England: Guilford Press.

Miller, W.R., & Rollnick, S. (2009). Ten things that motivational interviewing is not. *Behavioural and Cognitive Psychotherapy, 37,* 129–140.

Miller, W.R., & Rollnick, S. (2012). *Motivational interviewing: Helping people change* (3rd ed.). London, England: Guilford Press.

Miller, W.R., & Rose, G.S. (2009). Toward a theory of motivational interviewing. *American Psychologist, 64,* 527–537.

Moyers, T.B., Martin, T., Manuel, J.K., Miller, W.R., & Ernst, D. (2007). *Revised Global Scales: Motivational Interviewing Treatment Integrity 3.0* (MITI 3.0). Albuquerque: Center on Alcoholism, Substance Abuse, and Addictions, University of New Mexico.

Naar-King, S., & Suarez, M. (2011). *Motivational interviewing with adolescents and young adults.* London, England: Guilford Press.

Rogers, C.R. (1959). A theory of therapy, personality, and interpersonal relationships as developed in the client-centered framework. In S. Koch (Ed.), *Psychology: The study of a science (Vol. 3). Formulations of the person and the social contexts* (pp. 184–256). New York, NY: McGraw-Hill.

Rogers, C.R. (1980). *A way of being.* New York, NY: Houghton Mifflin.

Rollnick, S., Miller, W.R., & Butler, C. (2008). *Motivational interviewing in health care: Helping patients change behavior.* London, England: Guilford Press.

Rosengren, D. (2009). *Building motivational interviewing skills: A practitioner workbook.* London, England: Guilford Press.

Westra, H. (2012). *Motivational interviewing in the treatment of anxiety.* London, England: Guilford Press.

CHAPTER 7

Exercise and Smoking Cessation
Tackling Multiple Health Behavior Changes

Adrian H. Taylor and Tom P. Thompson

The harmful effects on health of cigarette smoking are well documented (World Health Organization, 2011), and public health strategies have been targeted at preventing the uptake of smoking and helping individuals with nicotine addictions to quit (American Psychiatric Association, 2000). Understanding why people start to smoke, mostly in the adolescent years, is as important as getting to grips with identifying effective support to help people quit. Although tobacco control strategies (e.g., taxing tobacco products, banning smoking in public places, conducting mass media educational campaigns) are widely implemented, individually oriented approaches are still required, and can be effective. The combination of approaches has resulted in a reduction in smoking prevalence from around 50% of adults prior to the first U.S. Surgeon General's report in the 1960s to 15% to 25% in most postindustrial societies. In contrast, tobacco companies have turned to developing countries to promote their products with alarming success. So what is the relevance of this topic in a book on exercise psychology?

From a review of 50 cross-sectional studies, Kaczynski, Manske, Mannell, and Grewal (2008) reported that physically active people were less likely to smoke (and smokers were less likely to be active). Prospectively, some studies (e.g., Rodriguez, Duton, Tscherne, & Sass, 2008) have shown that being substantially involved in sport and exercise somehow protects adolescents from becoming smokers. Similar findings have been reported for other unhealthy behaviors. We are sure that readers of this book will be able to come up with a range of possible explanations, based on their own and vicarious experiences. The implications are that promoting sport and exercise not only provides health benefits but may also reduce risky health-related behaviors.

In terms of helping smokers quit, there is scope for new therapies. Without help, only 3% to 5% of smokers successfully quit after 12 months, whereas using a combination of nicotine replacement therapy (NRT), bupropion or varenicline, and behavioral counseling at least doubles success rates (Cahill, Stead, & Lancaster, 2011; Hughes, Stead, & Lancaster, 2007; Stead, Perera, Bullen, Mant, & Lancaster, 2008). There is substantial research on why people relapse, including elevated cravings, low mood, and weight gain. Physical activity (PA) can favorably influence all these relapse factors, and it is recommended as an aid to smoking cessation within specialist smoking clinics (Everson-Hock, Taylor, & Ussher, 2010; Everson-Hock, Taylor, Ussher, & Faulkner, 2010), in self-help guides (Marcus, Hampl, & Fisher, 2004), and in reviews and guidelines (Ussher, Taylor, & Faulkner, 2012; U.S. Department of Health & Human Services, 2008). We review the evidence for beneficial effects in more detail in a section to follow, but the implications are that by promoting physical activity, it may be possible to help smokers quit. This chapter provides an overview of research on the following:

- Chronic effects of PA on smoking cessation
- Acute effects of PA on smoking-related measures
- Possible mechanisms involved in the effects of PA on smoking-related variables that may be important to consider when developing interventions
- The design of effective interventions that engage smokers, drawing on a case study we have encountered in our extensive work on counseling for multiple behavior change

Chronic Effects of PA on Smoking Cessation

A relatively stable change in one behavior (e.g., increased PA) is often accompanied by some changes in other behaviors (e.g., decreased smoking), but in many cases, this sort of rebalancing does not happen. There are many variables involved in behavior change. In this section, we examine the differences between people who take up PA and want to stop smoking and those who don't want to stop smoking but have also increased their PA.

For Those Who Don't Wish to Quit

Do interventions to increase physical activity with smokers who do not necessarily want to reduce or quit lead to a reduction in smoking or to more people quitting? We can probably all think of someone involved in sport and exercise who smokes. Even watching someone cycling or walking while smoking suggests there is no link between the two behaviors. These observations undermine the belief that getting involved in sport and exercise will lead to a change in smoking behavior. There are, however, some reasons why this change might happen, such as the following:

1. Exercise may enhance self-regulation or self-control over automated or impulsive behaviors such as reaching for a cigarette (Oh & Taylor, 2013), even if there is no strong desire for one. Smoking is often a highly contextually conditioned behavior: Animal and human research suggests that addictive behaviors such as substance use occur in places associated with the reward or pleasure (West, 2005). Taking a walk around the block in-

stead of a cigarette break outside the office with colleagues can help to disentangle the powerful and controlling stimulus–response reinforcement chain over time.

2. Exercise may influence emotions and moods (e.g., boredom) or core affect (e.g., valence/pleasure, activation; Ekkekakis, Parfitt, & Petruzzello, 2011), which in turn reduces the need to self-regulate these states with smoking. By learning to associate positive mood and affect with exercise, the need to seek pleasure from smoking may be reduced over time.

3. Engaging in exercise may lead to an enhanced sense of mastery, achievement, and self-perceptions (Taylor & Fox, 2005), which when low have been linked to a greater tendency to smoke (Rodriguez et al., 2008).

4. Engaging in exercise may lead to an identity shift (Taylor et al., 2014). For example, a smoker gains a sense of self by hanging around with other smokers. The smoking ban in UK pubs may well have strengthened that identity by bringing smokers together, huddled under shelters outside. By joining a sports team or exercise group, particularly with social engagement, a smoker may start to develop a new exercise identity, which, over time, replaces the smoker identity.

So, are increases in PA implicitly associated with smoking cessation or reduced smoking? A recent search of review articles, in which the focus was on promoting PA in primary health care, identified four systematic reviews that collectively included 54 original rigorous studies with a primary focus on promoting PA. Only four of these studies noted an increase in PA *and* reported smoking data after the intervention. All reported no effect of the PA intervention on smoking status. A secondary analysis of data from a recent study on the effects of a physical activity counseling intervention on clinical depression, among 361 patients (30% of whom were smokers) receiving treatment, also supported this result. Time to first cigarette after waking (a good proxy for smoking dependence) and number of cigarettes smoked did not reduce despite some increases in PA (van den Bosch, 2011).

In a pilot randomized controlled trial (RCT), not powered to detect intervention effectiveness, Taylor and colleagues (2014) reported that a behavioral support intervention called Exercise Assisted Reduction then Stop (EARS) appeared to have some value compared with brief advice (about support available for quitting) for smokers, should they wish to quit. In the intervention and control arms, respectively, 22% versus 6% made a quitting attempt; 14% versus 4% had expired air CO confirmed abstinence four to eight weeks post quit; at 16 weeks, 10% versus 4% had achieved point prevalence abstinence (i.e., a specified abstinence for a relatively brief period, such as one to seven days), and 39% versus 20% achieved at least a 50% reduction in the number of cigarettes smoked daily. In this study, the possible ways in which physical activity may support smoking reduction were explicitly discussed in a client-centered approach. The case study later in this chapter highlights some of the ways this intervention worked for one participant.

What About Smokers Who Do Want to Quit?

Do interventions to increase PA with smokers who want to quit lead to a reduction in smoking or to more people quitting? This question is concerned with the effectiveness of multiple health behavior changes, rather than with simply increasing PA. The timing may be simultaneous, or physical activity may be introduced before or after the start of an abrupt quitting attempt (in which a quit day is set and plans are made to gain pharmacological or behavioral support to be successful). Some reasons our clients have highlighted for why PA may be a useful adjunct behavior to support quitting attempts are as follows:

1. PA can acutely help smokers cope with elevated cigarette cravings and nicotine withdrawal symptoms. There is strong support for this observation, at least among temporarily abstinent smokers who are experiencing increases in cravings and withdrawal symptoms (Haasova et al., 2013a; Taylor, Ussher, & Faulkner, 2007). The case study later in this chapter identifies an example of how a smoker came to explicitly use PA.

2. PA can help distract thoughts away from cigarettes. Attempts to suppress thoughts about wanting a cigarette may only lead to stronger urges, whereas engaging in some form of PA that involves mental effort can remove a desire for a cigarette.

3. On average, smokers gain 4 to 5 kilograms in weight in the first year after quitting, with 34% gaining 5 to 10 kilograms and 13% gaining more than 10 kilograms (Aubin, Farley, Lycett, Lahmek, & Aveyard, 2012). This gain is due to both slowed metabolism and increases in emotional eating. Fear of weight gain often prevents smokers from attempting to quit and contributes to relapse among quitters (Brouwer & Pomerleau, 2000). Increasing PA may be one approach for preventing weight gain through increased energy expenditure and reduced emotional eating or snacking (Farley, Hajek, Lycett, & Aveyard, 2012; Oh & Taylor, 2012; 2013).

Smoking cessation counseling support can predominantly focus on avoiding smoking. For example, practitioners may discuss with clients what it has felt like to go without a cigarette and to seek to build the confidence to not smoke. In contrast, a focus on increasing physical activity and building confidence may change the focus of self-regulation and self-control. Goals to achieve an increase in PA are different from goals to reduce or quit smoking. In a group counseling session involving smokers who had recently quit, we observed a substantially different focus in the weekly sessions about their experiences in the past week depending on who opened the discussion. When we asked someone to begin whom we knew would talk about using exercise successfully to cope with cravings and withdrawal symptoms, successive quitters talked about their own PA experiences. If we did not mention exercise, then the conversation focused on how difficult it had been to not smoke.

So, do physical activity interventions help smokers who want to quit more than usual treatment and support? Ussher et al. (2012) conducted a comprehensive review of 15 RCTs that addressed this tightly defined question. The interventions involved attempts to increase PA, either in supervised group-based exercise sessions (plus

and strengthening the belief in the benefits of such actions is hard enough for most smoking cessation counselors, or so it seems.

In contrast, Marcus and colleagues (2004) recognized the links between smoking cessation and other behaviors. Intuitively, from surveys and through interviews, there is a clear case that PA can complement attempts to reduce or quit smoking. The challenge is to develop interventions that can aid multiple behavior changes in an efficient and effective way.

The following case study provides an example of working with a client who doesn't wish to quit (at least in the next month), but is interested in using physical activity to reduce smoking.

Reducing One Step at a Time: David's Story

Our case study follows David, a middle-aged man currently out of work who is looking for new employment. David has enrolled in a new intervention exploring ways to help him reduce his smoking habits and become more active. Only some of the processes David experienced may be applicable to individuals who are at different stages of readiness for either smoking or physical activity behavior change. The different stages of change for smoking reduction, cessation, and the adoption of higher levels of physical activity, as demonstrated through David's story, go some way to providing pragmatic examples of the theoretical processes in action. Various aspects of David's challenges, obstacles, and how he overcomes setbacks could be applied separately to other individual cases.

Clients such as David are common—they do not feel ready to quit smoking at the present time, but wish to do something to change their habits. Traditional support has focused only on stopping abruptly, usually with the use of nicotine replacement therapy (NRT), but with a significant number of people admitting to wishing to cut down (as opposed to quitting), it is clear that new strategies are needed for supporting people in making this change. Using NRT to help cut down is implemented only in the short term and is usually linked to a quit date (e.g., within four weeks), which excludes those who are not ready to think about quitting. Additionally, NRT can be costly, it may produce unwanted side effects, and its use long term is not recommended. David's story illustrates how the integration of physical activity can support the psychological processes and the techniques used to implement change. The task —looking at changing multiple behaviors simultaneously—is a challenging one but not an impossible one. A reduction in smoking (a stopping behavior) and an increase in physical activity (a starting behavior) can be mutually supportive.

At this first consultation, I (Tom) have not met with David before. All I am aware of is that this particular client does not feel ready to quit smoking abruptly at this point in time, and he is not contraindicated for moderate physical activity.

Tom (T): Good morning, David, is it? My name is Tom. Please, come in and take a seat.

David (D): Thank you, and thanks for seeing me. I've been meaning to look for some help for a long time now but never quite got round to it, you know?

T: OK, well done for taking this first step. Can I ask, why have you not got round to looking for help with your smoking?

D: Well, I guess, mainly because I don't really want to quit. Well, I don't feel like I can at the moment, but I feel I need to do something about how much I smoke. I've been to those Stop Smoking clinics a long time ago, and it never worked for me. I mean, I managed to stop for a few weeks once, but that was it. I just didn't feel ready or like I could handle such a drastic change. It felt like I was being told what to do and being preached at. I know I shouldn't smoke, and I can't be having someone telling me that all the time, especially when my family are the same!

T: Sounds like it wasn't easy! Well, I'm not here to tell you what you should or shouldn't be doing or changing, just here to support and help you explore ways you think you could make changes that suit you, as big or as small as you feel comfortable with. Was there anybody else who supported you through the process the last time you tried to quit? Did any friends or family attempt to quit with you?

D: No, it was just me. The family were supportive, but didn't really understand how hard it was for me, you know? For them it was a simple case of "just stop," but it's not that easy!

The immediate exchange has revealed David's somewhat negative experience in attempting to quit in the past. He has some skepticism of what he is about to enroll in, which is evident through his tone of voice, almost as though he is challenging me to tell him that he should stop smoking so he has an excuse not to engage with me. I sense he is quite a strong-willed character and is not afraid to speak his mind. I make it clear to him that I will not be doing any prescribing of goals and that everything that takes place is up to him in an attempt to put him at ease, distance myself from the practitioners he has worked with in the past, and begin to position myself alongside him in a supportive role.

Exploring reasons for previous failures and periodic successes can be a powerful opening technique for eliciting reflection over clients' own past behaviors and circumstances as to what caused the relative success or failure. In this brief dialogue it is clear that David was lacking support to promote self-determined behavior. With pressure to change coming from external sources and goals being set by someone else, the control element of David's behavior was stripped away from him when trying to change. In my experience, offering support for individuals through a heavily client-centered approach without imposing external targets on them is nearly always well received, and this process is often cited as one of the reasons for success when compared to a more traditional "telling" approach. To attempt to tell David what to do, particularly at this early stage, could be devastating to the engagement process and the development of trust and rapport between counselor and client.

Adopting a motivational interviewing (Miller & Rollnick, 2002) approach with clients such as David will be important for encouraging change. This approach will foster feelings of autonomy or control and satisfy one of the three constructs (autonomy, competence, and relatedness) of self-determination theory (SDT), which proposes that satisfaction of these three needs drives behavior. It builds on previous work with patients receiving physical activity counseling for depression (Haase, Taylor, Fox, Thorp, & Lewis, 2010).

It is possible that the competence dimension of SDT was not being addressed in David's past situations. It seems that he was pressured into making a quit attempt, and he didn't feel any sense of competence in achieving the changes, saying the changes were too drastic. It is clear to me that David needed a greater sense of control over his own behavior, and that using progressive goals would be key to avoid creating any sense of failure or undermining any feelings of competence. Further questioning over previous support when he failed to stop smoking revealed a sense that he lacked support and understanding from others. The third construct of SDT suggests that relatedness or companionship is what supports and maintains behavior. David clearly lacked companionship when trying to adopt his new behavior of "not smoking," and the reinforcement of his mental well-being through feeling related to others was absent. The failure to address these three fundamental behavioral determinants offers a reasonable indication as to why previous behavior change was not successfully sustained. In supporting David to set goals for change, encouraging and promoting change and ownership of his own sense of control, competence, and companionship will be important.

Following some more discussion about David's past smoking behavior, I steer the discussion toward his current behavior and attempt to explore how his smoking habits link with his daily routines and activities.

T: David, if you would, could you take me through your typical day? From when you wake up through to going back to bed, describing how your day is structured and what you get up to? And, as much as possible, when you smoke your 25 to 30 cigarettes each day.

D: Sure thing. Well, as I mentioned, I'm currently out of work and have been for about six months now, so my days are a bit different to when I was working. At the moment, I probably get up about 8 o'clock, and I'll pretty much smoke straightaway, before anything else, quite often a couple, one after the other, before jumping in the shower. Then I'll make a cup of coffee, and I always have a cigarette with a coffee! To be honest, the rest of the day at the moment isn't filled with much. I do a bit of job searching and that, down at the job center, but it's difficult at the moment. My wife works, and the kids go to school, so I just spend some time watching TV and drinking coffee (which means a cigarette). In the afternoon I will take the dog for a walk, and just waste time until the kids get back from school and the wife gets back from work. The evenings are spent with the family, having dinner and such, putting the kids to bed, and watching TV again, not doing a lot, really.

T: OK, great. You said you smoked 25 to 30 cigarettes a day, yet you have only mentioned a handful of those throughout your day—any more thoughts on when you might smoke, say, the other 20 you haven't mentioned?

D: To be honest, I don't really know! I just kind of smoke to fill the time, when I get bored and that. I guess a lot of the time I just smoke purely out of habit and without even thinking about it. I really couldn't list every cigarette I smoke throughout the day.

Encouraging David to talk through his typical day and routine acts as the beginning of a reflective process about his own behavior (Miller & Rollnick, 2002). As the counselor, I have avoided

any judgment statements and allowed David to come to the realization that most of his smoking is largely driven by habit and not necessarily by need. It is common among smokers that they will have little idea of what, when, and how much they actually smoke. The majority of smokers are aware of the real dangers and consequences of smoking, and outlining the risks can come across as judgmental and distance the client from the counselor. A much better, and client-centered, approach than reiterating the risks associated with smoking is to elicit from clients why they want to reduce or stop. It is likely they will have their own reasons for wanting to change their behavior, and by finding out what those reasons are, the importance for change can be developed in the right direction. For example, it would be futile to continually outline the dangers of smoking if they have openly admitted their motivation for stopping smoking is to feel fitter. Encouraging them to reflect on the pros and cons of change relating to their fitness levels and how they would feel would be much more helpful.

What David has also revealed through describing his typical day is a series of opportunities and threats to his desire to change. He has presented a list of stimuli that prompt him to smoke (i.e., cups of coffee, potential boredom) and activities that present opportunity for discussion around his physical activity (i.e., the dog walking, getting to the job center) and the potential to progress the discussion to how the two behaviors link. He has made no reference to any pleasurable physical activity, and is clearly inactive in his day-to-day life. One of the important ways physical activity can be used to help address smoking habits is to attempt to interfere with learned responses to cues by avoiding them or replacing them with alternative activities, something we discuss in later consultations. So far David has not revealed his motivation for wanting to change his smoking behavior. Therefore, at this stage I am unaware of the importance he holds over changing his smoking levels. Assessing the importance clients place on changing behavior allows me to gain an insight into potential barriers to change, and through further discussion, as suggested previously, attempt to increase the importance the clients place on changing behavior. If we assume that motivation for a behavior consists of two dimensions, that of importance and of confidence, these two dimensions will need to be assessed.

T: It seems your smoking is largely driven by habit throughout the day, and possibly boredom. Would you agree?

D: Yes, I think so.

T: And coming in to see me suggests that you want to do something about your smoking?

D: Yes, definitely.

T: So, if I may ask, what changes are you looking to make and why?

D: Well, I know I shouldn't smoke, as I've said, and recently I've noticed I'm coughing quite badly, and the other day highlighted that I need to cut down after I ran for a bus, only about 100 meters, and when I got to the bus I had such a bad coughing fit people were staring. It made me realize how unfit I am, and smoking is a big cause of that. I don't feel ready to quit completely at the moment—there's too much going on in my life for such a big change—but I would like to cut down how much I smoke. I'm not getting any younger!

T: Sounds like it was quite an eye-opening moment for you. How important is it for you to cut down your smoking? Could you rate it between 1 and 10, 1 being not at all important and 10 being incredibly important?

D: Oh, it's hugely important to me, you know? I have two young kids, and after the episode on the bus I don't want to be the kind of dad who can't take their children out to play or go swimming or something because I can't breathe! I would say it's a 9 out of 10, if not a 10.

T: So it is very important to you to make some changes. Any thoughts on how much you would like to cut down by and how quickly?

D: Well, I guess at least half to start with, probably within a week. I would like to stop all together, but feel like that's not realistic at the moment.

T: How confident would you be to cut down by half in the next week? Again, could you rate your confidence between 1 and 10, 1 being not confident, 10 being very confident?

D: Well, if I'm honest with myself, to do half in a week, probably only a 3 or 4 out of 10.

T: Well, that's OK; you have some confidence in yourself. What would make that confidence higher?

D: Not sure, really.

T: Would you mind if I told you about what other people have done in the same situation?

D: Go ahead.

T: Other people I have worked with have often found an initial target of reducing by half quite intimidating to begin with, and have broken down their targets a bit more. For example, setting a target of reducing by five cigarettes over the first week, or maybe by one a day over 7 days. What do you think about that?

D: What, only reducing by five? Oh, yeah, I could do that, put myself at an 8 or 9 out of 10 for that.

As is often the case, David has his own ideas about what changes he wants to make. The importance he holds over changing is quite high, but his confidence to change is relatively low. As discussed earlier, setting targets that individuals don't feel they can achieve can undermine their competence and could actually lower any confidence to change if they don't reach their target. To not take away their sense of control, offering stories of what others have found useful and asking what they think leaves them firmly in control of the decision making and goal setting. David also highlighted his motivation for change, that of wanting to feel healthier and be able to play with his children. The mention of wanting to feel healthier acts as a powerful cue for me to introduce physical activity. Through all of our dialogue, I am looking for cues to introduce the discussion of physical activity, and so far several have presented themselves. At this stage I do not want to act on them immediately to avoid coming across as being too pushy or not listening to his concerns.

David continues to talk about his private life in some more detail, which I go along with to maintain our growing sense of rapport. The conversation turns toward the coming week and what he has planned, which I see as a good opportunity to get back on track to discuss goals for the following week, focusing on when he smokes and the associated enjoyment. I am keen to encourage David to complete some kind of self-monitoring to help him reflect on how much he smokes and to help him put a structure to his smoking habits.

> T: It sounds like you have quite a busy week coming up. Something I'd like to talk about is how you feel about keeping a record of how much you smoke and when. It's something other people have found useful in assessing how much they smoke, and perhaps more importantly, identifying which cigarettes they enjoy smoking throughout the day and why. We have some simple diary sheets, which you might find useful. How would you feel about doing that?

> D: Yeah, sure. That won't be a problem. It's not something I've ever really done before, should be quite interesting.

> T: OK, great. What others have done is note down when and why they have a

cigarette and what they were doing at the time. It might be through habit, craving, something stressful happened, or maybe associated with something, like your morning coffee, and rate it based on how much satisfaction or enjoyment they get from each one. What do you think?

> D: Yeah, no problem. Will be interesting because, as you pointed out earlier, I'm not really sure how I get through so many cigarettes each day.

> T: Excellent, that would give you a really good starting point to start thinking about which cigarettes you could cut out. Some might be easier than others to begin with.

> D: Sure, I mean, thinking about it I can probably think of a few which I could drop without too much problem, like the ones I smoke one after the other in the morning. I could try and just stick to one first thing in the morning instead of the two or three. What do you think?

> T: That's something other people have found easiest as well, but it's really down to you and how you feel about doing that. How confident do you feel you could do that? Again, on a scale between 1 and 10?

> D: Well, probably about a 6 or 7, I suppose.

> T: That's pretty good. What do you think you could do to increase that to maybe an 8 or a 9?

> D: Well, I suppose I could get in the shower after having one cigarette before having another one. That would kind of force me to break it up a bit. Yeah, I feel pretty confident I could do that.

At this early stage, it is important for David to achieve any goals he sets and avoid any experiences of failure that might reinforce previous negative experiences of quitting and damage his self-efficacy. I feel happy with this initial goal, especially because he has agreed to self-monitor his smoking behavior, which has been shown to be a simple, yet powerful, behavior change technique. By asking him how he feels about cutting out cigarettes, he has provided his own strategies, which leaves him firmly in control of the goals and decisions, which may help to build his sense of autonomy. Interestingly, he has also come up with changing his behavior to interfere with his smoking habit rather than just using cognitive strategies, something that makes me optimistic that he will respond well to such strategies as we progress. Also, he has bought into the idea of recording when and how much he smokes, and is approaching it as a kind of experiment, saying it would be "interesting." This approach is non-threatening, and it leaves him with a sense that he is doing it for his own interest and not for my benefit, fostering his sense of control. If he had been resistant to the idea, I would have not pushed it at this stage, perhaps trying to explore it again in later sessions.

Tackling two behaviors simultaneously can be challenging (Everson-Hock, Taylor, Ussher, & Faulkner, 2010). David has mentioned he doesn't feel ready to quit because "there's a lot going on" in his life, so I feel it is best to address his smoking behavior in the first instance and later introduce physical activity. Because reducing his smoking is David's main motivation for seeing me, I don't want to begin any solid plans around his physical activity behavior at this early stage, but I do feel it is fitting to begin thinking about his daily activities with a view to building on his physical activity levels at the next session. I begin this dialogue asking about the importance he places on cutting down by using his health as a talking point, as he mentioned earlier. The intention is to reinforce positive outcome expectancies associated with him changing his behavior. Discussing the health benefits of reducing smoking invariably provides a good opportunity to introduce physical activity as an adjunct pursuit because it promotes similar health benefits to cutting down and quitting smoking.

T: Throughout the session today you have mentioned a few concerns you have over your health related to your smoking, for example, the bus incident, and wanting to be able to be fit enough to play with your children as you get older. I'd like to ask what kind of health benefits you think you would experience if you did cut down by, say, at least half?

D: Well, I would definitely say my breathing would get easier, you know, that's something I experienced a bit when I quit all those years ago, and hopefully I would be coughing less. I reckon I would also feel fitter and hopefully wouldn't have any more incidents like that one running for the bus! I mean, I know it will reduce my risk of cancer and all those things as well, but in the short term, I'm not getting any younger, and just want to feel fitter and better about myself.

T: Those are all very positive reasons for wanting to change your smoking, and all very real benefits you will experience if you do. In terms of feeling fitter and making your breathing easier, how do you think physical activity would link to that?

D: What, exercise? There's no way you'll get me into a gym or anything like that. I'd probably have a heart attack or cough my guts up. Why would I want to do that?

This response frustrates me because I failed to establish what I meant by physical activity, and I feel that David could distance himself from me if I cannot step back from a topic that is potentially alienating to him. I feel I have interrupted the flow of the session by abruptly introducing physical activity and can sense David's attitude toward me change slightly. Typically, people associate activity with vigorous exercise, which is invariably not something inactive smokers will associate themselves with. Whether or not they admit it, their confidence for completing such activities will be extremely low; therefore, physical activities could be threatening to them should I suggest it. I roll with this resistance and attempt to demonstrate empathy and to reframe physical activity in a way that is more accessible to him (adopting principles and techniques from motivational interviewing; Miller & Rollnick, 2002). I hope to get him back alongside me.

T: Yeah, I understand, and things like the gym are certainly not for everyone. I guess what I meant by physical activity was more general, in terms of anything that gets you up and about, maybe gets your heart pumping a little bit.

D: Like running for the bus?

T: Well, yes, but even things that are less energetic, like you mentioned walking your dog most days, things similar to that. How achievable are things of that nature for you, and how do you think that affects your health and how you feel?

D: OK, well, I do walk a fair bit with the dog, but it's not very intense. I don't really do a lot other than that, so can't imagine it helps that much.

T: How do you think you would feel if you didn't walk the dog regularly?

D: It's the only exercise I get, really, so I suppose it must be doing something for my health. I guess I would be a lot worse if I didn't do it. I know I probably don't do enough exercise.

T: If you were to increase your activity, even a little bit, like perhaps walking the dog for a bit longer, or walking slightly faster, what sort of benefits would you expect?

D: I guess the usual things, like feeling fitter, probably make my breathing a bit easier, might even lose some weight, I suppose, if I did more.

T: Sounds like you think the benefits would be similar to cutting down your smoking?

D: Yes, I suppose they are.

T: And you have expressed that these are all important things to you in what you want to achieve for your future goals. How much do you think your current behavior supports you in achieving these goals of feeling fitter and healthier?

D: Now that I think about it, not very much, I suppose.

Several key things have taken place in this exchange. First, David has emphasized the outcome expectancy he places on reducing his smoking, which acts a precursor to later self-revaluation that takes place. Second, with some prompting, he has reframed physical activity away from vigorous exercise to the much more achievable idea of moderate physical activity. Finally, developing a discrepancy between where he hopes to be in the future (in terms of his health) and his current behavior has started a process of self-reevaluation as he realizes that his current behavior may not enable him to reach his intended goals. The intention of making comparisons between stopping smoking and increasing physical activity was to initiate cognitions about how the two behaviors can complement one another, and I feel it was successful to some degree. We agree that as well as self-monitoring his smoking behavior, he is going to keep a record of what he does with his time in between each cigarette. I feel these targets are enough for David to think about after the first session, and I hope the information will act as a prompt to strengthen the reflection on the link between his behavior and smoking habits (particularly his physical activity, or limited physical activity, and his smoking). Progress toward the goals he has arrived at will give an insight into his level of self-regulatory skill when I next see him, which will be informative as to how to proceed. He leaves the first session with the self-monitoring sheets for recording his smoking behavior and daily routines, with the intention to try to cut out the several consecutive cigarettes first thing in the morning.

Reflecting on the first session, I feel it was mostly successful and have a reasonable level of confidence that David will return the following week. In terms of his readiness to change, for his smoking behavior, he demonstrated being at the contemplation stage for cutting down, and I hope by the next session he will be progressing through to the action stage. For his physical activity behavior, although he describes long-term goals of wanting to be able to do more, it is not something he was contemplating at the time of the session. Through prompting reflection on the benefits of becoming more active, he has shifted from the pre-contemplation into the contemplation stage with tasks that should help to develop thoughts around his behavior. Next session, I hope to support David in moving toward the action stage of initiating some increase in physical activity. I feel satisfied that introducing the behaviors sequentially, in terms of goal setting, was the right way to move forward with David.

When David returns the following week, his body language and general demeanor portray a sense of satisfaction with the previous week. He has his diary sheets with him, which is a positive sign. I ask to look them over and then encourage him to talk through how he found the task he set of monitoring his behavior.

> D: You know what, it was brilliant doing that. After the first two days, I realized straightaway that I was smoking more than I thought I was! I counted them up, and I was actually smoking 35 to 40 a day, which is more than I have always been convincing myself I smoke. That alone scared me. The fact I could have so little awareness and control over my smoking, it really was an eye opener.

> T: I see; that is quite a big discrepancy. So how did that affect you?

> D: Well, I thought, am I really smoking that much? You know, it kind of shocked me into thinking even more I need to cut down my smoking. That was it then, after the second day I thought to myself, I really need to change this. So, as you can see, for the third day onwards, I cut it down to about 20 to 25 a day, which to be honest wasn't a problem.

> T: So, just recording how many you're actually smoking made you realize how little control you had over it?

> D: Yeah, that's right, and I felt like I want to take control back, rather than being controlled by it.

> T: You mentioned it was easy to cut down to 20 to 25. How did you go about that?

> D: Like we talked about, I only had one in the morning before showering and getting going, that was easy enough, because I thought about it after that first cigarette and realized I didn't actually want another one really, so I just waited. Then you see, I was actually doing that quite a lot through the day when I wasn't doing much, with my cups of coffee smoking two or three one after the other, so I just cut those out because I didn't really want them, and rating them on how much I enjoyed them it was obvious I wasn't actually enjoying them, just doing it out of habit and boredom. So I would have a cigarette with my cup of coffee and then get on and do something to distract myself. It wasn't always easy, mind you, but it worked most of the time.

David's revelations over the past week are indicative of him taking active control over smoking habits, and they demonstrate improved awareness of how and why he smokes. As is often the case with heavy smokers, the simple act of self-monitoring prompts and reinforces the self-reevaluation of their behavior, often revealing they had little or no idea of their smoking habits that have become so ingrained in their day-to-day routines. I feel pleased at David's response to the task, particularly how he describes using some kind of distraction technique to help cope with missing habitual cigarettes. He has cut out the cigarettes he felt would be easiest for him to miss. This approach is frequently used when smokers begin to cut down—the first cigarettes are easy to cut out, and progress can be quick at the beginning. I am wary that as the easier cigarettes are cut out through simple behavioral changes, reducing the cigarettes David feels are pleasurable is going to be harder to tackle, and more powerful techniques will be needed to address reduction the further he goes.

With more discussion around the sheets he has kept on his smoking, we identify the cigarettes he places most value on and gains the most enjoyment from. These typically consist of the first one in the morning, ones with a cup of coffee, and ones after eating. The remaining cigarettes he attributes to smoking out of boredom when he has little to do during the day. He admits to not enjoying them much, but he has lower confidence than I would hope for to cut these out, rating his confidence around a 5 out of 10. David shows good levels of self-regulatory skills, so I decide to push him on how he feels he could cope without these cigarettes, seeing an opportunity to introduce physical activity while continuing to assess his confidence for sustaining the changes he has made.

T: Well, it seems you've made very good progress this week, and you are quite pleased with that, as you should be; it's not an easy thing to achieve. How confident do you feel that you can continue with the level you've reduced to this week?

D: I feel very confident, actually. The ones I cut out were just habit, pure and simple. I wasn't even really enjoying them, you know? Was just smoking them for the sake of it, and that's just stupid. I don't feel like I really miss them.

T: That sounds positive. So you've cut out the cigarettes you smoke one after the other, and looking at your diary, it now leaves you smoking at pretty evenly spread intervals throughout the day, and often smoking in response to doing something, like your coffee, or after having lunch.

D: Yeah, that's about right.

T: So how important is it for you to cut down some more?

D: Oh, really important. Like I said at the beginning, I want to get down to at least half, which I thought would be down to about 10 a day, but that would actually be more than half! But I would still like to get down to 10 a day, because then I would only be buying one pack of 10 a day rather than up to two packs of 20. I'd save so much money!

T: So, looking at the diary of your cigarettes, which ones do you think would be easiest for you to cut out next, over the next week perhaps?

D: Well, like we said, the one in the morning is probably my favorite, and the ones after food. I guess the times I smoke purely out of boredom, it would be good to get rid of those. That would cut out about another 10 a day if I could do that.

T: Looking at what you've been doing over the past week and when you smoke, as you probably noticed, when you're doing something active, you don't tend to smoke. It's interesting, when you walk your dog each day, you don't seem to smoke, and you don't seem to smoke for about an hour after that walk. Compared to times where you've been watching TV or using your computer, where you seem to smoke a lot more. Why do you think that is?

D: I don't know, really. I guess when I'm out walking I don't really think about it, and it kind of seems a bit silly smoking when I'm walking, you know, doing something good and healthy and then having a cigarette; it doesn't really go together. But then when I'm at home bored in front of the TV, it's something to do, and the temptations are there all the time.

T: When you go out walking, you go for about an hour and a half without a cigarette, which shows you can go for quite a long time without one, but when you're at home, it's more like every half an hour.

D: Yeah, that's about right.

It has been a really important exchange of information at this point for working the conversation toward physical activity. It sounds like the initial changes David has made to his smoking behavior will be sustainable for him, and I hope to build on these changes by encouraging him to progress his targets further. By building on the discrepancies between his two behaviors I am hoping David will connect his more active behavior with his lower smoking levels. Physical activity seems to have been implicitly affecting his smoking behavior, and I am hoping he will make this connection more explicit and start moving toward the contemplation and action stage of change to use physical activity to control his smoking habit.

T: From what you've said, you don't feel the need for a cigarette when you're out walking and go for an hour and a half without one, and then when you're at home you smoke nearly every 30 minutes. You're obviously able to go for longer without a cigarette, so how could you use that from day to day to help reduce further?

D: Well, I suppose the obvious thing for me to try would be to try and extend how long it is between each cigarette I have? You know, instead of every half an hour,

try and make it only every hour or something like that.

T: That's a reasonable idea. That would reduce the total amount you smoke each day. How confident are you that you could extend each cigarette to an hour in between each one then?

D: Pretty confident, I guess, because I do go for longer periods without one so I can do it, it's just coping with the boredom. I would have to distract myself.

T: Thinking about what your diaries show, what kind of things could you do to distract yourself?

D: Well, the best time for me not smoking is when I'm out walking the dog, you know, when my mind's off it, and I'm not thinking about it, so I suppose I could walk the dog for longer. He always needs more walking, and I'm the only one that does it.

T: Sounds like it could be a good idea. You usually walk the dog in the afternoon, right? What about the period in the morning when you smoke more, between breakfast and lunch?

D: I could take him for a walk in the morning as well, I guess. Wouldn't hurt, me or the dog.

T: How long would you walk for in the morning?

D: Probably about an hour, like in the afternoon.

T: Would that be easy enough for you to do?

D: Oh yeah, no problem. It would certainly take my mind off the cigarettes like in the afternoon. I could definitely do that. Some mornings I have to go to the job center so couldn't do it then. But I suppose I could walk down there instead of jumping on the bus.

T: Sounds reasonable. It seems that you think doing something active helps take your mind off the cigarettes. How could you use that for when you start craving one, and you haven't got time for a walk?

D: Well, I could get up and do something, like clean the house or cut the grass or something; the wife would be pleased!

David has started to make the explicit link between activity and controlling his smoking behavior and cravings. He has also started to think about changing his daily behaviors, such as walking to where he needs to be, which is encouraging. Because he responded well to the self-monitoring of his smoking, I decide to suggest self-monitoring his activity as a useful way to encourage reflection on his daily activity. Like his smoking, where he has implemented goal setting and self-monitoring, it would be good to see him use similar techniques for his activity. Again, with his permission, I frame the suggestion as vicarious experience.

T: Something other people have found useful for looking at their activity is using a pedometer, a little monitor you wear on your belt that counts how many steps you take each day. It gives them an idea of how much their activity changes on a day-to-day basis, and sometimes that links with how much they've smoked—so on days when they do less steps, they smoke more. Is that something you would be interested in trying?

D: Yeah, definitely, sounds good. It was useful to record how much I smoke, and I would be interested to see how much I walk when I'm with the dog.

To start bringing the session to a close, I ask David to reiterate the goals he has set himself for the coming week: to continue with the reduction he has already achieved and continue self-monitoring his smoking, to smoke no more than one cigarette every hour, to wear the pedometer each day and record his steps, to take his dog for an extra walk in the morning, and to think about doing something active when he finds his cravings are high. He has set an aim to reduce to 15 cigarettes a day by the end of next week, an aim with which he feels comfortable and confident. I am happy at this stage that he is still retaining a strong sense of control and autonomy over his goals and the changes he is making. Upon reflection, I am aware he talks little about interaction with his family and friends, particularly in the evenings, and how others influence his smoking. I add it to my agenda for the next session as something to explore.

Up to this point David's progress has been exemplary, and he has faced little in the way of setbacks and obstacles. Although this situation is positive, it is likely there will be setbacks, and discussing coping strategies for when setbacks do occur will also be important for sustaining his progress.

Over the next two sessions, David continued to self-monitor his behavior well, demonstrating good levels of self-regulatory skills, and reviewing the sheets he has completed has acted as a good way to identify successes and failures he may have experienced, framing any failures and setbacks as good learning experiences. I have been keen to shift the focus toward his physical activity, and over this period of a few weeks, he has experienced some difficulties, but by exploring different options relating to physical activity he has set himself further goals (largely revolving around walking as an activity), which he deems to be achievable and over which he feels confident in sustaining. He has begun to explicitly link how his activity levels affect his smoking behavior, and he has started to explore options for involving significant others in his activity. He reports that on some days he has smoked fewer than 10 cigarettes per day, something he is very proud of that has resulted in noticeable boosts in his confidence, such a boost that he has mentioned the idea of stopping smoking altogether. After some lengthy discussion around his desire to stop, he decides that he feels confident to make a quit attempt. Due to the progress he has made, I feel it is a good time to support him in his plans. In addition to the goal of quitting, he has made plans to explore physical activity options involving his family, such as swimming, and finding out information regarding the gym at the local leisure center. After these sessions, I am intrigued to see how well David does in achieving what are some pretty challenging goals.

When David returns the following week, he is all smiles. He has clearly achieved some, if not all of his plans. Although his progress has been exemplary up to this point, quitting altogether is incredibly difficult, and I would not be surprised if he had experienced some degree of failure. So I begin by inviting him to tell me about his week, letting him start at whatever point he chooses.

> D: Well, I did it! I had my last cigarette! I know we talked about cutting it down again a bit more before stopping, but after I went along to that gym, they did the induction there and then, I came out and felt so good about myself, I thought, nope, that's it. I didn't have another cigarette that day, and haven't since. If anything, coming out of the gym I would feel stupid, if not embarrassed about having a cigarette; it's just not something that goes together! I don't think I can manage going to the gym every day at the moment, like they told me I could, but I've been using my walking, exercise band, and the swimming, which we're doing twice a week, and I've been managing to cope. I've had the cravings, pretty badly at times, but I just make myself do something, and once I get over that initial craving, it kind of disappears. I know it's not been quite a week yet, but I feel confident I can keep this going.

> T: That's fantastic, David. Well done!

I am keen to reinforce any positive changes he has experienced since quitting and adopting the exercise. Off the back of this exchange I hope to discuss how he plans to maintain his abstinence and how to deal with any setbacks that may crop up in the future.

> T: So how do you feel now you've stopped for nearly a week?

> D: I feel great, liberated almost. I feel like I don't have that craving in the back of my mind all the time, like it's been silenced. After I take some exercise or come back from my walk, I feel energized and ready to go—it's almost better than a coffee! My breathing is definitely better. I don't feel quite so out of breath swimming now, and managed to do more lengths of the pool this week, so there's definitely an improvement there. The family are obviously happy I've stopped; they even commented that over the last few weeks I'm not coughing as much.

> T: What you've achieved is remarkable, well done. Looking forward, how are you going to sustain what you've achieved? How will you deal with things when you find your cravings might come back? Maybe something stressful happens or you find yourself getting bored again. What things will you do to help with that?

> D: The activity is definitely something I will continue with. I've actually started really enjoying it. What's the point in smoking if I'm doing these things? If the cravings do come back, I will do what I've been doing, get the exercise band out, go for a walk, things like that, keep myself active and busy. I hope to go back to work at some point, which will keep me busy during the day, and then I can still do my walking or the gym in the evening. I feel so good about myself after doing some activity, and feel the differences in my health. I am confident it will last this time. Besides, the family wouldn't let me slip back to smoking or

not going swimming now they're coming with me!

After this session David and I met twice more. He had continued with his activity patterns, and in the last session he told me he had a job interview that had boosted his self-esteem even more. He told me how he had been putting aside the money he used to spend on cigarettes to pay for his gym membership, and he still had enough left over to save toward a holiday for the family later that year. Toward the end of our sessions, I felt completely superfluous—he was in control of his own behavior and knew what he needed to do. For me, this outcome was evidence of success. He continued to be abstinent, and I am pretty sure he began losing weight!

Conclusion

The path to quitting or reducing smoking is rarely linear, and one size certainly does not fit all. David's story is particularly exemplary in terms of the goals he achieved and how well he achieved them. A case like this is quite rare, and more often than not, clients will not progress so readily and will encounter more challenging barriers to change, often due to not having such a strong capacity for self-regulation. There is a variety of support available for smokers wishing to quit, but overcoming a nicotine addiction is incredibly difficult. As the case study demonstrated, the challenge of cutting down and quitting can be addressed through a variety of strategies for promoting self-regulation of smoking behavior. Ultimately, it is individuals' motivations to quit, the importance they place on quitting, and their experience and management of withdrawal symptoms that will determine how successful they are at changing their smoking habits. As demonstrated, motivation and confidence can snowball if tackled in the right way. Early change can be slow as individuals begin to reflect on processes and behaviors, but as is often the case, once the reflective process and self-reevaluation begin, the change can become quite sudden.

Physical activity and its physical, mental, and emotional benefits make it an ideal adjunct to help counteract the negative effects of nicotine withdrawal. The timing of when physical activity is in-troduced to individuals who want to change their smoking behavior largely depends on their stages of readiness to change and their goals. The adoption of a new activity when going through the process of stopping a current one dovetails together in a nicely coherent fashion. Some smokers will find adopting a new activity harder than others, but it is not necessarily the amount or intensity of the activity that is important, more the benefit (both psychologically and physically) the individual experiences from it. By using physical activity as a replacement for their smoking, they can still satisfy their need for a sense of control that may have been stripped from them through their smoking addiction. Physical activity presents, in almost all cases, a chance to satisfy an individual's needs for autonomy, competence, and relatedness (see previous reference to SDT) within their lives when addressing their smoking behavior. As smoking is reduced, there is an ideal opportunity to engage in various forms of self-determined physical activity that rapidly become easier to do and, hence, result in improved perceived competence and physical self-perceptions.

References

American Psychiatric Association. (2000). *Diagnostic and statistical manual of mental disorders* (4th ed., Text Rev.). Washington, DC: Author.

Aubin, H.-J., Farley, A., Lycett, D., Lahmek, P., & Aveyard P. (2012). How much weight do smokers gain after quitting cigarettes? A meta-analysis. *British Medical Journal, 345,* e4439.

Bandura, A. (1986). *Social foundations of thought and action: A social cognitive theory.* Englewood Cliffs, NJ: Prenticehall.

Brouwer, R.J.N., & Pomerleau, C.S. (2000). "Prequit attrition" among weight-concerned women smokers. *Eating Behaviors, 1,* 145–151.

Cahill, K., Stead, L.F., & Lancaster, T. (2011). Nicotine receptor partial agonists for smoking cessation. *Cochrane Database of Systematic Reviews, 2011*(2).

Ekkekakis, P., Parfitt, G., & Petruzzello, S.J. (2011). The pleasure and displeasure people feel when they exercise at different intensities: Decennial update and progress towards a tripartite rationale for exercise intensity prescription. *Sports Medicine, 41,* 641–671.

Everson, E.S., Taylor, A.H., & Ussher, M. (2010). Determinants of physical activity promotion by smoking cessation advisors as an aid for quitting:

Support for the transtheoretical model. *Patient Education and Counseling, 78,* 53–56.

Everson-Hock, E.S., Taylor, A.H., & Ussher, M. (2010). Readiness to use physical activity as a smoking cessation aid: A multiple behavior change application of the transtheoretical model among quitters attending Stop Smoking Clinics. *Patient Education and Counseling, 79,* 156–159.

Everson-Hock, E.S., Taylor, A.H., Ussher, M., & Faulkner, G. (2010). A qualitative perspective on multiple health behaviour change: Views of smoking cessation advisors who promote physical activity. *Journal of Smoking Cessation, 5,* 7–14.

Farley, A.C., Hajek, P., Lycett, D., & Aveyard, P. (2012). Interventions for preventing weight gain after smoking cessation. *Cochrane Database Systematic Reviews, 2012*(1).

Faulkner, G.E., Arbour-Nicitopoulos, K.P., & Hsin, A. (2010). Cutting down one puff at a time: The acute effects of exercise on smoking behaviour. *Journal of Smoking Cessation, 5,* 130–135.

Haase, A.M., Taylor, A.H., Fox, K.R., Thorp, H., & Lewis, G. (2010). Rationale and development of the physical activity counselling intervention for a pragmatic TRial of Exercise and Depression in the UK (TREAD-UK). *Mental Health & Physical Activity, 3,* 85–91.

Haasova, M., Warren, F.C., Ussher, M., Janse Van Rensburg, K., Faulkner, G., Cropley, M., . . . Taylor, A.H. (2013a). The acute effects of physical activity on cigarette cravings: Systematic review and meta-analysis with individual participant data (IPD). *Addiction, 108,* 26–37.

Haasova, M., Warren, F.C., Ussher, M., Janse Van Rensburg, K., Faulkner, G., Cropley, M., . . . Taylor, A.H. (2013b, April). *The acute effects of physical activity on cigarette cravings: Exploration of potential moderators, mediators and physical activity attributes using individual participant data (IPD) meta-analyses.* Paper presented at Society for Nicotine & Tobacco Research annual conference, Boston, MA.

Hughes, J.R., Stead, L.F, & Lancaster, T. (2007). Antidepressants for smoking cessation. *Cochrane Database of Systematic Reviews, 2007*(1).

Janse Van Rensburg, K., Taylor A.H., & Hodgson, T. (2009). The effects of acute exercise on attentional biases to smoking-related stimuli during temporary abstinence from smoking. *Addiction, 104,* 1910–1917.

Janse Van Rensburg, K., Taylor A.H., Hodgson, T., & Benattayallah, A. (2009). Acute exercise modulates cigarette cravings and brain activation in response to smoking-related images: An fMRI study. *Psychopharmacology, 203,* 589–598.

Kaczynski, A.T., Manske, S.R., Mannell, R.C., & Grewal, K. (2008). Smoking and physical activity: A systematic review. *American Journal of Health Behavior, 32,* 93–110.

Marcus, B.H., Albrecht, A.E., King, T.K., Parisi, A.F., Pinto, B.M., Roberts, M., . . . Abrams, D.B. (1999). The efficacy of exercise as an aid for smoking cessation in women: A randomised controlled trial. *Archives of Internal Medicine, 159,* 1229–1234. Retrieved from http://archinte.ama-assn.org/cgi/content/full/159/11/1229

Marcus, B.H., Hampl, J.S., & Fisher, E.B. (2004). *How to quit smoking without gaining weight.* New York, NY: Pocket Books.

McEwen, A., Hajek, P., McRobbie, H., & West, R. (2006). *Manual of smoking cessation: A guide for counsellors and practitioners.* Oxford, England: Blackwell.

Miller, W.R., & Rollnick, S. (2002). *Motivational interviewing: Preparing people for change* (2nd ed.). New York, NY: Guilford Press.

Oh, H., & Taylor, A.H. (2012). Brisk walking reduces ad libitum snacking in regular chocolate eaters during a workplace simulation. *Appetite, 58,* 387–392.10.1016/j.appet.2011.11.006

Oh, H., & Taylor, A.H. (2013). Self-regulating smoking and snacking through physical activity. *Health Psychology, 32* [advanced online publication].

Prochaska, J.O., & DiClemente, C.C. (1983). Stages and processes of self-change in smoking: Towards an integrative model of change. *Journal of Consulting and Clinical Psychology, 51,* 390–395.

Rodriguez, D., Duton, G.F., Tscherne, J., & Sass, J. (2008). Physical activity and adolescent smoking: A moderated mediator model. *Mental Health and Physical Activity, 1,* 17–25.

Stead, L.F., Perera, R., Bullen, C., Mant, D., & Lancaster, T. (2008). Nicotine replacement therapy for smoking cessation. *Cochrane Database of Systematic Reviews, 2008*(1).

Taylor, A.H., Everson-Hock, E.S., & Ussher, M. (2010). Integrating the promotion of physical activity within a smoking cessation programme: Findings from collaborative action research in UK Stop Smoking Services. *BMC Health Services Research, 10,* 317.

Taylor, A.H., & Fox, K.R. (2005). Effectiveness of a primary care exercise referral intervention for changing physical self-perceptions over 9 months. *Health Psychology, 24,* 11–21.

Taylor, A.H., & Katomeri, M. (2007). Walking reduces cue-elicited cigarette cravings and withdrawal symptoms, and delays *ad libitum* smoking. *Nicotine & Tobacco Research, 9,* 1183–1190.

Taylor, A.H., Thompson, T.P., Greaves, C.J., Taylor, R.S., Green, C., Warren, F., . . . West, R. (2014). A pilot randomised trial to assess the methods and procedures for evaluating the effectiveness and cost-effectiveness of Exercise Assisted Reduction then Stop (EARS) among disadvantaged smokers. *Health Technology Assessment, 18*(4), 1–324.

Taylor, A.H., & Ussher, M. (2013). Physical activity as an aid to smoking cessation. In P. Ekkekakis (Ed.), *Handbook on physical activity and mental health* (pp. 449–464). New York, NY: Routledge.

Taylor, A.H., Ussher, M.H., & Faulkner, G. (2007). The acute effects of exercise on cigarette cravings, withdrawal symptoms, affect and smoking behaviour: A systematic review. *Addiction, 102,* 534–543.

U.S. Department of Health & Human Services. (2008). *Treating tobacco use and dependence: 2008 update. A report of the Surgeon General.* Rockville, MD: Public Health Service. Retrieved from www.surgeongeneral.gov/tobacco/ treating_tobacco_use08.pdf

Ussher, M.H., Taylor, A.H., & Faulkner, G. (2012). Exercise interventions for smoking cessation. *Cochrane Database of Systematic Reviews, 2012*(1).

van den Bosch, P. (2011). *Do physical activity interventions have any implicit effects on smoking status and alcohol consumption?* (Unpublished master's thesis). University of Exeter, England.

West, R. (2005). *Theory of addiction.* Oxford, England: Blackwell.

World Health Organization. (2011). *WHO report on the global tobacco epidemic.* Geneva, Switzerland: Author. Retrieved from www.who.int/tobacco/ global_report/en/

CHAPTER 8

Adjunct Exercise Therapy for Alcohol Use Disorders

Matthew P. Martens and Ashley E. Smith

Alcohol use disorders are an important public health problem, resulting in significant negative health-related, social, and economic consequences among those experiencing such disorders. These consequences often extend to friends, family, and others with whom the individual interacts. To combat alcohol use disorders, researchers and clinicians have developed a number of interventions that have shown some success at reducing or preventing alcohol-related problems, yet rates of alcohol use disorders remain high. Therefore, professionals in the field should continue to explore strategies that will help address this issue. The primary purpose of this chapter is to discuss how increasing exercise and physical activity may be an effective adjunct to treatment for alcohol use disorders. We first provide a summary of the literature on efficacious interventions for harmful alcohol use, the theoretical premise for exercise as an effective intervention, and relevant empirical research examining the relationship between exercise and alcohol use. Then, we present a case where, in the context of an empirically supported intervention for harmful alcohol use (motivational interviewing plus personalized feedback), we also attempt to help the individual increase her physical activity in an effort to both improve general health and facilitate reductions in alcohol use.

Epidemiology of Alcohol-Related Disorders

Prior to 2013, alcohol-related disorders were classified into two nonoverlapping categories: alcohol dependence and alcohol abuse (American Psychiatric Association, 2000). In 2013, the American Psychiatric Association revised the way that they conceptualized substance use disorders by providing only a single category consisting of 11 possible symptoms:

1. Taking the substance in larger amounts or for longer than you meant to
2. Wanting to cut down or stop using the substance but not managing to
3. Spending a lot of time getting, using, or recovering from use of the substance
4. Experiencing cravings and urges to use the substance
5. Not managing to do what you should at work, home, or school, because of substance use
6. Continuing to use, even when it causes problems in relationships
7. Giving up important social, occupational, or recreational activities because of substance use
8. Using substances again and again, even when it puts you in danger
9. Continuing to use, even when you know you have a physical or psychological problem that could have been caused or made worse by the substance
10. Needing more of the substance to get the effect you want (tolerance)
11. Developing withdrawal symptoms, which can be relieved by taking more of the substance

An individual with two or three symptoms related to alcohol use is considered to have a mild alcohol use disorder. Four or five symptoms are considered a moderate alcohol use disorder, and six or more symptoms are considered a severe alcohol use disorder.

Epidemiological studies have shown that many individuals experience alcohol use disorders. For example, findings from a national survey of adults in the United States indicated that approximately 8.5% of the population met diagnostic criteria for an alcohol use disorder in the preceding 12 months (Grant, Dawson, et al., 2004). These diagnostic rates are comparable to those reported in national surveys in other countries (e.g., Bijl, Ravelli, & van Zessen, 1998; Jenkins et al., 1997). In general, men, younger adults, and Caucasians are more at risk for alcohol use disorders than other demographic groups (Grant, Dawson, et al., 2004). Further, many people engage in potentially harmful levels of alcohol consumption without meeting formal diagnostic criteria for an alcohol use disorder. For example, one study of U.S. adults found that approximately 16% of the general adult population reported binge drinking (defined as five or more drinks on a single occasion) at least once in the past month, and studies of college students have reported past 2-week binge drinking rates of approximately 40% (Johnston, O'Malley, Bachman, & Schulenberg, 2010; Naimi, Nelson, & Brewer, 2010; Weschsler et al., 2002). Studies have consistently shown that individuals classified as binge drinkers are more at risk than non-binge drinkers of experiencing a host of negative alcohol-related consequences (e.g., Wechsler, Lee, Kuo, & Lee, 2000).

In addition to the harms associated with excessive alcohol use itself, research has shown that heavy drinking is associated with a variety of other mental-health-related problems. People with alcohol use disorders are more likely than others to meet diagnostic criteria for mood, anxiety, personality, and eating disorders (Dansky, Brewerton, & Kilpatrick, 2000; Grant, Stinson, Dawson, Chou, Dufour, et al., 2004; Grant, Stinson, Dawson, Chou, Ruan, & Pickering, 2004), whereas those classified as binge drinkers are more likely than others to report tobacco and illicit drug use (Wechsler, Dowdall, Davenport, & Castillo, 1995). Finally, the overall economic costs associated with excessive alcohol use are substantial. One recent study estimated that in 2006 the economic cost of excessive drinking in the United States was $223.5 billion, or $746 per person. The vast majority of these costs was due to lost productivity, health care, and criminal-justice-related expenses, and costs could largely be attributable to binge drinking (Bouchery, Harwood, Sacks, Simon, & Brewer, 2011).

Interventions for Alcohol Use Disorders

Considering the aforementioned prevalence rates of alcohol use disorders and other harmful patterns of alcohol use, it is important that individuals experiencing alcohol-related problems have opportunities to receive effective interventions. Four types of interventions that have received support in the research literature are motivational interviewing–based treatments, cognitive behavioral therapy, contingency management, and 12-step-based approaches. Although these are not the only types of treatments shown to be efficacious at treating alcohol use disorders, and in many instances clients may benefit from individualized treatments that combine multiple approaches, they do represent a diverse array of treatments that have been shown to reduce substance use behaviors. Each intervention is briefly reviewed here.

Approaches based in motivational interviewing (MI) focus on helping individuals identify and resolve ambivalence about changing their behaviors (Miller & Rollnick, 2002; see also chapter 6). MI-based interventions for problematic alcohol use have strong support in the research literature (Burke, Arkowitz, & Menchola, 2003; Visilaki, Hosier, & Cox, 2006), and they can often be effectively delivered in fewer sessions than other types of approaches. For example, one large study of alcohol treatment approaches found that 4 sessions of MI-based treatment were as effective as 12 sessions of cognitive behavioral therapy and 12 sessions of 12-step facilitation therapy (Project MATCH Research Group, 1997).

Cognitive behavioral therapy (CBT) focuses on helping clients adjust their thoughts, emotions, and activities that help maintain the problematic behaviors in question. In treatment for alcohol use disorders, CBT-based approaches are often incorporated into the context of relapse prevention, where therapists help individuals identify maladaptive thoughts that lead to excessive alcohol use and avoid situations where heavy drinking is likely to occur (Witkiewitz & Marlatt, 2004). These approaches also often involve helping clients develop alternative coping strategies for stressors that lead to alcohol abuse.

Contingency management (CM) treatments are based on basic principles of operant conditioning: People are more likely to continue to engage in a behavior when they receive reinforcement for the behavior (Skinner, 1953). Typically, CM treatments for substance use involve providing individuals with tangible incentives (e.g., cash, vouchers) for abstaining from the substance in question (Budney, Moore, Rocha, & Higgins, 2006; Petry, Martin, Cooney, & Kranzler, 2000). Theoretically, individuals will initially not use the substance to receive the external incentives, but will continue to abstain from its use as naturally occurring reinforcers also emerge (e.g., improved relationships with friends and family, employment opportunities). Although research has shown that CM-based approaches are effective at reducing alcohol use (Barnett, Tidey, Murphy, Swift, & Colby, 2011; Petry et al., 2000), there are several logistical issues that make them difficult to implement in real-world settings (e.g., having resources available to provide incentives for those in the treatment, objectively verifying that the client did not use alcohol).

Finally, 12-step-based approaches are the oldest and best-known treatments for alcohol use disorders. The most popular format for delivering a 12-step program for alcohol use disorders is through Alcoholics Anonymous (AA), although 12-step programs are also often implemented in formal treatment settings. In a 12-step-based approach, alcohol use disorders are conceptualized as a disease that is in some way associated with character defects (McCrady, 1994). A 12-step program involves "working" the steps in a sequential order, typically with the help of a sponsor who has previously successfully worked through each step. If the program is integrated into a formal treatment setting, then the individual's counselor or treatment provider will help with this process. Examples of these steps include admitting one is powerless over alcohol (step 1), turning one's life over to God or a "higher power" (step 3), and making amends to people one has previously harmed (step 9). Evaluating the efficacy of AA itself is challenging, but research has shown

that 12-step programs can be effectively incorporated into formal treatment settings (Ouimette, Finney, & Moos, 1997; Project MATCH Research Group, 1997).

Although research studies have supported the efficacy of each of the aforementioned treatments, they are not without limitations. Effect sizes in many of the studies evaluating these treatments are in the small to moderate range, and many individuals who receive these treatments do not respond to them. Further, in some instances, the treatments can be difficult to implement due to logistical considerations (e.g., lacking the resources necessary to implement contingency management) or because of philosophical issues (e.g., some people have difficulty with the higher power component of 12-step-based treatments). Thus, it is important for researchers and clinicians to continue to explore other interventions for alcohol use disorders, particularly those that are low cost and relatively easy to implement. Physical activity or exercise-based interventions may be one such promising strategy that can be used to boost the efficacy of existing alcohol use treatments.

Behavioral Economics Theory

Encouraging individuals to increase their levels of exercise as an adjunct to treatment for harmful alcohol use is consistent with principles of behavioral economics theory, particularly the concepts of substance-free reinforcement and delay-reward discounting (Bickel & Vuchinich, 2000). Research has shown that there is an inverse relationship between substance use and substance-free reinforcing activities; increasing individuals' participation in reinforcing activities that are inconsistent with substance use will theoretically decrease such use (Higgins, Heil, & Lussier, 2004; Murphy, Correia, & Barnett, 2007). For example, "Michael" is a young adult who consistently consumes at least four drinks several times a week at happy hour after work. If, instead, Michael chose to exercise after work and found this activity to be reinforcing (either the exercise activities themselves or the results and associated feelings after physical exertion), then it is likely that his alcohol use would decrease. This decrease would occur in part because he would be allocating more of his limited leisure time to activities that did not involve alcohol consumption. It could also occur because he decides that he wants to reduce activities (e.g., excessive drinking) that negatively affect the benefits he is experiencing from his exercise program.

Delay-reward discounting refers to the process of discounting the importance of rewards that will occur at some point in the future versus those that occur immediately. For many people, this discounting is a core feature of substance abuse (Madden & Bickell, 2010). Alcohol use provides immediate reinforcement for the individual experiencing problems with the substance (e.g., tension reduction, disinhibition), whereas benefits of decreased use are more distal (e.g., better long-term health). Thus, one strategy for interventions incorporating behavioral economics principles is to increase the salience of these delayed rewards, in the hope that doing so will help individuals change their day-to-day behaviors (Logue, 2000). For example, "Julie" is a woman who reports some interest in healthy living, but also engages in little physical activity and several episodes of binge drinking each week. A motivational intervention with Julie addressing how these behaviors are consistent or inconsistent with long-term health outcomes might result in an increase in one (physical activity) and a decrease in the other (alcohol use).

Whether guided by the concept of substance-free reinforcement or delay-reward discounting, a fundamental tenet of behavioral economics principles involves individuals engaging in alternative behaviors that will serve as deterrents to current problem behaviors (Bickel & Vuchinich, 2000). The four interventions for alcohol use disorders discussed earlier can all be used to help people struggling with alcohol use disorders increase alternative behaviors, such as exercise, that might facilitate treatment. A motivational interviewing–based intervention might include a component where individuals receive personalized feedback on their levels of physical activity, which would be followed by discussions of how physical activity might be related to alcohol use (our case study presented later in the chapter addresses this scenario). Cognitive-behavioral treatment might involve developing a structured plan for engaging in activities that do not involve alcohol use, one of which might be increasing exercise or other physical activity. A contingency management intervention could provide tangible rewards for leisure time activities that do not involve alcohol (e.g., exercise), and those participating in 12-step groups may seek out alternative activities that they can engage in together socially that support abstinence from alcohol and other drugs.

Research on Exercise and the Treatment of Alcohol Use

Despite increased exercise being theoretically consistent with decreases in alcohol use and relatively easy to incorporate into existing empirically supported treatments, only a handful of studies have investigated the potential benefits of attempting to increase exercise as a treatment for alcohol use disorders. In an early study addressing this topic, Sinyor, Brown, Rostant, and Seraganian (1982) found that incorporating a physical fitness program into a residential alcohol rehabilitation center was associated with improved rates of abstinence at a 3-month follow-up. Two studies among college student drinkers have also yielded positive findings. In one (Murphy, Pagano, & Marlatt, 1986), the researchers randomized heavy drinking college students to one of three 8-week intervention conditions: a running group, a meditation group, and a no-treatment control group. Results indicated no treatment effects for the meditation condition, but the running group decreased their alcohol use relative to the control group. In the other study, a group of college students who used alcohol were instructed to increase their physical activity or creative activities over the following 28 days (Correia, Benson, & Carey, 2005). Results indicated significant decreases in alcohol consumption over those days, although changes did not differ from a control condition. Another program-evaluation study indicated some positive effects on alcohol use among adolescents participating in a 12-week physical training program (Collingwood, Sunderlin, Reynolds, & Kohl, 2000). Other studies have shown that a brief bout of moderate exercise was associated with short-term reductions in urges for alcohol (Ussher, Sampuran, Doshi, West, & Drummond, 2004), and that a majority of adults in treatment for alcohol abuse or dependence would be interested in participating in an exercise program (Read et al., 2001). Finally, exercise interventions have been shown to have a positive impact on other mental health problems often associated with alcohol use disorders, particularly depression (Stathopoulou, Powers, Berry, Smits, & Otto, 2006; see also chapter 14 in this book). In sum, the research literature on the efficacy of exercise interventions for alcohol use is limited, and it could benefit from additional, large, well-controlled studies, but the existing literature does provide preliminary support for the potential positive impact of incorporating exercise into alcohol use disorder treatments.

Case Example

The following case example illustrates how a module on increasing exercise, and its potential relationship to reduced alcohol use, can be incorporated into an existing intervention for excessive alcohol use. In this case, a heavy-drinking college student, "Linda," has been referred by a physician at the university health center to a clinician at a university wellness center. At this center, the standard program for students involves a brief single-session empirically supported intervention that is delivered in a motivational interviewing–based style, and incorporates personalized feedback (e.g., Dimeff, Baer, Kivlahan, & Marlat, 1999). Students first complete a series of questionnaires about personal alcohol use habits, problems experienced from alcohol use, perceptions of alcohol use among other students, and other relevant factors. These data are used to generate a personalized feedback sheet, which includes information such as how students' drinking compares to campus norms, a summary of alcohol-related problems experienced, and other alcohol-related risks associated with their drinking habits.

If students also report low levels of exercise, this standard brief motivational intervention is supplemented with personalized feedback on the students' current physical activity levels (Martens, Buscemi, Smith, & Murphy, 2012). In addition to the alcohol use questionnaires, students complete questionnaires assessing typical weekly moderate and vigorous physical activity, which are then compared in the personalized feedback sheet to the U.S. national guidelines (United States Department of Health and Human Services, 2008). These questionnaires can involve simple self-reports (e.g., American College Health Association,

2009) or can serve as comprehensive measures of physical activity (e.g., Sallis et al., 1985). Students also receive feedback on their perceived barriers to regular exercise (e.g., Myers & Roth, 1997). After discussing the personalized feedback, the clinician (Ashley, second author) initiates discussions with students about how increasing physical activity might also help reduce their alcohol use, in addition to the other health-related benefits associated with regular exercise. Our presentation of the case begins with Ashley reviewing the feedback that details how Linda's own alcohol use, and perceived alcohol use among other students, compares to actual student norms.

Linda's Story

At the beginning of the session, I (Ashley) helped orient the client to the purpose and structure of the session. Specifically, I related to Linda that the purpose of this portion of the session was to review personalized information about her alcohol use that was created based on her responses to the questionnaires she recently completed. Consistent with motivational interviewing principles, I also made sure that Linda understood that I was not going to tell her that she needed to change her drinking or exercise behaviors, but would help her think about ways to make changes if, after reviewing the feedback, she was interested in doing so. Here, we join the session as I am reviewing the first portion of the feedback, which focuses on perceived drinking among other students. Both Linda and I have copies of the personalized feedback sheets.

> **Ashley (A):** So, Linda, we have taken the information you gave us and generated this feedback comparing your drinking to others students' drinking on your campus. As you can see, you reported consuming approximately 12 drinks per week in an average week, and you thought that the typical female student on your campus consumes 18 drinks per week. In fact, the campus norm or peer rate of drinking for women on your campus is approximately 5 drinks per week. Based on these numbers, you are drinking at the 97th percentile, meaning

you drink more than 96 percent of other women on your campus.

Personalized normative feedback can be effective in creating dissonance in the client and thereby increasing motivation to change behaviors. Many heavy-drinking college students believe that other students typically drink more than they do, when the actual norm is considerably less. Thus, some students think that they are drinking less than other students, but they are drinking considerably more than their peers. Pointing out and discussing this discrepancy can be a powerful tool for motivating behavior, and can be applied across multiple settings. For example, later in the session, we will see how I address a discrepancy between Linda's physical activity level and current national guidelines.

Linda (L): That doesn't seem right. Are you sure that those numbers are right?

A: These numbers are based on the campus's average drinking rates, which were determined based on a large campus-wide survey. They are also similar to national college drinking averages.

L: Well, don't people lie on those surveys? How do you know people were being honest?

A: That's a good question, Linda. In general, research has shown that college students are typically honest when asked to estimate their level of alcohol use. For example, I am assuming you were honest when answering your surveys a few minutes ago.

L: Yes, yes, I was. Okay, well, I guess I didn't realize I was drinking at a high rate because my friends drink the same amount, and I know a lot of people who drink much more than we do.

A: Yes, that is a common response. What do you make of the discrepancy between the campus norm drinking rates and your own?

L: Well, I guess there are some people who don't drink at all and some students only go out once a week. I have friends who don't drink or rarely drink, so I guess that goes into the lower average.

A: You're exactly right. So it is reasonable that the campus norms would be lower than your drinking rates. What's it like to hear that you drink more than 96 percent of your peers?

L: Well, I don't know. It's not good, I guess.

A: What do you mean?

L: I mean, it's kind of embarrassing that I drink that much more than most other students. And I guess it's also still hard to believe that it's true.

A: So it seems like it's difficult to hear that your drinking rate is so high compared to other students.

L: Yes. Like I said, most of my friends drink at least as much as I do. If I were to tell them that the campus average is only five drinks per week, they would just laugh.

A: So, you're saying that when you compare yourself to your friends, you feel like you drink at a normal or even a little below normal level, but compared to students in general, you drink quite a bit more.

L: Yes—that makes sense. I guess my friends would be in, like, the 99th percentile, then.

The last two statements represent effective use of reflective listening. In both instances, I reflected to Linda my perception of the meaning behind her comments, which should help her start to think about potentially changing her behavior. In the first reflection, I acknowledged that it seemed like it was difficult for Linda to hear this information, aiming to offer an empathic gesture. But, I also clearly noted that Linda's drinking is considerably higher than other students'. In the second reflection, I helped Linda understand the source of some of her misperceptions of other students' drinking. When compared to her friends, Linda did not believe that her drinking was above normal, but both she and her friends seem to be drinking at a rate well above the campus average. I did not impart my own perspectives here, but helped facilitate change by using Linda's own statements and beliefs.

A: I know we have covered a lot of information so far, and I wanted to ask if you have any questions for me at this time.

L: No. But, I think that if we'd been talking last year, I would be more at the average drinking rate you have there.

A: It sounds like you are saying that you were drinking less last year than you are now.

L: Yeah, I only went out one night a week, and I didn't go out every week, so it might have even been less.

A: So there have been substantial changes in your alcohol use from last year to your current drinking patterns.

L: I guess so. I think that's normal, though. You make new friends, and then you meet their friends, and I just started getting invited to more parties and get-togethers. That is how it is supposed to happen.

A: I can definitely see your point. You've made new and more friends in the past year, and that came with an increase in your alcohol consumption. I think that it's great to be more involved with your friends, but we know that there are some not-so-good things that sometimes happen as a result of alcohol use. If it's okay with you, we can move on to the next section of the feedback, which covers some negative consequences you have reported experiencing as a result of your alcohol use.

Linda and I then covered this portion of the feedback, and I continued to use a motivational interviewing–based style. Clinicians can include a number of different components in the feedback sheet in addition to perceived norms and alcohol-related problems, including reasons for drinking, calories consumed each week from alcohol, money spent on alcohol, and use of protective behavioral strategies, provided that they obtain the relevant information from the client. In the present example, Linda and I covered only the normative feedback and feedback on alcohol-related problems, because this intervention also included a physical activity component.

The case example continues with a discussion regarding Linda's self-reported levels of exercise.

A: I really appreciate your willingness to talk honestly about your alcohol use, and we can come back to that later in our meeting. However, because on your initial screening questionnaire you indicated that you do not regularly engage in exercise, I was wondering if we could spend a few minutes talking about that.

L: Sure. I thought we'd just be talking about my drinking today, but that's fine.

A: Great. Okay, you completed a series of questions regarding your weekly physical activity. You were asked to report the amount of moderate and vigorous exercise that you typically engage in on an average week. According to your reports, you engage in about 20 minutes of moderate-intensity aerobic activity twice per week and you engage in no vigorous-intensity aerobic activity on the average week. Is that correct?

L: Yes. That's about right. Sometimes I'll take a walk with a friend, and every once in a while I'll get inspired and go to the gym and ride the elliptical, but overall once or twice a week is about right.

A: So, you are averaging about 40 minutes of moderate aerobic activity per week.

L: That's right. Well, sometimes I can only get to the gym once a week, but, yeah, on average it's about two times. I used to do more, but at least I am getting a little bit of exercise in.

A: Yes, every bit counts. However, the U.S. Department of Health and Human Services suggests that the average adult engage in at least 2 hours and 30 minutes of moderate-intensity aerobic activity per week *or* at least one hour and 15 minutes of vigorous-intensity aerobic activity per week. Additionally, they recommend engaging in at least two or more days of muscle-strengthening activity per week.

An important point here is that, contrary to the intervention component addressing alcohol use, the feedback is focused on a national guideline rather than the typical behaviors of others. This technique is used because it is likely that there will be a bigger discrepancy between the client's behaviors and these guidelines than the typical physical activity among others, because a large percentage of adults and college students in the United States do not meet the recommended levels of physical activity each week. In this case, Linda is quite shocked to see that the recommendations are so high.

L: What! Are you serious? Two and a half hours per week! That's quite a bit of working out, and that's just the minimal guidelines?

A: It sounds like you are really surprised at these guidelines, but keep in mind that we are only talking about a half an hour each day, five days per week.

L: Well, I guess when you break it down like that it seems more manageable, but still . . .

A: Based on these guidelines, what do you make of the discrepancy between the recommendations and your current level of exercise?

L: Well, I used to work out a lot more. I guess I went to the gym four to five times per week last year, and I found some of the group exercise classes fun.

A: And how long would you exercise when you went to the gym?

L: I don't know . . . 20 to 30 minutes, I guess.

A: So last year you were regularly exercising about one and a half to two hours each week, which is pretty close to the national recommendations.

L: Yeah, I guess I was exercising pretty regularly.

Here I attempted to support Linda's self-efficacy, which is another important motivational interviewing principle. When Linda was provided with evidence that she could potentially change her current behavior, in the form of prior experiences, it was important that I reinforced and supported her possibilities for change. In this case, I showed Linda that, recently, her physical activity levels had been almost at the national recommended guidelines.

A: So, if it is okay with you, I was wondering if we could move on to the next portion of the feedback, which addresses some of the barriers to exercise that you report experiencing.

L: Sure.

The next section of the feedback covers self-reported barriers to exercise. If Linda indicates an interest in changing behavior, then we could discuss specific strategies for overcoming these barriers. Similar to the personalized feedback on alcohol use, I could address a number of topics in the feedback, including benefits of exercise, readiness to change exercise behavior, or dietary habits. The next portion of the session involves a discussion about the possible relationship between alcohol use and Linda's limited exercise.

> A: So, I'm wondering now if we can think about how our discussions of your alcohol use and physical activity fit into the larger context of being a healthy person. More specifically, I am wondering if the two are related to each other. For example, you said earlier that some of the not-so-good parts about your drinking included having less energy and gaining weight. How might your drinking rates, those consequences, and your lower exercise rates be connected?

In this portion of the session, I attempted to be a bit more directive than earlier in establishing a relationship between alcohol use and exercise, while still attempting to obtain information from Linda's perspective.

> L: I know I used to drink less last year. I guess that I felt more energetic and healthy when I exercised regularly, but that has become less of a priority this year.

> A: So, it sounds like you felt healthier overall last year, based on spending more time exercising and less time drinking.

> L: Yeah, I guess part of the reason I was drinking less last year was because I wanted to be fit, and that motivated me to get to the gym more often.

> A: Okay, so it seems like you felt healthier, more fit, and like you had more energy when you were drinking less and engaging in more physical activity, is that right?

> L: Yeah, and I used to go work out in the morning so that I wouldn't wait until the end of the day when I knew I was tired and likely to decide not to.

> A: That sounds like it was a great plan for you, and it helped motivate you to reach your exercise goals. How do you see your alcohol use being related to changes in your physical activity levels?

> L: Well, sometimes I used to run in the mornings, but I tried to run one day after drinking the night before and got really sick, so I try to avoid that now. Then I started going to the gym later in the day, but I would run out of time, and I can't really go on the weekends because I do homework during the day, and at night my friends and I go out to the bars.

> A: So it seems that your exercise level decreased as your drinking level increased?

> L: Yeah, I guess so.

Here, I attempted to help Linda see how, in her case, alcohol use and physical activity have an inverse relationship. The logical extension of this clarification is that making changes in one behavior (e.g., making a commitment to increasing exercise) might influence the other (e.g., less alcohol use).

> A: What is it like to reflect on these changes?

> L: I haven't really thought about the differences between last year and this year very much. I did feel better physically last year. I was new to college, and I knew I wanted to be fit. I had heard stories about gaining weight when you begin college, and didn't want that to happen to

A: What obstacles can you foresee getting in the way of you making these changes, and how might you be able to overcome them?

L: Well, I can see how drinking on nights before a group class or if there was a game or something the next day might make it hard to get motivated or get moving.

A: So it sounds like, in order to balance your social life and your desire to be more physically active, you might want to plan to not drink or cut back on drinking the nights before. Is that right?

L: Yeah, I think that would be a good plan.

A: Great. Are there any other ways you can think of to make some of the changes you talked about?

L: I think another good idea would be to sign up for the group classes offered at the gym ahead of time. I would have to purchase the student pass for unlimited classes, but I have done that before, and it is worth the money. Plus, if I buy that pass I think I would be motivated to attend more classes, and maybe some of my friends would want to come to those classes too.

A: That is a great idea! It sounds like you have some good strategies in mind for making some changes that seem important to you. How confident are you that you will be able to successfully put those strategies into use?

L: I'm fairly confident. I've done it before, and once I get into a routine, it just becomes another part of my day.

A: Well, I am noticing that our time is about up for today. I really appreciate your openness in our meeting and your willingness to discuss some difficult topics. It sounds like you are interested in both trying to reduce your alcohol use and increase your physical activity, and have some ideas on how you're going to do so. As you remember, we are only scheduled to meet this one time, but if you ever want to meet for a follow-up, just give us a call and we can touch base on your progress toward your goals.

L: Great. I really appreciate your time today.

This case example illustrates a brief intervention approach that has been shown to be efficacious among college students in numerous randomized clinical trials (see Cronce & Larimer, 2011). In general, brief interventions for alcohol use (e.g., a single 50-minute session or less) have been shown to deliver sustained treatment effects across a variety of populations (Burke et al., 2003; Visilaki et al., 2006). These interventions are relatively cost-effective, in that they often require only an hour (or less) of clinician time. There are costs associated with developing a system for creating the personalized feedback profiles, but these are generally relatively modest one-time costs. It is also relatively easy to incorporate novel modules or components into the interventions, as in our case example where we incorporated information on physical activity. We know from research that one important limitation to brief MI-based interventions is that their effect sizes, although statistically significant, are generally in the small to moderate range (e.g., Cronce & Larimer, 2011). These interventions should not be considered as replacements for longer-term treatments, and individuals experiencing significant problems with alcohol use should be referred to a more intense level of care than what we have presented here. These treatments do have considerable promise, though, as suitable interventions for individuals who may not yet meet diagnostic criteria for a serious alcohol use disorder, but are nonetheless experiencing some level of problems associated with alcohol.

Summary

For some individuals struggling with problems associated with alcohol use, increasing exercise might be a useful adjunct to other types of treatment. There are a number of efficacious interventions for alcohol use disorders, all of which could be modified to include a component focusing on increasing physical activity. Behavioral economics theory provides a clear conceptual link between increased physical activity and reduced alcohol use, and the limited evidence in the research literature provides preliminary support for the utility of exercise-based interventions. Our case example provided one illustration of how a component addressing increased exercise could be integrated into an existing empirically supported intervention model. We encourage clinicians and researchers to continue to explore strategies for integrating exercise-based interventions into a wide array of treatments for alcohol use disorders.

References

American College Health Association. (2009). American College Health Association-National College Health Assessment Spring 2008 reference group data report (abridged). *Journal of American College Health, 57,* 477–488.

American Psychiatric Association. (2000). *Diagnostic and statistical manual of mental disorders* (4th ed., Text Rev.). Washington, DC: Author.

American Psychiatric Association. (2013). *Diagnostic and statistical manual of mental disorders* (5th ed.). Arlington, VA: Author.

Barnett, N.P., Tidey, J., Murphy, J.G., Swift, R., & Colby, S.M. (2011). Contingency management for alcohol use reduction: A pilot study using a transdermal alcohol sensor. *Drug and Alcohol Dependence, 118,* 391–399.

Bickel, W.K., & Vuchinich, R.E. (Eds.). (2000). *Reframing health behavior change with behavioral economics*. Mahwah, NJ: Erlbaum.

Bijl, R.V., Ravelli, A., & van Zessen, G. (1998). Prevalence of psychiatric disorders in the general population: Results of the Netherlands Mental Health Survey and Incidence Study (NEMESIS). *Social Psychiatry and Psychiatric Epidemiology, 33,* 587–595.

Bouchery, E.E., Harwood, H.J., Sacks, J.J., Simon, C.J., & Brewer, R.D. (2011). Economic costs of excessive alcohol consumption in the U.S., 2006. *American Journal of Preventive Medicine, 41,* 516–524.

Budney, A.J., Moore, B.A., Rocha, H.L., & Higgins, S.T. (2006). Clinical trial of abstinence-based vouchers and cognitive-behavioral therapy for cannabis dependence. *Journal of Consulting and Clinical Psychology, 74,* 307–316.

Burke, B.L., Arkowitz, H., & Menchola, M. (2003). The efficacy of motivational interviewing: A meta-analysis of controlled clinical trials. *Journal of Consulting and Clinical Psychology, 71,* 843–861.

Collingwood, T.R., Sunderlin, J., Reynolds, R., & Kohl, H.W. (2000). Physical training as a substance abuse prevention intervention for youth. *Journal of Drug Education, 30,* 435–451.

Correia, C.J., Benson, T.A., & Carey, K.B. (2005). Decreased substance use following increases in alternative behaviors: A preliminary investigation. *Addictive Behaviors, 30,* 19–27.

Cronce, J.M., & Larimer, M.E. (2011). Individual-focused approaches to the prevention of college student drinking. *Alcohol Research & Health, 34,* 210–221.

Dansky, B.S., Brewerton, T.D., & Kilpatrick, D.G. (2000). Comorbidity of bulimia nervosa and alcohol use disorders: Results from the national women's study. *International Journal of Eating Disorders, 27,* 180–190.

Dimeff, L.A., Baer, J.S., Kivlahan, D.R., & Marlatt, G.A. (1999). *Brief alcohol screening and intervention for college students: A harm reduction approach*. New York, NY: Guilford Press.

Grant, B.F., Dawson, D.A., Stinson, F.S., Chou, S.P., Dufour, M.C., & Pickering, R.P. (2004). The 12-month prevalence and trends in DSM-IV alcohol abuse and dependence: United States, 1991-1992 and 2001-2002. *Drug and Alcohol Dependence, 74,* 223–234.

Grant, B.F., Stinson, F.S., Dawson, D.A., Chou, S.P., Dufour, M.C., Compton, W., . . . Kaplan, K. (2004). Prevalence and co-occurrence of substance use disorders and independent mood and anxiety disorders. *Archives of General Psychiatry, 61,* 807–816.

Grant, B.F., Stinson, F.S., Dawson, D.A., Chou, S.P., Ruan, W.J., & Pickering, R.P. (2004). Co-occurrence of 12-month alcohol and drug disorders and personality disorders in the United States. *Archives of General Psychiatry, 61,* 361–368.

Higgins, S.T., Heil, S.H., & Lussier, J.P. (2004). Clinical implications of reinforcement as a determinant of substance use disorders. *Annual Review of Psychology, 55,* 431–461.

Jenkins, R., Lewis, G., Bebbington, P., Brugha, T., Farrell, M., Gill, B., & Meltzer, H. (1997). The National Psychiatric Morbidity Surveys of Great Britain-initial findings from the Household Survey. *Psychological Medicine, 27,* 775–789.

Johnston, L.D., O'Malley, P.M., Bachman, J.G., & Schulenberg, J.E. (2010). *Monitoring the Future national survey results on drug use, 1975–2009: Volume II, college students and adults ages 19–45.* (NIH Publication No. 10-7585). Bethesda, MD: National Institute on Drug Abuse.

Logue, A.W. (2000). Self-control and health behavior. In W.K. Bickel, R. Vuchinich, W.K. Bickel, & R. Vuchinich (Eds.), *Reframing health behavior change with behavioral economics* (pp. 167–192). Mahwah, NJ: Erlbaum.

Madden, G., & Bickel, W. (Eds.). (2010). *Impulsivity: The behavioral and neurological science of discounting.* Washington, DC: American Psychological Association.

Martens, M.P., Buscemi, J., Smith, A.E., & Murphy, J.G. (2012). The short-term efficacy of a brief motivational intervention designed to increase physical activity among college students. *Journal of Physical Activity and Health, 9,* 525–532.

McCrady, B.S. (1994). Alcoholics anonymous and behavior therapy: Can habits be treated as diseases? Can diseases be treated as habits? *Journal of Consulting and Clinical Psychology, 62,* 1159–1166.

Miller, W.R., & Rollnick, S. (2002). *Motivational interviewing: Preparing people to change addictive behavior* (2nd ed.). New York, NY: Guilford Press.

Murphy, J.G., Correia, C.J., & Barnett, N.P. (2007). Behavioral economic approach to reduce college student drinking. *Addictive Behaviors, 32,* 2573–2585.

Murphy, T.J., Pagano, R.R., & Marlatt, G.A. (1986). Lifestyle modification with heavy alcohol drinkers: Effects of aerobic exercise and mediation. *Addictive Behaviors, 11,* 175–186.

Myers, R.S., & Roth, D.L. (1997). Perceived benefits of and barriers to exercise and stage of exercise adoption in young adults. *Health Psychology, 16,* 277–283.

Naimi, T.S., Nelson, D.E., & Brewer, R.D. (2010). The intensity of binge alcohol consumption among U.S. adults. *American Journal of Preventive Medicine, 38,* 201–207.

Ouimette, P.C., Finney, J.W., & Moos, R.H. (1997). Twelve-step and cognitive-behavioral treatment of substance abuse: A comparison of treatment effectiveness. *Journal of Consulting and Clinical Psychology, 65,* 230–240.

Petry, N.M., Martin, B., Cooney, J.L., & Kranzler, H.R. (2000). Give them prizes, and they will come: Contingency management for treatment of alcohol dependence. *Journal of Consulting and Clinical Psychology, 68,* 250–257.

Project MATCH Research Group. (1997). Matching alcoholism treatments to client heterogeneity: Project MATCH posttreatment drinking outcomes. *Journal of Studies on Alcohol, 58,* 7–29.

Read, J.P., Brown, R.A., Marcus, B.H., Kahler, C.W., Ramsey, S.E., Dubreuil, M.E., … Francione, C. (2001). Exercise attitudes and behaviors among persons in treatment for alcohol use disorders. *Journal of Substance Abuse Treatment, 21,* 199–206.

Sallis, J.F., Haskell, W.L., Wood, P.D., Fortmann, S.P., Rogers, T., Blair, S.N., & Paffenbarger, R.S. (1985). Physical activity assessment methodology in the Five City Project. *American Journal of Epidemiology, 121,* 91–106.

Sinyor, D., Brown, T., Rostant, L., & Seraganian, P. (1982). The role of a physical fitness program in the treatment of alcoholism. *Journal of Studies on Alcohol, 43,* 380–386.

Skinner, B.F. (1953). *Science and human behavior.* New York, NY: Macmillan.

Stathopoulou, G., Powers, M.B., Berry, A.C., Smits, A.J., & Otto, M.W. (2006). Exercise interventions for mental health: A quantitative and qualitative review. *Clinical Psychology: Science and Practice, 13,* 179–193.

United States Department of Health and Human Services. (2008). *2008 physical activity guidelines for Americans.* Retrieved from www.health.gov/PAguidelines/pdf/pagui de.pdf

Ussher, M., Sampuran, A.K., Doshi, R., West, R., & Drummond, D.C. (2004). Acute effect of a brief bout of exercise on alcohol urges. *Addiction, 99,* 1542–1547.

Visilaki, E.I., Hosier, S.G., & Cox, W.M. (2006). The efficacy of motivational interviewing as a brief intervention for excessive drinking: A meta-analytic review. *Alcohol & Alcoholism, 41,* 328–335.

Wechsler, H., Dowdall, G.W., Davenport, A., & Castillo, S. (1995). Correlates of college student binge drinking. *American Journal of Public Health, 85,* 921–926.

Wechsler, H., Lee, J.E., Kuo, M., & Lee, H. (2000). College binge drinking in the 1990s: A continuing problem. *Journal of American College Health, 48,* 199–210.

Wechsler, H., Lee, J.E., Kuo, M., Seibring, M., Nelson, T.F., & Lee, H. (2002). Trends in college binge drinking during a period of increased prevention efforts. *Journal of American College Health, 50,* 203–217.

Witkiewitz, K., & Marlatt, G.A. (2004). Relapse prevention for alcohol and drug problems: That was Zen, this is Tao. *American Psychologist, 59,* 224–235.

PART III

Exercise and People With Chronic Conditions

When individuals are dealing with pain and mobility concerns and perhaps confronting the issue of mortality earlier than is the norm, exercise may not be the top issue of interest, and it may be perceived with trepidation. Chapters 9 to 11 focus on the benefits and barriers of exercise for people with specific physical illnesses. Robert Motl, Yvonne Learmonth, and Rachel Klaren focus on the benefits of exercise for people with multiple sclerosis. In the next chapter, Michelle Rogerson and Mark Andersen explore the challenges of regular exercise for people with cardiac disease, who frequently have a history of inactivity. Karen Mustian and colleagues then present the role of physical activity before and after treatment for cancer patients and survivors. Instead of focusing on a specific disease or illness, in chapter 12 Melainie Cameron and Janelle White describe the struggle of promoting exercise for people with chronic pain, who often fear that exercise will aggravate their condition. In chapter 13, Cadeyrn Gaskin and Stephanie Hanrahan describe prejudices and other barriers confronting physically disabled people in exercise contexts. In the final chapter in this section, Kate Hays underscores the various ways that exercise can be used for people dealing with depression and anxiety.

CHAPTER 9

Using the Exercise Arrow to Hit the Target of Multiple Sclerosis

Robert W. Motl, Yvonne C. Learmonth, and Rachel E. Klaren

We begin this chapter by providing a background on multiple sclerosis (MS), its pathology and consequences, and current trends in its medical and rehabilitation management. The subsequent section highlights the commonality of physical inactivity for people with MS, followed by the benefits and promotion of active living in this population. We then introduce William, the lead character in our case study. This story provides examples of physical inactivity, barriers to and facilitators of behavior change, and beneficial outcomes that may encourage exercise adoption and maintenance in persons with MS.

Multiple Sclerosis: Pathophysiology and Physical Activity

Multiple sclerosis (MS) is a common and life-altering neurological disease among adults worldwide. This disease affects approximately 2.3 million people globally, with prevalence rates of 1 per 1,000 adults in Europe and North America (Multiple Sclerosis International Federation, 2013). The MS pathophysiology initially involves episodic periods of focal, immune-mediated demyelination and transection of axons within the central nervous system (CNS) of genetically susceptible persons (Bjartmar & Trapp, 2001; Hemmer, Nessler, Zhou, Kieseier, & Hartung, 2006; Trapp & Nave, 2008). This process results in the disruption of saltatory conduction of action potentials along myelinated axons in the brain, spinal cord, and optic nerves. The MS pathophysiology later transitions into a neurodegenerative

disease process, presumably associated with insufficient neurotrophic support, and results in the accumulation of irreversible neurologic disability (Bjartmar & Trapp, 2001; Hemmer et al., 2006; Trapp & Nave, 2008). The degree and location of axonal and neuronal damage within the CNS result in the heterogeneous expression of symptomatic, functional, and participatory consequences among persons with MS (Samkoff & Goodman, 2011).

The management of MS and its consequences has largely focused on pharmacological methods. There are five disease-modifying agents that have been developed over the past 2 decades that represent first-line treatments for slowing disease progression in MS (Gasperini & Ruggieri, 2012). For example, the early use of disease-modifying agents (e.g., interferons) has decreased the number of lesions seen through magnetic resonance imaging and the rates of both relapses and disease progression (Filippini et al., 2003). Unfortunately, disease-modifying agents delivered in clinical practice often yield suboptimal outcomes regarding treatment efficacy, perhaps because of side effects and poor patient compliance (Gasperini & Ruggieri, 2012). The disease-modifying agents are only modestly effective in slowing the eventual progression of disability in the second stage of MS (Confavreux, Vukusic, & Adeleine, 2003). The long-term course of MS is characterized by progression in mobility disability despite ongoing treatment with disease-modifying therapies (Confavreux et al., 2003). As of yet, there are not sufficient data indicating that more recently developed oral medications demonstrate better efficacy rates over time (Gasperini & Ruggieri, 2012). This limited long-term efficacy highlights the importance of considering other approaches for managing MS and its consequences.

Over the past 2 decades, there has been an increased amount of research regarding physical activity in persons with MS. The increased interest likely reflects the recognition that rehabilitation approaches such as exercise represent one possible way of restoring function in individuals with MS. There has been increased recognition that physical activity may have implications for modifying the MS-disease pathophysiology (Heesen, Romberg, Gold, & Schulz, 2006). This emerging area of research has focused on three primary areas: rates of physical activity and inactivity, beneficial consequences of physical activity, and theory-based correlates and behavioral interventions for changing physical activity.

Rates of Physical Activity and Inactivity

One of the most important reasons for focusing on the physical activity of persons with MS is the long history of conflicting messages regarding the appropriateness of physical activity for persons with MS. Often people with MS have been advised to "take it easy" and avoid excessive heat accumulation that might occur as a consequence of being physically active; the accumulation of heat can impair the propagation of action potentials and result in temporary worsening of symptoms in thermosensitive persons with MS (Davis, Wilson, White, & Frohman, 2010). Another important reason is that MS has long been considered a disease that "stops people from moving," as illustrated in mission statements of the National MS Society. The reduction in ambulatory capacity would seemingly have direct implications for MS physical activity rates (Klaren, Motl, Dlugonski, Sandroff, & Pilutti, 2013). MS is further associated with a heterogeneous array of symptoms, including fatigue, depression, pain, and weakness. Qualitative evidence indicates that symptoms are discussed as potential barriers or impediments reducing one's capacity or motivation for physical activity and exercise (Learmonth, Marshall-McKenna, Paul, Mattison, & Miller, 2012).

Persons with MS generally engage in less physical activity than adults without MS or any other chronic disease. For example, our group conducted a meta-analysis that quantified the difference in physical activity between individuals with MS and other populations (Motl, McAuley, & Snook, 2005). Overall, 53 effects were retrieved from 13 studies with 2,360 MS participants and yielded a weighted mean effect size (d) of -0.60 (95% confidence interval [CI] = -0.44, -0.77), indicating that persons with MS were significantly and moderately less active than the overall comparison groups. An even larger effect was obtained when comparing participants with MS to persons without MS or any other apparent disease ($d = -0.96$).

One recent study compared the physical activity levels of persons with MS and healthy controls using validated self-report and objective measures of physical activity (Sandroff et al., 2012). The samples included 77 persons with MS and 77 controls matched on age, height, weight, and sex who wore accelerometers for 7 days for measuring activity counts per day (i.e., total volume of ambulatory activity per day), steps per day, and time spent in moderate to vigorous physical activity (MVPA) each day. There were statistically significant differences between groups in accelerometer activity counts, accelerometer step counts, and time spent in MVPA (all $ps < .01$). The average effect size across measures was $d = -0.59$, indicating that persons with MS overall were moderately less physically active than the matched controls based on validated self-report and objective measures.

Overall, the existing research indicates that persons with MS are physically *inactive* compared with the general population of adults and persons with some chronic disease conditions. Such findings are potentially alarming given the well-documented prevalence of physical inactivity among the general population of adults and the associated increased relative risks of preventable diseases (e.g., obesity, cancer, diabetes, cardiovascular diseases; Hallal et al., 2012). This pattern of physical inactivity in persons with MS further increases the likelihood of preventable diseases over and above the presence of MS.

Beneficial Consequences of Physical Activity

There have been many excellent studies (Dalgas et al., 2009; Petajan et al., 1996; Romberg et al.,

2004; Sutherland, Andersen, & Stoové, 2001; van den Berg et al., 2006) that have been summarized in reviews (Motl & Pilutti, 2012; Sutherland & Andersen, 2001) and meta-analyses (Motl & Gosney, 2008; Pilutti, Greenlee, Motl, Nickrent, & Petruzzello, 2013; Snook & Motl, 2009) regarding the benefits of physical activity for persons with MS. We recently summarized the benefits of physical activity for persons with MS based on the international classification of functioning, disability, and health (ICF) model, an international standard to describe and measure health and disability, because exercise training has the potential to target and improve many components of the ICF disablement model in persons with MS (Motl & Pilutti, 2012). The review of data from clinical trials provided consistent evidence for the benefits of exercise training on muscle strength, aerobic capacity, and walking performance, along with some supportive evidence for beneficial effects on fatigue, gait, balance, and quality of life (QOL). The body of research examining exercise training and its effects on depression, cognition, and participatory outcomes was not sufficiently developed, although some preliminary evidence was promising. There was limited and inconclusive information regarding the effects of exercise training on markers of inflammation, neurodegeneration, and CNS body structures.

Our group has conducted meta-analyses regarding the effects of exercise and physical activity on fatigue (Pilutti et al., 2013), walking (Snook & Motl, 2009), and QOL (Motl & Gosney, 2008) in persons with MS. Regarding fatigue, the meta-analysis yielded a weighted mean effect size (ES) from 17 randomized controlled trial (RCT) designs with 568 MS participants of $g = 0.45$ (95% CI = 0.22, 0.68). The meta-analysis of exercise and walking outcomes yielded a weighted mean ES from 22 RCTs and non-RCTs with 609 MS participants of $g = 0.19$ (95% CI = 0.09, 0.28). The meta-analysis of QOL based on 13 RCTs and non-RCTs with 484 people with MS yielded a weighted mean ES of $g = 0.23$ (95% CI = 0.15, 0.31). The cumulative evidence supported that exercise training was associated with a moderate reduction in fatigue and small improvements in walking mobility and QOL among persons with MS. Such ESs are potentially clinically meaningful when compared, for example, with the overall effectiveness of disease-modifying medications for reducing exacerbations in persons with MS ($d = .30$; Filippini et al., 2003).

Overall, there is substantial evidence for the benefits of physical activity in persons with MS. The benefits of physical activity are many, including improvements in cellular processes and community participation, with the strongest improvements in aerobic and muscular fitness, fatigue, walking, and QOL. This evidence indicates that there is significant reason for promoting physical activity behavior in persons with MS.

Correlates and Behavioral Interventions for Changing Physical Activity

There has been an increased interest in the study of factors that correlate with physical activity for people with MS, because these variables can serve as targets of behavior change interventions. Theory should inform the search for correlates and the development of behavioral interventions for increasing physical activity (Glanz & Bishop, 2010). Theory guides the search for variables that are associated with physical activity and provides insight into the design of programs that successfully change the behavior (Glanz & Bishop, 2010).

Ideally, an examination of correlates should be based on a well-developed theory, such as Bandura's (1997) social cognitive theory (SCT), which identifies correlates, strategies, and pathways of behavior change. One of the primary active agents for behavior change in SCT is self-efficacy, defined as a situation-specific belief in one's ability to successfully undertake a course of action (Bandura, 1997). Research has supported self-efficacy as a primary correlate of physical activity in the general population (McAuley & Blissmer, 2000) and among persons with MS (Ellis & Motl, 2013). The importance of self-efficacy operating as a correlate of physical activity is that there are sources of information that can be targeted for changing this variable and, consequently, behavior (Bandura, 1997). SCT provides principles on how to change health behavior by targeting predictors (e.g., sources of efficacy information), whereas many other models of health behaviors do not inform on the process of change, but rather on the predictors of change alone. Such characteristics of SCT support its application for identifying correlates that can be targeted by an intervention for changing physical activity in people with MS.

Bandura (2004) forwarded a model whereby self-efficacy has both direct and indirect pathways with health behaviors including physical activity. The indirect pathway, in particular, includes physical, social, and self-evaluative outcome expectations; impediments and facilitators (i.e., sociostructural factors); and goal setting as possible intermediate variables between self-efficacy and health behavior. As Bandura (2004) noted, people with high self-efficacy expect more favorable physical, social, and self-evaluative outcomes; view impediments as more surmountable; and set higher goals for themselves than do people with low self-efficacy. Bandura (2004) further noted that people with more favorable outcome expectations, fewer impediments, and higher goals engage in more positive health behaviors compared with those who have the opposite profile. Parts of this indirect pathway have been tested and found to support the relationship between self-efficacy and physical activity in the general population of healthy adults (e.g., McAuley et al., 2009), and this pathway has recently been tested among people with MS using cross-sectional (Suh, Weikert, Dlugonski, Sandroff, & Motl, 2011) and longitudinal (Suh, Weikert, Dlugonski, Balantrapu, & Motl, 2011) designs. The cross-sectional study included 218 persons with relapsing-remitting MS (RRMS), and indicated that self-efficacy had indirect effects on physical activity via impediments, self-evaluative outcome expectations, and goal setting (Suh, Weikert, Dlugonski, Sandroff, & Motl, 2011). The longitudinal study examined the hypothesized relationships among changes in social cognitive variables and physical activity over an 18-month period in persons with RRMS. The 18-month changes in self-efficacy and goal setting had direct effects on residual change in physical activity, and self-efficacy further had an indirect effect on residual change in physical activity that was accounted for by change in goal setting (Suh, Weikert, Dlugonski, Balantrapu, & Motl, 2011).

Such research has served as the basis for behavioral intervention designs based on SCT for increasing physical activity and exercise behavior in individuals with MS. For example, we tested the effects of an intervention that was based on principles of SCT for increasing adherence across a 3-month exercise program in a sample of 26 persons with MS (McAuley et al., 2007). We randomized participants into either an intervention or standard care condition in the context of a 3-month exercise-training program. The intervention condition involved workshops that focused on the provision of information relative to physical activity participation based on SCT. Although the effects were generally not statistically significant, ES estimates indicated that persons in the efficacy enhancement condition attended 15% more exercise sessions ($d = .47$) than those in the standard care condition. This study represented the first empirical attempt to change physical activity behavior in persons with MS using a well-established theoretical framework to drive the intervention.

We have recently finished an examination of the effect of an Internet-delivered intervention based on principles of SCT for increasing physical activity across a 3-month period among persons with MS (Motl, Dlugonski, Wójcicki, McAuley, & Mohr, 2011). We randomly allocated persons with MS ($N = 54$) into either the Internet-based intervention condition or a standard care condition in a 3-month RCT. The Internet-based intervention condition was based on SCT and our previous research in MS (McAuley et al., 2007). The participants completed measures of physical activity, self-efficacy, outcome expectations, functional limitations, and goal setting before and after the 12-week period. The intervention group reported a statistically significant ($p = .01$) and large increase in physical activity over time ($d = 0.72$), whereas the control group had a small ($d = 0.04$) and nonsignificant change in physical activity ($p = .71$). The intervention group further reported a statistically significant ($p = .001$) and large increase in goal setting over time ($d = .97$), whereas the control group had a small ($d = -0.13$) and nonsignificant change ($p = .17$). The change in goal setting over time mediated the effect of the Internet intervention on physical activity. The goal setting was based on criteria for specific, measurable, achievable, realistic, and time-bound goals that are challenging yet attainable, and this might explain its predominance as the only intervention mediator. This study represented our initial attempt to change physical activity behavior using the Internet as a method of delivering content based on a well-established theoretical framework. Such results have been replicated in subsequent trials involving persons with MS (e.g., Dlugonski, Motl, Mohr, & Sandroff, 2012).

Overall, this research indicates SCT serves as a good backdrop for interventions designed for promotion and maintenance of physical activity in persons with MS. This framework is important considering that persons with MS are largely sedentary, and could benefit from engaging in sufficient physical activity. By adopting a SCT perspective within the context of behavior change, we can maximize the likelihood of long-term changes in physical activity with the potential for disease-modifying benefits.

Case Study: William's Tale

To bring the content of this chapter to life, we now describe William's tale. This story is about a participant in our research who is typical of many patients with MS who come to the clinic or volunteer for research studies involving exercise training. William's tale provides an example that may well be common to other professionals who work with MS patients in physical therapy clinics or other rehabilitation settings. This section integrates constructs of SCT because these proved to be invaluable in improving William's self-efficacy and motivation to exercise. In this section, we highlight important areas to target self-efficacy and behavior change based on SCT (Bandura, 2004), such as the following:

- Developing specific, measurable, achievable, realistic, and time-bound goals that are challenging yet attainable
- Identifying common barriers to initiation and maintenance of exercise and thinking of resolutions to overcome these barriers and facilitate behavior change
- Focusing on realistic outcome expectations for benefits of exercise
- Determining areas of social support from others through encouragement and social modeling

This case is depicted from the second author's point of view (YCL). YCL is a trained physical therapist and exercise leader who has experience working with patients who have disabling conditions. YCL has undertaken research to encourage physical activity and exercise in people with disabilities and, in particular, in those with MS. In this case, the third author (RK), a doctoral-level graduate student and exercise trainer, led the exercise program. RK is trained in kinesiology and has experience in leading exercise and applying SCT in disabled client groups. This situation is unique in some ways, yet it is similar to many models of MS care around the world where exercise prescription may be initiated by one health professional and continued by another. Overall, this story provides a good example of interdisciplinary delivery of exercise services based on SCT by multiple professionals.

William's Background

Our client, William, is a 44-year-old man who has lived with MS for over 20 years. Although William was initially unconvinced as to why he should exercise, he discovered over time that there were many benefits, and became a willing and motivated exerciser. The case study will focus on four main issues: (a) overcoming misconceptions and barriers surrounding the risks of MS and exercise and developing realistic expectations of benefits, (b) monitoring progress and providing relevant feedback toward goals, (c) observing William's progress in walking and fatigue levels and personal goal achievement over time, and (d) noting long-term outcomes and the importance of maintenance.

William lived alone, and he had recently been forced to retire from his work as a landscape artist due to his deteriorating mobility, which limited his ability to safely walk outside. William was a well-educated, strong-willed individual, and he was determined to not be beaten by MS. Despite his strengths, William's family was concerned about his physical deterioration that might be caused by his current sedentary life. His family was also anxious, and they worried about what William should be doing to help his symptoms; this support suggested that William had a strong family network that might be useful for improving his health behaviors. His disability level was such that he moved around his house with two canes and could look after his own basic cooking and cleaning on days when he didn't go to his twice-weekly art class, yet he used a mobility scooter outdoors and required his daughter's assistance when going to art class, shops, and on other trips.

When William was first diagnosed, he spent considerable time reading about MS and speaking to health professionals regarding what activities he could and should do. Unfortunately, he had received conflicting messages regarding how appropriate exercise may be for him. Ultimately, the misinformation led William, like many of his peers with MS, to avoid participation in exercise. At the time of our meeting, William was not convinced that he would receive any particular benefit from exercise.

Overcoming Misconceptions Surrounding MS and Exercise

Many people with MS may not make the first step toward beginning an exercise program without guidance from either a doctor or a therapist (Sweet, Perrier, Podzyhun, & Latimer-Cheung, 2013; Vickrey et al., 2000). In this case, William's daughter had seen a poster of a new exercise program being undertaken for people with MS in the clinic and university near where she lived. Highlighted on the poster were some of the possible benefits of exercise, such as improvement in strength and walking ability. The poster went on to describe that the program was designed by practitioners knowledgeable about MS, and it consisted of small sociable group-training sessions led by an exercise trainer. William's daughter did not hesitate to contact us, and from here, the case study begins.

My (YCL) initial contact with William was through his daughter, who called me when she visited him. When I then spoke with William, he seemed interested in listening to what I had to say, but maintained that there were other priorities in his life over exercise.

> YCL: Hi, William. So are you keen to learn more about our exercise program to benefit people living with MS?

> William (W): Well, I'll listen, but really I don't think it's for me. I'm really busy

looking after my house, and, you know, I like to go to my drawing class. We're really good; we have an exhibition in a few months, and we are busy, busy, busy preparing for that! Plus you know, well, exercise . . . I remember the doctor telling me years ago that it wasn't for me. "Take it easy," she said; she told me to save my energy for other more important things.

> YCL: That's good to hear you're keeping busy, William, and I don't want to put you off your exhibition. Lots of research has been done over the past 2 decades around physical activity and exercise for people with MS, so we know now that for many people, it will offer benefits. Your daughter tells me you have a few walking problems and can't get out the house too easily now?

> W: Yes, that's right, it's pretty bad. The MS has been getting worse over the past few years. My walking has deteriorated, and I've changed. I find it hard to be motivated, and I suffer with fatigue. But I'm still able to draw and things. However, yes, she's right. I'm not working now, and I can't walk about too easily. I use a scooter going to class, and I can't get to all the places I used to. But I do what I can, which isn't a lot. I always need a big rest the day I go to my art class, and can't do anything else, like the housework, cooking, or anything when I return home.

> YCL: I'm glad to hear you try to do things, and I'm sorry to hear that sometimes you're not able to do everything you want to. Well, have you thought about what makes it difficult to get out to these places? Or thought about ways to help?

> W: Of course I have; I know what the problem is. My legs won't work, and I get tired really easily. "Fatigue," that's what

they call it. I know these things. I've read all about it. As far as helping, well, I try and limit walking, although I can get around the house OK, and I try and do the housework and cook dinner on the days I'm not at class. On art class days, I always have to treat myself to takeout as I am too tired to prepare dinner myself. However, I've noticed though that I do feel better the next day after my art class, and over the holiday period last month, class was cancelled, [and] I really noticed that I missed it . . . I mean, my body missed it. Art class is great!

YCL: To get to the art class, and get around at the art class . . . what does that involve?

W: It's strange. I've got to walk around there and stand up to present my pictures, and that's hard, standing up. But I do feel a bit better when I do that. Why is that, I wonder?

YCL: Well, William, I'm a physical therapist who does research on exercise for people with MS, and over recent years, there has been a lot of work telling us that exercise can be beneficial. There is research that tells us that in general being more physically active is positive and will help improve some of your MS symptoms. When you aren't physically active, there may be deterioration, plus being inactive unfortunately puts you at risk for developing other health problems, including obesity, cancer, diabetes, and cardiovascular problems. However, there is good news: For someone like you, we could try different exercises to improve your walking ability, endurance, and leg strength, so not only encouraging more physical activity but encouraging structured exercise, too. Taking part in a structured exercise program a few times a week has been found to help people like you. In fact, we're starting a new exercise program

soon, and I wondered if you would like to learn more about it?

W: Wow, the MS is bad enough; I really don't want other problems, too. OK, I'll keep my daughter happy, you know, I love my daughter . . . she's great and does lots for me. She's getting married at the end of this year. I'll have a think. Could you maybe phone me in a few days? And then once I've thought about things, I'll call you back. Have you got any information you can send out to me?

YCL: Yes, of course, that's a good idea! I can e-mail you some information if you like.

W: Sure, that's good. I use the Internet sometimes, so I can check that out. I'm interested, but would like some time to think.

YCL: No problem, call me once you are ready.

I knew that it was important to address some key areas, concerns, and misconceptions he may have. Leaving William to make the next move to contact me was a big step, and, although there was a potential that he would not call back, the observation that he was requesting further information was a sign that he was motivated to learn more. Furthermore, he seemed to have a reasonable social network and encouragement from his daughter. Because I was keen for William to learn more about the exercise study, we sent him additional information by e-mail, including information on the study and links to relevant health articles online.

The initial conversation highlighted some important areas. There are many misconceptions surrounding MS and exercise. Overcoming these misconceptions is one of the main barriers for professionals who conduct work and research on exercise for people with MS. Understanding the effects of exercise in MS has improved over recent years, but individuals with MS still report many barriers and reasons as to why they may not exercise, such as fatigue, lack of appropriate exercise facilities, or health professionals who advise against exercise (Learmonth, Marshall-McKenna, et al., 2012).

I prepared for my next interaction with William, expecting to have to convince him of the reasons exercise may be good for him. William, however, had used the time since our last contact to read over the paperwork describing the program and the relevant articles on exercise and MS. He actually contacted me the next day to ask more about the program.

> W: I've been doing my homework. I've got lots of things I want to ask you. I don't know if it's right or wrong. The letter you sent me said that taking part in this exercise program might improve my walking, balance, fatigue, strength, and other things. How do you know that?

> YCL: Well, William, I'm glad you were able to take a look at what I sent, and, yes, there is evidence out there that doing the right exercise at the right level can be helpful. That's what we want to better establish with the exercise program.

Time was spent confirming with William what would be involved in the exercise program, which was based on current physical activity guidelines for older adults, following an exercise program similar to that recently described by Motl et al. (2013; i.e., a 6-month, thrice weekly, progressive exercise program led by an exercise professional that included aerobic, balance, and resistance exercises). For example, at the beginning of the program, William would undertake aerobic exercise for 10 minutes on a recumbent bike at a low aerobic intensity and then would progress through to 20 minutes working at a higher physiological intensity on another machine, for example, a treadmill. His balance and resistance training would be progressed following a similar incremental plan.

I also explained that I would monitor his progress during the study at set time points (before the study, 3 months and 6 months into the study,

and then after a further 6 and 12 months) when he would come back to the clinic. William listened to what I had to say, but was still hesitant to participate.

> W: I still don't really know how this would help me. . . . I am able to get around the house with two canes, and I can get to my classes with the scooter. I don't know if it's worth the effort for me.

> YCL: Sure, William. Well, let's discuss it some more. I want you to be comfortable that it's something you want to do. You've told me that you have problems walking and standing up.

> W: I do. I can't walk outside, which is annoying sometimes. . . . I would like to get out and see the architecture in the countryside more. I used to go to a big park near where I live a lot. There are old buildings and statues, although they are difficult to walk to. Plus, I get tired, and my leg fatigue makes me need to sit down. Plus, my feet, they don't do what I want them to—one of them drags along the ground a little. Can you help that?

> YCL: Well, I can't make any promises, but we can talk about doing small things to try and improve your walking. What else is a problem with your legs?

William went on to describe some of the common symptoms found in people with MS, many of which are discussed in an earlier section of this chapter. I was aware that these symptoms were all areas that the evidence suggested might be improved by participating in exercise. It was therefore important at this point to use my knowledge, and William's personal knowledge of living with his symptoms, to help him overcome some common misconceptions and understand the positive outcomes of exercise. Attempts to create strategies to guide and motivate William were needed, such as goal setting and explanations of the benefits of exercise. There was little evidence that William had high self-efficacy to exercise, thus, motivational interviewing, which has been successfully used to enhance activities related to health promotion in those with MS (Bombardier et al., 2008), was undertaken to help William learn the importance of physical activity and exercise and to improve his self-efficacy in this area. We discussed the potential benefits of exercise to both his current and future health and MS symptoms, and that the benefits of exercise would be reinforced throughout the program by both myself and RK, as has similarly been done in the past (Dlugonski et al., 2012; McAuley et al., 2007; Motl et al., 2011). Goal setting was incorporated into the discussion with William because it is a central component in positive behavioral change as indicated by SCT principles (Bandura, 2004). Furthermore, all subsequent discussions between William and me, and interactions with the exercise trainer, would aim to provide positive encouragement and feedback.

The exercise program was designed to help facilitate goal achievement as a means to encouraging a positive behavior change. We hoped that combining the constructs of the SCT (i.e., goal setting, outcome expectations, and positive encouragement) would help William to focus on ways to achieve this behavior change, identify his expectations, and successfully benefit from participating. We are not disputing the potential benefits of generic exercise, although best practice would encourage activity appropriate to the individual, with the physical therapist or exercise trainer working closely with the client. Because William was expressing increased interest, I went on to tell him more about the exercise program.

Monitoring Relevant Change

Once William was clear on the components of the program, I went on to discuss a plan for success with the exercise program. To that end, we explored ways to improve expected outcomes, overcome impediments, and acknowledge benefits of the new behavior.

YCL: William, our exercise program is starting soon. Is there anything you think may prevent you from taking part?

W: Well, I am a little apprehensive, actually. Getting to class three times a week will be hard because I can't drive. Plus, well, that's a lot to change, going from nothing to three times a week. I think I'll be tired, too.

YCL: It's good that you've thought about these things. You've said your daughter is happy to bring you to the classes, so you shouldn't worry about that. Attending the class, well, all you can do is start, and see how you get on. Starting is the first step to success. What do you expect to get out of physical activity and exercise?

W: I don't really know. The Internet said it may make me walk better, and, if that were the case, that would be brilliant. I could get out and about and maybe get rid of the old scooter sometimes. Maybe, you know, now that I'm thinking about it, I could use it to help me at the art class because I need some new scenery to draw. Getting out more would obviously be inspiring to me. Plus, you've told me if I am more physically active, I'm less likely to have other health problems. That's important to "live long and healthily"—that's what they say, isn't it?

YCL: Yes, you're right; you've identified some outcome expectations that might happen if you start the program. What may also be good is meeting new people —for this exercise program, you'll be working with others similar to you in a small group.

W: That would be nice, to meet others. We could then all work together!

YCL: It's often a good idea to set a goal or two as a way to provide motivation for you to continue with the program. Do you have an idea of what you may want to accomplish by the end of the 6 months?

W: Well for me, walking is my top priority, and you know the girl who called you? She's getting married soon, and if she could help me, I could walk with maybe just one cane, and, yeah, we could maybe do the wedding march down the aisle together. That would make me really proud. I don't know if that's possible, but . . . we could try.

At this stage, William was beginning to see potential in future areas he could look to improve. I felt it important that goal setting was made a formal part of the process, and noted that we would do that if he participated in the program. I hoped that doing so would help facilitate William's success in the exercise program.

YCL: Those are terrific, and we can maybe think about those in the future. Is there anything else, any other things you would like to accomplish?

W: Well, I don't know, but I am a little confused. You see, I do get tired a lot. Won't exercise make me tired? It certainly used to when I was healthier. Plus, my daughter does exercise and she's always tired after it. I don't think it'll be a good idea if it makes my fatigue worse, do you? Maybe this isn't for me.

There was evidence from William's comments and questions that he was second-guessing his ability, and he had already moved in one conversation from excitement to self-doubt. I noted that he might experience self-doubt during the exercise program, so, as is consistent with SCT, both RK and I would provide positive feedback at each of our interactions because it seemed important to immediately counteract this self-doubt, which could be a potential barrier in William's success.

Barriers to exercise, such as fear of exacerbating symptoms and fatigue (Learmonth, Marshall-McKenna, et al., 2012), may be common for people with MS. His comparison with his former self and others who did not have MS brought self-doubt to William's mind. It was important to use encouraging language to show that I was considering what he was saying and to try to build his self-confidence. It was also important for William

to know that he would not be working alone, so I used language that inspires collaboration (i.e., "we," "us," "our"). A knowledgeable, encouraging, and compassionate exercise leader has been found to act as a potential facilitator to exercise for those with MS (Learmonth, Marshall-McKenna, et al., 2012).

YCL: William, it's OK. Don't worry; it shouldn't be too difficult. We have looked at what types of exercise people with your level of MS have been able to do in the past, and we'll try our best to start you with a program that you can achieve. How does that sound? We'll use pacing to make sure you can take breaks when you need them, and the sessions won't start out very long.

W: I really don't know. I mean, it'll be too hard, and I get tired, you know. That "fatigue" they all talk about. Everyone with MS has it; I think that's what the doctors told me years ago. Save energy, and don't go out until you have to. And now, well, now I'm in a terrible state.

YCL: You are right; a lot of people with MS do deal with fatigue affecting their everyday lives, and we certainly consider that area when we are prescribing exercise to you. In fact, a lot of health care providers would now recommend exercise for those with MS. We'll work together, and there is a brilliant exercise trainer who has good knowledge of MS who will help, too. You will be able to rest when you need to, and if we need to modify the exercises, we can work together to all decide how best to do that. That way we can work to try and improve your fatigue.

W: Really?

YCL: Yes, because we'll be using pacing methods and gentle progression to build up your tolerance to exercise that may well carry over into what you are doing outside the exercise class.

W: I don't really understand. How will that help my fatigue?

It was becoming clear, by William's choice of language that he was becoming a little overwhelmed by the information we were discussing, and I knew it would be important to allow him some time to consider what we had talked about and decide whether he wanted to start the exercise program.

YCL: It's nothing complicated; don't worry, William. Often, pacing yourself can make fatigue more manageable. I think we have discussed a lot today, and if you like, we can discuss these areas more soon. I would suggest you take a few days to think about everything, and then contact me again. The next stage would be arranging an appointment to come into the clinic to begin the study where we can talk more and then perhaps take some measurements to see where you're at related to your walking ability and other areas.

In this short telephone conversation, I had helped William identify positive outcome expectations of the exercise program as well as impediments to his participation. We had also explored potential goals he may hope to achieve, all of which are important areas for increasing his self-efficacy and future success in the program. William contacted me a few days later to say that he was happy to consider the program and potentially "give it a try."

Monitoring Progress and Providing Relevant Feedback

So far, I had spoken with William only through the telephone and had sent him documentation through e-mail. Doing so was convenient for him, and this process highlights the service flexibility that many patients may appreciate. There was now, however, a need to meet with him in person. I prepared for the first meeting with William, remembering that he may well be having self-doubt

or hesitation, and that it would be important to try to address these potential barriers. Thus, the continued use of constructs embedded within social cognitive theory (i.e., overcoming perceived impediments, identifying facilitators, goal setting, effective outcomes) through motivational techniques was important. In addition, if William were to take part, at the first meeting I would use the time to assess his fitness and some of his MS-related symptoms, and identify outcomes that would establish any change throughout the program; doing so would be instrumental in providing documented evidence of the efficacy of the intervention as part of a research project.

William arrived early to his appointment, and he was keen to meet with me. William had read the e-mail describing the details of the program and looked at some of the recommended online articles. He also had some questions that I was able to answer. These questions related to the intensity of training, his weekly compliance, and the appropriate clothing to wear. I reminded him that he would have his heart rate monitored throughout the sessions, which would provide RK an objective way to keep track of how hard he was working. Further, we would use a scale to monitor his rating of perceived exertion (i.e., the Borg Scale; Borg, 1982) to measure how tired he would be, and the exercise intensity could then be adjusted accordingly. We also suggested he would probably benefit most if he could attend as often as possible, and that he should exercise in comfortable, loose clothing.

I reminded him of the importance of evaluating his progress. We would do this evaluation by taking a series of validated measurements before he began the program, and then we would repeat these at specific time points throughout the program. He was also reminded that he would be exercising alongside two other people with MS, and that, although I would initially be there for the first few exercise sessions, they would be led by RK. I also discussed with William that I would be in frequent communication with RK and that we might be discussing his progress on occasion.

We first gathered some basic demographic information from him and also established baseline values; the chosen outcome measures were consistent to those used in our previous related publi-

Table 9.1   Measurements Taken Throughout the Program and Attendance

Outcome	Before program	Three months of program	Completion of program
Attend more than 75% of the exercise classes (%)	0	95	87
Time to walk 25 feet (sec)	11.6	10.02	7.2
Distance walked in 6 minutes (m)	173	191	226
Leg strength (1RM) (lb) Quadriceps (leg extension) Calf muscles (calf press) Hamstrings (leg curl) Gluteal muscles (leg press)	10 15 12 26	10 18 12 26	12 20 14 26
Score on Fatigue Severity Scale	6	6	5
Score on Multiple Sclerosis Quality of Life scale	65	64	64
Score on 6-item self-efficacy scale	62	72	74

cation (Motl et al., 2013). Outcomes included the following:

• *Walking measures*—the 6-minute walking test (6MW; Butland, Pang, Gross, Woodcock, & Geddes, 1982), a validated measure of distance walked up and down a quiet corridor over 6 minutes; the Timed 25 Foot Walk (T25FW; Cutter et al., 1999), a validated measure of walking speed over 25 feet

• *Strength*—1 repetition maximum (1RM) of quadriceps, gluteal, hamstring, and calf leg muscles, involving William performing a maximal effort repetition of these muscle groups on resistance equipment

• *Fatigue*—the Fatigue Severity Scale (FSS; Krupp, LaRocca, Muir-Nash, & Steinberg, 1989), a validated questionnaire that involves nine questions related to fatigue

• *Quality of life*—the Multiple Sclerosis Quality of Life scale (MSQOL; Vickrey, Hays, Harooni, Myers, & Ellison, 1995), a validated questionnaire that includes 54 items relating to quality of life for people with MS

• *Self-efficacy*—the Exercise Self-Efficacy (EXSE) scale (McAuley, 1993), a validated six-item questionnaire to establish William's beliefs about his ability to exercise

To allow us to prescribe William's aerobic and resistance activity appropriately in addition to the strength testing, William also undertook a maximal exercise test on a recumbent stationary bicycle to determine his aerobic capacity (i.e., $\dot{V}O_2peak$) following protocol similar to what Motl and Fernhall (2012) described.

The baseline results for the walking, strength, fatigue, quality of life, and self-efficacy assessments are displayed in table 9.1 and are presented alongside the follow-up tests results. William's baseline scores for many measures were consistent with scores we have seen in our previous research in those with MS (Motl et al., 2012; Learmonth, Paul, Miller, Mattison, & McFadyen, 2012). This table also includes his attendance at the exercise sessions. Many of these results relate to his personal goals. These goals are discussed in the next section.

Changes in Walking, Fatigue Levels, and Goal Achievement Over Time

Central to the success of almost any exercise program are the monitoring of exercise, keeping records (e.g., using logbooks), and adjusting (and readjusting) goals. All of these activities feature in the story of William's adventure from the beginning to the end of his exercise program.

Beginning the Exercise Program. Following the initial consultation, William began attending the exercise class three times a week. RK and I initially led the class. Three participants with MS attended the program together who were all at a similar level of walking, balance, and strength. Other important components of SCT are social support and social modeling (Bandura, 2004). The group exercise setting was provided in an attempt to improve self-efficacy and facilitate a positive social support network. I had found in the past that group-based sessions encouraged overall adherence to exercise for people with MS (Learmonth, Marshall-McKenna, et al., 2012).

As mentioned previously, we had performed a maximum exercise test at the start of the program and established strength through 1RM effort of leg muscle groups. This measure is advised where possible, and it can be used to accurately prescribe exercise. To briefly summarize the program, it began with 10 minutes of aerobic exercise at 40% $\dot{V}O_2$peak, one set of resistance exercises (i.e., leg press, knee extension and flexion, ankle plantar flexion exercises) involving 8 repetitions at 40% to 50% 1RM, and one set of easy balance exercises (e.g., single-leg stand, heel-to-toe line walk, tandem stance, single calf raiser). After 3 months, all going well, William would progress to 20 minutes of aerobic exercise at 50% $\dot{V}O_2$peak, one set of resistance exercises involving 10 repetitions at 50% to 60% 1RM, and one set of easy, plus one set of moderate balance exercises (e.g., eyes closed or adding a knee dip). In the final weeks of the program, William was planned to undertake 20 minutes of aerobic exercise at 60% $\dot{V}O_2$peak, one set of resistance exercises involving 15 repetitions at 60% to 70% 1RM, and two sets of advanced balance exercises. At each session, William recorded his activity, provided feedback on level of exertion using the Borg scale, and marked his progress in his logbook. Maintaining a personal logbook, alongside feedback from RK and me, was expected to help William see progress and to serve as a resource for improving his self-efficacy.

Although the case study primarily focuses on an exercise-only intervention, we advocate that a holistic, interdisciplinary approach be taken with MS care. Health professionals involved in MS rehabilitation should seek to provide information on topics relevant to MS (e.g., self-management of symptoms, social interaction, mobility, activities of daily living), alongside topics relevant to general health, which have previously been included in past work to improve physical activity

adherence for people with MS (McAuley et al., 2007). Three weeks after William successfully attended the class three times per week, we discussed his progress. The following is an abbreviated version of the conversation.

YCL: You've done well attending the class; now, remember we'd spoken about what you'd hoped to achieve from taking part. Can we talk about that in more detail now?

W: Yes, I think I'll be continuing to attend because I've done well. I'm enjoying it, and get on well with Rachel and you, plus Tom and Naomi who train with me too are great. They help me see the potentials of exercise. So I want to keep exercising, and then continue longer after the class finishes. Plus, ever since the testing session, I've been thinking that walking is my main area I want to improve, and I like this idea of setting goals. So, yeah, that walking test we did in the corridor, we should work on that maybe. If I'm getting better, the numbers won't lie. And then I would like to walk Anna, my daughter, down the aisle on her wedding day. I've been thinking about that more and more. So can we work on that please?

YCL: Of course, that's terrific. We can think about goals together, and you can come up with some for yourself. We can make SMART goals, and we can write them down. You could perhaps take them home and stick them on the fridge?

W: What's SMART?

YCL: It's a tool that we use to help us make goals. It is an acronym, standing for specific, measurable, achievable, realistic, and time bound. For example, you could say that in 6 months' time, you want to be able to walk a specific distance, perhaps further than you currently can do? Of course it's important to be realistic within the time of the study.

William was displaying lots of positive signs of prospective success by attending the class and thinking about areas he would like to improve; after 3 weeks, he was displaying an increased self-efficacy to exercise. Research has shown that goal setting may be an important aspect to behavior change (Motl et al., 2011) and that it is a central construct in SCT (Bandura, 2004) for enhancing physical activity adherence. The SMART acronym is common in rehabilitation practice. The next vignette is an abbreviated version of the actual goal-setting interaction, whereby examples are given and suggestions made by both William and me.

I had found in previous clinical practice that asking clients to write goals in their own words provided accountability to their goals. I made sure that William understood what a good SMART goal would be, and clarified that his goals could be based on evidence, such as that for walking (Learmonth, Dlugonski, Pilutti, Sandroff, & Motl, 2013) and fatigue (Pilutti et al., 2013) outcome measures. We then discussed potential goals for William that he wrote down.

W: Well, I know my first one; it's easy to say, not so easy to do. I want to be responsible for attending the exercise class three times a week.

YCL: That's right, good idea. But maybe not worry about attending 100% of the time; let's say more than three-quarters of the classes?

W: OK! A good walking goal would maybe be that by the end of the 6 months of the program, I would be able to walk further, which would be like walking down the aisle. I could say in 6 months, I'll improve in that corridor test, the walking for 6 minutes. Then by Anna's wedding, I could hopefully surprise everyone by walking her down the aisle.

YCL: Good idea, although we can't guarantee that. However, studies suggest it may happen if you keep attending and are able to progress successfully in the exercises. We've found in our research that a change of more than about a quarter to a third would be significant, so although everyone is different, and we don't know if you definitely will improve your walking, we could still base a SMART goal on it.

W: I see, yes. Well, another goal could be that in 6 months I can walk a third more on that corridor than I could the first time. And I think that will link with being able to walk my daughter down the aisle, although that's not until next year. It makes sense that if I can walk better, I should be able to walk her all the way down the aisle; it's a big traditional church, I think the aisle is about 80 meters long.

YCL: Yes, it does make sense. Good, if you are happy with that then you can write it down.

W: My next goal could be for my tiredness—my fatigue. That could help me at home, and at my art class, if there was a fatigue improvement. What about a goal being "on days that I attend the art class, I am able to sort my dinner that evening?" Then I don't have to rely on Anna. Or, we could see if my scores on those fatigue questions changed? But, again, I don't know how realistic it would be.

YCL: Well, again, we've found in the past that scores could change by almost one point on the scale with exercise.

W: I see what you're getting at. It's good to use the research to see what is possible.

YCL: Yes, I think it certainly gives some indication. But remember, everyone is different, and things change day to day and week to week.

W: You are right, my fatigue does vary daily, and that's difficult to measure. We would probably want to use a larger difference, or we could combine this goal with something else, too.

YCL: Sure, what did you have in mind?

W: OK, so if in 3 months other people have improved by one point, if I got more than two points better, that would be a really big change. Then we could also say that in my day-to-day life, I could do more. So perhaps not having to order takeout the nights I go to art class. I'll write that down as a combined fatigue goal.

YCL: Sure, but let's write them down separately, because one might not necessarily equate to the other.

W: Sure. I'd like to write down another one, but this is perhaps more long term. It's linked, again, with my walking. I would like to write down that I am going to walk Anna down the aisle only using one cane. It's really the main goal I want to achieve.

YCL: I understand. The wedding is not until several months after the end of the program, but of course there will be other exercise options for you. Will you be able to stay in touch with me, and let me know how you are doing?

W: Of course!

YCL: Well done, William, you've identified some great goals, and we will check up on them as the program progresses!

William had done well identifying goals that were realistic, challenging, and attainable. We had discussed trying to make sure goals were realistic (by basing them on his current success of attending the class and on experiences of other persons with MS), challenging (by aiming to surpass what he is currently doing), and attainable (by associating the goals with outcomes previously seen to improve with similar exercise programs).

Two Months (16 Sessions) Into the Program.
It became apparent that William was beginning to take control of his exercise session by some feedback to me from RK, the exercise trainer, who was now leading the classes independently.

RK: I know you haven't seen William for three or four weeks now, but he's been coming along and managing well. We work on all his exercises as part of the group, and I think the social interaction is important to his success. He arrives early and is keen to start. I think he's hoping to impress you next month at his 3-month assessment.

YCL: Really? Tell me more about what he has been doing exercise-wise, and any other things that he may have said to you about how he is feeling, whether they are good or bad. Could you tell me a bit more on his progression with the exercises as well as if he has voiced any good or bad feelings?

RK: Sure. He has said he finds the exercises quite easy, and he's happy doing his aerobic exercise on the arm and leg ergometer, but in the past session, he was looking at the treadmill, and I think we may try that. He really likes the resistance exercises, but, like everyone in the small group, he isn't too keen on the balance exercises. He says that when his daughter is with him, he practices them at home.

YCL: Sounds good, just make sure safety comes first. Monitor him closely on the treadmill, and if appropriate, please ask him to wear a belt harness for you to hold on to. Has he mentioned how he is getting on in other areas of his life?

RK: Briefly. I remember him saying that he sometimes struggles to go to his art class the day after exercising. He gets tired after exercising, but in general feels more alert for class and doesn't want to stop. He has also been talking about how excited his daughter is getting for her wedding, and he is worried that he may not be able to achieve his goal for walking her down the aisle.

YCL: OK, I'm glad we were able to have this chat. I'll see him in 4 weeks.

Being able to liaise with William's exercise trainer provided invaluable feedback. I was able to learn that the level of the program seemed to be right for him. It was also emerging that his motivation and self-efficacy levels were improving, because he was attending classes, arriving early, and seeming keen. That he was "wanting to impress me" was positive, and it suggested he was receptive to positive feedback and social support.

Three Months (24 Sessions) Into the Program.   I next met with William back in the clinic. We repeated the outcome assessments in the same way as before the program and discussed how he was getting on with the areas we had used to monitor his progress (table 9.1). He had improved in some areas (walking speed and distance and self-efficacy for physical activity) but not in all. I felt not only that it was important to provide feedback to William on his progress, but also, in keeping with SCT, that it was essential to establish his views on his attendance and progress. It was also necessary to explore any barriers he was experiencing related to exercising.

YCL: We are halfway through the exercise program, and you seem to be doing well. RK tells me you've been attending well. Plus, from the questionnaire on self-efficacy, it appears that you now feel that you are able to continue exercising. How do you feel about that?

W: Well, that's good to hear; I'm really keen to keep going.

YCL: It seems you've improved in some of the walking tests, too.

W: Yes, but more than that, I think I've benefited in other areas. I've got more energy, [I] feel much more alert, and I can think things out clearer. I think I'm getting better at all of the exercises too. You would be impressed. I remember the goals we set. I think I'm getting there, but I am worried I might not. What do you think?

YCL: You've done well. Remember they are just targets, areas you hope to accomplish. Let's talk about them some more. Why don't you think you will achieve them? Is there anything we can do to help you overcome any problems?

W: I'm not sure. I guess just getting to the class is sometimes hard. I have to ask my daughter to give me a ride, and I feel bad, but she tells me that she really feels it's important, and she wants to help. It would be good if I could bring myself because I just worry if I don't always come, I'll not make the goals, and what will happen if I don't achieve them?

YCL: You've said your daughter doesn't mind bringing you. I'm sure that's true. Remember, if you don't meet your goals, it's OK. Your goals are modifiable, of course, and they are really just something for you to work towards. I don't want you feeling any pressure, keeping coming along and attending the class is the main thing. You're doing that, already achieving your main goal!

W: OK, and I think you're right about the exercise being beneficial. I think the people on the Internet, all those articles, I think they are on to something with exercise in MS; it's good. I want to keep coming along for the next few months. I am enjoying it a lot more than I thought I would. In fact, my friends at the art class and my family are starting to comment that I'm getting better, and they tell me I'm looking good. It's nice to get compliments!

There are lots of positive aspects from this meeting with William, and he is identifying improvements in himself and assessing his progress with respect to the goals he set. There is evidence of his progress based on his scores on his walking assessments and his reports of having more energy. His self-efficacy is becoming stronger than when he started as evidenced in his score on the EXSE and his desire to keep attending the class. Positive comments from his daughter and close friends in his art class on his progress are also further evidence of his progress; additionally, the comments seem to be helping William.

It was important, however, to make sure William did not feel pressured, and that achieving the goals did not become his only reason for taking part. Therefore, I took the opportunity to tell him that the goals were modifiable and reminded him that he had already achieved his first goal. We further discussed how the main focus of the program was to adopt an exercise routine into his daily behavior, and he was already achieving that as well.

Four Months (32 Sessions) Into the Program.
William continued with the program, with RK reporting high attendance and that he was managing all the exercises well. She reported that some had been modified slightly; he was taking longer breaks during each type of exercise and a break between sets of balance exercises.

> YCL: How has working with William been?

> RK: Pretty well, although I've noticed we need to take things slow. I thought we would have to stop a few times, but I've certainly found that as long as he takes ample breaks, it's OK. Although some days are better than others, there doesn't seem to be a pattern. . . . Some days are good; some are bad. But I know from my experience in MS that is normal to take exercise day by day depending on the participant's state.

> YCL: Yes, I think that you are well placed to make that judgment, and I'm glad you have highlighted it. It's important we keep William progressing safely, and since fatigue is a problem for him, it's good that he is able to take breaks. Is he directing the breaks or are you?

> RK: I always ask him at the start to make sure he tells me if and when he would like to take a break. Normally he will. Sometimes he takes a while chatting with the other people there, but I let them. I think they get a lot from the social side of exercise too.

This evidence is informative in that it suggests the necessity of a knowledgeable exercise trainer who understands MS and the modifiability of the exercise program. MS symptoms present differently each day, so it is important for trainers and health professionals to be aware that progress may be affected by changes in symptoms. It is also important for practitioners to be aware of potential symptom relapse, although these are reported rarely in the MS exercise literature. Should clients with MS begin displaying or reporting on signs of a potential relapse, it is important to remind them to seek further professional advice, or, where applicable, report these changes to the other members of the clinical team (e.g., a physician). The report from RK also highlights the importance of the social benefits of group exercise for people with MS, which has also been previously reported (Learmonth, Marshall-McKenna, et al., 2012).

Six Months (48 Sessions) Into the Program.
William returned at the 6-month follow-up period.

> YCL: Hi, William, you are looking well! You have completed the formal exercise program. Are you ready to see how you have progressed?

W: Yes, I am excited to see if I've gotten better. Although I know I have. I can walk better; give it a few weeks and I might be able to come and see you and not use the scooter. I'm still using it to get to art class, but when I'm there, I don't need it. I'm definitely managing to do more for myself at home now, too.

We then completed William's assessment (the results are displayed in table 9.1). William had improved his walking scores (i.e., after 6 months of the program William decreased his time needed to walk 25 feet by 38%), and his accounts of improved walking are evidenced in his reports of using fewer assistive devices at his art class. William also reported that he was able to cook for himself more, particularly on the days of his art class when previously he had been too tired to prepare dinner. His reported improvement in fatigue was evidenced in an improved score on the FSS by one point.

Long-Term Outcomes and the Importance of Maintenance

The exercise program lasted for 6 months, and it was our hope that the positive behavior changes William had made would become permanent in that he would begin to exercise independently and continue to work toward short- and long-term goals. At the end of the final assessment, I helped William plan for the future.

YCL: Well done, William. Now that you have completed the program, what do you think, and what's next?

W: I feel that I am stronger now and able to walk better. I feel like a new man. I would like to try and stay active. I've even looked to see what I can do next. Of course, I'll be busy in the next few months with my art class, the wedding, and exercise. But I will try and keep going.

YCL: Great, William! Well, I think there are some good exercise options out there, and I can provide you with some information on who to contact. Do you

think you'll keep exercising with the others from the class?

W: Well, yes, Tom, Naomi, and I are all going to try and get to the gym together, and we've already started going to an MS support group where I tell them all they should be exercising. Plus, I've found other good options for me to keep exercising. I'll try and keep in touch and let you know.

YCL: Great! I've enjoyed working with you, William. Well done! Maybe we should think about what you'd like to achieve next, keep you on target. That seemed to work for you for the program you've just finished.

W: Yes, you're right. Well, the wedding is coming up soon, and that's going to keep me doing the exercise. I want to try and keep doing exercise three times a week. As for long term, well, I'd love to be more independent, get back to driving, and make it easier for me to get to the gym. That's the next big goal.

This story tells us that William's self-efficacy has increased and that he was now truly motivated to keep exercising. He had sought out other forms of MS information through the support group, and was even acting as a spokesperson for the benefits of exercise. He appeared to benefit from the social network the class offered, and it is good that he planned to continue to actively look for options to allow him and his exercise friends to try to maintain their exercise program permanently. Keeping a long-term goal in mind also provided William with motivation.

A few months later, I received a brief e-mail from William.

Dear Dr. Learmonth,
Thank you so much for helping me begin an exercise program. I don't know why I was inactive for so long. I guess I wasn't aware that it would help, or even where I could exercise. I still go to my art class, and in the spring my aim is to walk in

a wonderful park near where I live and set up a perfect view of one of the old houses.

Anna is now married! Last month we walked arm in arm down the aisle together. She let me pick the tune too, so it was my favorite, The Prince of Denmark's March. *I needed to use a cane, but I marched all the way. We had an amazing day, my whole family was there, and they all thought I looked great. I believed them too!*

I have other news as well! I've been able to buy myself a nice manual wheelchair and for the past few weeks I've been taking that to the art class with me. It's nice because I can fold it myself, and my daughter finds it easier to get it in and out of the car. I think that if I keep getting stronger I may be able to do it myself. If I can, it means I could perhaps try driving again.

My friends from the exercise class now go to our local gym twice a week with me, and we keep doing some of the exercises we learned with you and Rachel. They work well, and we try each day to do a little more. We've even put together a little money and have our own personal trainer for one of the days. He is good and is learning a lot from us too. Plus, I do an hour of similar exercises at home, so I keep up the three times a week. Hope you are well and still persuading people to take part!

Regards,
William

Receiving this e-mail was a terrific motivator for us. It showed us that William was now working independently on his exercises and was fitting them in alongside his normal routine. He was on target with his future goals, and there were many suggestions that his self-efficacy was now much higher.

Summary

The chapter begins by providing an overview of MS, the problem of inactivity in MS, the beneficial consequences of physical activity in MS, and ways to enhance positive behavior change toward exercise. William's tale exemplifies a simple story of a man aiming to improve his health in time for his daughter's wedding, and provides the perfect backdrop for highlighting potential improvements through exercise for those with MS. William was

typical of many people with MS. He was initially inactive, but by using components of a theory (i.e., SCT) to encourage behavior change, we helped him take part in a 6-month exercise program and accrue benefits in many areas. Our case study with William describes an effective and thorough program and provides evidence of the beneficial use of exercise for persons with MS. We do acknowledge that there are many different difficulties (not all highlighted in this case study) that people with MS need to overcome to benefit from physical activity.

There is still limited information about the long-term efficacy of physical activity and exercise interventions for individuals with MS. Nevertheless, our group has the long-term goal of enhancing participation in physical activity programs and documenting the potential restorative power of exercise in the physical, mental, and neurological functions of people with MS.

References

Bandura, A. (1997). *Self-efficacy: The exercise of control.* New York, NY: W.H. Freeman.

Bandura, A. (2004). Health promotion by social cognitive means. *Health Education and Behavior, 31,* 143–164.

Bjartmar, C., & Trapp, B.D. (2001). Axonal and neuronal degeneration in multiple sclerosis: Mechanisms and functional consequences. *Current Opinion in Neurology, 14,* 271–278.

Bombardier, C.H., Cunniffe, M., Wadhwani, R., Gibbons, L.E., Blake, K.D., & Kraft, G.H. (2008). The efficacy of telephone counseling for health promotion in people with multiple sclerosis: A randomized controlled trial. Archives of Physical Medicine and Rehabilitation, 89, 1849–1856.

Borg, G.A. (1982). Psychophysical bases of perceived exertion. *Medicine and Science in Sports and Exercise, 14,* 377–381.

Butland, R.J., Pang, J., Gross, E.R., Woodcock, A.A., & Geddes, D.M. (1982). Two-, six-, and 12-minute walking tests in respiratory disease. *British Medical Journal, 284,* 1607–1608.

Confavreux, C., Vukusic, S., & Adeleine, P. (2003). Early clinical predictors and progression of irreversible disability in multiple sclerosis: An amnesic process. *Brain, 126,* 770–782.

Cutter, G.R., Baier, M.L., Rudick, R.A., Cookfair, D.L., Fischer, J.S., Petkau, J., … Willoughby, E. (1999). Development of a multiple sclerosis functional composite as a clinical trial outcome measure. *Brain, 122,* 871–882.

Dalgas, U., Stenager, E., Jakobsen, J., Petersen, T., Hansen, H.J., Knudsen, C., . . . Ingemann-Hansen, T. (2009). Resistance training improves muscle strength and functional capacity in multiple sclerosis. *Neurology, 73,* 1478–1484.

Davis, S.L., Wilson, T.E., White, A.T., & Frohman, E.M. (2010). Thermoregulation in multiple sclerosis. *Journal of Applied Physiology, 109,* 1531–1537.

Dlugonski, D., Motl, R.W., Mohr, D.C., & Sandroff, B.M. (2012). Internet-delivered behavioral intervention to increase physical activity in persons with multiple sclerosis: Sustainability and secondary outcomes. *Psychology, Health, and Medicine, 17,* 363–651.

Ellis, T., & Motl, R.W. (2013). Physical activity behavior change in persons with neurologic disorders: Overview and examples from Parkinson's disease and multiple sclerosis. *Journal of Neurologic Physical Therapy, 37*(2), 85–90.

Filippini, G., Munari, L., Incorvaia, B., Ebers, G.C., Polman, C., D'Amico, R., & Rice, G.P.A. (2003). Interferons in relapsing remitting multiple sclerosis: A systematic review. *Lancet, 361,* 545–552.

Gasperini, C., & Ruggieri, S. (2012). Development of oral agent in the treatment of multiple sclerosis: How the first available oral therapy, fingolimod will change therapeutic paradigm approach. *Drug Design, Development and Therapy, 6,* 175–186.

Glanz, K., & Bishop, D.B. (2010). The role of behavioral science theory in development and implementation of public health interventions. *Annual Review of Public Health, 31,* 399–418.

Hallal, P.C., Andersen, L.B., Bull, F.C., Guthold, R., Haskell, W., & Ekelund, U. (2012). Global physical activity levels: Surveillance progress, pitfalls, and prospects. *The Lancet, 380,* 247–257.

Heesen, C., Romberg, A., Gold, S., & Schulz, K.H. (2006). Physical exercise in multiple sclerosis: Supportive care or a putative disease-modifying treatment. *Expert Reviews of Neurotherapeutics, 6,* 347–355.

Hemmer, B., Nessler, S., Zhou, D., Kieseier, B., & Hartung, H.-P. (2006). Immunopathogenesis and immunotherapy of multiple sclerosis. *Nature Clinical Practice Neurology, 2,* 201–211.

Klaren, R.E., Motl, R.W., Dlugonski, D., Sandroff, B.M., & Pilutti, L.A. (2013). Objectively quantified physical activity in persons with multiple sclerosis. *Archives of Physical Medicine and Rehabilitation, 94,* 2342–2348.

Krupp, L.B., LaRocca, N.G., Muir-Nash, J., & Steinberg, A.D. (1989). The Fatigue Severity Scale: Application to patients with multiple sclerosis and systemic lupus erythematosus. *Archives of Neurology, 46,* 1121–1123.

Learmonth, Y.C., Dlugonski, D., Pilutti, L.A., Sandroff, B.M., & Motl, R.W. (2013). The reliability, precision and clinically meaningful change of walking assessments in multiple sclerosis. *Multiple Sclerosis, 19,* 1784–1791.

Learmonth, Y.C., Marshall-McKenna, R., Paul, L., Mattison, P., & Miller, L. (2012). A qualitative exploration of the impact of a 12-week group exercise class for those moderately affected with multiple sclerosis. *Disability and Rehabilitation, 35,* 81–88.

Learmonth, Y.C., Paul, L., Miller, L., Mattison, P., & McFadyen, A.K. (2012). The effects of a 12-week leisure centre-based, group exercise intervention for people moderately affected with multiple sclerosis: A randomized controlled pilot study. Clinical Rehabilitation, 26(7), 579–593.

McAuley, E. (1993). Self-efficacy and the maintenance of exercise participation in older adults. *Journal of Behavioral Medicine, 16,* 103–113.

McAuley, E., & Blissmer, B. (2000). Self-efficacy determinants and consequences of physical activity. *Exercise and Sport Sciences Reviews, 28*(2), 85–88.

McAuley, E., Hall, K.S., Motl, R.W., White, S.M., Wójcicki, T.R., Hu, L., & Doerksen, S.E. (2009). Trajectory of declines in physical activity in community-dwelling older women: Social cognitive influences. *The Journals of Gerontology. Series B, Psychological Sciences and Social Sciences, 64,* 543–550.

McAuley, E., Motl, R.W., Morris, K.S., Hu, L., Doerksen, S.E., Elavsky, S., & Konopack, J.F. (2007). Enhancing physical activity adherence and well-being in multiple sclerosis: A randomised controlled trial. *Multiple Sclerosis, 13,* 652–659.

Motl, R.W., Dlugonski, D., Wójcicki, T.R., McAuley, E., & Mohr, D.C. (2011). Internet intervention for increasing physical activity in persons with multiple sclerosis. *Multiple Sclerosis, 17,* 116–128.

Motl, R.W., & Fernhall, B. (2012). Accurate prediction of cardiorespiratory fitness using cycle ergometry in minimally disabled persons with relapsing-remitting multiple sclerosis. *Archives of Physical Medicine and Rehabilitation, 93,* 490–495.

Motl, R.W., & Gosney, J.L. (2008). Effect of exercise training on quality of life in multiple sclerosis: A meta-analysis. *Multiple Sclerosis, 14,* 129–135.

Motl, R.W., McAuley, E., & Snook, E.M. (2005). Physical activity and multiple sclerosis: A meta-analysis. *Multiple Sclerosis, 11,* 459–463.

Motl, R.W., & Pilutti, L.A. (2012). The benefits of exercise training in multiple sclerosis. *Nature reviews. Neurology, 8,* 487–497.

Motl, R.W., Pilutti, L.A., Sandroff, B.M., Klaren, R., Balantrapu, S., McAuley, E., … Fernhall, B. (2013). Rationale and design of a randomized controlled, clinical trial investigating a comprehensive exercise stimulus for improving mobility disability outcomes in persons with multiple sclerosis. *Contemporary Clinical Trials, 35,* 151–158.

Motl, R.W., Smith, D.C., Elliott, J., Weikert, M., Dlugonski, D., & Sosnoff, J.J. (2012). Combined training improves walking mobility in persons with significant disability from multiple sclerosis: A pilot study. Journal of Neurologic Physical Therapy, 36, 32–37.

Multiple Sclerosis International Federation. (2013). *Atlas of MS 2013.* London, England: Author.

Pilutti, L.A., Greenlee, T.A., Motl, R.W., Nickrent, M., & Petruzzello, S.J. (2013). Effects of exercise training on fatigue in multiple sclerosis: A meta-analysis. *Psychosomatic Medicine, 75,* 575–580.

Petajan, J.H., Gappmaier, E., White, A.T., Spencer, M.K., Mino, L., & Hicks, R.W. (1996). Impact of aerobic training on fitness and quality of life in multiple sclerosis. *Annals of Neurology, 39,* 432–441.

Romberg, A., Virtanen, A., Ruutiainen, J., Aunola, S., Karppi, S.L., Vaara, M., … Seppanen, A. (2004). Effects of a 6-month exercise program on patients with multiple sclerosis: A randomized study. *Neurology, 63,* 2034–2038.

Samkoff, L.M., & Goodman, A.D. (2011). Symptomatic management in multiple sclerosis. *Neurologic Clinics, 29,* 449–463.

Sandroff, B.M., Dlugonski, D., Weikert, M., Suh, Y., Balantrapu, S., & Motl, R.W. (2012). Physical activity and multiple sclerosis: New insights regarding inactivity. *Acta Neurologica Scandinavica, 126,* 256–262.

Snook, E.M., & Motl, R.W. (2009). Effect of exercise training on walking mobility in multiple sclerosis: A meta-analysis. *Neurorehabilitation and Neural Repair, 23,* 108–116.

Suh, Y., Weikert, M., Dlugonski, D., Balantrapu, S., & Motl, R.W. (2011). Social cognitive variables as correlates of physical activity in persons with multiple sclerosis: Findings from a longitudinal, observational study. *Behavioral Medicine, 37*(3), 87–94.

Suh, Y., Weikert, M., Dlugonski, D., Sandroff, B., & Motl, R.W. (2011). Social cognitive correlates of physical activity: Findings from a cross-sectional study of adults with relapsing-remitting multiple sclerosis. *Journal of Physical Activity & Health, 8*(5), 626–635.

Sutherland, G., & Andersen, M.B. (2001). Exercise and multiple sclerosis: Physiological, psychological, and quality of life issues. *The Journal of Sports Medicine and Physical Fitness, 41,* 421–432.

Sutherland, G., Andersen, M.B., & Stoové, M.A. (2001). Can aerobic exercise training affect health-related quality of life for people living with multiple sclerosis? *Journal of Sport & Exercise Psychology, 23,* 122–135.

Sweet, S.N., Perrier, M.-J., Podzyhun, C., & Latimer-Cheung, A.E. (2013). Identifying physical activity information needs and preferred methods of delivery of people with multiple sclerosis. *Disability and Rehabilitation, 35,* 2056–2063.

Trapp, B.D., & Nave, K.-A. (2008). Multiple sclerosis: An immune or neurodegenerative disorder? *Annual Review of Neuroscience, 31,* 247–269.

Van den Berg, M., Dawes, H., Wade, D.T., Newman, M., Burridge, J., Izadi, H., & Sackley, C.M. (2006). Treadmill training for individuals with multiple sclerosis: A pilot randomised trial. *Journal of Neurology, Neurosurgery, and Psychiatry, 77,* 531–533.

Vickrey, B.G., Shatin, D., Wolf, S.M., Myers, L.W., Belin, T.R., Hanson, R.A., … Delrahim, S. (2000). Management of multiple sclerosis across managed care and fee-for-service systems. *Neurology, 55,* 1341–1349.

Vickrey, B.G., Hays, R.D., Harooni, R., Myers, L.W., & Ellison, G.W. (1995). A health-related quality of life measure for multiple sclerosis. *Quality of Life Research, 4,* 187–206.

CHAPTER 10

Moving for Your Heart's Sake

Physical Activity and Exercise for People With Cardiac Disease

Michelle Rogerson and Mark B. Andersen

In this chapter, we examine physical activity, exercise, and cardiovascular disease (CVD) within an Australian context. In the first part of the chapter, we discuss the main factors that are associated with adherence to cardiac rehabilitation (CR) and physical activity (PA) for cardiac populations, and mention the various interventions conducted that aim to increase adherence to PA. In the second part of the chapter, we reconstruct conversations we have had from working in the rehabilitation field.

CVDs can be considered Australia's most costly diseases. They cost more lives than any other disease, accounting for 34% of all deaths, and have the highest level of health expenditure in Australia (Australian Institute of Health and Welfare [AIHW], 2011). Similar statistics are reported in other countries, such as the United States (Roger et al., 2011) and members of the European Union (Petersen et al., 2005). CVDs also result in a burden of disease, in terms of disability and premature death, second only to cancer (AIHW, 2011). Coronary heart disease (CHD), also known as ischemic heart disease or coronary artery disease, is the most common type of CVD. The two major clinical forms of CHD are angina and heart attack (AIHW, 2011).

Recovery from an acute cardiac event, such as a myocardial infarction, or coronary artery bypass graft (CABG) surgery is a long-term process. For optimal recovery, people need to make lifelong changes to PA, diet, and medication adherence. PA is helpful because it contributes to lowering physiological risk factors (Taylor et al., 2004), reducing

premature all-cause and cardiac-related mortality (Moholdt, Wisloff, Nilsen, & Slordahl, 2008) and morbidity (Blumenthal et al., 2004), as well as improving quality of life and psychological well-being (Blumenthal et al., 2005). Although the benefits of PA are widely accepted, many people with CVD do not engage in levels of PA sufficient for reaping its positive effects (Zhao, Ford, Li, & Mokdad, 2008). The reasons why people do or do not engage in PA are numerous and often complex; we address several of these issues in this chapter.

Cardiac Rehabilitation and Physical Activity

The World Health Organization, the National Heart Foundation of Australia (NHFA; Goble & Worcester, 1999), and the American Heart Association (Balady et al., 2000) recognize cardiac rehabilitation (CR) as being integral to, and necessary for, the comprehensive care of patients with CVD. CR programs should consist of multidisciplinary, professional teams to educate and advise clients during their recoveries, so they can resume full and active lives following cardiac events. Issues such as necessary treatments and life changes that may help reduce cardiovascular risk factors need to be considered to help prevent future cardiac episodes (Balady et al., 2000).

There are three recognized phases of CR: inpatient rehabilitation (phase 1), ambulatory outpatient rehabilitation (phase 2), and maintenance (phase 3; Goble & Worcester, 1999). Inpatient CR takes place in the hospital as soon as possible after the cardiac event. Ambulatory outpatient rehabilitation usually begins soon after discharge from the hospital; in Australia, it commonly continues for six to eight weeks (Goble & Worcester, 1999). This phase of rehabilitation is typically formal and structured, and it consists of a light to moderate PA program, as well as education, discussion, counseling, and behavioral interventions addressing topics such as basic anatomy and physiology of the heart, risk factors for heart disease and how to modify them for secondary prevention, skills for behavior change and maintenance, psychosocial issues, medications, and resumption of physical, sexual, and daily living activities. Maintenance CR is a lifelong, usually open-ended, stage that follows ambulatory rehabilitation. It involves sustained activities and behaviors for reducing cardiovascular risk factors and maintaining healthy and active living (Goble & Worcester, 1999).

In recently outlined recommendations, the NHFA (Briffa et al., 2006) stated "that people with established clinically stable cardiovascular disease should aim, over time, to achieve 30 minutes or more of moderate intensity physical activity on most, if not all, days of the week" (p. 71). This report also encourages regular low- to moderate-level resistance training under the supervision of an exercise professional. For people with advanced CVD, less intense and shorter bouts of activity than for clients with moderate CVD, as well as with more rest periods, may suffice. The American Heart Association and the European Society of Cardiology recommend similar levels to the Australian guidelines of moderate-intensity aerobic exercise for people who have experienced a cardiac event.

Evidence supporting the positive effects of CR and PA on the prevention and treatment of cardiac disease is compelling (Lawler, Filion, & Eisenberg, 2011). Despite the evidence, approximately half of all Australian adults, including those with CHD, do not engage in sufficient PA for health gain (AIHW, 2006). Similar rates of inactivity have been reported in the United States. Zhao et al. (2008) found that 60% of people with CHD and 51% of people without CHD were not meeting PA guidelines. Likewise, despite its well-

documented benefits, CR is vastly underused. Within Australia, 70% to 80% of potentially eligible clients do not attend CR programs (Scott, Lindsay, & Harden, 2003). Before developing strategies and interventions to promote exercise in people with CHD, researchers have suggested identifying and understanding the key factors that influence exercise adherence (and nonadherence) in cardiac populations.

Factors Influencing Adherence to Physical Activity and CR

Over the past two decades, researchers have investigated the factors associated with adherence to CR and PA in cardiac populations in a number of quantitative and qualitative studies. Intra- and interpersonal variables, in addition to environmental and organizational factors, have been identified as influencing whether people are likely to adhere to CR programs and PA. Some of the factors that might influence initiating and adhering to exercise and PA in cardiac populations include low social support, sex (female), low self-efficacy, unemployment, low previous PA levels, limited knowledge of benefits of exercise, low intention to exercise, poor overall health status, comorbidities, pain, low perception of severity of illness, smoking, limited knowledge of consequences of illness, presence of perceived barriers, high BMI, depression, perceived lack of time, limited interest or motivation, inclement weather, fear of engaging in exercise, and limited finances. For a review of the research on many of these factors, see Taylor, Wilson, and Sharp (2011). After first exploring the effects of depression, which is common in people with CHD, we discuss and provide supporting literature for the main factors that are consistently shown to be associated with adherence to CR and PA in cardiac populations.

Depression

Depression is common among people with CHD. Prevalence rates of major depression are between 17% and 27% in the months soon after an acute event, and many more people experience subclinical depressive symptoms (Rudisch & Nemeroff, 2003). For some people, depressive symptoms are still evident up to 12 months after a cardiac event (Grace et al., 2005). As well as being a risk factor for the development of CHD, depression is associated with poor outcomes following a cardiac event, including increased cardiac-related mortality and morbidity (van Melle et al., 2004). PA has been shown to reduce depression in people with CHD (Scholz, Knoll, Sniehotta, & Schwarzer, 2006), and it is as effective as antidepressant medication for managing mild to moderate depression (Blumenthal et al., 1999). Nevertheless, as previously discussed, many people with CHD do not engage in levels of PA sufficient for gaining its positive effects (Zhao et al., 2008). In addition, depression can exacerbate nonadherence to PA for both clinical (Seime & Vickers, 2006) and cardiac (Taylor et al., 2011) populations.

A small number of studies have examined why people with depression are typically more likely to experience problems with adhering to PA than people without depression. Seime and Vickers (2006) proposed that people with depression often focus primarily on the barriers to exercise, which makes them feel overwhelmed and decreases their sense of self-efficacy. Consequently, depressed individuals are likely to relapse or give up after attempts at exercise. Faulkner and Biddle (2004) provided a rare insight into the experiences of three individuals with clinical depression regarding their PA habits over a period of one year. The three individuals in their study reported barriers to PA that are common to people without mental health problems, such as limited time, boredom, and social anxiety, but the symptom of lethargy acted as a barrier for all three participants at some point during the study. Faulkner and Biddle also identified that although the prominent initial motives for staying involved in the exercise programs were centered on distraction techniques and providing structure to the day, after some time the motives became individualized for each participant (e.g., social interaction, health concerns, improving body image).

Some researchers and clinicians have highlighted important factors to consider and techniques that may be implemented when encouraging exercise adherence with depressed people. From a psychotherapist's perspective, Pollock (2001) highlighted the importance of the relationship between the professional and the person with depression. He argued that developing an exercise initiation and maintenance plan, which should be based on an analysis and assessment of the relevant barriers and facilitators to exercise for the individual, is essential. Pollock also suggested to professionals working with people with depression that the individual with depression should drive the assessment and that the professionals should eventually address the client's barriers and facilitators. This approach should ensure the exercise plan is unique to the individual, thereby increasing the chances of adherence to the exercise.

Similar to the suggestions of Pollock (2001), Seime and Vickers (2006) recommended that interventions to increase adherence to PA among depressed people should be individualized, rather than taking an exercise prescription approach of one-size-fits-all. Seime and Vickers also stressed the importance of addressing many aspects of PA with depressed individuals, such as the benefits of PA that are particularly salient to them, the types of PA they enjoy, the pros and cons of increasing PA, the perceived barriers to PA, the importance of social support, and tactics they believe will help overcome these barriers.

Self-Efficacy

One of the frequently investigated PA correlates in people with CVD is self-efficacy. Self-efficacy is defined as a person's perceived ability to master specific tasks and demands successfully (Bandura, 1997). Self-efficacy stems from social cognitive theory, which suggests that social, cognitive, and behavioral factors play an important role in whether an individual chooses to adhere to or avoid exercise. A distinction has been made between two types of self-efficacy: task self-efficacy (ability to perform a given task) and self-regulatory (or barrier) self-efficacy (ability to overcome barriers to successful performance; Bandura, 1997). The hypothesis is that people who have increased task self-efficacy or have increased barrier or self-regulatory self-efficacy will engage in higher levels of PA (Woodgate & Brawley, 2008). Studies have provided support for this hypothesis in cardiac populations by demonstrating a relationship between levels of self-efficacy and adherence to CR and PA (e.g., Maddison & Prapavessis, 2004). Self-efficacy has also been shown to change over the course of an exercise CR program. Maddison and Prapavessis reported an increase in both task and barrier self-efficacy during the early stages of a CR program, followed by a significant decline at the end of the program.

Given the consistent findings for self-efficacy being one of the strongest predictors of exercise adherence, the focus of future research and practice for exercise professionals should be on developing interventions to increase self-efficacy. One key aspect numerous researchers have highlighted is the need to distinguish between the various types of self-efficacy. Intervention strategies may need to be tailored to the specific setting of PA or CR (e.g., center-, community-, or home-based exercise) to modify both task and barrier self-efficacy. Determining when and how interventions could most effectively target each form of self-efficacy would prove interesting and valuable research. Interventions should also be theory driven, and they should help practitioners explore the association between self-efficacy and exercise adherence as a primary, rather than secondary, study outcome (Woodgate & Brawley, 2008). To increase the effectiveness of interventions designed to increase self-efficacy, researchers should also incorporate components to assist individuals in addressing and overcoming barriers to PA (Martin & Woods, 2012).

Social Support

Social support can be provided in a number of different ways, such as instrumental support (e.g., assisting with a problem), tangible support (e.g., supplying goods), informational support (e.g., giving advice), and emotional support (e.g., giving reassurance). For further discussion of these types of social support, see Lett et al. (2007) and Lett et al. (2005). Cardiac clients have reported receiving social support from family, friends, and health professionals, such as CR staff, cardiologists, and general practitioners. This support commonly comes in the form of verbal encouragement or instrumental activities (e.g., physically participating in the exercise program with the individual; Rogerson, Murphy, Bird, & Morris, 2012). For people with cardiac disease, there is mounting evidence that social support facilitates adherence to PA programs (e.g., Rogerson et al., 2012). In terms of support provided by health professionals, a

number of studies have highlighted the importance of client-centered care for positive health outcomes (e.g., Mead & Bower, 2002). Having a relationship between patient and health professional based on creating a strong therapeutic alliance, incorporating collaborative goal setting, engaging in effective communication, and taking a biopsychosocial perspective on illness are all critical components of patient-centered care (Mead & Bower, 2002). Given that physician recommendations for PA and CR have been identified as important predictors of patient participation in rehabilitation (Jackson, Leclerc, Erskine, & Linden, 2005), it is likely that relationships between patients and health professionals that are based on the components of client-centered care will result in higher levels of PA participation than those that are not.

Likewise, emotional and instrumental social support from spouses, family members, friends, and other participants in an exercise class have been identified as important in encouraging adherence in PA and CR (Moore, Dolansky, Ruland, Pashkow, & Blackburn, 2003). These findings are coming through particularly strongly in qualitative studies (e.g., Rogerson et al., 2012), in which participants have described the major predictors of PA adherence. People with cardiac disease have also highlighted the importance of having *peer-mentors* within a CR program to encourage increased social support and adherence to PA (Rogerson et al., 2012). This type of intervention is certainly one that warrants further investigation.

Perceptions and Knowledge

For people with CHD, perceptions of, and knowledge about, physical health, PA, and heart disease itself can affect adherence to PA and CR programs. An individual's perceived health status can be a major determinant of exercise adherence (Fleury, Lee, Matteson, & Belyea, 2004; Moore et al., 2003). In their qualitative study with post-CR participants, Fleury et al. found that the most common barrier to PA maintenance was physical condition. The participants identified physical limitations, including the perceived patterns and intensity of cardiac symptoms, in addition to symptoms of other comorbid conditions, as being the main barrier to maintaining PA. Moore et al. (2003) demonstrated similar results for women who had recently completed a CR program, showing comorbidity to be a significant predictor of exercise frequency and exercise intensity. The presence of a comorbid condition, such as diabetes, can limit mobility and may lead to pain during exercise, resulting in diminished desire to continue exercise behavior. In terms of increasing adherence to PA and CR, programs need to be tailored according to individuals' health status and comorbid conditions to ensure they can engage in the most helpful types of exercise without exacerbating symptoms.

Having positive beliefs and knowledge that exercise is beneficial to the individual are important predictors of increased exercise levels (Thow, Rafferty, & Kelly, 2008). Qualitative research with long-term, post-CR exercise adherers has demonstrated that people who have been successful in maintaining PA over the long term understand how PA can assist in controlling their health and, in particular, how it can help their heart conditions (Thow et al., 2008). Believing in the benefits of PA, however, may take some time, and people may need to first experience the benefits of engaging in PA for a period of time before it plays a motivating role in exercise adherence. Researchers have also found that having a good understanding of the consequences of heart disease and accepting the severity of the disease (Taylor et al., 2011; Thow et al., 2008) are associated with good adherence to PA. Conversely, those individuals who denied the severity of their illnesses were less likely to participate in long-term exercise programs than those who accepted the gravity of their conditions.

Interventions to Increase Adherence to Physical Activity

There have been some major advances in the PA intervention literature for cardiac populations, particularly over the past decade. There have been a number of randomized controlled trials investigating various interventions that enhance adherence to PA for people with CHD. The results of these studies have begun to provide interesting and important findings about programs and strategies that may be effective in helping people with CHD maintain regular exercise. This section of the chapter outlines one major review paper (i.e.,

Ferrier, Blanchard, Vallis, & Giacomantonio, 2011) on behavioral interventions to increase PA of cardiac clients, and discusses some of the specific interventions.

Given the low PA adherence rates of people with and without CHD, it appears that structured exercise programs, even if adhered to, are not often sufficient for maintaining adequate levels of exercise (Marcus et al., 2006). Many researchers have highlighted the importance of incorporating behavior modification techniques into interventions to increase the likelihood of adherence. In a recent review, Ferrier et al. (2011) examined behavior change techniques (BCT) that have been used in PA interventions to increase PA for people with CHD and heart failure. They found the most effective BCT used in interventions with people who were currently engaged in, or had recently concluded, CR programs were self-monitoring (including keeping a PA diary or wearing a pedometer), setting specific goals, identifying barriers, and developing plans for relapse prevention. For those people who had not participated in CR, unsupervised home-based interventions were effective at increasing PA adherence, particularly when techniques such as follow-up prompts, general encouragement, specific goals, and self-monitoring were used. Ferrier et al. (2011) suggested that BCTs led by the client or collaborative approaches with the researcher or health care professional are more effective at improving and maintaining PA adherence than a directive approach. These findings are consistent with Dishman and Buckworth's (1996) PA intervention review with healthy populations. Ferrier et al. (2011) concluded that interventions can result in improved PA outcomes, but the research in this area is still relatively limited. They suggested that researchers conduct interventions that target PA only, as compared to those attempting to address multiple health behaviors and to focus on people who have not attended CR programs.

Two interventions that have used BCTs, including specific goal setting, barrier identification, and relapse prevention, and have focused on developing cardiac clients' self-regulatory skills, are Sniehotta et al. (2005) and Scholz et al. (2006). Sniehotta et al. randomly assigned 240 participants to one of two psychological interventions ("planning only" or "planning plus diary" interventions) with a standard care control group. All participants were taking part in the standard care CR program at the time of recruitment. Both of the intervention groups participated in individual planning sessions toward the end of their CR program, which included both action planning (i.e., outlining when, where, and how they planned to be physically active) and coping planning (i.e., identifying potential barriers to their plans and solutions to overcome these barriers). One of the intervention groups (planning plus diary) also received, by mail, six weekly diaries after discharge from the CR program, which they were requested to complete and return to the researchers. Each diary included the individual plans of the participants, along with questions regarding their PA over the week and their confidence in adhering to their plans over the next week. The control group continued with standard cardiac care. Participants also completed a series of questionnaires at baseline, and 2 and 4 months later.

Sniehotta et al. (2005) found that participants in the intervention groups engaged in more PA at follow-up and had better adherence to recommended levels of exercise intensity than standard care patients. In addition, self-regulatory skills, including planning and action control, were significantly higher in the two treatment groups, compared to the control group. Particular improvements were noticed in action control in the participants from the planning-plus-diary condition. Participants in this condition had high behavioral intentions to exercise throughout the course of the study, and these intentions remained strong even at the 4-month point, at which time intentions of participants from the planning-only and control conditions decreased markedly. Sniehotta et al. concluded that interventions designed to improve self-regulatory skills can facilitate intended behavioral changes, such as PA, in people with cardiac disease.

Scholz et al. (2006) further developed their previous study (Sniehotta et al., 2005) by measuring the effects of a self-management intervention on depressive symptoms, in addition to PA adherence, and including a longer follow-up period. Scholz et al. randomly assigned 198 CR participants into either an intervention condition or a usual care control condition. The intervention was the same as the planning-plus-diary intervention Sniehotta et al. (2005) used. Therefore, both action planning and coping planning strategies were implemented, and diaries were completed by these participants. Participants in both the intervention and control condition completed a package of questionnaires, including the Center for Epidemiological Studies Depression Scale to measure depression, and a measure of goal attainment, at baseline, and 4 and 12 months later.

Scholz et al. (2006) found that participation in the intervention led to a significant increase in PA at both follow-up time points, and a decrease in depressive symptoms after 12 months. Surprisingly, they also found that perceived attainment of exercise goals, and not PA itself, was the mediator between the intervention and reduction of depression. Despite these unexpected results, Scholz et al. (2006) demonstrated that achieving personal goals during health behavior change may be of particular importance for lowering depressive symptoms.

Testing the effectiveness of a behavior modification program for increasing adherence to exercise in the year following CR, Moore et al. (2006) randomly assigned 250 participants to either an intervention group, termed CHANGE (Change Habits by Applying New Goals and Experiences), or the usual care-only group intervention. The CHANGE intervention, which also included usual care, consisted of five small-group cognitive behavioral change counseling sessions. Three were delivered over the final few weeks of the CR program, and the final two were done over the first 2 weeks after CR had concluded. The sessions addressed issues surrounding exercise maintenance, such as self-efficacy enhancement, problem solving, relapse prevention, peer modeling, goal setting, and self-assessment. Exercise frequency, intensity, and duration were measured via a portable wristwatch heart rate monitor, in addition to exercise maintenance, which consisted of the number of months in which participants continued exercising after the conclusion of the CR program. The results indicated that participants in the usual care group were 76% more likely than those in the CHANGE intervention to stop exercising in the year after CR. They also demonstrated, however, that all participants exercised less than recommended. Moore et al. (2006) concluded that the CHANGE intervention had been effective in reducing the likelihood of participants stopping exercise in the year after completing a CR program, but the intervention needed some improvements to ensure maintenance of exercise did not decrease over time.

In an attempt to determine the effectiveness of an intervention for people who did not participate in CR, Furber, Butler, Phongsavan, Mark, and Bauman (2010) randomly assigned 215 participants who could not, or chose not to, attend CR to either a 6-week intervention or a control condition. The intervention was based on social cognitive theory (Bandura, 1997), and it included self-monitoring of PA using pedometers, step calendars, telephone behavioral counseling, and goal setting. Follow-up support was provided that included feedback on goal achievement and general encouragement. The control condition participants were sent two PA information brochures by mail, and they completed the same questionnaires as the people in the intervention condition. Data on PA, psychosocial factors affecting PA, and demographic information were collected at baseline, 6 weeks, and 6 months. The results indicated that total PA and walking time and the number of total PA and walking sessions were significantly greater in the intervention compared to control condition at both 6 weeks and 6 months. Furber et al. also demonstrated that participants within the intervention condition had enhanced self-efficacy at 6 weeks and 6 months. The positive outcomes of this study demonstrate the potential for conducting low-intensity, low-cost, and community-based interventions for increasing PA among people with CHD who do not attend CR programs. An intervention of this type could provide major health benefits for this population, who are typically a hard-to-reach subsample of cardiac patients. In general, it seems that behavior modification programs, especially with contact between exercise professionals and clients in interpersonal collaboration, along with goal setting and planning strategies are some of the most effective ways to help people with CHDs increase their PA.

Despite these recent advances in knowledge, there are still few psychological interventions that have been conducted with people with CHD, and many strategies and techniques (discussed previously) that may be effective in increasing adherence to PA have received limited research attention. The scope for further research into the effectiveness of PA adherence interventions for this population is extensive.

Conversations From the Field

The variety of individuals, situations, and medical and psychological sequelae of having (and living with) CHD are legion, and instead of presenting a single case study, we have chosen to reconstruct pieces of conversations we have had from working in the rehabilitation field. This chapter may be more impressionistic than others in this book, but we have tried to cover a large amount of presenting issues that exercise professionals may encounter when they work with people with CHD. In each of the following sections, we present a central concern and what people have said regarding their health and exercise.

Negative Perceptions of Life Changes Resulting from Heart Disease

Within the CHD and exercise research, some of the most commonly expressed barriers to being physically active have been associated with individuals' negative perceptions of health and other life changes as consequences of their heart disease. Coming to terms with getting older, having a sense of losing their relationships with good health, and dealing with the shock of developing a heart problem may act as reality checks and intimate encounters with their own mortality. In particular, recognizing and acknowledging the need to slow down, experiencing the frustration associated with an increase in health-related problems, and no longer feeling invincible and confident in their health are common issues associated with an inability to be active. The following quotes summarize these feelings: "After you have a heart attack, you start to look at your various bodily functions and say 'well, you know I'm starting on the downward slide.'" "As you get older, you know you slow down or you know little things happen to you, but probably it was a bit of a shock to me when I had this heart attack. I really thought I was bullet-proof." "I resist this aging thing. I'm not very good at it. I keep thinking that I'm 25. Me? Grandchildren?"

Exercise professionals may wish to examine the literature on the life changes associated with disabling brushes with death along with works on existential psychology (e.g., death anxiety, identity crises) such as Yalom (2009). Another major life change that affects many people with CHD, in particular, is forced retirement. Retirement may not occur as anticipated; that is, when one is fit and healthy and when leaving work comes about in a planned manner. In addition to causing emotional difficulties, leaving work may also add financial strain. A client in CR commented, "That's the biggest thing [not working] . . . if you know you're going to retire, you can build up to it." Another said, "I was probably looking forward to sort of retiring fit and healthy." These perceived changes in one's life can have negative effects on physical activity levels.

Depression or Low Mood

Some clients spoke about the causes of depression, which included an inability to work and be physically active, financial concerns, loneliness, and trouble sleeping. One client described a number of these issues: "Emotionally it can get pretty hard. It's frustrating not being able to do much. Money-wise it's hard too because it's putting a hell of a strain on the wife. And loneliness is a very big thing."

The effects of depression and low moods may include feeling teary and emotional, having low motivation and energy, feeling useless, having permanent or temporary decreases in PA, and increasing sedentary behaviors. One client claimed that depression and low mood are what stopped him from being active, saying, "It's not the physical side that stopped me from getting up and walking around the block, it's more the mental side of things." Although depression seems to be an overarching theme, it is also connected to many other variables such as physical restrictions, low motivation, negative perceptions of life changes, and limited social support. Many people are aware of the problems associated with depression, but are unable to overcome this barrier to being physically active.

Low Motivation

Limited interest in or desire to exercise is a common barrier. Some clients acknowledge laziness or boredom with exercise as the problem, but others, although aware of the benefits, could see no obvious reason or necessity to be physically active. One person, who was waiting for a bypass operation, described his lack of motivation as, "I have no incentive at the moment to get fit, really nothing." Another could not perceive any benefit from exercise, and had no real desire to improve his health. He explained: "I don't really feel rejuvenated or anything after the walk, so my mind says, 'What benefit can I get out of it . . . who cares if I drop dead tomorrow?'"

Perceived and Actual Physical Restrictions

People often develop other physical problems after their heart events, and these restrictions can become frustrating barriers stopping them from being physically active. One client commented: "It's been this vicious circle that I was in, that, while doing exercise, I suffered plantar fasciitis, and it was painful. It was more painful than a heart attack." For some people, it seems there is a belief that exercise needs to be at a higher intensity than they thought they could manage to be considered beneficial, as demonstrated by the following comment: "The walking kills me because of the leg. I can walk very slowly for a fair distance, but that's not much good. You've got to put a bit of effort into it, and by putting an effort in, you just can't go as far." Medications may also affect perceived ability to be physically active. One client, who felt severely restricted by her heart medication, explained, "When I was warfarin-free, it was wonderful and it was exciting to feel the aerobic response of my heart, but I don't feel that when I'm on warfarin."

Negative Perceptions and Uncertainties of Exercise

Various negative perceptions of exercise may stop people with CHD from engaging in regular PA. Fears of causing more damage to the heart, damaging other body parts, or running out of energy are real concerns, and these fears often result in people being cautious or hesitant to engage in exercise, as illustrated in the following quote: "I was really frightened [when walking] because you don't have the same stamina . . . you don't have the same reserves and resources within your body. Your energies are all totally depleted after heart surgery."

For others, uncertainty about the benefits of exercise, and the correct type and amount required for people with heart disease acted as a barrier. "I just don't really know how much I can do now, especially when I get a bit out of breath. But I am not sure if I get anything much from my walks if I don't get out of breath."

Perceived External Obstacles

External obstacles, or factors perceived to be outside one's control, may also be barriers to PA. A concern for some is that the exercise they enjoyed was too expensive (e.g., playing golf or using a gym regularly). Due to the extra financial strain often placed on families because of forced retirement or increased medical costs, people sometimes remove nonessentials from their budgets, often resulting in decreases in physical and social activities. One client knew that he would enjoy, and would be physically able, to exercise in a gym, but he was restricted financially, as he explained: "I can't afford the petrol to get to the gym. That's one of the other biggest killers since I stopped working. To go to a gym and do weights and things like that—that all costs money."

Effects of Past Sedentary Behavior

Effects of past sedentary behavior and falling back into habits of inactivity may contribute to current low activity levels. One female client noted, "As time goes on, you slip back to the old way, you know. But I've always been like that," and "I haven't really been a great exercise person. Where some people will go to the gym and that sort of thing, I've never been that sort of person."

Physical Limitations: My Body Can't Do It

Another barrier to being active is physical limitations. Having an injury that restricts PA, particularly walking, may cause frustration and disruption to exercise. In numerous studies, physical limitations have been found to affect PA levels in both cardiac and noncardiac populations (e.g., East, Brown, & Thwells, 2004; Fleury et al., 2004). Due

to the low mood and frustration that physical limitations impose, it appears evident that exercise professionals should identify and address (e.g., prescribing PA that doesn't aggravate existing physical conditions) not only physical restrictions of the heart, but also other physical injuries or complaints that are likely to affect PA levels.

Facilitators of Physical Activity

Facilitators of PA refer to the common factors that encourage participation in PA. Such factors include having a reason for exercising, experiencing the psychological and physical benefits of exercise, having positive influences from others, enjoying exercise, and using psychological strategies.

Others as Reasons for Exercising

We know it sounds obvious, but exercise professionals might wish to explore in-depth (e.g., beyond "my doctor said I should") the reasons clients have for engaging in and maintaining exercise. In working with people in CR, one theme that emerges often (and is accompanied by strong emotions) is doing the exercise for someone other than themselves. Clients have spoken about having someone worth fighting for and owing it to someone else to take part in the necessary exercise and improve their health. One client said, "I owe it to my partner. That is important. You've got to get better for your partner." This desire to exercise for others is often coupled with the need to consider health as the number one priority in their lives, the importance of keeping positive and moving forward, a desire to do the exercise, or a desire to keep living. The following quote demonstrates how this coupling helped motivate some participants to be more active: "I'm not ready to go lie down and die. I want to watch these boys grow and so forth and watch them play footy and things like that, and enjoy them growing up, my grandsons."

The Positive Influences of Others

Many people in CR mention the importance of partners, family, and close friends in maintaining PA. They are highly motivated by support from significant others, either through receiving encouragement to be active or having an exercise companion. The following comments highlight this important facilitator: "What's helped is also the buddying system. My wife tends to come out two or three times per week, so she's been very supportive that way." Support from CR staff is also important for many clients. The ability of the staff to increase confidence, provide guidance and encouragement, and monitor participants' health and progress during CR programs seem to be central factors in the maintenance of PA. These ideas are reflected in the following quote:

> The time I spent at the [cardiac] rehab was fabulous because we had the people there who were checking how we were feeling and our levels, and checking us as we went through the hour of exercise. They were very professional. I was always given encouragement to keep going, and I could have a chat to the girls at rehab if I needed to. They were really lovely people.

For some people who do not have strong family or friend support, exercise may provide them with chances to interact socially with other people: "You get to see other people, and you're not by yourself all the time." Some clients have mentioned how important it is to have positive role models for exercise. If they could see that someone else with similar characteristics, and in a similar situation to themselves, had been successful at maintaining PA and achieving good health, they were much more likely to follow their exercise programs: "I met this guy at rehab who had not exercised much in the past, but had started, little by little, and now exercises every day and says how great it is. I thought, 'If he can do it, surely I can, too.'"

Experiencing the Psychological and Physical Benefits of Exercise

Exercise professionals often notice that once exercise programs begin, clients start experiencing the psychological and, to a lesser extent, the physical benefits of exercise. They also note how these changes aid in maintaining PA. Some clients commonly continued to exercise because psychologically it made them feel better by relaxing

them, by taking their minds off problems such as pain or stresses, or by helping them feel good because they had achieved something important by exercising.

> The exercise to me is a vital thing . . . once I'm doing that [exercise], my mental attitude changes and [I] feel much better for it. . . . There's no doubt in the wide world that the exercise after the operation is essential, both for your body and your mind.

Another exerciser spoke about how the exercise helped with his mental state. He said, "It makes you feel good within yourself and gives you a mental uplift, too, when you're doing physical things. Walking relaxes you, and it also gives you time to think. You get right away from the environment you're in, and you can run things through your head." Physical benefits, such as feeling the heart and body working well, achieving a healthy weight, and knowing they are doing something positive for their bodies may act as motivators to keeping some people physically active.

Using Psychological Strategies

Psychological strategies, such as goal setting, practicing positive self-talk, eliminating excuses, and prioritizing exercise by writing it in a diary, may act as facilitators for PA. Here are some quotes about goal setting and self-talk: "My view is that it's important to always have goals in front of you," "Having goals which are meaningful to you and the family are worthwhile . . . goal setting is important because it gives you a target," and "[I say,] 'come on, you can do this; you've only got one more to go. If you can get over there, you'll be right.'"

For some people, eliminating the excuses that encourage inactivity may be helpful in ensuring they participate in adequate levels of physical activity. One client who knew what effect making excuses would have on his PA program said, "Get rid of the excuses. I very quickly tore down those avenues that allowed me to take a route and not do it so often."

Back to Depression: What We Know and Where We Are

Being diagnosed with CVD, or experiencing a myocardial infarction, can be a major catalyst for changing the way people perceive their lives, their health, their work situations, and their financial status. After their cardiac event, many individuals report feeling older, less healthy, and more vulnerable in relation to their health than they did before their heart problem. Many people with CHD have to retire from their work, which, in some cases, may bring about depressed mood, frustration, and a sense of guilt. The clients quoted in this chapter viewed these factors as negative, and they commented that feeling this way hindered their efforts to continue to maintain PA. East, Brown, and Thwells (2004) found that CR clients often experienced a sense of loss related to their inability to return to what they considered their "normal" lives. East et al. suggested that heart disease should be "viewed as a chronic illness with long-term consequences rather than an acute problem from which people quickly recover" (p. 208). It is likely that for people with CHD who are also experiencing depression, the ability to deal with and accept the changes associated with their health and life situations caused by their CHD would be decreased, compared to those people without depression. The changes that people with CHD experience in their perceptions of life and health-related issues should be considered valid and important in their overall recovery and rehabilitation, particularly with reference to how these altered perceptions may affect PA maintenance. Some clients may require a referral to a psychologist to thoroughly explore these issues. Depression in clients with CHD may not be readily apparent, and exercise professionals in a variety of service fields should be vigilant for signs and symptoms of this barrier to initiating and maintaining PA. Some people with CHD may downplay or dismiss their symptoms of depression because of the view that such changes would be expected or normal after a major health scare, but depression in CHD can negatively affect numerous aspects of life, including PA maintenance, and there are likely confounding and complex relationships among depression, CHD, and maintenance of PA. Due to the complex nature of treating depression and the extensive training required to effectively do so, health professionals who are not specifically trained in this area are encouraged to refer clients to a psychologist to work through the associated issues.

For many individuals in CR, when they felt particularly depressed or sad, the idea of exercising was difficult, or impossible, to contemplate. Instead, they took up more sedentary activities, such as sleeping, watching television, or just doing nothing. According to Seime and Vickers (2006), these types of sedentary behaviors, in addition to low motivation, low self-esteem, and pessimism, are all common during periods of moderate to severe depression. Faulkner and Biddle (2004) also found that, for their participants, when depressive symptoms worsened, PA was hard to maintain and enjoy. The challenges for exercise professionals in these instances are, first, to find out whether it is possible for people to overcome these periods of sadness or depression and to use exercise as a way of improving psychological well-being and, second, to determine the most effective ways of encouraging increased PA during these difficult times.

Although one might expect that experiencing a heart attack or being diagnosed with CHD would be enough of a reason to begin or continue to exercise, for a number of people, this may not be the case. Most people with CHD understand the benefits for their hearts and overall health in keeping active, but that knowledge does not appear strong enough to overcome the low motivation, interest, or desire to engage in exercise. Lack of, or low, motivation has been associated with nonadherence to PA across a number of studies of people with CHD (Fleury et al., 2004).

The Future of Exercise for People With Heart Disease

Although not specifically addressed in this chapter, there are certainly specific barriers and facilitators to PA that people of different cultural backgrounds experience (see chapter 3 in this book). In particular, for those populations experiencing rises in prevalence and severity of CHD (e.g., the Indian subcontinent, Southeast Asia, Pacific islands), more in-depth, culturally relevant information should be obtained about what helps and hinders their maintenance of regular PA, as well as the effects that depression can have on their abilities to be active.

The literature and excerpts from conversations in this chapter suggest that CHD and depression affect each other in ways that negatively influence PA. On one hand, the perceived implications of having heart conditions tend to make people feel depressed, and people who are depressed tend to do less PA. On the other hand, being depressed seems to bias people to perceive that their heart conditions restrict their lives in many ways, including making PA less manageable. For example, one major barrier identified in the quotes was negative perceptions of life changes resulting from heart disease. The negative perceptions of health and life in general experienced by people with CHD could have been associated with increases in depression, which then reduced their motivations to undertake PA.

Exercise professionals may find psychological strategies (e.g., self-talk, imagery, breathing) for enhancing participation in PA helpful for a number of potential clients. Another approach for exercise professionals that warrants further attention is introducing positive role models to CR clients, particularly those with similar characteristics and abilities to cardiac clients with depression. Some of the people in this chapter believed that role models had been helpful in motivating them and assisting them in increasing their PA. Also, some other people in this chapter, who were already active, commented that they would have been happy to talk to, and encourage, people who had just recently experienced heart problems and who were struggling to make the necessary behavior changes. According to Bandura's (1997) concept of self-efficacy, vicarious experience or social modeling is one way to increase self-efficacy, and high self-efficacy can positively influence health behaviors. From the people's voices in this chapter, it appears that some of them experienced fears about engaging in exercise, which may have been due to low self-efficacy and confidence to exercise. Exercise professionals might find it useful to employ a modeling strategy. For example, a previous CR client who had successfully maintained PA and other health behaviors could

attend a current CR program to provide encouragement and support to recent cardiac patients.

Past sedentary behavior seems to be a barrier to current PA adoption and maintenance. Previous research indicates that the likelihood that people with CHD and depression will be inactive is high. The challenge for health professionals and researchers alike, therefore, is to minimize the negative effects of having an inactive past on current attempts to increase PA levels. Exercise professionals in cardiac settings may find that taking a thorough history of past PA in all its forms, and especially past PA that was enjoyable, may lead to different ways of introducing PA that may help prevent relapses to previous inactive behaviors. Helping people increase their physical activities will almost always be an uphill battle, and we must remember that besides all the physical, psychological, and behavioral barriers to exercise that people with CHD experience, these clients also have all the other reinforcements and inducements to sedentary living (e.g., home entertainment systems, computer and online gaming, and evolutionary tendencies to conserve energy) that everyone faces.

References

Australian Institute of Health and Welfare. (2006). *Australia's health 2006*. Canberra, Australia: Author.

Australian Institute of Health and Welfare. (2011). *Cardiovascular disease: Australian facts 2011*. Cardiovascular disease series. Cat. no. CVD 53. Canberra, Australia: Author.

Balady, G.J., Ades, P.A., Comoss, P., Limacher, M., Pina, I.L., Southard, D., . . . Bazzarre, T. (2000). Core components of cardiac rehabilitation/ secondary prevention programs: A statement for healthcare professionals from the American Heart Association and the American Association of Cardiovascular and Pulmonary Rehabilitation Writing Group. *Circulation, 102,* 1069–1073.

Bandura, A. (1997). *Self-efficacy: The exercise of control*. New York, NY: Freeman.

Blumenthal, J.A., Babyak, M.A., Carney, R.M., Huber, M., Saab, P.G., Burg, M.M., . . . Kaufmann, P.G. (2004). Exercise, depression, and mortality after myocardial infarction in the ENRICHD trial. *Medicine & Science in Sports & Exercise, 36,* 746–755.

Blumenthal, J.A., Babyak, M.A., Moore, K.A., Craighead, W.E., Herman, S., Khatri, P., . . . Krishnan, K.R. (1999). Effects of exercise training on older patients with major depression. *Archives of Internal Medicine, 159,* 2349–2356.

Blumenthal, J.A., Sherwood, A., Babyak, M.A., Watkins, L.L., Waugh, R., Georgiades, A., & Bacon, S.L. (2005). Effects of exercise and stress management training on markers of cardiovascular risk in patients with ischemic heart disease. *Journal of the American Medical Association, 293,* 1626–1634.

Briffa, T.G., Maiorana, A., Sheerin, N.J., Stubbs, A.G., Oldenburg, B.F., Sammel, N.L., & Allan, R.M. (2006). Physical activity for people with cardiovascular disease: Recommendations of the National Heart Foundation of Australia. *Medical Journal of Australia, 184,* 71–75.

Dishman, R., & Buckworth, J. (1996). Increasing physical activity: A quantitative synthesis. *Medicine & Science in Sports & Exercise, 28,* 706–719.

East, L., Brown, K., & Thwells, C. (2004). 'Knocking at St. Peter's door'. A qualitative study of recovery after a heart attack and the experience of cardiac rehabilitation. *Primary Health Care Research and Development, 5,* 202–210.

Faulkner, G., & Biddle, S.J.H. (2004). Exercise and depression: Considering variability and contextuality. *Journal of Sport & Exercise Psychology, 26,* 3–18.

Ferrier, S., Blanchard, C.M., Vallis, M., & Giacomantonio, N. (2011). Behavioural interventions to increase the physical activity of cardiac patients: A review. *European Journal of Cardiovascular Prevention and Rehabilitation, 18,* 15–32.

Fleury, J., Lee, S.M., Matteson, B., & Belyea, M. (2004). Barriers to physical activity maintenance after cardiac rehabilitation. *Journal of Cardiopulmonary Rehabilitation, 24,* 296–307.

Furber, S., Butler, L., Phongsavan, P., Mark, A., & Bauman, A. (2010). Randomised controlled trial of a pedometer-based telephone intervention to increase physical activity among cardiac patients not attending cardiac rehabilitation. *Patient Education Counseling, 80,* 212–218.

Goble, A.J., & Worcester, M.U.C. (1999). *Best practice guidelines for cardiac rehabilitation and secondary prevention.* Melbourne, Australia: Heart Research Centre.

Grace, S.L., Abbey, S.E., Pinto, R., Shnek, Z.M., Irvine, J., & Stewart, D.E. (2005). Longitudinal course of depressive symptomatology after a cardiac event: Effects of gender and cardiac rehabilitation. *Psychosomatic Medicine, 67,* 52–58.

Jackson, L., Leclerc, J., Erskine, Y., & Linden, W. (2005). Getting the most out of cardiac rehabilitation: A review of referral and adherence predictors. *Heart, 91,* 10–14.

Lawler, P.R., Filion, K.B., & Eisenberg, M.J. (2011). Efficacy of exercise-based cardiac rehabilitation post-myocardial infarction: A systematic review and meta-analysis of randomized controlled trials. *American Heart Journal, 162*(4), 571–584.

Lett, H.S., Blumenthal, J.A., Babyak, M.A., Catellier, D.J., Carney, R.M., Berkman, L.F., . . . Schneiderman, N. (2007). Social support and prognosis in patients at increased psychosocial risk recovering from myocardial infarction. *Health Psychology, 26,* 418–427.

Lett, H.S., Blumenthal, J.A., Babyak, M.A., Strauman, T.J., Robins, C., & Sherwood, A. (2005). Social support and coronary heart disease: Epidemiologic evidence and implications for treatment. *Psychosomatic Medicine, 67,* 869–878.

Maddison, R., & Prapavessis, H. (2004). Using self-efficacy and intention to predict exercise compliance among patients with ischemic heart disease. *Journal of Sport & Exercise Psychology, 26,* 511–524.

Marcus, B., Williams, D., Dubbert, P., Sallis, J., King, A., Yancey, A., . . . Claytor, R. (2006). Physical activity intervention studies. What we know and what we need to know. *Circulation, 114,* 2739–2752.

Martin, A.M., & Woods, C.B. (2012). What sustains long-term adherence to structured physical activity after a cardiac event? *Journal of Aging and Physical Activity, 20,* 135–147.

Mead, N., & Bower, P. (2002). Patient-centred consultations and outcomes in primary care: A review of the literature. *Patient Education and Counseling, 48,* 51–61.

Moholdt, T., Wisloff, U., Nilsen, T.I., & Slordahl, S.A. (2008). Physical activity and mortality in men and women with coronary heart disease: A prospective population-based cohort study in Norway (the HUNT study). *European Journal Cardiovascular Prevention and Rehabilitation, 15,* 639–645.

Moore, S.M., Charvat, J.M., Gordon, N.H., Pashkow, F., Ribisl, P., Roberts, B.L., & Rocco, M. (2006). Effects of a CHANGE intervention to increase exercise maintenance following cardiac events. *Annals of Behavioral Medicine, 31,* 53–62.

Moore, S.M., Dolansky, M.A., Ruland, C.M., Pashkow, F.J., & Blackburn, G.G. (2003). Predictors of women's exercise maintenance after cardiac rehabilitation. *Journal of Cardiopulmonary Rehabilitation, 23,* 40–49.

Petersen, S., Peto, V., Rayner, M., Leal, J., Luengo-Fernandez, R., & Gray, A. (2005). *European cardiovascular disease statistics.* London, England: British Heart Foundation.

Pollock, K.M. (2001). Exercise in treating depression: Broadening the therapist's role. *Journal of Clinical Psychology: In Session, 57,* 1289–1300.

Roger, V.L., Go, A.S., Lloyd-Jones, D.M., Adams, R.J., Berry, J.D., Brown, T.M., . . . Wylie-Rosett, J. (2011). Heart disease and stroke statistics—2011 update: A report from the American Heart Association. *Circulation, 123*(4), e18–e209.

Rogerson, M.C., Murphy, B.M., Bird, S., & Morris, T. (2012). "I don't have the heart": A qualitative study of barriers to and facilitators of physical activity for people with coronary heart disease and depressive symptoms. *International Journal of Behavioural Nutrition and Physical Activity, 9,* 140.

Rudisch, B., & Nemeroff, C.B. (2003). Epidemiology of comorbid coronary artery disease and depression. *Biological Psychiatry, 54,* 227–240.

Scholz, U., Knoll, N., Sniehotta, F.F., & Schwarzer, R. (2006). Physical activity and depressive symptoms in cardiac rehabilitation: Long-term effects of a self-management intervention. *Social Science & Medicine, 62,* 3109–3120.

Scott, I.A., Lindsay, K.A., & Harden, H.E. (2003). Utilisation of outpatient cardiac rehabilitation in Queensland. *Medical Journal of Australia, 179,* 341–345.

Seime, R.J., & Vickers, K.S. (2006). The challenges of treating depression with exercise: From evidence to practice. *Clinical Psychology: Science and Practice, 13,* 194–197.

Sniehotta, F.F., Scholz, U., Schwarzer, R., Fuhrmann, B., Kiwus, U., & Voller, H. (2005). Long-term effects of two psychological interventions on physical exercise and self-regulation following coronary rehabilitation. *International Journal of Behavioral Medicine, 12,* 244–255.

Taylor, A.H., Cable, N.T., Faulkner, G., Hillsdon, M., Narici, M., & Van Der Bij, A.K. (2004). Physical activity and older adults: A review of health benefits and the effectiveness of interventions. *Journal of Sports Sciences, 22,* 703–725.

Taylor, G.H., Wilson, S.L., & Sharp, J. (2011). Medical, psychological, and sociodemographic factors associated with adherence to cardiac rehabilitation programs: A systematic review. *Journal of Cardiovascular Nursing, 26,* 202–209.

Thow, M., Rafferty, D., & Kelly, H. (2008). Exercise motives of long-term phase IV cardiac rehabilitation participants. *Physiotherapy, 94,* 281–285.

van Melle, J.P., de Jonge, P., Spijkerman, T.A., Tijssen, J.G., Ormel, J., van Veldhuisen, D.J., . . . van den Berg, M.P. (2004). Prognostic association of depression following myocardial infarction with mortality and cardiovascular events: A meta-analysis. *Psychosomatic Medicine, 66,* 814–822.

Woodgate, J., & Brawley, L.R. (2008). Self-efficacy for exercise in cardiac rehabilitation: Review and recommendations. *Journal of Health Psychology, 13,* 366–387.

Yalom, I.D. (2009). *Staring at the sun. Overcoming the terror of death.* San Francisco, CA: Jossey-Bass.

Zhao, G., Ford, E.S., Li, C., & Mokdad, A.H. (2008). Are United States adults with coronary heart disease meeting physical activity recommendations? *The American Journal of Cardiology, 101,* 557–561.

CHAPTER 11

Exercise for Cancer Patients and Survivors
Challenges, Benefits, Barriers, and Determinants

Karen M. Mustian, Lisa K. Sprod, Lara A. Treviño, and Charles Kamen

Cancer patients and survivors who want to exercise face many obstacles, whether they were regularly exercising prior to their cancer diagnosis and treatment or not. The biopsychosocial challenges experienced by patients and survivors stemming from the news of a diagnosis of cancer, the disease itself, the toxicities and side effects (acute, chronic, and late effects) of treatment, and the difficult life adjustments required for family, work, and social activities pose impediments to the adoption and maintenance of a regular exercise program. Patients begin to experience these challenges early in their cancer trajectories from the moment of diagnosis, and they continue to experience them throughout treatment. In addition, many of these challenges persist after treatments are complete, and new challenges may arise for survivors months, years, and decades later. Exercise can be prescribed as an effective therapeutic intervention to provide supportive care to cancer patients and survivors for preventing and reducing toxicities and side effects, and, ultimately, overcoming these challenges throughout the entire cancer trajectory. In this chapter, we present a summary of the types of challenges cancer patients and survivors experience, describe the barriers to and determinants of adoption and maintenance of exercise regimens, describe how exercise can be prescribed as an effective treatment for these challenges, and present a case study.

Challenges Faced by Cancer Patients and Survivors

Treatments for cancer often include surgery, chemotherapy, radiation therapy, hormone therapy, or some combination of these modalities. These treatments lead to myriad physical, psychological, and social problems and side effects that interfere with a cancer patient's ability to complete treatments as prescribed, function independently, perform activities of daily living, and maintain a high quality of life (Mustian, Sprod, Janelsins, Peppone, & Mohile, 2012; Mustian, Sprod, et al., 2013). Psychological and social disorders and toxic side effects are especially burdensome in older adults who are at greatest risk for functional impairment after cancer treatment (Galvão, Taaffe, Cormie, et al., 2011; Mohile, Heckler, et al., 2011; Mohile, Fan, et al., 2011; Mohile, Mustian, Bylow, Hall, & Dale, 2009). Among the most onerous physical side effects stemming from cancer and its treatments are nausea, vomiting, hair loss, dermatitis, muscle atrophy, cachexia, cardiopulmonary toxicity, neurological toxicity, compromised immune function, chronic inflammation, gene expression changes, and decreased bone formation (Mustian et al., 2012; Mustian, Sprod, et al., 2013). The most prevalent and troublesome psychological problems and side effects include cancer-related fatigue, cognitive impairment, sleep problems, depression, pain, anxiety, impaired mood, poor body image, and reduced self-esteem (Mustian et al.,

2012; Mustian, Sprod, et al., 2013). The most common and disruptive social side effects include the inability to work, maintain family and social relationships, participate in leisure activities, effectively understand and navigate the health care system, or make decisions easily (Mustian et al., 2012; Mustian, Sprod, et al., 2013).

Benefits of Exercise for Cancer Patients and Survivors

Exercise interventions are effective for reducing many of the preceding biopsychosocial disruptions, disorders, and side effects cancer patients and survivors experience. In this section, we highlight findings from a few key research studies demonstrating some of the biopsychosocial benefits of exercise for cancer patients and survivors.

Aerobic exercise alone can improve many conditions and side effects. For example, breast cancer patients who participated in a home-based, moderate-intensity walking program performed four to six days per week, 10 to 45 minutes per day, showed improvements in cancer-related fatigue, sleep disruption, depression, and anxiety (Mock et al., 2001). Similarly, a progressive aerobic exercise intervention, performed three times per week, beginning with 15 minutes per session and progressing to 45 minutes per session, resulted in improvements in anxiety in breast cancer patients undergoing treatment (Courneya et al., 2007). Aerobic exercise has also been shown to be beneficial for prostate, lung, and gastrointestinal cancer patients (Dimeo, Thomas, Raabe-Menssen, Propper, & Mathias, 2004; Galvão et al., 2013; Galvão et al., 2009; Galvão, Taaffe, Cormie, et al., 2011). In addition to aerobic exercise and walking, resistance training is beneficial for cancer patients and survivors. A 12-week resistance training intervention with prostate cancer patients, performed three times per week, resulted in improvements in cancer-related fatigue, cognitive function, and quality of life (Segal et al., 2003). Combined aerobic and resistance exercise interventions have been used successfully among cancer patients and survivors, and they have led to reductions in myriad symptoms and side effects. For example, breast and prostate cancer patients undergoing radiation who participated in a 4-week aerobic and resistance training program showed improvements

in cancer-related fatigue and sleep quality (Mustian et al., 2009; Sprod et al., 2010).

Nontraditional modes of exercise, sometimes referred to as mindfulness-based modes of exercise, are also effective for improving the symptoms and side effects cancer patients and survivors experience. For example, Yang style tai chi chuan performed three times a week for 60 minutes per session at a moderate intensity for a 12-week period produced improvements in aerobic capacity, muscular strength, flexibility, insulin resistance, inflammation, bone formation, quality of life, self-esteem, and cancer-related fatigue (Janelsins et al., 2011; Mustian, Katula, & Zhao, 2006; Mustian, Palesh, & Flecksteiner, 2008; Peppone et al., 2010; Sprod et al., 2012). Yoga participation one or two days per week over a 4- to 12-week period has also been shown to result in improvements in sleep quality, insomnia, anxiety, mood, cancer-related fatigue, quality of life, inflammation, and circadian rhythms in cancer patients and survivors (Bower et al., 2011; Carson, Carson, Porter, Keefe, & Seewaldt, 2009; Chandwani et al., 2010; Mustian et al., 2011; Mustian, Palesh, et al., 2013; Rao et al., 2008; Speed-Andrews, Stevinson, Belanger, Mirus, & Courneya, 2010; Ulger & Yagl, 2010).

Barriers to Exercise for Cancer Patients and Survivors

Cancer patients undergoing treatment and survivors following completion of treatment may have difficulties adopting exercise programs, even though the program may improve physical, psychological, and social function. Barriers to exercise have been studied to understand why some patients and survivors adopt exercise programs and some do not. The barriers to exercise that have been identified fall into two categories: disease-specific and treatment-related barriers and non-disease-specific and non-treatment-related barriers. Disease-specific barriers to exercise are directly connected to the disease itself; cancer treatments may also prevent patients from engaging in physical exercise (Blanchard, Courneya, Rodgers, & Murnaghan, 2002; Courneya et al., 2008; Courneya, Keats, & Turner, 2000; Mustian, Sprod, et al., 2013; Perna, Craft, Carver, & Antoni, 2008; Rogers, Courneya, Shah, Dunnington, &

Hopkins-Price, 2007; Rogers et al., 2008). Examples of disease-specific and treatment-related barriers to exercise are side effects from the cancer or the treatments, such as nausea, chronic inflammation, bone fractures, cancer-related fatigue, cognitive impairment, sleep problems, depression, pain, anxiety, impaired mood, and muscular, cardiopulmonary, neurological, and immune toxicities (Courneya et al., 2008; Mustian et al., 2012; Mustian, Sprod, et al., 2013). Non-treatment-related barriers to exercise are not directly connected to treatment, but they may be a part of the cancer experience. Examples of non-treatment-related barriers are poor body image, reduced self-esteem, non-prioritizing of exercise, limited time or motivation, and inability to care for one's self or family (Blanchard et al., 2002; Courneya et al., 2000; Courneya et al., 2008; Mustian, Sprod, et al., 2013; Perna et al., 2008; Rogers et al., 2007; Rogers et al., 2008). In addition, family members or health care providers sometimes create barriers by discouraging patients and survivors from exercising due to unfounded concerns that it is detrimental and limited knowledge regarding how patients and survivors can exercise safely and derive desirable benefits (Blanchard et al., 2002; Courneya et al., 2000; Courneya et al., 2008; Perna et al., 2008; Mustian et al. 2012; Mustian, Sprod, et al., 2013; Rogers et al., 2007; Rogers et al., 2008). The distinction between disease-specific and treatment-related or non-treatment-related barriers is not always clear, and separating the two is not as important as correctly identifying what barriers exist for a cancer patient or survivor and providing interventions (such as problem solving) for successfully removing these barriers so that patients and survivors are able to exercise throughout their cancer experiences.

Disease- and Treatment-Related Barriers

Disease- and treatment-related barriers to exercise in cancer patients undergoing treatment and in survivors include fatigue, nausea, vomiting, and pain (Courneya et al., 2008). In a supervised exercise training program in breast cancer patients receiving chemotherapy, of the 36 different barriers patients reported for missing exercise sessions, 53% were related to the disease or treatment (Courneya et al., 2008). These barriers are common side effects of the disease and treatment

and, based on differences in treatment, these barriers may differ among cancer types. For example, head and neck cancer patients reported that their barriers to exercise adoption were cancer-related fatigue, shortness of breath, and difficulty swallowing (Rogers et al., 2008). Breast cancer patients, however, reported cancer-related fatigue, nausea, vomiting, and pain as their most common treatment-related barriers to adopting exercise programs (Courneya et al., 2008). These barriers are more applicable to cancer patients undergoing treatment and patients undergoing palliative care who are experiencing acute toxicities and side effects; nevertheless, they may also affect cancer survivors who experience chronic or late side effects from treatment. Chronic side effects of treatment are symptoms that begin during treatment or within a few weeks following the completion of treatment and continue for weeks, months, or years. Late side effects of treatment are symptoms that were not present during or immediately after treatments but arose months or years after the completion of treatment. Acute, chronic, and late side effects encompass all types of disorders and side effects, including physical symptoms (e.g., fatigue, musculoskeletal problems), psychological symptoms (e.g., distress, anxiety, cognitive difficulties), and social symptoms (e.g., inability to maintain relationships, work, or participate in leisure activities; Stein, Syrjala, & Andrykowski, 2008).

Non-Treatment-Related Barriers

Non-treatment-related barriers to exercise in cancer patients and survivors include poor body image, reduced self-esteem, nonprioritizing of exercise, limited time or motivation, inability to care for one's self or family, limited self-discipline, and procrastination. Lack of time, or being too busy to exercise, was the number one barrier that cancer patients reported in a randomized clinical trial testing a home-based exercise intervention (Courneya et al., 2005). Patients' emotional states may also affect their motivations to exercise (Rogers et al., 2007). Negative affect and frequency of perceived barriers to exercise were significantly and inversely associated with exercise behavior in early-stage breast cancer patients. The more severe their negative affect and the higher their number of perceived barriers, the less likely the patients were to engage in physical exercise (Perna et al., 2008). These barriers are more commonly reported among cancer survivors than among patients undergoing treatment. Barriers to physical exercise in palliative care patients have not been empirically studied, and only a limited number of studies have examined the effects of physical activity in these individuals (Lowe, Watanbe, & Courneya, 2009). Cancer patients and survivors likely face far more barriers than are currently identified in the existing literature because this area of research is limited. Professionals should spend a considerable amount of time assessing and identifying the barriers that present challenges for each individual cancer patient and survivor when providing interventions for successfully overcoming these barriers.

Determinants of Exercise Adoption

Some determinants of exercise adoption that have been identified have been based on the theory of planned behavior. Briefly, the theory of planned behavior states that attitudes toward the behavior, perceived behavioral control, and subjective norms (e.g., social norms) shape a person's intentions to perform the behavior and, ultimately, the performance of the behavior (Ajzen, 1991). Intentions to exercise and perceived behavioral control of adopting an exercise program were the best predictors of whether colorectal cancer patients and patients undergoing bone marrow transplants were likely to adopt an exercise program following treatment (Courneya et al., 2000). In addition, there may be some gender differences regarding prediction of adoption of an exercise program based on the model components. For example, in breast cancer patients, exercise intention was the best predictor of adoption, whereas in prostate cancer patients, perceived behavioral control was the better predictor (Blanchard et al., 2002). Professionals should take these gender differences into account when developing exercise programs for cancer patients and survivors.

Determinants of Exercise Adherence and Maintenance

Cancer patients' and survivors' adherence to exercise programs has been examined on a limited basis both during and after completion of treatments, but cancer patients' maintenance of exercise programs (i.e., continuing to exercise over the long term, as opposed to adhering acutely to an exercise prescription) has not been examined (we were unable to find any published studies that reported on long-term maintenance of exercise behavior at this time). Results from studies testing home-based walking interventions showed that survivors who were no longer receiving treatment, and who received the intervention, reported significantly better exercise adherence than those in the control condition (Pinto, Rabin, & Dunsiger, 2009). Predictors of adherence to these home-based exercise interventions were gender, normative beliefs, perceived behavioral control, and baseline exercise self-efficacy (i.e., belief in one's ability to exercise). Patients who were undergoing curative treatment also demonstrated good adherence to a structured, home-based walking and progressive resistance exercise intervention by significantly increasing the number of steps they walked daily, compared to the control group patients, who decreased their daily steps (Mustian et al., 2009). The exercise intervention group also reported a 79% adherence rate to the progressive resistance portion of the exercise intervention, indicating that the home-based walking and progressive resistance exercise intervention is easily adhered to and well tolerated by cancer patients undergoing treatment (Mustian et al., 2009).

Tai chi chuan has also proven easy to adhere to and tolerable among breast cancer survivors. Mustian and colleagues (2008) showed a significantly higher adherence rate (72%) to a 12-week Yang style tai chi chuan exercise program compared to a 67% adherence rate to a psychosocial support group. Common reasons patients reported for discontinuing with their assigned intervention group were dislike of their group intervention, work and family obligations, and severe persisting side effects from treatment. Those who reported discontinuing their group assignment due to not liking their interventions were patients assigned to the psychosocial support group who wanted the tai chi intervention. In summary, cancer patients and survivors adhere relatively well to structured group and individual interventions, community- and home-based interventions, as well as aerobic, anaerobic, and mindfulness modes of exercise. Additional evidence is needed to determine adherence to exercise programs by cancer patients undergoing palliative care.

Prescribing Exercise for Mental Health Outcomes

Historically, the goal for exercise prescriptions has been to elicit improvements in physical outcomes such as cardiopulmonary and muscular function, and improvements in psychosocial outcomes have been secondary benefits along the way to achieving increases in physical function. Nevertheless, positive changes in psychosocial outcomes such as decreases in depression, anxiety, fatigue, and increases in quality of life should also be considered as primary endpoints for exercise prescriptions, particularly in cancer patients, and they can be achieved with much smaller doses of exercise than what is necessary to achieve changes in physical function. For example, a cancer patient or survivor may experience less depression, lower anxiety, increased vigor, and improved quality of life immediately after a single bout of exercise that lasts for only 5 to 15 minutes and is of low intensity, whereas it is not possible to achieve gains in physical function with this dose of exercise. For any professional who is considering prescribing exercise with the goal of improving psychosocial outcomes, it is important to keep in mind that the doses prescribed can, and in many cases should, be lower for cancer patients and survivors, especially when just beginning the exercise regimen or performing them during cancer treatments, and for previously sedentary individuals.

To prescribe safe and effective exercise interventions for cancer patients and survivors, there are a number of factors to consider. First, professionals should assess any potential contraindications to physical activity or exercise, specifically, but not limited to, orthopedic, cardiopulmonary, neurologic, or oncologic contraindications (Mustian et al., 2012). Because it takes a relatively small dose of physical activity to improve many psychosocial health outcomes, it is important to encourage cancer patients and survivors to be physically active, even if only for a short time each day. Small things, such as taking the stairs rather than the elevator or parking farther away from the store to increase physical activity, can produce significant and meaningful improvements in psychosocial outcomes.

The American College of Sports Medicine (ACSM) has established recommendations for physical exercise participation by cancer patients and survivors (Mustian et al., 2012). In general, the ACSM recommends that cancer patients and survivors start with low doses and slowly progress to 150 minutes of moderate-intensity or 75 minutes of vigorous-intensity physical exercise per week, with an additional two or three weekly sessions of resistance training and stretching each week targeting all of the major muscle groups (Mustian et al., 2012). If this dosage of exercise is not achievable, participation in some, rather than no, physical exercise is recommended; physical exercise, even at levels not reaching the recommendations as previously mentioned, will still provide psychosocial health benefits for cancer patients and survivors (Mustian et al., 2012). It is also advisable to individually tailor exercise interventions based on numerous factors, including the health status, disease trajectory, and current fitness level of the patient or survivor (Mustian et al., 2012). Cancer patients and survivors who have comorbid conditions, or who are at higher risk of complications resulting from participation in physical exercise, should be referred to an exercise professional, whose minimum qualifications include a bachelor's degree from an accredited exercise science or kinesiology program. Primary certification through the ACSM as a cancer exercise trainer or equivalent specialty certification program (e.g., British Association of Sport and Exercise Sciences, BASES; Exercise and Sports Science Australia, ESSA; National Strength and Conditioning Association, NSCA) ensures increased competency in the unique needs of cancer patients and survivors by the exercise professional conducting the baseline assessments and providing the exercise prescriptions (Mustian et al., 2012).

Examples of the types of improvements in cancer-related psychosocial outcomes that have resulted from participation in physical exercise interventions follow. Moderate-intensity exercise, between 55% and 75% of maximum heart rate, including 10 to 90 minutes of aerobic exercise, performed three to seven days per week, is beneficial for improving quality of life in cancer survivors who have early stage cancer (Holmes, Chen, Feskanich, Kroenke, & Colditz, 2005; Mustian et al., 2009; Mustian et al., 2012). Accumulating at least 30 minutes of physical activity throughout the day results in improvements in psychosocial side effects and quality of life (Mustian et al., 2012). Resistance training at a moderate to vigorous intensity, 3 days per week (2–4 sets of 8–15 repetitions of different exercises for the major muscle group) is also beneficial for improving psychosocial side effects and quality of life in cancer survivors (Courneya et al., 2007; Mustian et al., 2012; Segal et al., 2003). Psychosocial outcomes may also be improved through mindfulness-based modes of exercise. Yoga and tai chi have been shown to improve psychosocial side effects and quality of life in cancer survivors who engage in these modes of exercise one to three times per week for 60 to 90 minutes per session (Janelsins et al., 2011; Mustian et al., 2006; Mustian et al., 2012; Mustian, Palesh, et al., 2013; Peppone et al., 2010; Sprod et al., 2012). In addition, cancer patients with metastatic disease may benefit from low-intensity exercise with positive psychosocial outcomes (Adamsen et al., 2003; Crevenna et al., 2003; Headley, Ownby, & John, 2004; Oldervoll et al., 2006; Oldervoll et al., 2011; Porock, Kristjanson, Tinnelly, Duke, & Blight, 2000).

In the following case study example, we show how a psychologist or exercise professional might work with cancer patients or survivors to identify goals and cancer-specific challenges, barriers, and determinants of exercise and to eventually prescribe exercise for a client.

Mrs. Bobzean's Tale

When we first met, Mrs. Bobzean was a 58-year-old Caucasian woman who was overweight. She was married, and had one daughter and three grandchildren. She lived with her husband. Mrs. Bobzean presented to the health club where I, the first author, worked, reporting that she had been recently diagnosed with Stage 3A breast cancer. She had undergone a radical mastectomy of her right breast, and was preparing to begin adjuvant chemotherapy to reduce risk of recurrence from occult disease. A nurse at the cancer center where she was receiving treatment told her that she should consider beginning an exercise program, because losing weight could reduce her risk of breast cancer recurrence, and that it was fine to start exercising even as she was about to begin chemotherapy.

I first met with Mrs. Bobzean and assessed her for any medical contraindications to beginning an exercise program. I discovered that she was a moderate risk patient, according to the ACSM's *Exercise Guidelines for Cancer Patients and Survivors* (Mustian et al., 2012), based on her weight and cancer diagnosis; she had no other known comorbidities. Therefore, Mrs. Bobzean did not need to see any other medical specialists for clearance to exercise. Knowing the potential treatment-related and non-treatment-related barriers that might affect Mrs. Bobzean's willingness to exercise, I sat down with her and assessed her readiness to begin an exercise program prior to providing her exercise prescription.

> **Karen (K):** Thank you, Mrs. Bobzean, for telling me a little bit about your cancer treatment. What are you hoping that we can accomplish here today?
>
> **Mrs. Bobzean (Mrs. B):** As I mentioned, a nurse at the cancer center told me that it might be good if I started exercising. So here I am!
>
> **K:** Well, I'm very glad that you've come in. I want to let you know that I am an exercise psychologist and am certified as an American College of Sports Medicine Cancer Exercise Trainer, so I have specific training in the types of exercise that might be beneficial to cancer patients. I'd be happy to help design a program that will fit your needs and help you feel better while you complete your chemotherapy.
>
> **Mrs. B:** That sounds like exactly what I'm looking for.
>
> **K:** Great! First I want to ask you a little bit about your previous experiences with ex-

ercise. Have you exercised in the past prior to your diagnosis with cancer?

Mrs. Bobzean reported that before being diagnosed with cancer, she did not have an active lifestyle due to caring for her three grandchildren and her ailing husband, who had been undergoing treatment for lung cancer. She had never before gone to a gym to work out. Prior to her cancer diagnosis, her recreational activities involved bowling once per week in a bowling league and taking a walk with her husband for about an hour most evenings through their neighborhood; these walks ended when her husband was diagnosed with lung cancer.

> **K:** Well, walking and bowling are great forms of physical activity. So, you were regularly exercising with your husband during those walks each evening. That is wonderful to hear. Have you been able to continue to be physically active and exercise since your diagnosis?

> **Mrs. B:** Unfortunately, no. I have tried to walk more, but I don't have the time to just go for a walk after work like I once did. I am far less active than I was prior to my cancer diagnosis and my surgery. I know it's important, but I just don't have the time or energy. I get so tired even trying to get out of bed. I have to nap a lot, and doing simple things like getting dressed make me bone tired. It is also uncomfortable for me to do some types of movements since my mastectomy.

I was pleased to hear that Mrs. Bobzean seemed to understand the importance of physical activity and that she wanted to be active. I wanted to reassure her that the fatigue, limited range of motion, and difficulty managing all her daily activities were treatment-related side effects that most cancer patients experience; these barriers are not only common but also manageable. This conversation prompted me to think about making sure I got a comprehensive picture of all the barriers that may affect Mrs. Bobzean's ability to exercise.

> **K:** It is common for breast cancer survivors to experience fatigue and limited range of motion initially as a result of surgery, and most patients find it difficult to resume all their normal activities of daily living immediately. Although physical activity may seem like the very last thing that you have time for, it may in fact offer a tremendous benefit for you by helping you recover more quickly from your surgery and by helping you get through your chemotherapy with fewer side effects; it may also reduce the severity of the ones you are already experiencing. Before we really start to talk about what types of exercise and how much you may need to do, I want to really understand your typical day and week. You said you don't have the time to exercise. What obligations are taking up your time?

> **Mrs. B:** I work full time as an administrative assistant. I am also the primary caregiver for my husband, who is undergoing treatment for lung cancer, and I often also look after my three grandchildren. It seems like I am always at work or busy helping my family nights and weekends. I rarely have a free minute to myself, and if I do, I'm so tired I usually sit down to relax and fall asleep.

> **K:** I see. You're a very busy woman! Those are important activities, and it is understandable that you would be extremely tired when you add those activities on top of trying to recover from your surgery. I'm wondering if there's anything else that's coming up for you now as you think about beginning an exercise program.

> **Mrs. B:** Well, no. No, there's nothing else.

I had heard a bit about some of Mrs. Bobzean's non-treatment-related barriers at this point, but I wanted to be thorough. Thinking back to the theory of planned behavior, I decided to assess some issues that might influence Mrs. Bobzean's adoption of an exercise plan, such as attitudes, behavioral control, and norms.

> K: Oftentimes when people think about beginning an exercise program, they may feel unsure about where to begin. Or, they might be concerned that they won't do the exercises right, or that the exercises will be too difficult for them to grasp.

> Mrs. B: Um, now that you mention it, I am a little bit worried about exercising in a gym. I'm pretty old now, and I don't know how I'm going to feel working out with a bunch of young kids.

> K: Mmm hmmm. I see.

> Mrs. B: Also, since my surgery, I wear a prosthesis. I don't know how it's going to feel for me to change clothes in the locker room in front of all those other women or to exercise with it. I think I'll be embarrassed to take my prosthesis off in the locker room or exercise without it.

> K: Yes, that's definitely an issue for us to think about. Anything else?

> Mrs. B: I'm a little worried about pain. And what if the exercises tear something on my right side, where I had the mastectomy? I know the nurse said it was a good time for me to start exercising, but I am worried about hurting myself.

> K: These are all really important questions and concerns. I'm making notes about them so we can be sure to address them as we plan your program.

After a little more back-and-forth, I felt that I had a thorough grasp of the barriers and determinants of adoption that might have been influencing Mrs. Bobzean. I knew that the main determinant of exercise adoption for breast cancer patients ac-

cording to the research I reviewed is intention, so I decided to assess that specifically.

> K: Given everything we've talked about so far, Mrs. Bobzean, what would you say your intention is to start exercising, with 0 being no intention at all and 10 being ready to start right now?

> Mrs. B: Well, honestly, I think I'm probably at a 7 right now.

> K: A 7 is a great place to start! Let's talk about what this exercise program might involve and see if that changes your rating.

I knew that Mrs. Bobzean had treatment-related barriers, including pain and fatigue. She had non-treatment-related barriers, including caring for her grandchildren and sick husband, and concern about working out in a gym. She reported fairly high intention to participate in physical activity; the number of barriers, however, had kept her from participating in exercise. Because Mrs. Bobzean was limited in the amount of time she could devote to physical activity, I decided to find ways to incorporate exercise into her activities of daily living, with a focus on things she could do at home and with her grandchildren. I also realized that given the time constraints and side effects she would likely experience while completing chemotherapy, finding things she could do without going to the gym might be the best way to increase her physical activity.

> K: How old are your grandchildren, and how often do you babysit?

> Mrs. B: My grandchildren are 3, 6, and 8, and I watch them about three to five days a week when I get home from work. My daughter works in the evenings and needs the help.

> K: I'll tell you what I'm thinking. Given how busy your schedule is, I'm thinking we might be able to find ways to get you active during your daily routine. What

types of things do you and your grand-children do in the evenings?

Mrs. B: I usually cook dinner while they watch television or play video games; my husband is usually watching TV or sleeping as well. We all eat dinner. After dinner, I clean up and do the dishes. Then I like to take a little break on the couch, but I usually fall asleep and don't wake up right away. When I do wake up, it is time to get the kids a bath and put them to sleep, and I also have to help my husband get ready for bed.

K: It makes sense that you want to relax, and we want you to have time to do that. I'm also thinking that it's really important that children get at least an hour of physical activity each day. Do you live near a park or in a neighborhood where it is safe to walk around in the evenings?

Mrs. B: Our neighborhood is safe and has sidewalks. My husband and I used to walk around the cul-de-sacs every night.

K: Great! You might be able to take your grandchildren for a walk around the neighborhood after dinner. This would help you increase your daily physical activity and restart your exercise and benefit the kids as well.

Mrs. B: I don't like leaving my husband for too long. How long do I need to go walking for?

K: Well, that is a great question. It is highly likely that you will not have to walk for more than 15 to 30 minutes in order to begin to see benefits. Do you think that your husband can walk with you on a short walk for about 15 minutes?

Mrs. B: He doesn't want to. I have asked him, and he is just so down and out from his lung cancer, and he has many more side effects than me. He is convinced he is going to die, and there is nothing really he can do. So he just watches TV, sleeps, and eats—he doesn't work anymore; he can't, really. I am not gonna die! I decided my grandkids and my daughter need me, and this ain't the hill that's gonna get me.

K: Well, would you feel comfortable leaving your husband for 15 to 30 minutes each evening? The reason I am asking is because we know that cancer patients report as little as 15 to 30 minutes of moderately paced walking as little as three times a week can reduce the fatigue you mention you are having. How do you think it would work to leave your husband while he watches TV and to try taking a 15- to 30-minute walk with your grandchildren at least one day next week? I am also interested in how you will feel afterwards.

Mrs. B: Oh, just one time for 15 to 30 minutes next week? I can probably take them for a 30-minute walk at least once next week. I will just have to convince my grandchildren to leave their video games and TV shows—I could see if they want to walk to the fountain in our neighborhood.

K: Great! That sounds like a fantastic idea and good way to start. What would you say your intention is to take a 15- to 30-minute walk next week, on a scale from 0 to 10?

Mrs. B: A 10! I definitely think I can do it.

K: I look forward to hearing about it. I think it will be a great experience. Let's plan to meet at the end of next week to talk about how it went.

As part of setting this small goal, I also provided Mrs. Bobzean with a pedometer so she could get instant feedback about her current activity level each day. I also discussed other ways to help her incorporate physical activity into her daily life. As an administrative assistant, Mrs. Bobzean spent much of her day sitting in front of a computer. I encouraged her to take short walks during her breaks and a longer walk during lunch. If there was not a safe or convenient place to walk outside of her place of employment, I told her that she could walk around the office or up and down the stairs. I listened for barriers and tried to come up with creative alternatives.

At my second meeting with Mrs. Bobzean, I found that she did walk for 30 minutes with her grandkids on two separate evenings. I found out that she felt invigorated and energized afterward and that she had really enjoyed the change of pace with her grandkids. I encouraged her to continue walking and monitoring her steps on the pedometer, and I also suggested that she could engage in resistance training during her work breaks with small handheld weights or resistance bands. I reminded her that participating in physical activity would not require expensive purchases, and that finding time to exercise was an investment in her future and that it would help her get through her chemotherapy. I encouraged her to purchase some resistance bands before our next meeting so that I could show her some simple exercises that she could do at work or home.

At our third meeting, I asked Mrs. Bobzean how her walking is going. She again reported that she had walked on two separate evenings with her grandkids for about 30 minutes. I also asked if she had been able to purchase resistance bands.

> **Mrs. B:** Um, no, I didn't get a chance to do that this week.
>
> **K:** Oh no! That's too bad. What got in the way?
>
> **Mrs. B:** I just really didn't have time this week. But I'll definitely do it over this next week.

I wanted to be certain to encourage Mrs. Bobzean while also remaining sensitive to her busy schedule. I wanted to focus specifically on assisting her in problem solving around any bar-

riers she might have been facing. As an exercise psychologist, I knew that learning to help clients problem-solve so that they can achieve their exercise goals is one of the most important skills I had mastered.

> **K:** I know you do have a very busy schedule, Mrs. Bobzean. If you don't mind, I'd like to go back and talk about some of the barriers that can come up around exercising. Part of my job is to help you problem-solve around these barriers so that you can still exercise even with your busy schedule. I want to ask a little bit about some things we touched on two weeks ago. I remember you mentioned feeling unsure about working out for a couple of reasons, including worrying about feeling pain or injuring yourself. How are those worries now?
>
> **Mrs. B (growing tearful):** Now that I've started chemotherapy, I just feel so sick all the time. I'm nauseous and tired, and I know I should exercise. (She begins crying.) But I just can't do it! I can't even make dinner for everyone on some nights. I just order pizza or get fast food for the kids, and my husband and I feel terrible about it.

While it is always difficult to sit in the room with a tearful client, I understand that tears are a normal part of the process of coping with cancer. It is common for cancer patients to feel distressed during treatment, and there are going to be some things that they have to cut back on doing some days—it is important for her to understand that these need not be permanent and that she should give herself permission to take care of herself throughout this process. As an exercise psychologist, when confronted with a client's distress, I realize I need to make a decision about whether the client is in need of additional mental health services, or whether this distress is a normal response to cancer, and its treatment does not require referral. In making this decision, I often consult with a clinical psychologist or other mental health worker with specific expertise in this area. In this situation, I talked to Mrs. Bobzean for a while and determined that she was feeling distressed on the day of our meeting, but that the feelings were transitory and she was still overall optimistic about her treatment and about exercise. I was able to sit with her distress, responding empathically and nonjudgmentally to her feelings and normalizing her distress while offering hope for her continued recovery and improvement. I provided her with the name of a clinical psychologist with whom I had worked in the past, in the event she decided that she wanted more intensive help and support.

> **K:** Well, you've done so well with the walking, let's see if we can find ways to make resistance training more a part of your daily routine the same way you have incorporated more walking.
>
> **Mrs. B:** I wonder if I could do some resistance band exercises while I'm watching television with my husband in the evening?
>
> **K:** I'm sure that you could! With the approval of your husband's oncologist, the two of you could even start doing some light exercises together.
>
> **Mrs. B:** Oh, that would be wonderful. I really miss the walks we use to take together. It was our special time to talk. I also feel like he should get some exercise too—it might make him feel better. I'll ask his oncologist about it at his next clinic visit.

In the weeks that followed, Mrs. Bobzean began to incorporate more physical activity into her daily routine, such as walking with her grandchildren and walking during her breaks at work. I encouraged her to monitor her pedometer. Ideally, I told her that she should work toward walking 10,000 steps per day, but I recognized that this goal was not realistic in the beginning and that she may have difficulty achieving this benchmark during her chemotherapy treatments. Instead, I worked with her to set a goal of increasing the

number of steps she walked by 10% per week. I told her that she would most likely start feeling more energized as she was more physically active, and this increased energy would provide additional motivation to continue making physical activity a priority.

There are other pieces of information that I imparted to Mrs. Bobzean as I continued working with her. I assessed for additional treatment-related barriers, such as neuropathy, which I knew could interfere with exercise adherence. I continually assessed her level of fatigue and pain because I knew these were barriers about which she was particularly concerned. After she finished chemotherapy and wanted to continue to increase her physical activity, I helped her to problem-solve barriers related to body image (age, prosthesis, hair loss from chemotherapy, and others) so that she could begin to exercise at the health club where I worked (she received a free 3-month membership as a cancer survivor). I continually used the dual pillars of problem solving and motivation enhancement to guide my work with Mrs. Bobzean. When I saw her exercising in the club, I stopped to encourage her and praise her for her dedication to remaining active. She eventually worked up to the ACSM recommended dose of 150 minutes of exercise per week. She even became so motivated that she asked me to show her how to use a new Nike Fuelband that she bought and was using, along with the application on her cell phone, instead of monitoring her activity with a pedometer. As Mrs. Bobzean moved into long-term cancer survivorship, she integrated physical activity into her life in a way that it had not been integrated before, and she reported feeling more energetic and healthier than ever.

Concluding Thoughts

In conclusion, we recommend that cancer patients and survivors continue to remain physically active during and after cancer treatment. Assessing treatment-related and non-treatment-related barriers is critical in establishing a safe and effective exercise program for individuals affected by cancer. The skills of problem solving and motivation enhancement can be used to overcome these barriers and to help cancer patients incorporate physical activity into their long-term survivorship plans.

References

Adamsen, L., Midtgaard, J., Rorth, M., Borregaard, N., Andersen, C., Quist, M., . . . Knutsen, L. (2003). Feasibility, physical capacity, and health benefits of a multidimensional exercise program for cancer patients undergoing chemotherapy. *Supportive Care in Cancer, 11,* 707–716.

Ajzen, I. (1991). The theory of planned behavior. *Organizational Behavior and Human Decision Processes, 50,* 179–211.

Blanchard, C.M., Courneya, K.S., Rodgers, W.M., & Murnaghan, D. M. (2002). Determinants of exercise intention and behavior in survivors of breast and prostate cancer: An application of the theory of planned behavior. *Cancer Nursing, 25*(2), 88–95.

Bower, J.E., Garet, D., Sternlieb, B., Ganz, P.A., Irwin, M.R., Olmstead, R., & Greendale, G. (2011). Yoga for persistent fatigue in breast cancer survivors: A randomized controlled trial. *Cancer, 118,* 3766–3775.

Carson, J.W., Carson, K.M., Porter, L.S., Keefe, F.J., & Seewaldt, V.L. (2009). Yoga of Awareness program for menopausal symptoms in breast cancer survivors: Results from a randomized trial. *Support Care Cancer, 17,* 1301–1309.

Chandwani, K.D., Thornton, B., Perkins, G.H., Arun, B., Raghuram, N.V., Nagendra, H.R., . . . Cohen, L. (2010). Yoga improves quality of life and benefit finding in women undergoing radiotherapy for breast cancer. *Journal of the Society for Integrative Oncology, 8*(2), 43–55.

Courneya, K.S., Friedenreich, C.M., Quinney, H.A., Fields, A.L.A., Jones, L.W., Vallance, J.K.H., & Fairey, A.S. (2005). A longitudinal study of exercise barriers in colorectal cancer survivors participating in a randomized controlled trial. *Annals of Behavioral Medicine, 29,* 147–153.

Courneya, K.S., Keats, M.R., & Turner, A.R. (2000). Social cognitive determinants of hospital-based exercise in cancer patients following high-dose chemotherapy and bone marrow transplantation. *International Journal of Behavioral Medicine, 7,* 189–203.

Courneya, K.S., McKenzie, D.C., Reid, R.D., Mackey, J.R., Gelmon, K., Friedenreich, C.M., . . . Segal, R.J. (2008). Barriers to supervised exercise training in a randomized controlled trial of breast cancer patients receiving chemotherapy. *Annals of Behavioral Medicine, 35,* 116–122.

Courneya, K.S., Segal, R.J., Gelmon, K., Reid, R.D., Mackey, J.R., Friedenreich, C.M., . . . McKenzie, D.C. (2007). Six-month follow-up of patient-rated outcomes in a randomized controlled trial of exercise training during breast cancer chemotherapy. *Cancer Epidemiology, Biomarkers & Prevention, 16,* 2572–2578.

Crevenna, R., Schmidinger, M., Keilani, M., Nuhr, M., Fialka-Moser, V., Zettinig, G., & Quittan, M. (2003). Aerobic exercise for a patient suffering from metastatic bone disease. *Supportive Care in Cancer, 11,* 120–122.

Dimeo, F.C., Thomas, F., Raabe-Menssen, C., Propper, F., & Mathias, M. (2004). Effect of aerobic exercise and relaxation training on fatigue and physical performance of cancer patients after surgery. A randomised controlled trial. *Supportive Care in Cancer, 12,* 774–779.

Galvão, D.A., Spry, N., Denham, J., Taaffe, D.R., Cormie, P., Joseph, D., . . . Newton, R.U. (2013). A multicentre year-long randomised controlled trial of exercise training targeting physical functioning in men with prostate cancer previously treated with androgen suppression and radiation from TROG 03.04 RADAR. *European Urolology.* [Epub ahead of print]

Galvão, D.A., Spry, N., Taaffe, D.R., Denham, J., Joseph, D., Lamb, D.S., . . . Newton, R.U. (2009). A randomized controlled trial of an exercise intervention targeting cardiovascular and metabolic risk factors for prostate cancer patients from the RADAR trial. *BMC Cancer, 9,* 419.

Galvão, D.A., Taaffe, D.R., Cormie, P., Spry, N., Chambers, S.K., Peddle-McIntyre, C., . . . Newton, R.U. (2011). Efficacy and safety of a modular multi-modal exercise program in prostate cancer patients with bone metastases: A randomized controlled trial. *BMC Cancer, 11,* 517.

Headley, J.A., Ownby, K.K., & John, L.D. (2004). The effect of seated exercise on fatigue and quality of life in women with advanced breast cancer. *Oncology Nursing Forum, 31,* 977–983.

Holmes, M.D., Chen, W.Y., Feskanich, D., Kroenke, C.H., & Colditz, G.A. (2005). Physical activity and survival after breast cancer diagnosis. *Journal of the American Medical Association, 293,* 2479–2486.

Janelsins, M.C., Davis, P.G., Wideman, L., Katula, J.A., Sprod, L.K., Peppone, L.J., . . . Mustian, K.M. (2011). Effects of Tai Chi Chuan on insulin and cytokine levels in a randomized controlled pilot study on breast cancer survivors. *Clinical Breast Cancer, 11,* 161–170.

Lowe, S.S., Watanbe, S.M., & Courneya, K.S. (2009). Physical activity as a supportive care intervention in palliative cancer patients: A systematic review. *Journal of Supportive Oncology, 7,* 27–34.

Mock, V., Pickett, M., Ropka, M.E., Muscari Lin, E., Stewart, K.J., Rhodes, V.A., . . . McCorkle, R. (2001). Fatigue and quality of life outcomes of exercise during cancer treatment. *Cancer Practice, 9*(3), 119–127.

Mohile, S.G., Fan, L., Reeve, E., Jean-Pierre, P., Mustian, K., Peppone, L., . . . Dale, W. (2011). Association of cancer with geriatric syndromes in older Medicare beneficiaries. *Journal of clinical oncology: Official journal of the American Society of Clinical Oncology, 29,* 1458–1464.

Mohile, S.G., Heckler, C., Fan, L., Mustian, K., Jean-Pierre, P., Usuki, K., . . . Morrow, G. (2011). Age-related differences in symptoms and their interference with quality of life in 903 cancer patients undergoing radiation therapy. *Journal of Geriatric Oncology, 2,* 225–232.

Mohile, S.G., Mustian, K., Bylow, K., Hall, W., & Dale, W. (2009). Management of complications of androgen deprivation therapy in the older man. *Critical Reviews in Oncology/Hematology, 70,* 235–255.

Mustian, K.M., Janelsins, M., Sprod, L., Peppone, L., Mohile, S., Frizzell, B., . . . Morrow, G. (2011). YOCAS® Yoga significantly improves circadian rhythm, anxiety, mood and sleep: A randomized, controlled clinical trial among 410 cancer survivors. [Abstract] *Supportive Care in Cancer, 19(Suppl. 2),* S317–318.

Mustian, K.M., Katula, J.A., & Zhao, H. (2006). A pilot study to assess the influence of tai chi chuan on functional capacity among breast cancer survivors. *Journal of Supportive Oncology, 4*(3), 139–145.

Mustian, K.M., Palesh, O.G., & Flecksteiner, S.A. (2008). Tai chi chuan for breast cancer survivors. *Medicine and Sport Science, 52,* 209–217.

Mustian, K.M., Palesh, O.G., Janelsins, M.J., Sprod, L.K., Peppone, L.J., Chandwani, K.D., . . . Morrow, G.R. (2013). A multi-center randomized controlled trial of yoga for sleep quality among cancer survivors. *Journal of Clinical Oncology, 31,* 3233–3241.

Mustian, K.M., Peppone, L., Darling, T.V., Palesh, O., Heckler, C.E., & Morrow, G.R. (2009). A 4-week home-based aerobic and resistance exercise program during radiation therapy: A pilot randomized clinical trial. *Journal of Supportive Oncology, 7*(5), 158–167. Retrieved from www.ncbi.nlm.nih.gov/pmc/articles/PMC3034389/#__ffn_sectitle

Mustian, K.M., Sprod, L.K., Janelsins, M.C., Peppone, L.J., Carroll, J., Mohile, S.G., & Palesh, O.G.

(2013). Exercise for cancer patients: Treatment of side effects and quality of life. In B. Carr & J. Steel (Eds.), *Psychological aspects of cancer: A guide to emotional and psychological consequences of cancer, their causes and their management* (pp. 279–289). New York, NY: Springer.

Mustian, K.M., Sprod, L.K., Janelsins, M.J., Peppone, L.J., & Mohile, S.G. (2012). Exercise recommendations for cancer-related fatigue, cognitive impairment, sleep problems, depression, pain, anxiety, and physical dysfunction: A review. *Oncology and Hematology Review, 8*(2), 81–88. Retrieved from www.ncbi.nlm.nih.gov/pmc/articles/PMC3647480/

Oldervoll, L.M., Loge, J.H., Lydersen, S., Paltiel, H., Asp, M.B., Nygaard, U.V., . . . Kaasa, S. (2011). Physical exercise for cancer patients with advanced disease: A randomized controlled trial. *The Oncologist, 16,* 1649–1657.

Oldervoll, L.M., Loge, J.H., Paltiel, H., Asp, M.B., Vidvei, U., Wiken, A.N., . . . Kaasa, S. (2006). The effect of a physical exercise program in palliative care: A phase II study. *Journal of Pain and Symptom Management, 31,* 421–430.

Peppone, L.J., Mustian, K.M., Janelsins, M.C., Palesh, O.G., Rosier, R.N., Piazza, K.M., . . . Morrow, G.R. (2010). Effects of a structured weight-bearing exercise program on bone metabolism among breast cancer survivors: A feasibility trial. *Clinical Breast Cancer, 10,* 224–229.

Perna, F.M., Craft, L., Carver, C.S., & Antoni, M.H. (2008). Negative affect and barriers to exercise among early stage breast cancer patients. *Health Psychology, 27,* 275–279.

Pinto, B.M., Rabin, C., & Dunsiger, S. (2009). Home-based exercise among cancer survivors: Adherence and its predictors. *Psycho-Oncology, 18,* 369–376.

Porock, D., Kristjanson, L.J., Tinnelly, K., Duke, T., & Blight, J. (2000). An exercise intervention for advanced cancer patients experiencing fatigue: A pilot study. *Journal of Palliative Care, 16,* 30–36.

Rao, R.M., Nagendra, H.R., Raghuram, N., Vinay, C., Chandrashekara, S., Gopinath, K.S., & Srinath, B.S. (2008). Influence of yoga on mood states, distress, quality of life, and immune outcomes in early stage breast cancer patients undergoing surgery. *International Journal of Yoga, 1*(1), 11–19.

Rogers, L.Q., Courneya, K.S., Robbins, K.T., Malone, J., Seiz, A., Koch, L., & Rao, K. (2008). Physical activity correlates and barriers in head and neck cancer patients. *Support Care Cancer, 16,* 19–27.

Rogers, L.Q., Courneya, K.S., Shah, P., Dunnington, G., & Hopkins-Price, P. (2007). Exercise stage of change, barriers, expectations, values and preferences among breast cancer patients during treatment: A pilot study. *European Journal of Cancer Care, 16*(1), 55–66.

Segal, R.J., Reid, R.D., Courneya, K.S., Malone, S.C., Parliament, M.B., Scott, C.G., . . . Wells, G.A. (2003). Resistance exercise in men receiving androgen deprivation therapy for prostate cancer. *Journal of Clinical Oncology, 21,* 1653–1659.

Speed-Andrews, A.E., Stevinson, C., Belanger, L.J., Mirus, J.J., & Courneya, K.S. (2010). Pilot evaluation of Iyengar yoga program for breast cancer survivors. *Cancer Nursing, 33,* 369–381.

Sprod, L.K., Janelsins, M.C., Palesh, O.G., Carroll, J.K., Heckler, C.E., Peppone, L.J., . . . Mustian, K.M. (2012). Health-related quality of life and biomarkers in breast cancer survivors participating in tai chi chuan. *Journal of Cancer Survivorship: Research and Practice, 6,* 146–154.

Sprod, L.K., Palesh, O.G., Janelsins, M.C., Peppone, L.J., Heckler, C.E., Adams, M.J., . . . Mustian, K.M. (2010). Exercise, sleep quality, and mediators of sleep in breast and prostate cancer patients receiving radiation therapy. *Community Oncology, 7,* 463–471. Retrieved from www.ncbi.nlm.nih.gov/pmc/articles/PMC3026283/

Stein, K.D., Syrjala, K.L., & Andrykowski, M.A. (2008). Physical and psychological long-term and late effects of cancer. *Cancer, 112*(Suppl. 11), 2577–2592.

Ulger, O., & Yagl, N.V. (2010). Effects of yoga on the quality of life in cancer patients. *Complementary Therapies in Clinical Practice, 16,* 60–63.

CHAPTER 12

It Hurts to Move
The Catch-22 of Physical Activity for People With Chronic Pain

Melainie Cameron and Janelle White

Fearing that movement will aggravate their condition, people with chronic pain tend to reduce their levels of customary activity. Physical inactivity has consequences, including reduction in muscle mass and flexibility, bone density, balance, proprioception, and cardiovascular and respiratory capacity for exercise (U.S. Department of Health and Human Services, 1996). It also contributes to a shrinking world, reducing social interaction and support and increasing isolation, loneliness, and risk of depression. Physical inactivity places people at increased risk of chronic and complex diseases, and it is the fourth leading risk factor for mortality, accounting for 6% of deaths worldwide (World Health Organization, 2009; 2010).

Because most human beings have at some stage overexerted themselves and experienced postactivity soreness and tiredness, many people assume that physical exertion will increase pain and fatigue. Common wisdom for people in pain is to "rest up" and "take it easy." The paradox for those of us who work in exercise for rehabilitation is that, despite common wisdom, physical activity may actually reduce both pain and fatigue.

Reductions in pain and fatigue associated with exercise may be surprising to clients who expect to experience continual decline predicted by the natural progression of many clinical conditions. These surprises offer teachable moments, windows that practitioners can use to reveal to clients the intrinsic and personal importance of exercise.

The International Association for the Study of Pain taxonomy defines pain as "an unpleasant sensory and emotional experience associated with actual or potential tissue damage, or described in terms of such damage" (Merskey & Bogduk, 1994). The emotional component of this definition, linked continuously by the word "and" to the sensory component of the definition, surprises many practitioners. Pain, by definition, is affective.

Typically, pain is classified as acute, subacute, or chronic (persistent). Persistent pain is defined as pain on a daily basis for at least three months. Some types of pain are not indicative of physiological damage to tissue. Rather, pain might be present due to stress and strain or flagging potential tissue damage. It may serve as a warning to cease an activity or change a posture. Some pain, however, does not serve as a particularly helpful early warning system for physiological damage; in particular, persistent pain may have no useful purpose at all. Neuroplastic changes in the nervous systems of people with persistent pain can lead to the development of altered pain perceptions, such as allodynia (i.e., pain perceived from a stimulus that would not usually provoke pain, such as a light breeze or the weight of a single layer of cloth; Thorgaard Skou et al., 2013; Tu et al., 2013).

Furthermore, the relationship between pain and function is not as clear-cut as it would intuitively appear. For example, we now understand that the prevalence and incidence of back pain in history, and in communities currently without disability insurance, are not markedly different from levels currently observed in Western societies, but levels of disability (reduced function) differ widely

(Waddell, 2004). This disparity suggests that social structures influence pain behavior, if not pain per se.

Put simply, pain behaviors are the things we do when we are in pain that show others we have pain. Some pain behaviors, such as limping to avoid loading an acutely sprained ankle, are helpful in preventing further damage to tissues and worsening pain. Most pain behaviors commence this way, as constructive alterations to routine behavior when pain is acute, but pain behaviors can also be socially and psychologically rewarded and reinforced, and if prolonged, some pain behaviors become unhelpful, and may actually compromise function. For example, an adult with acute low-back pain may avoid prolonged forward bending postures such as those adopted when vacuuming floors because these postures provoke pain (i.e., they adopt antalgic postures). If said adult is a parent of teenage children, then a social benefit might be returned for this pain behavior if the teenagers take on a greater proportion of housework while the parent is in pain. This secondary gain reinforces the pain behavior, which may be prolonged after the behavior itself ceases to be helpful for the modulation of pain, and actually delays the resolution of pain.

Pain is not simply the passage of electrical signals from nociceptors to the cerebral cortex. Pain is a construct of the brain in response to nociceptive firing, influenced by a complex social, psychological, physiological, and chemical milieu. What we do, say, and believe, how we interact with others, what we eat, and how we medicate ourselves all influence our experiences of pain.

Studies of people with painful conditions who engage in regular exercise training do not consistently show improvements in pain (Davis & MacKay, 2013; Fransen & McConnell, 2009; Fransen, McConnell, Hernandez-Molina, & Reichenbach, 2009). Some clients report that regular exercise training reduces pain. There are a few known mechanisms by which pain modulation occurs during physical activity: (a) the release of endorphins (the body's own endogenous opioids) during vigorous activity will have a similar effect to synthetic opioids and will modulate pain transmission by binding to mu (μ) opioid receptors in the substantia gelatinosa of the dorsal horn of the spinal cord (Ossipov, 2012), (b) vibration and position sense, transmitted by type A beta fibers, may modulate ("gate") in the dorsal horn the transmission of poorly localized, persistent pain along type C fibers (Ossipov, 2012), (c) distraction from cognitions about pain may occur while engaged in exercise—pain perception is closely linked to the attention that we give to it (Bjarke Vaegter, Handberga, & Graven-Nielsen, 2013), (d) a sense of physical accomplishment may override pain via both emotional and cognitive processing in the limbic system (Bjarke Vaegter et al., 2013), and (e) abdominal breathing during aerobic exercise may increase relaxation in tight, painful muscles (Perri & Halford, 2004). Some of these physiological mechanisms occur only with particular types of exercise, and other mechanisms are socially influenced, hence the somewhat inconsistent effects of exercise on pain perception.

Functional improvements with regular exercise training are somewhat more consistent and predictable (Hurkmans, van den Giesen, Vliet Vlieland, Schoones, & Van den Ende, 2009; Davis & MacKay, 2013). Even clients with chronic and complex diseases are not exempt from the physiological response to exercise training. For example, skeletal muscle, when exercised regularly against resistance, will maintain or increase in strength and size (hypertrophy). It takes severe muscle wasting disorders, such as amyotrophic lateral sclerosis (ALS), to undo the effects of regular resistance training on muscle strength. (Curiously, ALS, although a chronic, complex, and serious disease, may be painless.) Exercise does not cure chronic, painful conditions, but it can improve quality of life, and sometimes extend life for clients with terminal conditions.

Adherence to structured exercise programs may be particularly challenging for people with chronic painful conditions who experience considerable symptom fluctuation. Supervised, graded, and individualized exercises, and self-management approaches in which clients take control of their exercise schedule, may increase exercise adherence (Jordan, Holden, Mason, & Foster, 2010).

Goals of Pain Management

There is contrast between the goals of pain management in acute and chronic conditions (Flor &

Turk, 2011). For clients with acute pain, goals are based around relief, recovery, and prevention of progression to a chronic condition. For clients with chronic (persistent) pain, the goals of pain management are often based on three broad concepts:

1. **Restoration of function.** This goal includes using the biopsychosocial model and considering improvements in the areas of physical, psychological (emotional), and social functioning. Practitioners using this approach acknowledge that the function may not be restored to previous levels, but it allows the client to renegotiate new desirable levels of function. The client may even choose one specific area on which to focus at a time. This tactic can be commenced simply through asking clients, "What would you be doing now if your pain was not an issue?"

2. **Pain reduction.** For people with chronic pain it is important to check that any underlying causative factors (e.g., disease processes) are being addressed and treated to provide optimum conditions for pain reduction. Although a range of pharmacological interventions is often helpful for the effective management of chronic pain, there is also a need to fine-tune the often long list of medications that clients may be taking. This approach has the dual purpose of reducing the unwanted side effects of certain medications and allowing specific targeting of the different types of persistent pain etiology, which can reduce the unnecessary use of certain medications.

3. **Correction of pain consequences.** These consequences can also be viewed through the biopsychosocial lens. Some may be purely physical, where there may be atrophy of muscle due to limited or minimal use. Correction of posture may be necessary after many months or years of poor posture due to pain. Other painful conditions may be developing due to changes in posture, gait, or overuse that need to be addressed. Incorporated into the psychosocial realm of the consequences of pain are any maladaptive changes that may have occurred relating especially to a client's coping skills, behaviors, and mental health status.

The Biopsychosocial Approach to Pain

Persistent pain is complex, and the client experiencing it may be understood through the biopsychosocial model (Flor & Turk, 2011). In applying the biopsychosocial model to clients with persistent pain, we summarize each of the three individual components, yet acknowledge that each influences the other.

The Biological

Biological understanding implies that practitioners must seek to clearly comprehend the multifaceted etiology of persistent pain (neuropathic, malignant, nonmalignant, and chronic regional). There may or may not have been causative factors in clients developing pain, and neuroplastic changes may be a factor in those individuals with persistent pain. Biological understanding also includes knowledge of medications that can work to alleviate persistent pain (e.g., analgesics, tricyclic antidepressants, anti-epileptics, corticosteroids). Because persistent pain is complex, referral to a pain specialist or neurologist may also be helpful. It is important to acknowledge that multidisciplinary care and long-term analgesic medication may be valuable adjuncts to exercise therapy.

The Psychological

In considering the psychological component of this approach to pain, practitioners maintain awareness of clients' moods, presentations, and verbal and nonverbal behaviors. Clinical care in this domain could involve administering pencil and paper screening tests for signs of depression or anxiety (e.g., Depression, Anxiety, and Stress Scale [DASS]; Lovibund & Lovibund, 1995), or asking questions about depression and anxiety and avoidance behaviors, and ensuring that clients are referred for care from psychologists or psychiatrists if mental health issues are identified. Depression and anxiety are common in clients with persistent pain, and these conditions may amplify pain perception and worsen clients' pain levels significantly, which may in turn lead to clients withdrawing further and avoiding social interactions and physical activities.

The Social

An awareness of the social issues that clients with persistent pain may experience includes acknowledging which activities the clients enjoyed prior to becoming less active due to their pain. Avoidance behaviors may lead to negative social consequences such as losing jobs, reducing social contact with friends, and decreasing intimacy with partners. People with persistent pain can be subject to considerable social stigma. Astute practitioners are interested in talking about what their clients would most like to have back in their social lives, and will work with them to set goals around resuming these activities.

Case Study 1

The following case example is a fictional aggregate of encounters we have seen or heard about from our clients. It is a tale about how exercise therapy can go badly wrong. You may be inclined to cringe while reading and think to yourself, "I would never do or say that!" Our clients, however, tell us far too many stories of practitioners who behaved just like Penny did working with Ava.

Ava is a 68-year-old woman of Croatian background. She completed high school to year 10 in Croatia, and then began working in her parents' bakery. About four years later, as a newly married 19-year-old, she immigrated to Australia with her husband. She and her husband bought a house in a Melbourne suburb and raised four children, all of whom are now adults living away from the family home. Her husband died 3 years ago, and Ava now lives alone, but her children visit often. Ava speaks English well, with a pronounced Croatian accent. She never learned to drive, but is confident to navigate public transport around the city. About four weeks ago, Ava found a lump in her left breast, which prompted her to see her general practitioner for a breast examination. The mass was identified as a primary breast cancer, and several metastases were found in the bones of her lower limbs. Ava had a partial mastectomy to remove the lump and surrounding invaded breast tissue. She has commenced radiotherapy to contain the metastases. Ava lives with daily pain from these metastases.

Her general practitioner has prescribed Fentanyl (transdermal opioid patches) to manage this persistent pain. Ava is finding her activities of daily living challenging; she has ongoing fatigue, and struggles with housework. She has been referred to an exercise practitioner (Penny) from the hospital oncology department with a request for an exercise program designed to maintain lower-limb bone mineral density.

> **Penny (P):** Good morning, Ava. How are you today? Are you ready to have some fun doing exercises with me?
>
> **Ava (A):** I am sorry, but I just feel miserable. The last thing I want to do right now is exercise. The cancer and the radiotherapy make me feel so sick. All I want to do is go home to my sister in Croatia to die.
>
> **P (continuing upbeat):** Well, you can only go to see your sister if you have good, strong legs. Exercise with me, and we'll try to get you on your way soon.

Ava has expressed a lack of interest in exercise and a desire to die. With her upbeat tone and driven focus on exercise, Penny appears to have disregarded both these factors. Forcing exercise, or any other therapy, onto clients without their consent is unreasonable in ambulatory clinical care with clients who are competent to make informed health care decisions. Penny has a responsibility to allow and respect Ava's unwillingness to participate in exercise. A wiser approach would be to explain to Ava why exercise is important for her health and well-being at this stage of her life and to allow her to make an informed choice about what she will do, rather than jollying her along without regard for her feelings.

Ava acquiesced to Penny's exercise plans at the first appointment. She found the exercises difficult, but she attempted all of them, and tried hard to please. She did not attend her second appointment as scheduled.

When Ava and Penny first met, Ava was probably in the precontemplation stage of behavior change (see table 12.1); she was referred to see

Penny by the hospital oncologist, and said that she was not even thinking about exercise. Clients in the precontemplation stage have not thought through any of the issues associated with the change, and are ill-prepared to commence. Pushing clients to undertake the actions of change at this stage may be counterproductive. By disregarding Ava's stage of behavior change, Penny has overlooked the possibility that exercise intervention might "backfire" at this time.

Penny telephoned Ava to follow up and reschedule another session.

> P: Hello, Ava. It's Penny here. I'm just calling because I was expecting you for an appointment today, but you didn't turn up. Is everything okay?
>
> A: Well, really, no. (She pauses.) I could hardly move for 3 days after I saw you on Monday, and so I don't think I'm really meant to be doing exercise right now. I think I'm too sick to exercise.
>
> P: Come on, Ava. The oncologist has said you need to exercise to keep your bones strong, so that they don't break. It's the perfect time for you to exercise, and I know that exercise would be a great way for you to feel better and help manage your pain.

Penny has overlooked Ava's report of postexercise pain. Instead of responding to the emotional component of Ava's report (i.e., affect associated with pain), Penny has attempted to use the authority of a medical specialist to convince Ava that exercise is the correct therapy for her. This directive approach assumes that the practitioner knows best, and does not identify that Ava is probably in a stage of behavior change inconsistent with the commencement of exercise (see table 12.1).

At the time of the missed second appointment, Ava may have progressed to the contemplation stage of behavior change. The contemplation stage is one of thinking about change; Ava is now thinking about exercise, but much of her contemplation is negative. She is considering whether exercise is going to be of benefit to her in the face of a seemingly relentless disease. An important aspect of the contemplation stage includes considering arguments against making a change to a health behavior (e.g., too sick or too tired to exercise) as well as the reasons in favor of that change. In this stage of change, Ava remains unprepared to engage in exercise.

Considerable skill is required for practitioners to navigate this territory with clients. A practitioner may be convinced that exercise, although uncomfortable for the client, is doing no harm, and is likely to drive beneficial physiological changes. Convincing the client to try some exercise that leaves them feeling more pain afterward, however, may result in the client refusing to do further exercise and becoming distant or angry when asked to continue exercise. Following Penny's telephone call, Ava attended another appointment. Penny continued to direct Ava to exercise at levels that produced discomfort and did not hear or heed her client's emotional responses to pain. Penny became frustrated that Ava seemed to complain and whine throughout the session, and Ava thought that Penny was heartless.

> P: You really need to walk faster. I'll turn the treadmill up for you now. (She reaches for the treadmill controls.)
>
> A: When I walk fast, I am really sore afterwards. I'd rather walk at this pace.
>
> P: No, no! Brisk walking—that's what we wrote in the exercise program. We need to get your bones strong. (She reaches across Ava to increase the treadmill speed.)
>
> A: That's fast enough. My legs are already feeling tired. I was very sore after the last session. I thought we would take things easier this time.
>
> P: If this exercise program is going to do you any good, then you have to challenge yourself, Ava.

Table 12.1   Promoting Exercise at Each Stage of Health Behavior Change

Stage of change	What typifies this stage?	Do	Don't
Precontemplation (nonbeliever)	Clients do not believe in the value of exercise for their situation; consequently, they aren't even thinking about exercise.	Make brief, clear, valid, educative statements as to the value of exercise relevant to these clients. Give accurate, factual appraisal of risk to clients in this stage (e.g., "A waist circumference of 100 cm means that your risk of developing type II diabetes is higher than for other men your age.").	Proselytize, using upbeat manner and charisma or amplified fear of catastrophe, to convert the client to your beliefs. Use a higher authority (e.g., specialist, boss, doctor, God) to justify exercise for these clients.
Precontemplation (believer)	Clients believe in the value of exercise, but are not thinking about it for their current situations.	Ask questions to prompt thinking (e.g., "Have you thought about doing exercise to become stronger?").	Overwhelm client with plans for exercise or structured programs.
Contemplation	Clients are thinking about exercise, but may be unsure of what to do or how to do it.	Ask clients what they might need to know now to be ready to engage in exercise. In response, offer guidance as to types and principles of exercise for rehabilitation (e.g., "Training with resistance or weights is beneficial for improving glucose control in people like you who have type II diabetes.")	Assume that you know what clients don't know, or need to know. Be overly directive, telling clients what they must do or must not do. Be vague about the value of exercise.
Preparation	Clients are preparing for exercise, gathering specific information and equipment, and planning a schedule to allow exercise.	Provide accurate details of exercise programs and opportunities to allow clients to plan for participation (e.g., dates, times, locations, costs, lists of required equipment).	Assume that clients will be able to work out the details of an exercise program for themselves (i.e., that they have enough information to plan).
Action	Clients have begun some exercise, but have not yet experienced intrinsic benefits from exercise, nor made it a life habit.	Affirm clients' actions, and help them identify the earliest signs of benefit from exercise (e.g., small gains in strength, endurance, bone mineral density). Ask clients what exercise means for them.	Critique clients' early efforts as insufficient. Focus on long-term goals at the exclusion of early improvements. Tell clients what you believe exercise should mean for them.
Maintenance	Clients exercise regularly, and can readily identify some benefits from doing so.	Affirm clients' actions. Help them to plan strategies for managing changes to usual routine (e.g., holidays), so as to avoid setbacks.	Expect that nothing will change for clients once they have established exercise routines.
Relapse	Relapse occurs when clients experience setbacks, including advancement of disease, new symptoms, provocation of pain due to excessive exercise, and boredom with existing exercise.	Encourage clients to resume exercise as soon as they feel able. Offer clients a few clear alternate methods for exercise during setbacks.	Scold clients for discontinuing with exercise. Overwhelm clients with many exercise choices.

For details of stages of behavior change, see Marcus et al., 1992; Marcus, Eaton, Rossi, & Harlow, 1994.

A: Don't be so bloody patronizing! Just getting out of bed this morning was a challenge for me. When have you ever been really sick? You don't have the first clue how I feel!

P: No, Ava, you are right, I really don't know how you feel, but I do know that exercise is really good for you, even when you are sick.

Penny and Ava have been working at cross-purposes. Ava felt terrible, and sought an ally. Her diagnosis of cancer was quite recent, and it led to some rapid changes in her life. Ava was likely to be angry about many things, and by not listening or responding to Ava's feelings, Penny risked the brunt of Ava's anger. Because Penny was confident that exercise is therapeutic, she pushed Ava to work harder, disregarding what was actually good for Ava at the time. Of course, Ava and Penny have different understandings of what *good* means in this context. To Ava, good meant feeling comfortable and pain-free throughout exercise, but to Penny, good meant obtaining substantial physiological and functional improvements with exercise.

Reflections on Practice

Working with clients rarely runs to a script. Here we offer suggestions as to ways that Penny might have reflected on her interactions with Ava.

Reflection. After the second session with Ava, Penny could consider the language Ava used: "When have you ever been really sick? You don't have the first clue how I feel!" Realizing that she does not understand Ava's feelings, Penny could shift her focus from trying to make Ava exercise to empowering Ava to make choices about her health.

Another helpful thing we can do for our clients is to provide them with time, our attention, and a safe place to tell their stories. Penny could reflect that she doesn't actually have any clue how Ava feels. It could be therapeutic of her to ask how Ava feels and to listen while Ava tells her story.

Biopsychosocial Model. Recognizing that holistic care of Ava will involve a team working within a biopsychosocial model, Penny could have sought permission to make contact with the other health professionals involved in Ava's care and to arrange a team meeting to include Ava, her family members involved in care, and other health care practitioners (e.g., oncologist, dietician, pain specialist, general practitioner).

Negotiating Alternatives. After talking with Ava to discover the activities that she used to do before her persistent pain began, Penny may be able to negotiate alternative exercises to walking on the treadmill.

Knowledge Building and Relevance to Client. Penny could try to ascertain the level of knowledge that Ava has about her condition and the side effects of any medication that she is taking. Knowing that adults generally prefer to see relevance to any tasks they have been assigned to justify them undertaking them, Penny might take the time to explain to Ava the purpose of any exercises she recommends.

Setting Achievable Goals. Penny could guide Ava toward setting some small yet achievable goals (e.g., walk 80 steps today) so that Ava can see small wins from each exercise session.

Supervision. Penny might seek advice from a colleague or mentor to guide her reflections on her interactions with Ava. Penny's supervisor could prompt her to consider that sometimes clients need us to be not so much experts as collaborators who build caring relationships with them.

Clients Come With Some Expertise. Penny is, undoubtedly, knowledgeable about the physiological benefits of exercise on bone mineral density, but her behavior toward Ava is condescending. Ava "hears" Penny's behaviors and patronizing attitudes, rather than Penny's words, and Penny's expertise is lost amid the noise. It may be helpful for Penny to understand that in people with chronic pain, perceived injustice is associated with increased pain, disability, and depressive symptoms (Scott, Trost, Bernier, & Sullivan, 2013), and that if her interactions with clients are viewed as unfair, they may be counterproductive. Further, if Penny could be guided to understand that Ava is the *expert on herself,* and that these two experts might work together, then perhaps a constructive, therapeutic relationship could develop.

Let's Try That Again

We rarely get a second chance to make a first impression with clients, to try that again. Clients who are hurt, offended, or harmed by our interaction may seek alternate care, and we may not know that we pushed them away. Although we present this revision as a "second take," we encourage practitioners to reflect on their ongoing interactions with clients and modify their engagement along the way. For example, if Penny and Ava are to make progress, they will need to collaborate, set shared goals, and work toward them together. Both parties will need to concede some ground from their ideas of what is good and useful and doable exercise for Ava. We suggest that Penny could facilitate an alternate unfolding of the second appointment if she were to speak differently with Ava.

> P: I think it might be helpful for you to walk a bit faster. Would you like to give that a try?
>
> A: My legs are already tired. Must I really speed up?
>
> P: No, you don't have to. You are in charge of the treadmill controls right there (she points, but does not reach across Ava), but if you can walk a bit faster, then I expect that you will get a bit more benefit from the exercise.
>
> A: What sort of benefit? Sore legs don't feel like much of a benefit. I'm not trying to lose weight, you know—Dr. George [oncologist] said I shouldn't worry about that anymore because the cancer would probably knock weight off me.
>
> P: Well, no, sore legs aren't fun at all. The purpose of walking faster is to stress the bones in your legs a bit more. Bone is alive. When you stress it, it becomes stronger in response. You have spots of cancer in your leg bones, and they make the bones weaker and increase the like-

lihood that your bones might break. The point of this exercise is to help your bones become as strong as possible to give you the best chance to avoid fractures in your legs.

> A: Well, I could try to go a bit faster. Is it okay if I just creep the speed up slowly? I really don't think I can rush today.
>
> P: Of course, take your time. And I'll make sure that we leave a gap between this appointment and the next one so that you can get over your legs feeling sore. Also, would you like to think about some other things you could do to recover from these exercise sessions, like having a massage or doing a hydrotherapy session in the pool? I've also got an information sheet with some tips for things you can try at home to make your legs feel a bit less sore after exercise. If you like, I can also chat with your pain specialist to make sure that your pain medications are doing what they should be.

Penny has now given some decisional control back to Ava, explaining why she considered this increase in exercise beneficial and offering empathy and some strategies to reduce Ava's postexercise leg soreness. By interacting in this way, Penny was able to bring Ava into a collaborative partnership. Penny relinquished some of her high expectations of a demanding exercise program, and Ava was prepared to attempt some of the tasks Penny suggested. Penny has begun to sound like a caring other, and Ava is ready to risk trusting her judgment.

Case Study 2

Marj is a 75-year-old widow who has multiple comorbidities. She has rheumatoid arthritis (RA), osteoarthritis, type II diabetes, advanced cardiovascular disease, and depression with anxiety. She lives on her own. Her husband died 10 years ago from emphysema. She has lived with persistent pain since undergoing open-heart surgery 10 years ago. Three years ago, she was diagnosed with RA, although she reports that symptoms, including pain, preceded formal diagnosis by several years. Now Marj reports severe pain and swelling of her hands and wrists and moderate pain in her hips and shoulders. Like many people her age, Marj also has osteoarthritis in her spine. The combined effects of these arthritides mean that it is particularly difficult for her to get going in the morning.

Marj takes several medications for her conditions, including warfarin, beta blockers, and oral hypoglycemics. She tries to manage her arthritis pain using daily paracetamol (acetaminophen) and nonsteroidal anti-inflammatory medication because she is allergic to most opioids. Because of the risk of serious cardiovascular complications, Marj's rheumatologist will not prescribe a COX-2 specific anti-inflammatory (inhibits the cyclo-oxygensase-2 enzyme that is responsible for inflammation and pain). At this stage, Marj shows no signs of acute joint erosions, so she is not using any of the biologic agents or disease-modifying antirheumatic drugs to limit RA disease progression.

Marj was an avid lawn bowler who regularly competed and played socially. Bowling, however, has become increasingly difficult as her mobility decreased. It was not until she took her name off the list of regular bowls events, stopped going out, and needed help with the gardening (which she loved) that her daughter suggested that she try a different approach such as seeing an exercise practitioner. She was reluctant at first, saying, "I can barely move! How am I supposed to exercise?" She had thought that her doctors had done all they could, and that she just had to live with her pain, as many people her age often do. After receiving some encouragement and seeing her cardiologist to get clearance, she started attending a 12-week arthritis exercise group.

Ten weeks into the program, her daughter, Carlie, came to visit one day and noticed her mother moving potted plants. Carlie thought this activity was excellent improvement and wondered if her mother had even noticed. She mentioned her mother's increased activity to Peta, the exercise practitioner leading the group. At the next class, Peta initiated the following conversation:

Peta (P): I caught up with your daughter, Carlie, during the week. She said she thinks you seem to be able to do more gardening since you have been exercising.

Marj (M): Oh, she's a funny one—always wants to see the best in me.

P: I expect that's because she loves you.

M: Perhaps. She's done it for years, trying to snap me out of my depression, trying to buoy up my mood.

P: Well, regardless of Carlie's motivations, do *you* think you can do more now than you used to be able to?

M: I have been doing some gardening . . . just a bit of potting to raise some seedlings. Carlie came over last week while I was up to my elbows in potting mix. I do love my garden. Somehow, I never feel quite so sad or flat when I'm in my garden. Before this class, yes, I was wondering if I would have to give up gardening altogether. I stopped doing heavy work—building garden beds and turning compost and netting trees—years ago. My son and grandson come over sometimes to do that stuff for me.

P: Carlie said she'd seen you moving pots around, and she thought that you'd stopped that kind of heavy work too.

M: Well, they weren't the really heavy ones, you know. Not tree pots or anything. But yes, I guess I do feel able to do a bit more than before.

P: Bit of a pleasant surprise then—being able to do a bit more?

M: Well, yes. I wasn't really expecting that exercise would do much except make me more sore and tired. I enjoy the classes, you know. It's good to be here, and I've met some lovely people too, but no, I wasn't expecting to feel different. I never expected to feel more capable; I thought that had all gone when the rheumatoid arthritis came along.

P: Oh, I am pleased for you. Feeling more capable is one of the best things that regular exercise can bring. If we continue to progress your exercises slowly and gently, then I expect that you won't feel too tired or worn out, but do tell me if you ever think we've overdone it in this class. The last thing I want to do is exhaust you—that would just put you off this class altogether. (She pauses.) Tell me, do you notice pain when you are in the garden?

M: Hmm, pain is still there, for sure. Pain is always there. (She pauses.) But I probably pay less attention to the pain when I am in the garden. I get caught up in what I am doing with the plants and kind of forget about it for a bit. Unless I get stuck in one position, like weeding—then I really feel the pain when I try to get up.

P: Doing exercise often produces that funny mix of effects, where you can do more, but don't necessarily feel less pain. I'm not going to promise that exercise will make your pain go away, but if you keep on with the exercise training, I'm pretty confident that you'll be able to do even more in that garden of yours.

Pain is a domain of great importance to clients, and it often demands a substantial amount of attention from them. Clients who exercise regularly but do not experience improvements in pain may become frustrated or cease exercise because their primary objective has not been achieved. Clients' frustrations with unresolved pain might not be discussed unless practitioners raise the matter for conversation. Rather, clients who are dissatisfied (Ava in case study 1) may simply cease partici-

pating in exercise sessions. Peta anticipated that Marj might experience such dissatisfaction with the outcomes of an exercise intervention, and provided information to help Marj refocus her expectations of exercise on an activity of personal importance (i.e., gardening) rather than pain. Peta gently guided Marj to identify the benefits gained from regular exercise training (i.e., the ability to do more gardening), and also to recognize that although she (Marj) had not anticipated this effect, she could enjoy it. Although an experienced practitioner may have been able to forecast this outcome, Peta knew that "a pleasant surprise" is a much easier recognition for a client to swallow than "I told you so."

Frustration in the face of persistent pain is also a challenge for practitioners. We work with clients for whom the natural progression of their conditions may be decline, and we may share clients' frustrations when they do not make exercise-related gains as rapidly as we would hope or if their pain does not improve at all. Due to their conditions, people with persistent pain may at times be unpleasant, grumpy, recalcitrant to try new activities, or frightened of provoking their pain, or they may have unrealistic expectations that we will be able to "cure" them of their pain.

Clients' frustrations may also manifest in excessive exercise or physical activity. For example, there is a risk that Marj, now focusing more on gardening than pain and feeling somewhat stronger and more capable, might choose to tackle a large project such as spreading compost or pruning trees and provoke an increase in pain following more vigorous activity. Peta could balance her encouragement of Marj with a caution to pace herself.

P: I am so pleased for you, Marj. You are able to do more of something you love, and that's just wonderful. I would ask you, though, to remember to pace yourself. If you overdo it in the garden, for example, tackling a big job all in one day, you could feel much worse rather than better.

M: Don't you worry about that. I am not about to go out and do anything silly.

P: I don't think it is silly to want to really achieve something you love, but I would suggest that if you want to take on a big garden project, you let me know and we could plan it out together. Most of those big jobs can be broken into small parts so that you can do them a piece at a time. That way you won't do too much in one day and become really sore.

Summary of Strategies for Practitioners

Pain is an unpleasant sensory, emotional, and affective experience. Pain does not necessarily equal physiological harm to tissue. We recommend that practitioners respect clients' reports of pain and the accompanying emotions while educating them about the relationships (or lack of relationships) among hurt, harm, and physical function. The purpose of the clinical encounter is to connect with the client to help bring about positive change, not to "sell" exercise as a product. Clients and practitioners have their own stories to tell, and if both stories are to be heard, then both parties must contribute, listen, and share. We offer suggestions of educational strategies that are suited to clients' stages of health behavior change (see table 12.1).

References

Bjarke Vaegter, H., Handberga, G., & Graven-Nielsen, T. (2013). Similarities between exercise induced hypoalgesia and conditioned pain modulation in humans. *Pain, 155,* 158–167.

Davis, A.A., & MacKay, C. (2013). Osteoarthritis year in review: Outcome of rehabilitation. *Osteoarthritis and Cartilage, 21,* 1414–1424.

Flor, H., & Turk, D. (2011). *Chronic pain: An integrated biobehavioral approach.* Seattle, WA: IASP Press.

Fransen, M., & McConnell, S. (2009). Exercise for osteoarthritis of the knee. *Cochrane Database of Systematic Reviews, 2009*(4).

Fransen, M., McConnell, S., Hernandez-Molina, G., & Reichenbach, S. (2009). Exercise for osteoarthritis of the hip. *Cochrane Database of Systematic Reviews, 2009*(3).

Hurkmans, E., van der Giesen, F.J., Vliet Vlieland, T.P.M., Schoones, J., Van den Ende, E.C. (2009). Dynamic exercise programs (aerobic capacity and/or muscle strength training) in patients with rheumatoid arthritis. *Cochrane Database of Systematic Reviews, 2009*(4).

Jordan, J.L., Holden, M.A., Mason, E.E.J., & Foster, N.E. (2010). Interventions to improve adherence to exercise for chronic musculoskeletal pain in adults. *Cochrane Database of Systematic Reviews, 2010*(1).

Lovibund, S.H., & Lovibund, P.F. (1995). *Manual for the Depression Anxiety Stress Scales* (2nd ed.). Sydney, Australia: Psychology Foundation.

Marcus, B.H., Banspach, S.W., Lefebvre, R.C., Rossi, J.S., Carelton, R.A., & Abrams, D.B. (1992). Using the stage of change model to increase the adoption of physical activity among community participants. *American Journal of Health Promotion, 6,* 424–429.

Marcus, B.H., Eaton, C.A., Rossi, J.S., & Harlow, L.L. (1994). Self-efficacy, decision-making and the stages of change: An integrative model of physical exercise. *Journal of Applied Social Psychology, 24,* 489–508.

Merskey, H., & Bogduk, N. (Eds.). (1994). Part III: Pain terms, a current list with definitions and notes on usage. In H. Merskey & N. Bogduk (Eds.), *Classification of chronic pain: IASP Task Force on Taxonomy* (2nd ed., pp. 209–214). Seattle, WA: IASP Press.

Ossipov, M. (2012). The perception and endogenous modulation of pain. *Scientifica.* Retrieved from www.hindawi.com/journals/scientifica/2012/561761/qq

Perri, A., & Halford, E. (2004). Pain and faulty breathing: A pilot study. *Journal of Bodywork and Movement Therapies, 8,* 297–306.

Scott, W., Trost, Z., Bernier, E., & Sullivan, M.J.L. (2013). Anger differentially mediates the relationship between perceived injustice and chronic pain outcomes. *Pain, 154,* 1691–1698.

Thorgaard Skou, S., Graven-Nielsen, T., Rasmussen, S., Simonsen, O.H., Laursen, M.B., & Arendt-Nielsen, L. (2013). Widespread sensitization in patients with chronic pain after revision total knee arthroplasty. *Pain, 154,* 1588–1594.

Tu, C-H., Niddam, D.M., Yeh, T-C., Lirng, J.-F., Cheng, C.-M., Chou, C.-C., . . . Hseih, J.C. (2013). Menstrual pain is associated with rapid structural alterations in the brain. *Pain, 154,* 1718–1724.

U.S. Department of Health and Human Services. (1996). *Physical activity and health: A report of the Surgeon General*. Washington, DC: Author.

Waddell, G. (2004). *The back pain revolution*. Edinburgh, Scotland: Churchill Livingstone.

World Health Organization. (2009). *Global health risks: Mortality and burden of disease attributable to selected major risks*. Geneva, Switzerland: Author.

World Health Organization. (2010). *Global recommendations on physical activity for health*. Geneva, Switzerland: Author.

CHAPTER 13

It's About Moving

Enabling Activity and Conquering Prejudices When Working With Disabled People

Cadeyrn J. Gaskin and Stephanie J. Hanrahan

Although disability is often discussed in medical terms, it can also be thought of as a social experience. In addition to having bodies that may not function as well as those of others, disabled people have to contend with how others react when they see, hear, or otherwise find out about the presence of disability. Often, these reactions are far from helpful, and they reveal deep prejudices toward disabled people.

Involvement in physical activity offers many benefits and presents numerous challenges for disabled people. As we outline in this chapter, exercise and many other forms of physical activity can promote the physical health and psychological well-being of disabled people. Physical activity also provides a context in which disability-related mental health issues can manifest. First, however, we introduce the idea of disability and expand on the issues touched on in the introductory paragraph.

Ideas about what constitutes disability and how disabled people should be treated have changed markedly throughout time, and they differ between cultures. Presently, there are two major ways of thinking about disability: the medical model of disability and the social model of disability. The dominant medical model emanates from the health professions and locates the problem of disability within the individual. Under this model, health practitioners define, diagnose, and attempt to treat the "impairments" that disabled people have. That is, health practitioners are trained to perceive dis-

abled people as being somehow broken and in need of fixing so that they may obtain something more or less approximating normal function. Although many powerful organizations (e.g., health care practitioner associations and guilds, health care providers, and universities) and their employees and members typically present the medical model of service delivery and treatment as a highly scientific and objective process, conceptualizations of what constitutes normal functioning are heavily value laden, and they change over time and between cultures.

In contrast, the social model of disability comes from civil and human rights movements of the 1960s and locates the problem of disability within society. From this perspective, people's physical or mental impairments do not cause disability; rather, the problems stem from the unaccommodating world around them. Poor building or civic design (e.g., steps with no handrails and footpaths with no curb cuts), prejudiced attitudes, and limited access to information (e.g., the unavailability of documents written in Braille) are examples of ways in which society disables people. Rather than changing individuals, as is advocated with the medical model of disability, proponents of the social model of disability have argued that it is society that needs to change.

Differences between these two perspectives arise in the language of disability. Many readers of this chapter may have already found our use of the term *disabled people*, instead of *people with disa-*

bilities, quite jarring. The American Psychological Association (2010), for example, has advocated for using person-first, disability-second language (e.g., people with multiple sclerosis, children with autism) to avoid equating people to their disabilities. The term *disabled person* is discouraged, because it may infer that the whole person is disabled. Under the social model of disability, however, the term *disabled person* is not pejorative because it is a commentary on society rather than a reflection on the individual; it is society that has caused the disability (i.e., it is society that places limits on what disabled people can achieve), not individual impairment. For these reasons, we have preferred the term *disabled people* in this chapter.

There is an uneasy tension between the medical model, which includes psychology, and the emancipatory ideals of the social model of disability. There remain circumstances in which disabled people can be legally detained and treated against their will and despite any objections from significant others in their lives. In contrast to the traditional stance of criticizing psychology for pathologizing disabled people, contemporary disability writers have argued that psychology has much to offer in advancing our understanding of disability (e.g., Thomas, 1999). In this respect, through the introduction of the concept of *psycho-emotional disablism* to the disability literature, Thomas recognized that not only does society oppress people who have impairments, but such experiences shape how these individuals perceive themselves and how they interact with others. For example, being excluded from physical play or sporting activities at school because of physical, cognitive, or sensory impairments may lead people to perceive that they have poor physical abilities and to avoid physical activity.

From a public health standpoint, the argument for encouraging disabled people to perform physical activity is compelling. Preventable and treatable chronic health conditions—such as obesity (Liou, Pi-Sunyer, & Laferrère, 2005), fatigue, chronic pain, depression, and anxiety (Kinne, Partrich, & Doyle, 2004)—are highly prevalent in disabled people. Some studies with disabled people have revealed the presence of secondary conditions in almost all participants (Nosek et al., 2006), and other research has shown that some comorbid conditions are up to four times more common in disabled people than in the general population (Nosek et al., 2006). Participation in regular physical activity is known to ameliorate many of the physical and mental conditions that disabled people experience (Warburton, Nicol, & Bredin, 2006).

The Physical Activity Guidelines Advisory Committee (2008) in the United States provided a detailed review of research related to the effects of physical activity on disabled people. The majority of the studies reported involved three to five exercise sessions of 30 to 60 minutes duration per week, so more research is needed to determine dose–response relationships. Generally, the extensive review indicated that the overwhelming majority of both random and nonrandom controlled trials found that physically disabled people who engaged in physical activity showed significant improvements in cardiorespiratory fitness, muscle strength, flexibility, walking speed and distance (in ambulatory individuals), bone mineral content and density (with weight-bearing exercise), quality of life and well-being, functional independence, depression, self-esteem, quality of sleep, interpersonal relationships, and anxiety. The report also indicated that physical activity leads to significant reductions in triglycerides, total cholesterol, and pain.

In interviews with physically disabled adults, Blinde and McClung (1997) found that not only physical, but also social, aspects of the self are enhanced through physical activity. Participating in activity programs redefined physical capabilities and expanded social interactions and experiences. Participating in physical activity can also be empowering (possibly because sometimes disabled people face limited achievement opportunities). Physically disabled male college students indicated that participation in physical activity can provide opportunities for three different types of empowerment: facilitation of goal attainment, perceived competence as a social actor, and social integration (Blinde & Taub, 1999).

Experiences in physical activity programs may differ depending on whether the programs are integrated (i.e., include people with and without disabilities) or segregated. An integrated program can be either freeing or constraining (Devine, 2003). Integrated exercise programs can be freeing when the physical and social environments allow individuals to participate on an equal footing with able-bodied participants and when there are opportunities for social integration and achievement. Integrated exercise programs, however, may be perceived to be constraining if individuals feel they are excluded from the group for either ability or social reasons. The influence of integrated programs on able-bodied individuals should also be considered. Perhaps participating in integrated exercise programs could help able-bodied people develop capacities for empathy, acceptance, tolerance, and open-mindedness (Hanrahan, 2007).

Even though there is overwhelming evidence of the physical, psychological, and social benefits of physical activity for disabled people, the majority of individuals with disabilities are sedentary. Epidemiological studies, predominantly from the United States, have shown that most disabled people are insufficiently physically active (Centers for Disease Control and Prevention, 2007).

Psychosocial Issues That Manifest in the Exercise Environment

Physical activity and exercise environments may present many challenges for disabled people. The difficulties in negotiating exercise settings (e.g., pushing a wheelchair or using a white cane in confined spaces) and executing desired movements, as well as the attitudes of others toward disabled people being physically active, make the exercise environment one in which psychosocial issues relating to disability can manifest. In this section, we introduce some of the issues that may arise in work with disabled people. Our aim is to sensitize the reader to these issues, rather than to give a categorical account of what life is like for disabled people. The life experiences of disabled people are as diverse as for able-bodied people. Attending a school that is well equipped to meet the needs of disabled children, for example, can be a vastly different experience than one where the staff has little or no experience with disabled children. People disabled from birth may have quite different childhoods than those who acquire disabilities later in life. People born in the 1960s will have had different childhood experiences than those born in

the 1990s. And so forth. Perhaps the only experience that is common among disabled people is one of coping with the prejudices of others toward them. Although understanding some of the more common experiences of disability informs practice, it is important to understand, from clients' perspectives, what life is like for them.

Collectively, physical activity researchers have drawn on the experiences of disabled people across the lifespan. In presenting this information, we have chosen to group major findings according to stages of development. There is an Eriksonian (1985) flavor to our writing in that we often relate physical activity to the pursuit of major psychosocial goals. Erikson's psychosocial stages of development (see table 13.1) may be particularly useful in this context because (a) his emphasis on social influences is consistent with our leanings toward viewing disability as a social phenomenon, (b) many of the stages have substantial physical components, and (c) the life cycle focus of his model fits well with the physical activity and disability research, which has involved people from a broad range of life stages. Although we discuss the issues that disabled people may face during different phases of their lives, it is important to bear in mind that the physical maturation from one stage to the next does not mean that one set of psychosocial issues is replaced by another. Often new psychosocial issues come to sit alongside the remnants of older issues that have not been adequately addressed. Feelings of inferiority developed during childhood, for example, may persist in some fashion throughout life. In addition, the cumulative effects of psychosocial experiences of disability will differ depending on if the disability is congenital or acquired, and the age and life circumstances at which the disability originated.

Childhood

In this stage of development, children make their entrances into school life where they receive systematic instruction in the skills that they will use to become productive members of society (Erikson, 1985). Although it is common for disabled children to receive education in regular schools alongside their able-bodied peers, some disabled children attend separate schools (e.g., schools for deaf children) or are placed in separate support units for disabled children that are colo-

Table 13.1   Erikson's Psychosocial Stages of Life

Psychosocial stage	Indicative ages	Nuclear conflict	Ego quality
Oral-sensory	Birth to 18 months	Trust versus mistrust	*Hope* (the belief that one's wishes will be fulfilled)
Muscular-anal	18 months to 3 years	Autonomy versus shame and doubt	*Willpower* (the determination to exercise freedom of choice and self-control)
Locomotor-genital	3 to 5 years	Initiative versus guilt	*Purpose* (the courage to develop and work toward valued goals)
Latency	5 to 12 years	Industry versus inferiority	*Competence* (the belief in one's ability to perform important tasks)
Puberty and adolescence	9 to 19 years	Identity versus role confusion	*Fidelity* (the ability to maintain loyal relationships despite differences in value systems)
Young adulthood	18 to 40 years	Intimacy versus isolation	*Love* (the capacity for mutuality of devotion among people)
Adulthood	40 to 65 years	Generativity versus stagnation	*Care* (concern for family and community)
Maturity	65 years and over	Ego integrity versus despair	*Wisdom* (detached, but active, concern with life)

Note. Erikson conceptualized the human life cycle to encompass eight psychosocial stages. At each stage, there is a nuclear conflict (critical turning point in psychosocial development), which represents an opportunity for the development of new ego qualities. Although described sequentially, with indicative ages, some people may not enter or exit stages at the ages stated, may regress into previous stages, or may appear to avoid the challenges of a particular stage through skipping to a later stage. The nuclear conflicts may best be viewed as continua, rather than as dichotomies. The relative success in addressing the nuclear conflict at one stage may influence a person's capacity to meet later psychosocial challenges.

cated within regular schools. There can be large differences between mainstream and specialized formats in terms of their disabling effects on children (Gaskin, Andersen, & Morris, 2012). Although the rights of children with special education needs to inclusive education in regular schools have become a cornerstone of public policy (United Nations Educational, Scientific and Cultural Organization, 1994), there is much debate on conceptual and practical issues with regard to its implementation (Lindsay, 2003). Unfortunately, the practice of inclusion in schools has not always followed well-intentioned policy (Graham & Spandagou, 2011). School principals (head teachers) have differing opinions on what it means to deliver inclusive education for disabled students, and the extent to which schools are inclusive may be dependent on principals' conceptions of *inclusive* education, characteristics of

school environments, and the attitudes and capacities of staff.

With regard to inclusion in physical activity, the attitudes of able-bodied peers, professionals (e.g., coaches, teachers), and family members have a significant influence on disabled people's participation in physical activity (Hutzler, 2003). Although physical activity can have positive associations for many disabled children (Bedini & Anderson, 2005), others may find being active to be punishing due to experiencing negative evaluations of their physical competencies compared with their able-bodied peers', having to endure painful physiotherapy, and being excluded from participating in physical activity (Gaskin, Andersen, & Morris, 2010; 2011; 2012).

Some disabled children engage in physical activity during physiotherapy sessions (Anttila, Autti-Rämö, Suoranta, Mäkelä, & Malmivaara, 2008). Although the intentions of physiotherapists may be to restore physical functioning (in line with the medical model), disabled children can find their therapy experiences painful and may not understand why they have to perform the prescribed exercises (Gaskin et al., 2012). Physiotherapy may also take them away from occasions when their peers are participating in enjoyable physical activities. Factors that deter young people from adhering to physiotherapy regimens include the boredom associated with doing repetitive exercises, frustration with not understanding why they have to do physiotherapy and not being able to achieve treatment objectives, strict physiotherapists, uncomfortable physical experiences (fatigue, pain, physical distress), and functional decline (Redmond & Parrish, 2008). In contrast, giving young disabled people the choice of whether or not they do physiotherapy and allowing them to have input into treatment goals and regimens is likely to enhance adherence. Perhaps the best way to enhance the lives of disabled children through physiotherapy is to make a shift from primarily focusing on repetitive practice of motor skills to being proactive in the promotion of physical activity in daily living (Damiano, 2006). Such an approach would involve the incorporation of the research evidence on physical activity and disability into practice through the use of intense active training protocols, mobility-enhancing devices, and lifestyle modifications.

Negative experiences with physical activity (e.g., limited competence, physical pain, and social exclusion) seem to contribute to the development or intensification of feelings of inferiority, low self-esteem for physical activity, and, for many, a reluctance to engage further in physical tasks (Gaskin et al., 2010; 2011; 2012). Evidence of the development of these feelings of inferiority can be seen in children's comments about physical activity, in which they seem to display internalized ableism (the incorporation of prejudices against people who are not able bodied) and identification with their able-bodied classmates (Hutzler, Fliess, Chacham, & Van den Auweele, 2002). Feelings of inferiority have been reflected in disabled adults' reports of their childhood experiences with physical activity (Gaskin et al., 2010; 2011; 2012). Regarding able-bodied people as normal, and themselves as abnormal (and not able to do some

things), may be perceptions that are repressed (or suppressed) in some children with disabilities (Bedini & Anderson, 2005). The idea of normality, however, seems to be idiosyncratic, and many disabled children downplay the importance of such a label differentiating themselves from others. Nevertheless, these types of evaluations do occur, and they may influence psychological well-being.

Adolescence

The disabling factors that some people face during their early school years continue as they transition to high school (McMaugh, 2011). Disabled adolescents have to contend with the disabling structural practices of the schools they attend, as well as the attitudes of peers and teachers toward disabled people. Social experiences with peers vary dramatically among people, with some adolescents forming strong, supportive friendships with some of their peers but also encountering bullying and victimization from others (McMaugh, 2011). In terms of physical activity, some disabled students have experienced routine exclusion from sporting and social activities (Gaskin et al., 2010; 2012; McMaugh, 2011). Rather than opting out of activities that may be physically difficult or health compromising, students are often placed in situations where inclusion is not an option. Some students find this exclusion from physical activity with their peers highly distressing (Gaskin et al., 2012).

Adolescence is a time when individuals' identities develop (Erikson, 1985) and, for some disabled people, physical activity can have an important role in how they perceive themselves (Gaskin et al., 2010). In one example of the experiences of a young person with disability (Ben), involvement in sport and exercise seemed to be a way of compensating for feelings of inferiority developed during childhood, and a means of developing a coherent identity (Gaskin et al., 2010). In many Western cultures, sport and physical activity have a dominant role in defining hegemonic forms of masculinity (Connell & Messerschmidt, 2005). Disabled people are also subject to the ideals of men and women that are portrayed in the mass culture; sometimes, they will go to extraordinary lengths to try to meet these standards (Gaskin et al., 2010). For example, they may focus on building fitter bodies or excelling at increasingly higher levels of competition. In his Olympic and Paralympic idols, Ben saw achievement personified, and he desired to be like these sports people. Because of this identification, Ben developed a strong commitment (maybe overcommitment) to sport and physical activity.

The example of Ben, however, may be an outlier. It seems more likely that adverse experiences with physical activity during childhood may lead to a lifetime aversion to being active. One example of a young woman with a disability (Amy) serves to illustrate this point (Gaskin et al., 2012). For Amy, physical activity in childhood amounted to social exclusion (she was removed from physical education classes, and she found it difficult to involve herself in the physical games of her peers), clinical interventions (painful physiotherapy, wearing callipers), and limited opportunities to demonstrate competence. When she entered high school, however, Amy made friends easily, because socialization between her peers occurred through conversation rather than physical games. That is, sedentary behavior was socially acceptable among Amy's group of friends.

Young Adulthood

Leaving the school years behind and entering adult life means that there may be different physical, structural, and social barriers with which disabled people have to contend. Attempting to join a fitness club, for example, may be met with refusal if disabled people are perceived as liabilities (Cousminer, 2003). If entry is permitted, however, some disabled people may find that they are limited in what they are able to do. For example, people using wheelchairs may find it impossible to maneuver around equipment that has been placed close together (Gaskin et al., 2011). The negative beliefs of some gym members and staff (e.g., "disabled people do not belong in fitness clubs," or "disabled people take up too much staff time and attention") may also discourage disabled people from embarking on exercise programs (an example of psycho-emotional disablism). To address such issues and facilitate access to fitness clubs, some disabled people have had to rely on the help of others (e.g., doctors speaking with fitness club staff, family members assisting with movement around equipment).

Young adulthood is a time when the building of close and loyal relationships with others is the main psychosocial goal (Erikson, 1985). This stage of life presents new challenges, not least of all, romantic intimacy. The myth that the presence of disability equates to asexuality is one that persists in society (Milligan & Neufeldt, 2001). Physically disabled people are presumed to have sexual dysfunction, thereby limiting their opportunities for gratification, and meaning that their sexual needs are deemed to be either absent or suppressed. Intellectually disabled people, by contrast, are perceived to have typical sexual function, but not the social judgment required to engage in responsible sexual relationships. Although such myths are contradicted in the literature (e.g., Sakellariou, 2006), people in mainstream society do not engage with this discourse, and so prejudices are maintained.

Some disabled people may engage in physical activity in attempts to normalize their bodies and realign them with body-beauty ideals of attractiveness (Gaskin et al., 2011; Guthrie & Castelnuovo, 2001). A good example of how physical activity ties in with sexuality comes from the case of David, a young man with cerebral palsy (Gaskin et al., 2011). David experienced the frustrations of not being able to form romantic relationships that many disabled people face. David began using a wheelchair in early adolescence, and perceived that if he were able to learn to walk again then women would find him attractive. Through engaging in physical activity, David was trying to regain the ability to walk, in the hope that success would make him attractive to potential partners. As with other men with cerebral palsy (Gaskin et al., 2010), David's motivation to perform physical activity can be intertwined with major psychosocial goals.

Middle Adulthood

The focus of middle adulthood is on making contributions to society, whether that be through raising the next generation, developing a career, or finding some other way of being productive (Erikson, 1985). The onset or deterioration of a medical condition can hamper productivity during this phase of life. The presence of impairments may make activities of daily living more time consuming than they were earlier in life. With possibly increasing demands from work and family, some disabled people may feel that they have no time to exercise. The re-examination of life goals and desires, which may typically occur during this psychosocial stage, may also lead to a nondisabled partner choosing to leave the relationship (Marini, Glover-Graf, & Millington, 2012). Such an occurrence may be detrimental to disabled persons' engagement in physical activity if they were reliant on their partners for financial, physical, or social support.

Throughout adulthood, motivations to perform physical activity are quite varied, with social factors having a significant influence on the extent to which people are physically active. For many disabled people, maintenance of physical function is a prominent reason to be physically active (Goodwin & Compton, 2004; Guthrie & Castelnuovo, 2001). Although some disabled people derive enjoyment from being physically active, others perceive it as something they do to comply with the advice of medical practitioners, to address their fears of the consequences of not exercising (Guthrie & Castelnuovo, 2001), or to try to achieve narrowly defined social ideals regarding bodily appearance and function (Gaskin et al., 2011; Guthrie & Castelnuovo, 2001).

Older Adulthood

Being able to reflect on one's life as worthwhile and meaningful is the hallmark of successful adjustment to older adulthood (Erikson, 1985). People at this stage in life also have to contend with increasing physical and cognitive limitations, as well as sensory impairments. Functional decline may be nothing new to some disabled people, but the increasing loss of independence will still be unwelcome for most.

For older adults, physical activity can help maintain and enhance many aspects of subjective well-being (Stathi, Fox, & McKenna, 2002). Being physically active can provide opportunities for achievement, stave off physical and cognitive functional decline, assist people in leading busy lives, and help them to keep a positive outlook on life. Physical activity can assist older people to continue interacting with the world outside of their homes and to maintain their family lives and social activities.

Case Study

This case of the disabled client (Maria) and the personal trainer (Paul) is a fictional aggregate based on our practice and experiences of disabled people trying to become active and our encounters with personal trainers. Maria, a 30-year-old teacher, is contemplating the idea of starting to exercise. She was born with spina bifida, and she has scoliosis (deformity of the spine), reduced sensation in her legs and feet, and partial paralysis in her lower body and legs. She is, however, ambulatory, and she has never used a wheelchair. Maria's doctor has told her that her sedentary behavior has become a major health risk. She has procrastinated about starting to exercise for a couple of years, and has been ambivalent about her doctor's warning. Recently, however, a friend of hers had an acute myocardial infarction, which prompted her to rethink whether she should be more active. She agreed to attend a meeting with a personal trainer (Paul) that her partner scheduled for her. In this initial meeting with Paul (P), Maria (M) is talking about why she has not already started an exercise program:

> **M:** I know I should be more active, but it can take me so much longer to do things than it does other people, and I just can't find the time to fit it in my schedule.
>
> **P** (ignoring the issue of time management and focusing on exercise, the lifeblood of personal trainers): I suppose it depends on how much a priority exercise is for you. You've been telling me that you're afraid of what might happen if you don't exercise.
>
> **M:** Yeah. Mandy had that heart attack, and she's only a bit older than I am. Also, another friend of mine just got diagnosed with type 2 diabetes. (She pauses.)
>
> (Paul again fixates on exercise and shies away from discussing Maria's anxieties.)
>
> **P:** So you're saying that you really do want to exercise?

M: I don't know about "want." I really don't like it. "Should" is probably more accurate. I should be exercising.

Paul was conscious of not telling Maria that yes, she really should exercise if she wants to minimize the stated health risks. First, she has already realized that exercise has health benefits, and second, it is not usually effective for trainers to preach to their clients. When Maria paused, he jumped in (perhaps a bit quickly) with the idea that she wants to exercise. She immediately corrected him by underscoring the difference between feeling as if she should exercise and wanting to exercise. Paul is now thinking that he has a few options, including talking about exercise not necessarily being that horrible, considering different types of exercise, challenging her about whether or not she really intended to ever exercise, or exploring why she may not want to exercise. He decides on the latter. Although he may tend to fixate on exercise to the exclusion of other topics, Paul at least is aware that his commenting on exercise not being that bad would be forcing his attitudes and beliefs on his client. He recognizes that he might understand Maria better if he can comprehend why she doesn't like exercise (an activity that has always been a major part of his life).

P: You say you should exercise, but that you really don't want to. What is it about exercise that you don't like?

M: What is there that I don't like? It takes time, and it hurts. There is definitely nothing enjoyable about it.

P: I'm wondering how you have come to see exercise as not being enjoyable.

M: Well, I've never exercised as an adult, but I have horrible memories of exercise as a kid. Physio sessions were the dreaded part of my week as a kid, and then when it came to PE classes at school, I either got a pass to the library or did something lame like keep score for everybody else.

P: So in school you were never really given the opportunity to participate in physical activity?

M: No, never. No one would have picked me to be on their team, anyway.

Paul either doesn't pick up on or avoids Maria's experiences of rejection and exclusion. As a personal trainer, he keeps the focus on physical activity.

P: So PE classes were all about team sports?

M: Yeah, usually. I guess the only exception was gymnastics, but there is no way I was going to be doing back handsprings.

Paul now realizes that he has latched on to the issue of PE experiences in school and has ignored what Maria said about physiotherapy sessions.

P: You mentioned physio sessions. Did they involve a lot of exercise?

M: It was usually the physio moving my limbs for me, but it involved a lot of stretching that really hurt. I hated it.

Paul is about to ask Maria if she thought there was any benefit from having gone to the physio sessions, but then he decides not to, because what would he do if she said no? Also, even if she did think the sessions were beneficial, what did that have to do with her engaging in nonphysio exercise sessions as an adult? Instead, he decides to explore her definition of exercise, because exercise is more than physio sessions or PE classes.

P: So do you equate the idea of exercise with either physio sessions or PE classes?

M: Yeah, I guess I do. I've never really done anything else.

P: Sometimes people equate exercise with structured classes or boring, repetitive exercises . . . .

M (interrupting): Yes, that is what I think exercise is—boring, repetitive, and painful. Either that or sport, and I'd suck at sport. I almost didn't come today because I was afraid that you'd start immediately by making me participate in some kind of boot camp. I told my partner that if that happened I'd never come again.

Paul has always enjoyed being active and struggles to understand how people cannot find activity to be enjoyable. His first inclination at this point is to start talking about what he likes about different forms of exercise, but he then realizes that because of Maria's different history and experiences with physical activity that his talking about how wonderful it is would probably just make her think that he has no idea about her situation. Paul doesn't want Maria to think that he is anything like the slave driver she seems to have in her head. In part due to his fear that she may never come back if he tries to hard-sell the idea that exercise can be fun, Paul changes tack and begins a discussion about what she does like.

P: OK. Instead of talking about what you don't like, how about you tell me what you do like?

M: That's just it. I don't like anything about exercise.

P: Sorry, I didn't make myself clear. What do you like generally in life—not specific to exercise?

M: Well, I love my job. I teach primary school. Kids at that age are great. They are still curious and get excited about learning, and you don't have the dramas to deal with that high school teachers do.

P: You love your job. What else do you like? What do you like to do when you aren't working?

M: Well, my partner and I like going to movies and sometimes just staying at home and playing board games. It probably sounds really old-fashioned, but we have a cupboard full of board games. I love it when I beat him!

Paul is excited to learn that Maria has a competitive streak. He's thinking that he should be able to figure out a way to use it. While still contemplating how he might be able to tie physical activity into her teaching, he prompts her for additional information about her activities.

P: What about on the weekends or holidays? What do you like to do when you have time off?

M: Chris, my partner, his family has a property out in the bush. So, sometimes we go there. It's great to get out of the city and be in nature. I obviously don't do any work on the property, but they have this great veranda that looks out over the pond. I love sitting out there and just communing with nature. Also, a couple of years ago we went to the coast—again, I really liked the sound of the waves, the smell of the ocean. It's just great being outside.

P: Do you ever go swimming in the pond or the ocean?

M: No, I might wade in a bit, but I definitely don't go swimming. First, I don't know how to swim, and second, I'm not too keen on anyone seeing me in bathers. I mean I know that most people find something to complain about regarding their bodies—just listening to my girlfriends rant on makes that obvious—but my body isn't what you'd call normal, and I hate it when people stare.

As a personal trainer, Paul does not feel equipped to wade into a discussion about social physique anxiety. Although demonstrating empathy for her concerns would probably be useful, he at least respects Maria's wishes about avoiding water-based activities, even though he likes pool-based exercise programs because of the possible non-weight-bearing cardio and resistance activities.

> P: Fair enough. I won't push you into taking up swimming. Aside from being more active being useful in terms of helping you to avoid illnesses, can you think of any other benefits of being more active?

Paul is a bit frustrated that he doesn't seem to be getting anywhere, but then he reminds himself that he had been getting bored with the repetitiveness of his boot camp clients, and that he wanted a change and a challenge. He actually likes the idea of a client who isn't focused only on appearance and whose mood doesn't seem to be dictated by slight fluctuations in weight. Paul has gotten some ideas about what Maria likes that he thinks he will be able to use in creating an activity program for her, but he is now trying to help Maria come up with positive reasons for engaging in exercise aside from just avoiding ill health.

> M: Well, I suppose that if I was more active and a bit fitter, I could play more with the kids during recess and maybe even join Chris for some mild kinds of activities. He likes being active, so I tend to stay at home whenever anything more energetic than sitting at a movie is involved.

> P: So it sounds to me as though you think there might be some benefits of being more active, but that you don't want boring, repetitive exercises, anything that resembles boot camp, or anything involving swimming.

> M: Yeah—I guess that's right, but I don't think that leaves you with much.

> P: I think I'll be able to come up with something. Do you want to include Chris in what we do or would you rather just participate on your own?

> M: It would be great if Chris and I could do it together, but I'm not going to go to his gym. I don't fit in there. I also don't want Chris to be bored doing really basic stuff.

> P: Well, I don't want you to be really bored either. How about we meet on Saturday, you bring Chris along, and we see what happens?

Maria and Paul make plans to meet at his studio on Saturday. When the time for the session arrives, Paul wants to start by showing his enthusiasm and also hopes to allay Maria's fears about exercise. He is interested in getting Maria to be active. He is not interested at this point in time in creating the ideal exercise program in terms of cardiovascular endurance, strength, power, or flexibility. He just wants Maria to be open to the experience of starting to move a bit more, an introduction that in the future may lead to a more traditional exercise program.

> P: Hi, Maria. You must be Chris. I'm glad you could both make it.

> M: Yeah, I was a bit hesitant, but we are here.

> Chris (C): Nice to meet you.

> P: Before we get started, I just want to say that I really like the professional challenge you have given me: helping you to become more active but avoiding what you consider to be boring or repetitive exercises. I like being tested and having the chance to be creative—definitely more interesting than the average exercise program. We are going to try a couple of things today that may or may not work. All I ask is that you give the activities a genuine try and that afterwards you are both entirely honest with me when you evaluate them.

M: That sounds fair.

C: OK.

P: I'll have you start with something relatively simple, but don't worry—if you find it too easy we can definitely make it more challenging. To start with, I'd like the two of you to hit this balloon back and forth between you 10 times without the balloon touching the floor.

They do the activity. Maria seems a bit hesitant the first hit or two, but successfully completes the task. Chris looks a bit bored.

P: So that must be too easy; you succeeded on your first attempt. This time you'll be doing the same thing, but with two balloons. You can't touch the same balloon twice in a row. I've brought two different colors so it will be easy to tell which is which. The goal is still to 10, but 10 for each balloon, so probably easiest if you count to 20.

Maria and Chris have a few attempts, but either a balloon hits the ground or one of them hits the same balloon twice in a row before they get to 20. Chris is looking less bored, but he is still not completely engaged in the activity. Maria is starting to look frustrated. Every time a balloon has hit the ground, it has been when it is her turn. She tends to miss when the balloon floats to her left. To help Maria's frustration, Paul decides to change things by devising a game that provides different levels of difficulty for Maria and Chris and also brings in an element of competition between the two of them, something Maria previously indicated she enjoyed.

P: Now that you've had a bit of a warm-up, time for something a bit more competitive.

Paul ties a string between a pole and a piece of exercise equipment. The string is about the height of Maria's shoulders. He then draws two playing boxes—one on each side of the string. One is about 2 square meters, the other about 3 square meters. He then directs Maria to the smaller square and Chris to the larger square.

P: First, Chris, are you right or left handed?

C: Right.

P: OK, from now on you can only use your left hand. Maria, you can use whatever hand you want. If you hit the balloon out or if the balloon hits the ground within your square, the other person gets a point. You can hit it twice in a row if you want to. It's kind of like balloon volleyball. Any questions?

C: What are we playing to?

P: Let's start with a game to 15.

M: I serve first.

Maria and Chris play the game. Chris is ahead early, but Maria starts to figure out how to take advantage of the fact that Chris can use only one hand while covering a larger space. Chris wins 15-12.

P: So how was that?

C: I can't believe I've started to sweat just hitting a balloon!

M: That was good. Can we play again? I know I can beat him!

P: Did I hear that correctly? You want to be active?

M: Well, this isn't exercise, it's just having fun!

Paul wants to indicate that the activity is a form of exercise, but does not want to extinguish the positive attitude that Maria has toward the activity, so he just has them play again without saying anything else. When the score is 10-10, Maria falls when rushing to hit the balloon. Paul is battling in his head how to react to the fall. He wants to help her, but does not want to coddle her because she has a disability. At the same time, he thinks that if one of his able-bodied clients fell, he would help them up. He decides to offer her a hand up, but does not say anything.

M: Oh, I guess I went for a bit too much. If my balance was better, I would have gotten that.

P: You are OK?

M: Yes, I just feel stupid. I mean, Chris never falls down and he has to cover a larger space.

P: I'm sure Chris has fallen in his life.

C: Sure I have.

M: But falling as a kid doesn't count.

C: I fell heaps of times when I went skiing, and I've tripped myself more than once in my adult life.

M: It's not the same.

P: True. It isn't the same. Chris doesn't have spina bifida. All my clients have different abilities and different skills. My job is to try to help them do what they can with what they've got.

M: I can't believe you just said that.

P: What?

M: That Chris and I are different because I have spina bifida and Chris doesn't.

Paul wasn't sure about being so blatant, but at the same time, he believes in being realistic and doesn't want Maria to waste her energy pitying herself.

P: Well, uh . . .

M (interrupting): It's great. Most people pussyfoot around my disability. I like that you just said that.

P: Good. So, as I said, my job is to help people be active with whatever skills and abilities they have. You mentioned that you wouldn't have fallen if you had better balance. Have you ever done anything to improve your balance?

M: Not since I was a little kid.

P: Would you be interested in doing something now?

M: I suppose.

Paul describes and demonstrates a few balance exercises and has Maria try them. He provides multiple exercises from which Maria will be asked to pick one to do at home. Having some choice in the exercise gives the client some autonomy in what she is going to do.

P: Of those three exercises, is there one you think you could do once or twice a day for the next week?

M: I think I could do the last one we did.

P: Great. When and where will you do the exercise?

M: I could do it while I'm brushing my teeth—after all, I'm just standing there.

P: Excellent. Pairing the balance exercise with a regular activity like brushing your teeth is a great way of fitting it into your schedule, and the act of brushing your teeth will also remind you to do the exercise. Now, do you want to finish the balloon volleyball game? I think the score was 10 to 10.

C: Actually, with that last point, I think I was up 11-10.

M: You aren't competitive, are you?

C: What about you? You had us stay up until 1:00 in the morning so you could finish beating me at Monopoly!

M: True.

Maria and Chris finish the game and then play a third. Chris wins both of them, but the scores are close. Maria seems to appreciate that Chris plays all out and doesn't just let her win points.

M: Wow, that is the most active I've been in years!

P: Was it boring or painful?

M: No, it was actually fun, but I might be sore tomorrow.

P: Some stretching could help with that. Are you game to do a few stretches?

M: Why not?

Paul leads Maria and Chris through some gentle stretches, indicating that they should not stretch to the point of pain. He finishes the session with a reminder about the balance exercises, and they agree to meet again the following week. Paul has plans over the coming sessions to increase Maria's activity through the introduction of more games, with the idea that she might eventually want to work on specific fitness and strength to improve her performance. As Maria becomes more confident in her physicality, Paul thinks he might eventually introduce water-based activities that may potentially allow her greater freedom of movement than land-based activities. One possibility might be to join a water-based program with other people with mobility problems, which might decrease her social physique anxiety, or take advantage of Maria's enjoyment of nature and have her and Chris start with some simple wading in the pond on his family's property when no one else is around to watch. Paul is also contemplating how to potentially harness Maria's love of teaching as a motive for getting fitter. She could become more

active during recess by playing games like balloon volleyball with the kids.

In sum, although Paul keeps Maria's disability in mind when selecting activities and exercises, his main challenge is changing her negative perceptions of exercise and helping her develop her exercise self-efficacy.

Final Thoughts

Although this chapter focuses on exercise and disabled people, it is perhaps worth reflecting on how remarkably similar disabled and able-bodied people are. There is an incredibly large body of evidence that demonstrates that both disabled and able-bodied people benefit from being physically active. Also, the powerful social motives that influence people to be active are common among disabled and able-bodied people. Nevertheless, some differences do exist. Bodies that may not function as well as people may wish and societal barriers present challenges to participating in physical activity. Through reading and reflecting on this chapter, we hope that exercise professionals will become enablers of physical activity in the lives of disabled people.

References

American Psychological Association. (2010). *Publication manual of the American Psychological Association* (6th ed.). Washington, DC: Author.

Anttila, H., Autti-Rämö, I., Suoranta, J., Mäkelä, M., & Malmivaara, A. (2008). Effectiveness of physical therapy interventions for children with cerebral palsy: A systematic review. *BMC Pediatrics, 8,* 14.

Bedini, L.A., & Anderson, D.M. (2005). I'm nice, I'm smart, I like karate: Girls with physical disabilities' perceptions of physical recreation. *Therapeutic Recreation Journal, 39,* 114–130.

Blinde, E.M., & McClung, L.R. 1997). Enhancing the physical and social self through recreational activity: Accounts of individuals with physical disabilities. *Adapted Physical Activity Quarterly, 14,* 327–344.

Blinde, E.M., & Taub, D.E. (1999). Personal empowerment through sport and physical fitness activity: Perspectives from male college students with physical and sensory disabilities. *Journal of Sport Behavior, 22,* 181–202.

Centers for Disease Control and Prevention. (2007). Physical activity among adults with a disability—United States, 2005. *Morbidity and Mortality Weekly Report, 56,* 1021–1024.

Connell, R.W., & Messerschmidt, J.W. (2005). Hegemonic masculinity: Rethinking the concept. *Gender and Society, 19,* 829–859.

Cousminer, D. (2003). Assisted workouts: Starting my own workout program. *Journal of American College Health, 52,* 47–48.

Damiano, D.L. (2006). Activity, activity, activity: Rethinking our physical therapy approach to cerebral palsy. *Physical Therapy, 86,* 1534–1540.

Devine, M.A. (2003). Constraining and freeing: The meaning of inclusive leisure experiences for individuals with disabilities. *Journal of the Canadian Association for Leisure, 28,* 27–47.

Erikson, E.H. (1985). *Childhood and society* (35th anniversary ed.). New York, NY: Norton.

Gaskin, C.J., Andersen, M.B., & Morris, T. (2010). Sport and physical activity in the life of a man with cerebral palsy: Compensation for disability with psychosocial benefits and costs. *Psychology of Sport and Exercise, 11,* 197–205.

Gaskin, C.J., Andersen, M.B., & Morris, T. (2011). Physical activity and fantasies in the life of an adult with cerebral palsy: The motivator, looking for love. *Qualitative Research in Sport, Exercise and Health, 3,* 238–262.

Gaskin, C.J., Andersen, M.B., & Morris, T. (2012). Physical activity in the life of a woman with cerebral palsy: Physiotherapy, social exclusion, competence, and intimacy. *Disability and Society, 27,* 205–218.

Goodwin, D.L., & Compton, S.G. (2004). Physical activity experiences of women aging with disabilities. *Adapted Physical Activity Quarterly, 21,* 122–138.

Graham, L.J., & Spandagou, I. (2011). From vision to reality: Views of primary school principals on inclusive education in New South Wales, Australia. *Disability & Society, 26,* 223–237.

Guthrie, S.R., & Castelnuovo, S. (2001). Disability management among women with physical impairments: The contribution of physical activity. *Sociology of Sport Journal, 18,* 5–20.

Hanrahan, S.J. (2007). Athletes with disabilities. In G. Tenenbaum & R. C. Eklund (Eds.), *Handbook of sport psychology* (3rd ed., pp. 845–858). Hoboken, NJ: Wiley.

Hutzler, Y. (2003). Attitudes toward the participation of individuals with disabilities in physical activity: A review. *Quest, 55,* 347–373.

Hutzler, Y., Fliess, O., Chacham, A., & Van den Auweele, Y. (2002). Perspectives of children with physical disabilities on inclusion and empowerment: Supporting and limiting factors. *Adapted Physical Activity Quarterly, 19,* 300–317.

Kinne, S., Partrich, D.L., & Doyle, D. L. (2004). Prevalence of secondary conditions among people with disabilities. *American Journal of Public Health, 94,* 443–445.

Lindsay, G. (2003). Inclusive education: A critical perspective. *British Journal of Special Education, 30,* 3–12.

Liou, T.-H., Pi-Sunyer, F.X., & Laferrère, B. (2005). Physical disability and obesity. *Nutrition Reviews, 63,* 321–331.

Marini, I., Glover-Graf, N.M., & Millington, M.J. (2012). *Psychosocial aspects of disability: Insider perspectives and counseling strategies.* New York, NY: Springer.

McMaugh, A. (2011). En/countering disablement in school life in Australia: Children talk about peer relations and living with illness and disability. *Disability & Society, 26,* 853–866.

Milligan, M.S., & Neufeldt, A.H. (2001). The myth of asexuality: A survey of social and empirical evidence. *Sexuality and Disability, 19,* 91–109.

Nosek, M.A., Hughes, R.B., Petersen, N.J., Taylor, H.B., Robinson-Whelen, S., & Byrne, M. (2006). Secondary conditions in a community-based sample of women with physical disabilities over a 1-year period. *Archives of Physical Medicine and Rehabilitation, 87,* 320–327.

Physical Activity Guidelines Advisory Committee. (2008). *Physical Activity Guidelines Advisory Committee report, 2008.* Washington, DC: US Department of Health and Human Services.

Redmond, R., & Parrish, M. (2008). Variables influencing physiotherapy adherence among young adults with cerebral palsy. *Qualitative Health Research, 18,* 1501–1510.

Sakellariou, D. (2006). If not the disability, then what? Barriers to reclaiming sexuality following spinal cord injury. *Sexuality and Disability, 24,* 101–111.

Stathi, A., Fox, K.R., & McKenna, J. (2002). Physical activity and dimensions of subjective well-being in older adults. *Journal of Aging and Physical Activity, 10,* 76–92.

Thomas, C. (1999). *Female forms: Experiencing and understanding disability.* Buckingham, England: Open University Press.

United Nations Educational, Scientific and Cultural Organization. (1994). *The UNESCO Salamanca statement and framework for action on special needs education.* Paris, France: UNESCO.

Warburton, D.E.R., Nicol, C.W., & Bredin, S.S.D. (2006). Health benefits of physical activity: The evidence. *Canadian Medical Association Journal, 174,* 801–809.

CHAPTER 14

Let's Run With That
Exercise, Depression, and Anxiety

Kate F. Hays

In the realm of exercise and mental health, as with many other aspects of our lives, there is a discrepancy between knowledge and behavior. On nearly a daily basis, whether in scientific journals or the popular press, we see reports on the benefits of physical activity. Regular exercise is associated with, among other things, reduced weight gain, improved sleep patterns, and reduced risk of mortality, coronary heart disease, stroke, diabetes, cancer, osteoporosis, and obesity (Haworth, Young, & Thornton, 2009).

Most news reports, journal articles, and books focus on the various physiological and physical health benefits. Beyond that, substantial information points to mental benefits, whether in regard to cognitive or affective functioning. Among these latter reports, considerably more space is devoted to benefits related to well-being—primary prevention of mental disorders—than to recovery, or tertiary prevention. This attention is not surprising; many more people are psychologically healthy than are emotionally distressed or mentally ill. Furthermore, a large and nonclinical population base allows for easy access and a large research pool.

It is accurate, and almost tautological, to say that mood improvements and decreases in tension result in increased well-being. Can that same shift among those who are psychologically healthy (from mild stress to a generally positive perspective) be extrapolated to those with mental illness (predicting a change from clinical depression or anxiety to improved functioning and feeling)? The mechanisms of change in people with clinical conditions may not be identical to the processes in those who experience only mild discomfort. Yet the clients who walk into a psychotherapist's office present with various mental health issues—most frequently, depression or anxiety (or some combination of both). Can exercise be of mental as well as physical benefit to them? In this chapter, I explore that question in regard to actual practice. Research information and an interactive model are followed by case examples.

The Clinical Challenge

Depression affects approximately 10% of the adult population in the United States each year. Nearly 20% experience a major depressive episode at least once in their lifetimes (Craft & Perna, 2004; Gartlehner et al., 2007). Whether because of an actual increase or an artifactual one—such as greater public awareness or the influence of the pharmaceutical industry—rates of diagnosis have risen sharply, and they show no likelihood of diminishing. During 1991 and 1992 in the United States, 3.33% of the adult population was diagnosed with major depressive disorder (MDD); 10 years later, the percentage had more than doubled, to 7.06%. These increases were consistent across almost all sociodemographic population subgroups (Compton, Conway, Stinson, & Grant, 2006).

Anxiety, similarly, affects a considerable proportion of the population. Anxiety disorders requiring treatment affect about 40 million (18%) Americans each year (Kessler, Chiu, Demler, & Walters, 2005).

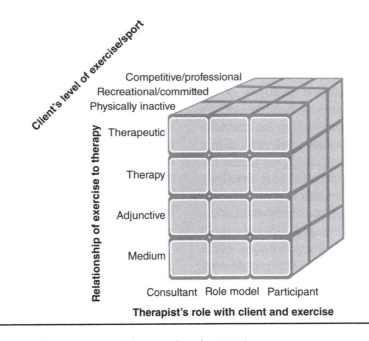

Client's level of exercise/sport

Competitive/professional
Recreational/committed
Physically inactive

Relationship of exercise to therapy

Therapeutic

Therapy

Adjunctive

Medium

Consultant   Role model   Participant

Therapist's role with client and exercise

Figure 14.1   Dimensions of exercise and therapy involvement.

offering suggestions or prescriptions regarding exercise in relation to mental health, may serve as a role model, or may participate with the client in physical activity during psychotherapy. The third element involves the relationship of exercise to the therapeutic encounter itself. In this regard, exercise may be valued for its therapeutic benefits, exercise alone may be the therapy of choice, exercise may be adjunctive to psychotherapy, or physical activity may be the medium in which the psychotherapy is conducted.

A matrix model (figure 14.1) illustrates the potential interaction of these three dimensions. For example, a professional athlete chose to work with a therapist who had been a high-level performer, anticipating that the therapist would understand his contextual experience and value his expertise. In another example, a committed exerciser, in a negative spiral, remained inactive and depressed following an illness. Brief consultation reminded the client that exercise had served an antidepressant function in the past. The client returned to running and mental well-being.

In the case descriptions that follow, two cells of the matrix are explored in depth, via session dialogue and reflection. (Actual details have been masked for purposes of confidentiality.) The first case concerns a client who was depressed and

physically inactive. I served as a consultant regarding exercise, and exercise was adjunctive to psychotherapy. In the second case, an anxious client was a recreational exerciser. I participated in moderate exercise with the client, using this activity as the medium in which psychotherapy occurred. I am reminded of the Latin phrase *solvitur ambulando:* All is solved by walking. Both cases involved walking—whether done by the client as the primary form of exercise or done by myself and the client during a therapy session.

Case Study 1: Talking the Walk

Shortly before her 65th birthday, Rachel called me for an initial appointment. She had been in psychotherapy with Steven, a colleague of mine, for several years. He had seen her through bouts of depression, binge drinking, recovery hospitalizations, and family challenges. Now, Steven met with Rachel monthly, in a supportive role designed to help maintain her behavior change. He had strongly encouraged her to exercise, a multipurpose method that might address many of her conditions. She had a history of recurring depression (with symptoms including intense sadness, loss of interest and energy, a sense of worthlessness, and low self-esteem); she was also overweight, with arthritis in her knees, and had recently been diagnosed with diabetes. Rachel, too, recognized that exercise would be helpful regarding her weight, diabetes, mobility issues, and mood. She also understood herself enough to know that she was feeling monumentally stuck. Both Rachel and Steven thought it would be helpful for her to work with a psychologist who could address exercise motivation with her.

First Session

A short, stocky woman with grayed curls, Rachel moves slowly and deliberately, planting her feet widely as she comes into my office. She sighs as she settles deeply into the easy chair. Sitting across from her, I comment that I will be asking various questions and writing down what we talk about today; once I get to know her, though, I won't be keeping notes during the session. I use a pre-printed form that I have created for intake interviews with sport or performance clients, based on one Taylor and Schneider (1992) originally developed. Because she is already in therapy, and because she has been referred specifically regarding physical activity, I touch more lightly on clinical issues than if this were a regular clinical interview. I start with a general inquiry:

> **Kate (K):** Tell me what's going on.

> **Rachel (R):** I get overwhelmed with things that happen, things that need to get done. I know that I'm likely to get depressed at certain times of the year. I'm here really because I'm in terrible physical shape. I'm diabetic. I'm overweight. I feel physically terrible. It hurts to walk. I'm a couch potato.

At this point, I'm mostly aware of a sense of dread. It's easy to establish rapport with Rachel—that's the least of my worries. I'm thinking: "What have I gotten myself into?" I was pleased and excited when Steven contacted me in the first place, to inquire whether I'd be willing to work with Rachel. He's a well-known and much-respected practitioner. I'm feeling performance pressure—mostly, in relation to him. More pragmatically, as a psychologist who often conducts psychotherapy, I'm wondering how to help Rachel, yet not interfere with her psychotherapy. As an antidote to

my own capacity for catastrophizing, I decide to obtain some history regarding her background in exercise and physical activity, successes as well as failures.

> **K:** It sounds like moving around at this point is quite a challenge. Tell me about you and exercise.

> **R:** It was really different when I was younger. In high school, I played volleyball, baseball, and basketball. I went skiing regularly. I liked swimming and biking. Most of all, I loved ice skating. I'm not sure where it all went. I got married, had three children—and there just wasn't time for me.

Inquiring more, I obtain a general sense of what Rachel's life is like. Her children are grown and married, with children of their own. She is actively involved with them all, and everyone gathers at her home at least weekly for Friday evening dinner. She and her husband have been married for 45 years, in what she describes as a companionable marriage. Always passionate about textile weaving, she rarely makes time for this activity, because she is general manager of her husband's busy dental practice.

> **R:** I'm at Jason's office 4 days a week—have been there since the kids left—and it's a harried, demanding situation. I'm receptionist, do the accounts, deal with any stuff that comes up. There are other things I'd like to be doing, but I feel I owe him; he stuck by me all those years that I was drinking.

We explore this information as well as her patterns of emotional eating. I begin getting a picture of a woman who, for a variety of reasons, puts her own needs and preferences last. Helping her validate her self-worth and values may be an uphill climb. I also wonder if that is my job here. And if we don't address these issues, will she let herself exercise?

In response to my questions, Rachel details various attempts that she's made at different points

If I were to be physically active . . .		
	Pros	Cons
Reactions of self	Proud of myself. Feel better (mentally).	Being in exercise class and not able to do it—look silly, out of shape. Feel mortified in bathing suit. Fear about not persevering. Where will I work this in? What will I have to give up to do it?
Reactions of others	Proud of me: • husband • children • friends [names listed]	Daughter will feel that I don't have enough time for her.
Consequences to self	Lose weight. Feel better (physically). Increased energy.	Feel sore.
Consequences to others	Husband would get more physically active.	

Figure 14.2 Rachel's initial "decisional balance" responses regarding physical activity.

to become more physically active, or to lose weight, or both. Fifteen years prior, she had lost about 100 pounds: "Mostly, I stopped eating." Not surprisingly, the weight returned (and then some). Subsequently, a medical clinic put her on an exercise regimen. She disliked the enforced structure. She tried to get into another clinic but didn't meet their criteria for inclusion. A few years ago, she bought a treadmill, created a program for herself, and stayed with it for a few months. At one point, she reached 40 minutes of exercise at a time. Now, the treadmill sits at the back of her closet.

I wonder, What *is* going to motivate Rachel? As part of my assessment, she and I discuss and complete a Decisional Balance Scale (Prochaska, Norcross, & DiClemente, 1995; see also the case study in chapter 6). This open-ended matrix offers a pro–con list regarding change and the consequences of change to oneself and others, as well as one's own and others' reactions. I ask questions of Rachel and write out her responses (see figure 14.2). This exercise serves a number of functions: Rachel is able to see a number of the thoughts that support and inhibit her likelihood of exercising. She and I now have a shared picture regarding her motivation. Diagnostically, it is also clear that she is more attuned to motivational aspects regarding

other people than herself. For example, she can immediately list a number of others who would feel proud of her, as well as the awareness that her self-consciousness inhibits her and her daughter's preferences are perhaps more important than her own.

As we complete this worksheet, I recognize that even though she has come to see me because she wants to become more active, and even though she understands the ways that exercise can be helpful to her, Rachel is not yet in the *preparation* or *action* stage of change (Prochaska et al., 1995). If I just prescribe specific types and quantities of exercise at this point, I will meet with resistance or failure to comply. Rachel is, however, well into the *contemplation* stage. It will probably be most useful to help her do some problem solving, obtain more information, and strengthen her social supports for physical activity. Whatever she starts with, I need to keep in mind her high level of self-consciousness and negative body image.

Brainstorming together, we come up with a list of possible forms of exercise, again paying attention to the positive and negative potentials for each. Although swimming would be easy on her knees and good overall exercise, the challenge of being in a locker room and changing in front of others stops her cold. On the other hand, taking the treadmill out from the closet seems like it might work. It's exercise that she could do without exposing herself to others.

During this conversation, Rachel develops a long-term goal for herself: to be able to go ice skating with her granddaughter. Looking at the woman in front of me, the image feels incongruous, yet that hope—combining as it does her central values of family, remembered joy, and desire to be fit—is also well worth honoring and celebrating. I remind her of her capacity for persistence; she has learned a lot through alcohol recovery.

I also offer Rachel a few tips for beginning exercisers: I encourage her to start slowly and make gradual changes. I describe ways she can keep a simple written notation of her exercise type, frequency, intensity, and duration. Given the upcoming holidays and her ongoing connection with Steven, we agree to meet in a month.

Second Session

K: I am really curious, Rachel, to hear how this month has been for you. What have you noticed about you and exercise?

R: Well, even though I have trouble imagining putting my bathing suit on at a gym, as we discussed last time, I guess I could go there with my bathing suit under my clothes. I hadn't thought of that. So I checked out three different clubs that have swimming pools. Two are near home and one is close to my husband's office. I was talking with my friend Sarah the other day—and it turns out she uses one of them regularly. So I'm thinking I'll actually join that one.

K: You've been really busy! I'm very impressed. Seems like just by writing out that list, you were able to come up with some counterarguments to your "yes, buts"!

R: Yes—maybe I'm learning something from all those years of working with Steven and keeping those darn thought records.

Well, that's not all: I actually got my son to drag the treadmill from the closet into the bedroom. Dusted it off and started it up. I decided to start small, as you said, so the first week I only did 10 minutes at a time. But I made myself get on it three times that week. It wasn't too hard. I took a few days off after I scalded myself, cooking—but now I'm up to 15 minutes each time—and still doing three times a week.

K: That is awesome! You know, in some ways, by the time you picked up the phone to call me, I think you had already committed yourself to making some changes. And you've got not only all your CBT experience to support you, you also have years of knowing about lapses and how to keep them from becoming relapses.

I truly am impressed. For a depressed person to make these changes this fast is not what I would have anticipated. Have I miscalculated in thinking she was in *contemplation*? Perhaps she has leapt into the *action* stage and bypassed *preparation* altogether.

I wonder if this may be a time in her life when Rachel can use exercise as a gateway to other aspects of health care and attention to her own well-being. My task now is to help her with persistence in this renewed behavior. It is time, as well, to help her begin attending to the important connections between exercise and both physical and mental health.

I also am aware that, when a client seems responsive to my interventions, I tend to pick up momentum. Here, I need to stay at Rachel's pace of change, appreciating the seriousness and longevity of her depression.

K: We talked last time about the idea of keeping written track of what you do about exercise. Have you had a chance to do that?

R: Well, I've been so busy, I really haven't. It didn't seem like it was worth it. Besides, 10 or 15 minutes on the treadmill is no big deal.

K: Maybe it's no big deal compared to what you think you should be doing—but compared with not exercising at all, it's a great start. Actually, the getting started part is in some ways the most difficult. Well, okay, the other really difficult part is keeping going.

(Injecting some lightheartedness—in this case, consciously playing with the issues of motivation and persistence—never hurts.)

And that brings me back to writing down what you've done. As I said before, it doesn't have to be an elaborate diary—you could just mark on your calendar "10" or "15" or whatever the length of time is that you walk on the treadmill. I'll write down for you, here, why it's so useful to note what you've done:

- It gives you information

  - about your consistency
  - about the "FIT" [frequency, intensity, and time/duration]

- It gives you a record that you can look back on
- It shows you the progress you make
- It reinforces the patterns you've established

It seems to me that you tend to discount your own progress or change. Writing down what you've actually done will show you that change over time. And besides, there's something really important that I would like you to start recording: your mood before you use the treadmill—or do any kind of exercise—and your mood after. Again, we can keep it really simple: How about a 1 to 10 scale, where 1 is "I don't even want to get out

of bed" and 10 is "I'm feeling fantastic." Just check yourself before and after you exercise—and remember to write those numbers down, too.

My intention here is to offer easy, simple methods of reinforcement that Rachel can use—and in particular, ones that will give her information to help shift her motivation from extrinsic (i.e., to please the new helping person) to intrinsic ("Ah! This really does have an effect and impact!").

In this process, I'm also deliberately modeling the idea of writing things down. Additionally, I'm giving her something, albeit a piece of paper with my (I hope, legible) handwriting. She may experience that paper merely as points to recall from our meeting; it may also be a way that she experiences our connection even in absence—a *transitional object* in psychologese.

Third Session

Although walking continues to be somewhat painful for her, Rachel has maintained regular, scheduled time to do so. When the weather cooperates, she walks outside now. She comments that she is walking for "only" 20 minutes at a time. She has, however, been noting the frequency and duration of her walking, and is surprised and impressed with its effect on her mood. The most dramatic change, she reports, was one day when she recorded a mood shift from a 3 to an 8. She's begun viewing the treadmill as an opportunity rather than a menace that stares balefully at her and tells her she *must* exercise. Now, it's an invitation. If she wakes up in a low mood, she is starting to feel assured that she can count on the treadmill to give her the physiological "lift" that she needs. She feels excited about the possibilities of change, especially if exercise is going to help her feel more energized.

Over time, Rachel and I worked on a number of issues. We often needed to come back to the same themes of self-care and the mind–body interaction. She was responsive to referral to a registered dietitian for assistance in weight loss. Because she was continuing to work with Steven, we soon started meeting for a half hour rather than a full hour, using the time as supportive check-in.

Steven announced his impending retirement. With three-way discussions, we decided that Rachel and I would expand our charge to include Rachel's entire well-being. She and I continued meeting monthly, for the most part—at times of crisis, we met more frequently—but now, our meetings were an hour in length. Our focus broadened to discussing ways in which Rachel could address some of her larger life goals. We talked frequently about her desire to feel more aesthetic fulfillment in her life, whether by having time to weave or attend theater and concerts. This yearning kept getting sidetracked by various family crises that Rachel felt pulled into. Because I am someone with a passion for the creative and the aesthetic, I supported her attention to those longings of hers, yet attempted not to impose my own expectations of how she should be living her life and where her priorities should be.

Although I often work with clients for a fairly short term, I saw Rachel for a total of 34 sessions, over a 3-year period. There were many starts and stops in her progress, lapses followed by re-engagement, but always with a sense that we were headed, overall, in a constructive direction.

We completed treatment—with the caveat that she could return at any time—when Rachel felt confident about her commitment to regular exercise (5 days a week, either walking or swimming) as an essential aspect of her ongoing depression management. She had also built into her schedule a weekly block of time for cultural engagement, whether for her own or others' activities. Ice skating with her granddaughter, however, never happened.

Case Study 2: Walking the Walk

Therapists have been exercising with clients for at least 100 years, since Sigmund Freud conducted therapy while walking with Gustav Mahler (Feder, 2004). Despite the longevity of this practice, there is surprisingly little research on this aspect of the client, therapist, exercise interaction (Hays, 1994; 1999). Exercising with clients—a situation in which physical activity serves as the medium in which therapy is conducted—may occur for various reasons. An emotional impasse can be shifted; agitation, anxiety, or interpersonal tension can be moderated; catharsis can be facilitated or

enhanced; or rapport can be developed via a different relational mode (used in particular with children or adolescents). Appropriate cautions need to be taken into consideration, including (at least) client and therapist physical condition, as well as issues of confidentiality and potential boundary blurring (Hays & Sime, 2014).

Referred by her couples therapist for individual therapy, 27-year-old mental health professional Shana described herself as follows: "[I have] lost direction in my life. I feel stuck in my relationship and at work. I'm thinking about going back to school. I feel trapped in many aspects of my life." She characterized her early life as chaotic. Shana was the youngest of three, the daughter of alcoholic parents. Her mother was hospitalized following a suicide attempt. Removed from home by welfare authorities, Shana's experience in foster care brought its own major challenge; she was sexually abused in that household.

At least on the surface, Shana appeared to be an ideal therapy client. She was interested in working with me, she was psychologically sophisticated, she had been in therapy before, and she was highly aware of both her history and current thoughts and emotions.

Second Session

> **Shana (S):** I remember the day—I was 11—that my mother ODed. I don't know what she was taking, but I'm sure, with alcohol, that it was a pretty lethal combination. And she knew it! It's not as if it just happened. Yeah. I came home from school—I never wanted to come home from school, I never knew what I'd find. . . . I think this was the worst, though—and there was this note just left on the table for whoever walked in.
>
> I guess I knew enough to call the hospital. (She shudders.) But you know, that's just one moment in this endless litany. Oh, I am so fucked up! (Tears leak out of her eyes.)

As Shana pours out her story, I think to myself, "This is going too fast." Yes, she's had a lot of therapy—but at our initial meeting, I also experienced how brittle and self-conscious she was. Is she likely to decompensate—that is, become emotionally less functional? Might she dissociate? Can I help her contain and modulate her rush to pour out her life, so that she can process it in manageable amounts? Can I help her ground herself in the present rather than fling herself back into her past? By exposing herself to me, this near-stranger, is she—just as abruptly—then going to have to close herself down? Can I help her learn that interactions with others are not all-or-nothing? Can we develop some sense of safety and trust in this relationship and process?

I am asking myself these questions as part of a clinical differential diagnosis. Her history of trauma, abrupt self-revelation, agitation, and hypercritical self-reflection all raise questions of an anxiety disorder, post-traumatic stress disorder (PTSD), perhaps in combination with a personality disorder. While considering these assessment questions, I also want to validate her experience and, at the same time, help her "contain" it in effective ways.

K: That's a lot, Shana. The memories are so strong for you. I can see and hear that. I'm very willing to learn more about where you've been—and I know that that's part of your healing and coming to terms with what you experienced.

You may have heard this phrase before: "That was then and this is now." It seems simple but I think it's very important: The "then" really did happen and was devastating. It's important to recognize and acknowledge it. And at the very same time, you have learned over the years so many ways to cope.

You and I talked last time about diaphragmatic breathing, and how much it helps you settle back into yourself. Would it be useful to take a couple of minutes right now to do some of that breathing? Are there other ways that you can calm yourself right now?

S: (Takes three moderately deep breaths and then launches, anew.) Yeah, that works. . . . But this is so embarrassing. You see? This is all so bad. I'm really . . .

(She goes silent.)

There's a lot of power in silence, judicious silence (Hanrahan, 2005). At the same time, I'm feeling concerned, wondering *where* Shana's thoughts are going. Is she actively dissociating in my office? Certainly, her history would suggest this possibility. Should I let her just sit there, and see what happens?

S: (She gives herself a shake, takes another deep breath, and exhales forcefully.) OK, that's not fair to you. I'm OK, really I am. It's just . . . (She starts to drift off again.) Oh, I don't know. I get caught up in what happened. I know this sequence so well! It's what happens with my girlfriend, too. I start to let her in, and then I just shut down. And then I blow up. And then it sort of subsides, and then we're fine for a little while, and then I think it's safe and start telling her things again and then . . . I mean, I know this pattern, so why don't I just stop it?

K: Shana [using her name again, partly to help her stay grounded in the present and in our particular situation], you have such understanding of your usual ways of interacting these days, and you have such access to what you experienced in the past. Maybe our job will be to help you know what to do with all of this, in a way that helps you ultimately feel some sense of control and some flexibility. That way, you can feel like you've got some choices about yourself and the way you connect with other people.

S (dubiously): Yeah.

This session was instructive, although challenging. Shana postponed the next session, apparently because of an emergency situation in her work setting. The on-again, off-again quality of our sessions felt unstable. Sometimes Shana would postpone meetings—again, at least ostensibly because of work obligations. She left one session partway through, saying that she couldn't think of what to talk about. At other times, she would start to talk and then shut down, explaining yet again that she *knew* I would see (and judge) how emotionally damaged she was. Alternatively, she would minimize and discount both her traumatic history and its impact on her current functioning.

Sixth Session

Shana arrives promptly but starts out:

> S: I don't know what to talk about today. You know, after our last session I thought of something that we should talk about. It seemed important at the time. I remember that much—but now I can't even remember what I was going to talk about. (She lapses into silence.)

By now I have had enough experience with Shana to recognize that these silences are not necessarily serving a therapeutic function. Rather, they seem like opportunities for negative self-judgment at best and—probably—dissociation at worst.

Both Shana and I are wearing sturdy shoes and the weather outside is sunny, spring-like, and inviting. Through information gathered during the intake process and in subsequent conversation, I am aware that Shana exercises regularly.

> K: Shana, it seems as if sitting in silence sometimes doesn't help you move forward. I wonder if we might continue this conversation on a walk. We probably won't run into anyone we know in this neighborhood—but if we do, I suppose we could just say hi and keep on going. I don't think it would be particularly obvious that what we're doing is therapy. What do you think?

> S: Phew! That's a really good idea. I feel as if I'm crawling out of my skin, just sitting here. And I don't think it's going to get any prettier.

I am aware that this is the first time, in all our contact, that I've experienced any level of enthusiasm in Shana's demeanor. It seems as if this suggestion has actually increased her level of trust. Perhaps I have offered her a way—during therapy—that she can engage in some self-regulation.

We walk for about five minutes, silently. Shana bends down regularly to pick up and throw some pebbles. And then she says:

> S: Oh! Of course! That's what I was thinking of. Duhhh! Well, that's pretty obvious. OK. It's about one of those therapists I saw. OK. So this one was right after I finished college. I finally talked to my therapist about what happened in that foster home. Oh. And I guess I talked about wondering about who I was sexually, anyway. And then . . . maybe it was poor timing. My therapist went on vacation. By then I knew enough about myself that I could tell that I was bleeding emotionally. So I went to a hospital out of town—I didn't want her or anyone to know—and got myself admitted.

> The next time I saw that therapist, she had found out, anyway. (She falls silent and we walk for a minute.) She . . . she said she wouldn't work with me anymore. (She pauses.) She didn't ever tell me why. What do you think?

It's my turn to pause. Mostly I feel outrage at this therapist who has—at least as Shana experienced it (whether this tale is accurate or not)—perpetrated against her in yet another way, abandoning her at a time of crisis and in response to her disclosure. Despite my reaction, I don't think that's the core of what Shana needs to hear from me at the moment.

> K: Shana, I appreciate you letting me know what happened. That sounds so difficult. It seems like it was another situation where you had to look out for yourself, you had to take care of yourself, because the person who was supposed to be the caretaker didn't do

so. And then—that you were punished for taking care of yourself. That's quite a pattern to experience through your life.

S (quietly): Yeah.

K (mirroring the somberness of the moment): And I guess it helps explain part of the reason that it's been such a challenge for us to move forward in our work, despite both of our best intentions.

S: Yeah.

We circle back to the office and speak a bit about the "walking intervention." Shana expresses surprise that being outside—and perhaps being side by side rather than face to face—has been a useful way to engage the therapy. She seems interested in trying this again sometime; I indicate my willingness. We complete the usual end-of-session transactions regarding payment and scheduling.

Shana came in, again sporadically, for a few more sessions. During one of these times, we again went for a walk in response to her high level of agitation in the office. In that session, less self-punitive than previously but nonetheless self-critical, Shana said, "Maybe I'm not ready for therapy." We discussed her treatment readiness thoroughly. Making use of her sense of competence as a mental health professional, I suggested she try out a third-person perspective. I asked her, "Suppose someone just like you came in to see you and made that comment. How might you respond?" Shana thought she'd probably remind the person that therapy is a process and that she should just stick it out. Although she left the session 10 minutes before it was scheduled to end, she said she'd give therapy one more try. The following week, she came—although late—and said she had decided she just wasn't ready for therapy and that at this point it was adding to her stress. I did what I could to honor her decision yet leave the door open to a return to psychotherapy. I suggested that we meet for a check-in in 4 months' time—the new year, and perhaps a new start. Although she took this offer seriously, Shana said that she was likely not to come in. After the new year arrived, she called a few days before that

scheduled session to say that financial matters precluded her starting up therapy again.

Conclusion

As these real-life cases illustrate, and despite the seductive hope of the Latin phrase *solvitur ambulando*, physical activity can't solve all issues of mental health and illness. At the same time, research and practice clearly underscore the various ways in which exercise *can* be used, often with predictably good effect. The agenda for the future is clear. More research can help pinpoint the interaction between exercise and clinical recovery, more systematic training of mental health professionals will bolster practice, and more information from practitioners will in turn further inform the research and practice agenda.

References

American Psychiatric Association (2010). *Practice guideline for the treatment of patients with major depressive disorder.* Retrieved from http://psychiatryonline.org/data/Books/prac/PG_Depression3rdEd.pdf

Babyak, M., Blumenthal J.A., Herman, S., Khatri, P., Doraiswamy, M., Moore, K., . . . Krishnan, K.R. (2000). Exercise treatment for major depression: Maintenance of therapeutic benefit at 10 months. *Psychosomatic Medicine, 62,* 633–638.

Barlow, D.H. (Ed.). (2007). *Clinical handbook of psychological disorders: A step-by-step treatment manual.* New York, NY: Guilford Press.

Callaghan, P. (2004). Exercise: A neglected intervention in mental health care? *Journal of Psychiatric and Mental Health Nursing, 11,* 476–483.

Compton W.M., Conway, K.P., Stinson, F.S., & Grant, B.F. (2006). Changes in the prevalence of major depression and comorbid substance use disorders in the United States between 1991–1992 and 2001–2002. *American Journal of Psychiatry, 163,* 2141–2147.

Craft, L.L., & Perna, F.M. (2004). The benefits of exercise for the clinically depressed. *Primary Care Companion to the Journal of Clinical Psychiatry, 6,* 104–111.

Dunn, A.L., Trivedi, M.H., Kampert, J.B., Clark, C.G., & Chambliss, H.O. (2005). Exercise treatment for depression: Efficacy and dose response. *American Journal of Preventive Medicine, 28,* 1–8.

Exercise is Medicine (n.d.). Retrieved from http://exerciseismedicine.org

Feder, S. (2004). *Gustav Mahler: A life in crisis*. New Haven, CT: Yale University Press.

Gartlehner, G., Hansen, R.A., Thieda, P., DeVeaugh-Geiss, A.M., Gaynes, B.N., Krebs, E.E., . . . Lohr, K.N. (2007). *Comparative effectiveness of second-generation antidepressants in the pharmacologic treatment of adult depression*. Rockville, MD: Agency for Healthcare Research and Quality. AHRQ Publication No. 07-EHC007-EF.

Greist, J.H., Klein, M.H., Eischens, R.R., Faris, J., Gurman, A.S., & Morgan, W.P. (1978). Running through your mind. *Journal of Psychosomatic Research, 22*(4), 259–294.

Hamer, M., Stamatakis, E., & Steptoe, A. (2009). Dose-response relationship between physical activity and mental health: The Scottish Health Survey. *British Journal of Sports Medicine, 43,* 1111–1114.

Hanrahan, S.J. (2005). On stage: Mental skills training for dancers. In M.B. Andersen (Ed.), *Sport psychology in practice* (pp. 109–128). Champaign, IL: Human Kinetics.

Haworth, J., Young, C., & Thornton, E. (2009). The effects of an "exercise and education" programme on exercise self-efficacy and levels of independent activity in adults with acquired neurological pathologies: An exploratory, randomized study. *Clinical Rehabilitation, 23,* 371–383.

Hayes, S.C., Strosahl, K.D., & Wilson, K.G. (1999). *Acceptance and commitment therapy: An experiential approach to behavior change*. New York, NY: Guilford.

Hays, K.F. (1994). Running therapy: Special characteristics and therapeutic issues of concern. *Psychotherapy, 31,* 725–734.

Hays, K.F. (1999). *Working it out: Using exercise in psychotherapy*. Washington, DC: American Psychological Association.

Hays, K.F. (2010, October). *Exercise and psychotherapy: Mental benefits and therapists' perspectives*. Paper presented at the annual conference of the Association for Applied Sport Psychology, Providence, RI.

Hays, K.F., & Sime, W.E. (2014). Clinical applications of exercise therapy for mental health. In J.L. Van Raalte & B.W. Brewer (Eds.), *Exploring sport and exercise psychology* (3rd ed., pp. 209–239). Washington, DC: American Psychological Association.

Herring, M.P., O'Connor, P.J., & Dishman, R.K. (2010). The effect of exercise training on anxiety symptoms among patients: A systematic review. *Archives of Internal Medicine, 170,* 321–331.

Johnsgard, K.W. (2004). *Conquering depression and anxiety through exercise*. Amherst, NY: Prometheus.

Kessler R.C., Chiu W.T., Demler, O., & Walters E.E. (2005). Prevalence, severity, and comorbidity of twelve-month DSM-IV disorders in the National Comorbidity Survey Replication (NCS-R). *Archives of General Psychiatry, 62,* 617–627.

Landers, D.M., & Arent, S.M. (2001). Physical activity and mental health. In R.N. Singer, H.A. Hausenblas, & C.M. Janelle (Eds.), *Handbook of research on sport psychology* (2nd ed., pp. 740–765). New York, NY: Wiley.

Leith, L.M. (1998). *Exercising your way to better mental health*. Morgantown, WV: Fitness Information Technology.

Mohler, J.M. (2005). *Determinants of mental health providers' use of exercise as a treatment for psychological distress* (Unpublished doctoral dissertation). Loyola University, Baltimore, MD.

Mojtabai, R., & Olfson, M. (2010). National trends in psychotropic medication polypharmacy in office-based psychiatry. *Archives of General Psychiatry, 67,* 26–36.

Otto, M., & Smits, J.A.J. (2011). *Exercise for mood and anxiety: Proven strategies for overcoming depression and enhancing well-being*. New York, NY: Oxford University Press.

Quinn, C. (2010). Training as treatment. *Nursing Standard, 24*(22), 18–19.

Pasquariello, C.D. (2011). *Let's get physical: The role of physical activity in the training of graduate mental health students* (Unpublished master's thesis). Virginia Commonwealth University, Richmond, VA.

Pollock, K.M. (2001). Exercise in treating depression: Broadening the psychotherapist's role. *JCLP/In Session: Psychotherapy in Practice, 57,* 1289–1300.

Prochaska, J.O., Norcross, J., & DiClemente, C. (1995). *Changing for good*. New York, NY: Harper.

Robertson, R., Robertson, A., Jepson, R., & Maxwell. M. (2012). Walking for depression or depressive symptoms: A systematic review and meta-analysis, *Mental Health and Physical Activity, 5,* 66–75.

Rosenblatt, A.H. (2012). *Factors related to psychologists' recommendation of physical exercise to depressed clients*. (Unpublished doctoral dissertation). Adler School of Professional Psychology, Chicago, IL.

Sacks, M.H., & Sachs, M.L. (1981). *Psychology of running*. Champaign, IL: Human Kinetics.

Summers, R.F., & Barber, J.P. (2012). *Psychodynamic therapy: A guide to evidence-based practice*. New York, NY: Guilford.

Taylor, J.J., & Schneider, B.A. (1992). The Sport-Clinical Intake Protocol: A comprehensive inter-

CHAPTER 15

Overtraining in Professional Sport

Exceeding the Limits in a Culture of Physical and Mental Toughness

Stephanie J. Tibbert and Mark B. Andersen

A great deal of exercise activity occurs in the realm of sport, from junior recreational sport to professional teams. Sport is exercise, and many of the processes that occur in sport also occur in similar ways in exercise settings. Sport and exercise psychology are not dichotomous fields. The overlap is extensive, and we believe exercise (and how exercise can go wrong) in sport settings needs attention. This chapter concerns overexercising in the domain of professional sport, but a discussion regarding implications for other physical activity contexts is presented following the case study.

In daily life we walk a tightrope between stress and recovery and attempt to maintain a balance between a host of stressors and adequate recovery. When this balance is not maintained we may find that our ability to perform is reduced. Two individuals may be playing the same sport, or following the same training program, but one may flourish, producing personal best performances, and the other may fail to complete the basic training program. The early research investigating overtraining (OT) attributed plateaus or decreases in performance mainly to training stress, but many factors, including personality, relationships, experiences, sport and exercise environments, and current life situations, will affect the stress/recovery balance, which in turn will affect well-being, performance, and health (Richardson, Andersen, & Morris 2008).

Definitions

Researchers have used numerous terms to describe athletes' unexplained performance decrements and loss of positive training adaptation, such as OT, overtraining syndrome (OTS), burnout, staleness, overreaching, and underrecovery. The mercurial terminology has hampered understanding of OT-related phenomena, but the inconsistencies appear to have arisen because there are a variety of outcomes and many risk factors, not just one or two pathways for most athletes. In the following section, we review the current definitions identified in the literature.

Overreaching, Overtraining, and Overtraining Syndrome

Individuals specifically train to overload their bodies to produce compensatory adaptations resulting in enhanced performance. The effect of the overload is a short-term performance decrement while their bodies adapt. Functional overreaching describes the adaptation period, but lasts only for a short period (e.g., days or weeks). Nonfunctional overreaching is characterized by a relatively long period of performance decrement that is not in line with the time it usually takes for athletes' bodies to adapt. Long-term performance decrements associated with imbalances between training or non-training stressors and the corresponding recovery may be integral to the development of OT (Meeusen et al., 2006). There appears to be a gray area concerning differences between nonfunctional overreaching and OT. Although Meeusen et al. provided some distinctions between OT and nonfunctional overreaching definitions, it is still unclear when, or if, nonfunctional overreaching turns into OT. It appears that functional overreaching, nonfunctional overreaching, and OT are on a continuum of increasingly severe forms of athlete imbalances between stress and recovery. Nevertheless, alternative descriptors of OT exist, both as positive and negative adaptations to training (e.g., Lehmann, Foster, Gastmann, Keizer, & Steinacker, 1999), and as a process and an outcome (Kreider, Fry, & O'Toole, 1998). Hooper and Mackinnon (1995) suggested that OT is the process, whereas OTS is one of the eventual outcomes from stress/recovery imbalance (SRI), along with illness and injury, which represent the end state of nonadaptation resulting from OT behaviors.

Burnout

Maslach (1982) initially developed the concept of burnout to describe outcomes of job stress among people employed in helper–recipient relationships (e.g., nurses). Later, Smith (1986) produced a list of symptoms of burnout in sport, including boredom and a loss of motivation, which are at odds with the extremely high levels of motivation often associated with OT. Richardson et al. (2008) argued that the loss of motivation inherent in burnout is a key factor in distinguishing it from OT, although burnout may be one outcome of the OT process. Burned-out athletes may be fed up with training, demotivated, and emotionally exhausted, but the physical breakdown associated with OTS is often not present (Richardson et al., 2008).

Staleness

Staleness refers to the state of sustained fatigue or underperformance athletes may experience. Silva (1990) suggested that staleness represents an early stage in the development of OTS. Richardson et al. (2008) suggested that staleness and OTS were similar and recommended that adding another construct to the already confusing OT lexicon is not a good enough reason to use the term.

Underrecovery

Kellmann (2002) focused on the recovery aspect of athletes' training, arguing that inadequate recovery between training sessions is the main cause of OTS. Kellmann (2002) defined recovery as an "inter- and intra-individual multilevel (e.g., psychological, physiological, social) process . . . for the re-establishment of performance ability" (p. 10) and identified that recovery is unique to each individual. Looking at the broad view of recovery enables a holistic approach to understanding why athletes may be in SRI, rather than just reviewing training volumes and intensities (Richardson et al., 2008).

Kellmann (2002) is one of several researchers to view performance decrement in a holistic light. Kenttä and Hassmén (2002) observed that "nontraining stressors have more recently gained a wider acknowledgement in regard to overtraining and burnout in athletes" (p. 69). Richardson et al. (2008) also suggested using the term OT to describe negative processes or behaviors in response to stress/recovery imbalance or performance decrements. Outcomes of OT include OTS, illness, and injury. In this chapter, we use the other associated terms only in reference to the work of researchers who have used them.

Prevalence of Overtraining

Greenleaf, Gould, and Dieffenbach (2001) found that 40% of American Atlanta and Nagano Olympians indicated that OT had negative effects on their performances at the Olympic Games. Kenttä, Hassmén, and Raglin (2001) reported that 37% of young aspiring athletes identified themselves as being stale previously at least once in their careers, with the incidence of staleness being higher (48%) in individual sports than team sports. When interviewing members of four U.S. Olympic teams who did not meet expectations, Gould, Guinan, Greenleaf, Medbery, and Peterson (1999) stated that athletes identified OT as a major cause of perceived failure. Durand-Bush and Salmela (2002) reported that several of the 10 Canadian Olympic athletes they interviewed described feeling overtrained and reported a desire for increased recovery during their careers. Following a survey about nonfunctional overreaching and OT with 367 athletes competing at club to international level, Matos, Winsley, and Williams (2011) reported that approximately one-third of young athletes had experienced nonfunctional overreaching or OT at least once already in their careers.

Although there have been numerous articles reporting the prevalence of OT in elite athletes, there appear to be a number of inconsistencies, making the research difficult to generalize. The research groups investigating prevalence have used different terms and definitions of OT. Kenttä et al. (2001) and Morgan, Costill, Flynn, Raglin, and O'Connor (1988) used the term *staleness*, whereas Durand-Bush and Salmela (2002) and Greenleaf et al. (2001) used the term *overtraining*, and when similar words were used, different explanations of the term were evident. Morgan et al. (1988) used the term *staleness*, but did not explain staleness to the athletes. Similarly, Gould, Dieffenbach, and Moffat (2002) identified athletes as overtrained if they indicated that they thought they had overtrained in preparation for the Olympics. Gould et al. also did not explain whether they had provided a description of OT to athletes prior to asking about overtraining. Matos et al. (2011) used a definition derived from Kenttä et al. (2001) for their prevalence study with young athletes. Matos et al. asked athletes, "Have you ever experienced a significant decrement that persisted for long periods of time (i.e., weeks to months) although you kept training and you felt extremely tired every day?" (p. 1288). Loss of performance is often a hallmark of OT (Richardson et al., 2008), but using retrospective recall might not prove reliable regarding performance decrements because there are variables that may affect athletes' perceptions. These variables may include not performing as well as they had hoped or comparing themselves with others, which perhaps made the athletes feel they were not performing as well as they felt they should be. The limitations regarding descriptions and definitions of OT and OTS indicate that using these studies as evidence of OT prevalence should be done with caution.

Overtraining Syndrome and Illness

One aspect of OTS that may affect prevalence rates relates to athletes who become injured or ill prior to any OTS diagnosis. Mackinnon (2000) reviewed the OT and immunity literature and concluded that overtrained athletes are not immune

deficient by clinical standards, but they are susceptible to upper respiratory tract infections during and following heavy training. There seems to be substantial research on exercise, immunology, and illness, and even though regular physical activity has positive effects on the immune system, prolonged exhausting exercise appears to have negative consequences. Richardson et al. (2008) suggested that illness might be both a contributor to and an outcome of OT, and explained that when athletes have an imbalance between stress and recovery, they become vulnerable to infections and illnesses, which may stress the body further, leading to substantial SRIs and potentially OTS. It seems that the interactions of OT processes and behaviors with illness is circular, with stress/recovery imbalance and illness appearing to both contribute to and result from the other. Also, some initial signs of stress/recovery imbalance (e.g., illness) can be part of the OT process.

Overtraining Syndrome and Injury

In a similar manner to illness, injury may affect athletes before meeting whatever diagnostic criteria for OTS researchers are using. In comparison to the illness literature, there is limited research connecting overuse injuries and OTS. Flynn (1998), in one of the few articles on injury and OT, suggested that OT might lead to musculoskeletal breakdown prior to OTS becoming apparent. In some sports, this scenario would appear quite likely, as Richardson et al. (2008) suggested. For example, a swimmer with a similar volume of training to a runner may be likely to continue until OTS sets in, whereas a runner might develop overuse injuries before reaching the OTS stage. Injuries from overload often arise from an accumulation of stress, with a gradual onset, making detection (and early intervention) difficult. Kibler and Chandler (1998) explained that weakened or fatigued muscles might not manage the load of the training program and instead transfer these forces to the skeletal system, resulting in stress fractures that are part of the process of OT. Richardson et al. suggested that when athletes begin training cycles with muscle weaknesses, imbalances, or low flexibility, overload-related injuries might follow. It appears from the current literature that injury can be a contributing factor to OT as well as a potential outcome.

Detection and Symptoms

Fry, Morton, and Keast (1991) listed more than 90 symptoms reported by overtrained athletes that spanned performance, psychological, and physiological factors. The variety of symptoms indicates that few practical, valid, and reliable markers can be used to enable clear and quick diagnosis of athletes who are entering this state (Kenttä et al., 2001). Nevertheless, some frequently reported symptoms appear to be consistently associated with OT, such as underperformance, increased incidence of infectious illnesses (e.g., upper respiratory tract infections), loss of appetite, unexpected weight loss, sleep disturbances, mood disturbances, and concentration difficulties (Fry et al., 1991; Kenttä & Hassmén, 1998; Morgan et al., 1988). Researchers have investigated many of these physiological and psychological symptoms in attempts to determine some clear markers of OT, but although there seem to be some commonly reported symptoms (e.g., increased resting heart rate), OT appears to follow a pathway specific to individual athletes. Additional physiological markers have included decreased heart rate during maximal exercise (Hedelin, Kenttä, Wiklund, Bjerle, & Henrikkson-Larsen, 2000), hormonal responses to exercise (Uusitalo, Huttunen, Hanin, Uusitalo, & Rusko, 1998), and blood lactate concentrations during incremental graded exercise (Jeukendrup & Hesselink, 1994), but Kellmann (2010b) stated, "Physicians and physiologists stress that no firm physiological marker exists [to detect overtraining]" (p. 294). Kenttä and Hassmén (1998) suggested that psychological indicators of OT are more sensitive and consistent than any physiological markers. Two psychological indicators commonly reported with OT include increased mood disturbance and reduced subjective ratings of well-being (Richardson, 2005). Substantial research has focused on mood state changes associated with OT.

Researchers investigating OT have repeatedly used the Profile of Mood States (POMS; McNair, Lorr, & Droppleman, 1992) to monitor changes in mood with training (e.g., Morgan, Brown, Raglin, O'Connor, & Ellickson, 1987). The POMS is a questionnaire that was originally designed to monitor the moods of psychiatric outpatients. The POMS provides a measure of total mood disturbance along with six mood-state subscales (tension, depression, anger, vigor, fatigue, and confusion). Five of the six scales measure negative mood states, and one measures a positive mood; a decrease in negative mood states does not automatically indicate mood benefits, merely a reduction in negative mood. Morgan et al. (1987) used the POMS to monitor swimmers throughout a competitive season and identified that a healthy mood-state profile appeared to be connected to good performance. The seemingly healthy profiles progressively deteriorated during the season, but when there was a significant reduction in training stress, a healthy POMS profile re-emerged for the swimmers. Martin, Andersen, and Gates (2000) investigated the effectiveness of the POMS in monitoring training stress in 15 cyclists. Martin et al. noted that changing the cyclists' training intensity did not significantly influence global mood or specific mood states. Between athletes whose performances improved and those whose performances did not improve, there were no apparent differences in mood states. The researchers suggested that using the POMS was not effective for differentiating between productive overreaching and counterproductive OT at an individual level.

Kellmann (2010a) suggested that although the POMS may identify some early indicators of OT, "the POMS does not provide information about the causes of overtraining" (p. 98). Understanding the causes of OT may provide researchers and practitioners with strategies to detect and manage OT. Kellmann and Kallus (2001) developed the Recovery Stress Questionnaire for Sport (RESTQ-Sport) for use in sporting populations to gather information not available by using the POMS. The RESTQ-Sport identifies the extent of athletes' physical or mental stress and athletes' capabilities to recover. Recently, the effectiveness of the RESTQ-Sport to monitor changes in stress and recovery has been investigated. Nederhof, Zwerver, Brink, Meeusen, and Lemmink (2008) studied three female speed skaters, one who was recovering from nonfunctional overreaching (NFOR), one who had received a diagnosis of being in a state of nonfunctional overreaching, and one who was apparently healthy. Athletes completed both the POMS and the RESTQ-Sport to determine if differences were evident for the three athletes.

Both questionnaires displayed differences among the three participants. The healthy athlete displayed a typical athlete profile on the POMS, low on the five negative mood scales and high on the positive mood scale. The recovering athlete who had not been training for 3 months displayed scores around the middle, which is generally regarded as a nonathlete profile, whereas the NFOR athlete scored high on the fatigue scale and low on the rest of the scales, including the positive vigor scale. The POMS identified the different stages of OT for the athletes. The RESTQ-Sport scores also showed differences among the three athletes, with the current nonfunctional overreaching athlete and the recovering nonfunctional overreaching athlete producing higher general and sport-specific stress scores than the healthy athlete. The current nonfunctional overreaching athlete displayed a profile with low general recovery. Nederhof et al. reported that the current nonfunctional overreaching athlete had high levels of total stress in combination with low levels of recovery, indicating that training stress was only one factor contributing toward the imbalance between stress and recovery. The researchers concluded that the RESTQ-Sport had better diagnostic value for OT and OTS than the POMS. A limitation with this study is the small sample size ($N = 3$). Additional research investigating the effectiveness of the RESTQ-Sport with larger sample sizes of athletes in different stages of OT might prove fruitful.

Risk Factors

A number of researchers have attempted to identify risk factors associated with OT and burnout (Gould et al., 1999; Gould, Tuffey, Udry, & Loehr, 1996; Krane, Greenleaf, & Snow, 1997; Matos et al., 2011; Richardson et al., 2008) to enhance understanding as to why some athletes struggle to maintain the balance between stress and recovery and others appear to cope in an identical training environment. Reviewing the published literature, there appear to be many reasons why athletes overtrain, including environmental influences, personality traits, influential relationships, and sport cultures. Kenttä and Hassmén (1998) identified that physiological, psychological, and social stressors could contribute to the staleness syndrome. Krane et al. (1997) reported a variety of intrapersonal, interpersonal, and sociocultural factors that drive athletes to overtrain, including perfectionism, supermotivation, and parent and coach pressures to win. Matos et al. (2011) suggested that the development of a one-dimensional identity, limited autonomy, feelings of disempowerment, perfectionist traits, experience of having received conditional love, and unrealistic expectations were risk factors for OT in young athletes. Kellmann (2002) proposed that the reason why athletes display different degrees of vulnerability might be interindividual differences in recovery potential, exercise capacity, nontraining stressors, and stress tolerance. The variety of published risk factors indicates that further research would be beneficial.

Richardson (2005) set out to enhance understanding regarding the many variables suggested to be risk factors to OT. He interviewed 27 elite-level coaches and athletes regarding their opinions, perceptions, and experiences of OTS in Australia. From his qualitative research, Richardson produced arguably the most comprehensive model of OT risks and outcomes to date (see figure 15.1).

Within this model, Richardson suggested four categories of OT risks: athlete intrapersonal variables, interpersonal variables, situational factors, and sport sociocultural contexts, or environments in which the other three factors are deeply embedded. Richardson suggested that risk factors might do one of two things to upset the balance of stress and recovery that could lead to OTS: increase athletes' desires to train or increase athletes' demands for recovery. The dynamic nature of this model indicates that at any time, any number of factors can influence the OT process.

Athlete Interpersonal Factors

The people who surround athletes may influence attitudes and behaviors regarding stress, recovery, and OT. Richardson et al. (2008) suggested the following as a nonexhaustive list of interpersonal factors that could influence athlete overtraining: past and present relationships with parents, coaches, and significant others; attitudes and behaviors of others related to OT; illness and injury; success and failure; patterns of reinforcement for OT behavior; and contingent dispersal of love and approval.

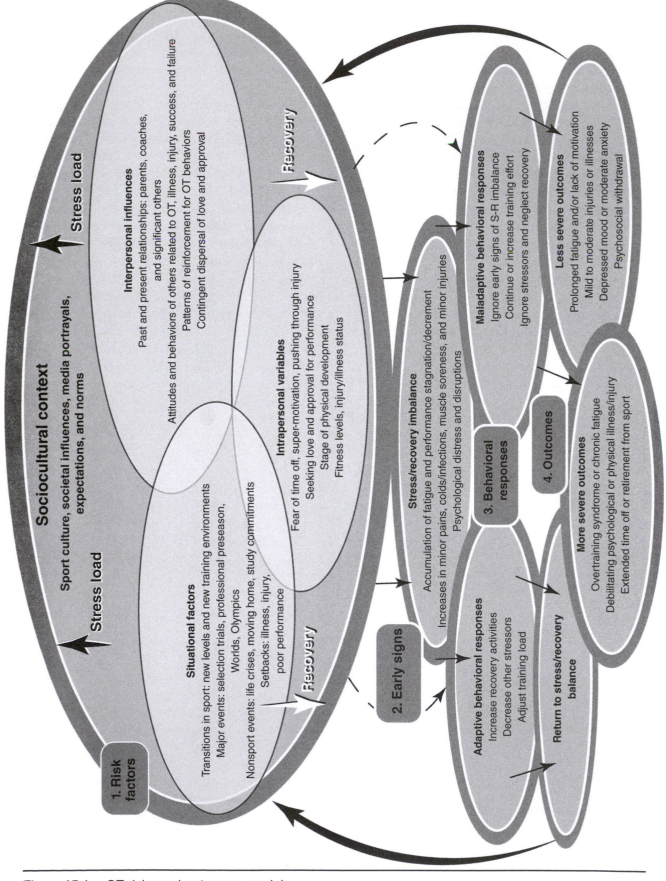

Figure 15.1 OT risks and outcomes model.

Richardson et al. (2008) suggested that the most salient risk factors for OT were the influences of coaches and parents and the sociocultural contexts. Athletes' susceptibility to OT might increase if they internalized parents' and coaches' OT ideals through patterns of reinforcement and contingency-based expressions of love and approval. In the OT literature, there is support for these findings. Krane et al. (1997) identified abusive coaches who drove athletes to overtrain and described an athlete who would do anything her coaches asked her to do to try to receive some love and approval. Kellmann (2002) suggested that coaches influence rest and recovery behaviors during competition and training camps. Wrisberg and Johnson (2002) displayed quotes from participants who reported feeling humiliated, denigrated, and verbally abused by coaches, which prompted athletes to turn to OT behaviors as a way to cope.

Richardson et al. (2008) suggested when athletes receive praise and approval for excessive training or underrecovery behaviors, there may be an increased susceptibility of OT for those individuals. Additionally, coaches who have achieved success in the past by promoting the more-is-better approach may encourage athletes to internalize this approach, taking on board the idea that they too will achieve success if they can keep going. Budgett (1998) identified that gaining success of any kind in sport might reinforce the attitude that tough training is the way to succeed. Coaches appear to influence athletes to develop the attitude that when it comes to training, more is better, which might lead to OT. It would seem logical to assume that there may be similarities between the role of the coach in sport and the role of the exercise practitioner in the exercise environment, although there is minimal research in this area. When an individual enters an unfamiliar environment and gets recognized for hard work or persistent attendance regardless of how the individual's body is adapting, behaviors and attitudes conducive to OT may appear. An extreme example of these phenomena associated with OT would be the worldwide (separate programs in over 25 different countries) television reality show *The Biggest Loser.*

The psychological climate established by those in authority can clearly influence behavior with regard to training and recovery. Additionally, family and friends who praise hard-training individuals, making them feel that they are doing something good when they train excessively, might increase susceptibility to OT.

Intrapersonal Variables

Athletes' personalities, behaviors, and beliefs may help in attaining success in sport, but particularly low or high levels of certain traits and behaviors may exacerbate stress levels, prompting increased needs for recovery and increasing susceptibility to stress/recovery imbalance. The risk factors identified in the model include supermotivation, high fitness levels, and injury/illness status, as well as pushing through injury and seeking love and approval for performance. There seems to be a fine line between when such characteristics are helpful for performance and when they become risk factors. Richardson et al. (2008) suggested that athletes at risk of OT may be placed at the high end of one or more of those characteristics.

Supermotivation. Possessing high levels of motivation, demonstrated by having a strong commitment to goals and dedication to training, is undoubtedly important for success in sport (Mallett & Hanrahan, 2004), but possessing extremely high levels of motivation to achieve success and to set new standards may be a risk factor for OT (Budgett, 1998; Gould et al., 1996; Richardson, 2005). The OT literature highlights that athletes who are excessively motivated may ignore how their bodies feel and potentially neglect recovery because they are so determined to reach their goals. This profile may lead an athlete toward stress/recovery imbalance by training excessively.

Pushing Through Injury. Richardson et al. (2008) suggested that pushing through injury was an intrapersonal and social risk factor for OT. Athletes will push through injury for a variety of reasons, including gaining love and attention, meeting financial obligations, having the media reinforce the belief that playing injured is heroic, and thinking that pushing through injury is the route to achieve success. Whatever reason athletes have for pushing through injury, the likelihood is that athletes who engage in this behavior might potentially exacerbate injuries, upsetting the stress/

recovery balance. This pushing through pain may also be part of many sport cultures.

Seeking Love and Approval for Performance. Richardson et al. (2008) suggested that athletes who look for love and approval for their performances might train excessively in attempts to elicit positive reactions from significant others. Matos et al. (2011) suggested that young athletes might try to dedicate themselves to training and aim for sporting success to meet parent and coach expectations, but a perceived failure in meeting the expectations can result in increased training, feelings of guilt, and threatened self-esteem, all of which may contribute to OT.

Situational Factors

The situational influences described in the OT risks and outcomes model (Richardson et al., 2008) include aspects of the environments and cultures, internal and external to the sport, that increase athletes' susceptibility to stress or affect athletes' needs for recovery.

Nonsport factors. A variety of nonsport factors have been identified in the literature as situations that may elevate stress levels and upset stress/recovery balance, such as difficulties with a roommate (Wrisberg & Johnson, 2002), financial or family problems (Scanlan, Stein, & Ravizza, 1991), a move home, and involvement in school or university (Richardson et al., 2008). Athletes, like everyone else, have to cope with day-to-day concerns—not just negative situations, but also positive life events, such as becoming a parent or starting a new relationship—that may elevate stress levels and affect recovery needs.

Sport-specific events. The descriptions of sport-specific events that may increase the risk of OT by elevating stress levels or affecting athletes' needs for recovery include transitions in sport, setbacks due to injury, illness, poor performance, and completion of a professional preseason. Hanin (2002) suggested that athlete responses to poor performance could affect the balance of training and recovery, potentially motivating athletes to push excessively in training to eliminate uncertainty and enhance self-confidence. Richardson et al. (2008) suggested that during transitions, athletes were likely to experience additional stress, which would benefit from extra recovery time that might not be available. Transitions might include joining a new team, moving to a higher level of the sport, switching time zones, or performing in different physical environments.

Sport Sociocultural Context

These risk factors refer to the attitudes, norms, and imperatives imposed by the sociocultural environment that can push athletes to increase training or increase the demands for recovery. Richardson et al. (2008) proposed that when athletes struggle to maintain an image of toughness, as imposed by the sport's subculture, they have an increased susceptibility to OT. Hanin (2002) suggested that sport cultures and subcultures could emphasize the benefits of quantity over quality in training, thereby increasing the risk of SRI. Coaches who frequently endorse attitudes such as *no pain, no gain* and *more is always better* create a sport culture of risk instead of promoting positive self-care and self-awareness (Brustad & Ritter-Taylor, 1997). Referring to these demands placed on athletes by coaches, an interviewee, quoted in Richardson et al., suggested that there appear to be certain values and norms accepted in sport that are abusive, and would not be acceptable in other areas of life, such as the education system. Wiese-Bjornstal (2010) identified the role of sport culture in potentially maladaptive athlete behaviors. She suggested that athletes learn what the expectations and norms of the sport cultures are through socialization experiences and that the expectation is for them to be tough and play through injury and pain. The problem with expectations that everyone hide their pain, feel the need to be tough, and play through injury is that OT becomes the norm in sport. Gould, Jackson, and Finch (1993) and Wrisberg and Johnson (2002) provided examples where athletes felt ashamed, condemned, or stressed out for not living up to the expectations of the sport culture. Playing injured, hiding emotions, and ignoring pain appear to be tactics athletes use to try to live up to the norms and expectations in some sport cultures, but these tactics appear to be maladaptive responses to signs of SRI that potentially lead to injury, illness, and OTS. Again, it seems that parallels can be drawn between the sport and exercise cultures, where exercisers may overtrain in an attempt to live up to the expectations of a conditioning coach or become socialized into believing that the norm in an exercise environment is to train through pain and injury.

Overtraining and Mental Toughness

The link between mental toughness and OT would appear to be in a buffering capacity, given that mental toughness is associated with consistent good performance in athletes (Gucciardi, Gordon, & Dimmock, 2008), and OT leads to performance deterioration. Purvis, Gonsalves, and Deuster (2010) suggested that mental toughness or resilience might act as a buffer against the development of OTS. Purvis et al. indicated that although no research had examined mental toughness in athletes with OTS, mental toughness training may be beneficial for the prevention of OTS and associated symptoms. It appears logical that some characteristics and behaviors of mental toughness may appear to buffer stress, as Purvis et al. suggested, reducing the susceptibility to stress/recovery imbalance, but some of the OT risk factors identified in the literature appear similar to characteristics of mentally tough athletes (e.g., persevere until goals are met, view adversity as a challenge, make sacrifices and subjugate other experiences outside sport, push through pain, play with injuries). Trying to be mentally tough may mean athletes play injured, ignore pain, view emotions as weaknesses, and strive to go beyond physical boundaries to gain contingent love and, thus, increase their susceptibility to stress/recovery imbalance.

The following case example comes from a 14-month relationship I (first author) had with an Australian Football League (AFL) player. I sat down with Ethan several times over this period. We were not in treatment together, but in my encounters with him, I explored the possible connections between perceived mental and physical toughness demands within the culture of football and how individual athletes negotiated those cultural imperatives. A lot of the exercise psychology literature seems to suggest that personal problems in training and exercise, such as OT, are housed within individual athletes. Ethan's stories, we believe, have something important to tell exercise psychologists, coaches, strength and conditioning coaches, and personal trainers when problems in

the exercise and training domains appear, and that we also need to look externally for the contingencies of reinforcement and punishment in the subculture that may help maintain maladaptive behaviors. Many of the interventions we implement to address OT may come to naught because they are counteracted by ubiquitous cultural pressures.

The Chronic Overtrainer: Ethan's Story

I met with Ethan five times over a 14-month period to discuss how he was coping with training and performing as an elite athlete. Ethan was a regular senior team player in his ninth year at the club. This season was the first time in his career Ethan had experienced an interrupted preseason due to a back injury during off-season training. The interviews follow Ethan's struggle to manage his back and additional injuries in an elite football environment.

First Meeting

During our first interview, Ethan talked about his passion for football, which had developed early in his life. He loved pushing himself in training and reaped the benefits of his hard work when, at a young age, an AFL team recruited him.

Upon achieving his dream of becoming a professional AFL player, reality hit home quickly when he struggled to make any impact at the club. Ethan used his frustration as motivation to work harder: "It spurred me on to keep hammering away and earn the respect of players, not to whinge, but just get on with the job." He made this statement passionately, and it seemed important that he could work hard without complaining. Ethan kept training hard to try to get noticed, but he was not selected to play senior football until his third year at the club. His debut had not been spectacular, and he spent most of his third and fourth years in football yo-yoing between the reserves and the senior team. At the beginning of Ethan's fifth season, the club appointed a new head coach who applauded his work ethic. Ethan viewed his first four years in professional football as a time that demonstrated his resilience:

> E: I'd just keep on fighting and fighting. I don't like to be seen as mentally weak. I

used to love watching *Rocky* movies, and I kind of feel a bit like him. He was up against the odds, and he came through and won. In my early years, I was down and out, [and] people had written me off. I was always in the [media] lists of who was going to get de-listed at the end of the season, but that spurred me on. You know those people that doubted me; they shouldn't doubt me, because I know I'm strong. I'll get what I want . . . It spurs me on a bit, sticking it up those people who did doubt me.

When Ethan was talking about his doubters, he sounded angry and even a bit vengeful. Ethan seemed to have taken their opinions personally and could not let the criticism go, but he was proud that he had not given in and had continued to fight to get to where he wanted to be. He labeled his determination as being "mentally tough."

E: I think just *never giving in* is mental toughness. There's a saying at the club, "failure doesn't cope well with perseverance." I like that saying. I think that's mental toughness.

S: Can footballers be too mentally tough?

E: No! I don't think you can be [too mentally tough]. No, that [mental toughness] gives me my edge and helps me perform. It helps me stay focused. I like being known as mentally tough, nothing's going to break me down . . . It can give me an edge on players, not only opposition, but at training too. You're going to have to play very well or train really well to beat me, because I'm going to be there in the mind [of other players] the whole time.

It sounded like Ethan needed to be the toughest, hardest-working player in the team. He explained that if he had not adopted this way of playing he would not have lasted long at the club.

E: I had talent, but I didn't have the super, super-talent that some kids have got where they can just get through sometimes. I knew that I had to take a different path to get me through. The only reason I am still here is because I've worked a lot harder than them [more talented players] . . . Without mental toughness and the way I am, I don't reckon I'd be here.

In his first years at the club, the coaches told Ethan he did not have enough natural talent to be successful, and so he needed to find another pathway. When the coaches began to give Ethan more opportunities in the senior team, it was due to his massive work ethic and tough style of football. Ethan explained that his way of playing football was the way to gain his coaches' and teammates' respect.

E: I know my teammates get a real buzz out of me throwing myself across someone's boot . . . I don't have any fears out on the ground. It sort of comes from the competitive side . . . just wanting the ball and doing anything to get it. Whether there's someone bigger in front of me, I want the ball more than that person.

Ethan talked about needing to be ahead of the other players because senior player positions were so competitive.

E: There's always new players wanting your position. I think that's why I do it [train so hard]. I'm getting a little bit more relaxed as I get more comfortable about where I am in the team.

Ethan's superior fitness, coupled with his ability to push himself through pain, meant that he had a certain status within the club. Players and coaches with whom I had previously spoken mentioned Ethan as the player everyone wanted to beat in training. Ethan loved being the player others aspired to be, and he seemed to thrive on managing a workload that others could not. This preseason, however, was different for Ethan; he had a long-term back injury that meant he could not "thrash himself constantly in the gym." This preseason he had to work on maintaining his ability instead of improving it. I wondered if OT had anything to do with his injury. Ethan explained:

> E: I've got bulging discs in my back from off-season. That was from pushing really hard on leg weights, plus upper body weights, and cross-training. I mean, it was the prescribed program. I had a jarring sort of feeling in my back. I didn't know if it was tightness or fatigue. I pushed through it, and I thought it would go away, but we came back to pre-season training, and three days in, I woke up and couldn't move it. For about a week, I couldn't move, and that really shook me up . . . I was just following the program. I was annoyed with myself at the time, but I was a bit annoyed with the coaches, too. I was doing everything within the guidelines, but I was probably going a bit heavier than I should have been, especially in the off-season. Sometimes you keep going and going in the off-season and not bring your body down or have some down time. I've done that so much in the past, and I've got through until now when I hurt my back. That taught me a lesson. It's just the beast within.

I asked Ethan if pushing too hard had resulted in any other injuries throughout his career. Ethan laughed when he talked about OT being at the root of most of his injuries—numerous stress fractures, an ankle injury, a shoulder injury, and now his back. Although he knew his injuries seemed to be partly due to training too hard, Ethan struggled to hold himself back:

> E: The back was a real overuse sort of injury. It sort of taught me that pushing too hard is silly. I've read a lot on over-training. I know I should be doing that, not overtraining, but I just can't help it sometimes . . . I wanted to do everything

to make sure that I had a good pre-season, but not really listening to my body enough to think, "Stop and get this checked out." In footy culture, you sort of don't want to be known as a whinger. Everyone gets sore. Everyone gets niggles. It's probably a macho sort of thing, like, "I'll be right." With those sorts of things, you push through them.

Ethan had pushed through and the result was a serious back injury. The way Ethan talked about not being known as a "whinger" made me wonder if what seemed like his personal drive to push himself excessively may be due to internalizing the cultural demands of his football club.

Ethan began to explain what went on in his head when he overtrained. He understood that he needed to control his desire to push through and train excessively, but understanding the need for control and applying control were two different things.

> E: It's just that little man in the back of my head that tells me that I have to do something extra. I'll have to do it [whatever training has popped into his head], because I've thought of it, and I think it's the right thing to do for me to get to where I want. I'll just do it even if I'm tired. I know that recovery is important. I know it . . . Yeah, I still have to relax a bit. I've just got to control myself . . . I have to get people to remind me sometimes. I know it [recovery] works, and I am getting better at it.
>
> S: Sounds like a tough job controlling that little man in your head.
>
> E: I can control it more now, but in the past I couldn't. I just would keep going. If I didn't do that extra thing, I would be annoyed that I didn't do that extra little bit to try and improve. It's the way I think. (He laughs.) It's hard to explain. My mind tells me to do it, and I just do it. No matter how I was feeling in the past, my mind would just say, "I think you should

do this," so I'd just do it. There wasn't a point where I didn't do it. I would always do it. I didn't want to know, if I didn't do it, what that sort of feeling felt like. It's just like the little man on your shoulder telling you that "you should do it, and I think that would be best for you."

S: So, it sounds like you would always do the extra training?

E: (He laughs.) I've always done it. If I didn't, I'd think about it the whole time, and I reckon I would eventually do it in the backyard. Seriously, I would think about it and think about it, "Why didn't I do it?" Eventually I'd do it. Then I can relax for the rest of the day. If I didn't do it, I'd think about it. I've always done it.

Ethan knew there were times that he needed to rest, but he seemed unable to block out the little man in his head. It sounded like the cultural voice of the football environment was so ingrained that he found no respite until he had succumbed to OT. I was not sure if Ethan would listen to any practitioner who advocated different ways to train other than pushing himself into injury time and time again.

Early Competitive Season

When Ethan and I met again, the competitive season was well underway, and he was happy with his performance so far. I asked Ethan how he was feeling, and he replied that he was finding it "harder and harder as each week goes on to get [his] body right." I asked Ethan for clarification.

E: Every week you get a few different corks and bumps . . . some take a bit longer than others to get rid of, um, to try and shake with extra treatments. My back issue . . . is the one that is really a little bit harder to shake. I'm pretty right on top of that, doing extra Pilates to get that right. It's just trying to get extra treatment that sometimes can take a mental toll on you. Knowing that you are racing against the clock to get your body 100% right before the game starts. Doing the extra ice baths and icing, [and] getting up [during] the night, especially when it's cold, when you just want to sort of relax and take your mind off things.

S: Sounds hard to take your mind off the injury.

E: I find it hard to take my mind off things at the best of times. You need, um, some downtime . . . [when you are injured]; you are constantly thinking about your body, trying to get it right. Your mind is always ticking over, I suppose. It's just staying on top of it during the week and having to constantly think about it.

Ethan had now been managing his back and completing the extra recovery at home for almost six months. Ethan began to tell me about the little things he had to do to protect his back:

E: I can't do as many ground balls. I have to change my weights program . . . I have to make sure my posture is good. I can't go to the gym and thrash out weights. I have to think about my back all the time, but it's not affecting my performance on game day.

S: Sounds like a change of focus for you.

E: You obviously want to try to improve yourself and do a personal best and stuff like that in the gym, [but] the game is the most important part of the week. That's what I have to get my back right for. So, it's not doing a personal best during the season for your weights. It's about doing a good solid weights session with good posture ready for game day.

Ethan's time and effort this season were going into getting his body ready to play on game day. It was clear that he still wanted to push himself hard, but he had tried that already, and the result was a reoccurrence of the back injury:

E: I had a small flare-up, as I got away from doing the basic things. I have to stay on top of it 100% of the time. I can't fall away from . . . not doing too many ground balls and too much extra work after training. I was getting away from that a bit. So again, a little injury reminded me. My body does that to me sometimes; it's good. I have been doing a bit of reading on bulging discs, and I think once you have bulging discs, you are always going to have them. It definitely did scare me. When I flared it back up the second time, that really shook me up, because I thought this was going to keep happening.

After the second flare-up, Ethan realized that if he overdid his training, he was not going to be able to play football. He knew he had to listen to his body now, but as is apparent from the quotes throughout this chapter, Ethan has a strong tendency to minimize things (e.g., a small flare-up, a little injury). Such minimization is consistent with not wanting to show weakness or vulnerability, and such *partial silencing* seems consistent with the internalization of the sport's culture. Ethan continued to talk about the lessons he was learning this season:

E: I feel a little bit heavy in the legs. I am starting to think about that more, because in the past I would just try and work through it, and think that I would be able to get through it. Sometimes you just need to freshen up the legs a little bit. Stay off the legs and no running, 'cause the 2 hours on the weekend [game day] is what's most important. I try to drill that through my own head.

S: So it sounds like you are beginning to be able to hold yourself back when you are feeling tired or heavy.

E: That's another good positive for me, starting to recognize those things [heavy legs]. The data has shown me from the

GPS [global positioning system] that when I am fatigued, my power output just drops right away. . . . If I am feeling good, my performance will be a lot better.

Ethan realized that he was not able to perform well when he was fatigued, but it still sounded like a struggle to reign in his tendency to push himself excessively. It seemed like he was trying hard to learn the lessons his body was trying to teach him, but his work ethic and attitude had helped him attain his tough guy status within the club, and giving that up did not sound as though it would be easy. When Ethan talked about getting respect and rewards in football, it was for behaviors that encapsulated pushing through and playing when he was tired or injured, but he knew he could not perform at a high level when he was tired and injured. It seemed that in football there was an expectation for players to perform injured, tired, and in pain, but Ethan was recognizing that he did not perform as well in these situations. The cultural imperatives seemed to be part of the struggle within Ethan between what he knew was best and what was culturally expected.

Ethan began to talk about other expectations at the club; he had watched the coaches humiliate plenty of his teammates when they were upset or worried about poor performances. He decided to portray the tough footballer image and not display vulnerability or emotion at the club. Ethan's choice to hide his vulnerability at the club had helped him become successful, but in doing so he was tacitly advocating for the unrealistic expectations set up within his football culture. Silencing pain and distress and not showing emotion were encouraged *absences*. Ethan understood he had to adhere to the footballers' code, but he was also aware that he needed an outlet for his emotions where he would not be criticized. Outside football, he recognized that he needed to be *Ethan*. He began to tell me about how he managed his feelings outside of the club:

E: I know we [footballers] can be pains in the arses. We are pretty highly strung. The emotion of elite sport (he laughs), it can take a toll . . . and strain relationships. When you are injured and losing, it's pretty hard not to take it home. I take it home and think about what I could have done more. I take it really bad. She [his partner] actually lets me be me a lot of the time.

S: Sounds good to have that external support.

E: It's very important to have your own . . . support network, because they see you when you are probably at your lowest. You try to be upbeat as much as you can at the footy club. You are not the only one with injuries . . . What's the point in moping around and looking like a sook if other guys are dealing with things themselves and in their lives? I just suck it up, get on with it, and try to do the best I can to get out there as quick as I can. There is no point in moping around, because they won't care at all; so just get on with it.

Ethan knew he could not show his real feelings at the club, so he assumed a tough guy façade by demonstrating that he could manage his rehabilitation in record time, without displaying any negative emotions or weaknesses. Ethan let the tough footballer image drop only when he was at home with his family and friends, where he could deal with his feelings. He needed to have an environment where he could collapse in a heap and still be loved, because he would lose his status within the club if he displayed those same feelings at training or competition.

End of the Competitive Season

Prior to our third conversation, I had heard that Ethan was injured, but I did not know the extent of his injury. Ethan arrived on crutches, moving slowly, and looking as though he was in pain. A week before our interview, Ethan had damaged his knee during the last quarter of a match. Although Ethan sustained his injury in the last quarter of the match, when his team was so far ahead it would have been nearly impossible to lose, he implied that his coaches and teammates were proud that he had played out the rest of the match:

E: I just went up for a marking contest during the game and came down on one leg . . . and sort of twisted a little bit as I landed. I, um, broke some cartilage . . . I got up after that marking contest and went to take off again, and it felt quite crunchy. I thought I may have jarred it and tried to run it out. . . . I ended up coming off for about five or six minutes and got it checked out by the physios and the doctors. I was sort of running up and down the boundary, and the adrenalin was still pumping, so I was able to get back out for the last five or six minutes and play out the quarter. Yeah, I wasn't moving at 100%, but it was right to play.

S: So playing injured didn't cause any more damage?

E: It's hard to know, but, yeah, I'm pretty sure the damage had already been done in the marking contest when I came down on it. No, I don't think there was more damage done.

Ethan appeared to consistently minimize any pain or injuries he incurred. That minimization seemed to move into denial that he may have incurred more damage by playing with already busted cartilage. Even talking to me (with no repercussions for showing vulnerability), he seemed to need to downplay injuries. The sport culture of "only the weak show pain or complain while injured" prevailed. The following day, Ethan went to hospital to get scans and X-rays, which led to surgery that evening to repair some of the damage.

E: I had the operation on Monday night and didn't go back to the footy club until Thursday. . . . On Thursday, Friday, and Saturday, I was on the bike just rolling my legs over in a brace and doing upper body weights, and just handling the footy a little bit. Then I had Sunday off. Monday, I threw the crutches away. Everything was going really well, did a bit, oh you know, did what I was supposed to do by the physios and doctors, and Monday night it started to get a little bit sore again. When I went to bed, it was okay. I woke up on Tuesday, and all of Tuesday was a shocking, shocking day. I could hardly walk on it at all. I'm back on the crutches again now. I'll just keep pushing on to get back out there to play in the finals [a 4-week period where the top eight teams battle it out to make it to the final premiership match].

It sounded like Ethan's drive to overtrain was also rearing its head in his rehabilitation when he said "did a bit, oh you know, did what I was supposed to do." It sounded like Ethan may have pushed harder than he was supposed to, but he continued to talk about his recuperation.

E: It was a good feeling throwing them back in the crutches bin, and I made a big deal of it, but, yeah. (He laughs.) I had to pull them back out [the following day]. It was a bit of a slap in the face, but I had to get back on them, because it was sore yesterday.

Ethan had never experienced a backward step in his rehabilitation before, and he looked like he was struggling with the uncertainty of when he could play again. Nevertheless, Ethan had set himself a goal of playing the following week. Our interview was the day following taking the crutches back out of the bin, and Ethan was not able to put any weight on his injured limb. I could not understand how he thought that he might be able to play the next match, but Ethan was determined, and he was spending every waking minute trying to get his knee better.

E: If I have a spare hour, I whack on—there is a machine called a Game Ready, and it ices and compresses the joint. I slept with the Game Ready on at night [Monday]. It's programmed to turn on for half an hour and then turn off for an hour. It is the best way you can recover from training. I've got the wobble board to do proprioceptive work. If I am just sitting at home, I've got the Game Ready on, or I've just got [my knee] up, trying to reduce the swelling. I'm always thinking, "How I can get it better?" I'm eating foods that are high in iron and taking glucosamine, really strong ones, and doing all the right things with my diet. I am constantly thinking, "What can I do to get me out there quicker?" Those sorts of things, so leaving no hour spare.

S: Seems like you are working hard on your recovery. Are you tempted to play even if it's sore? (This was Ethan's old pattern.)

E: Maybe if it was a different sort of injury . . . but this knee is quite serious. Losing cartilage, wherever, is very, very serious. It doesn't grow back the way it was the first time. . . . I don't want to break any more of that strong stuff away, because I know it ends a lot of guys' careers. I've played with guys that just haven't been able to deal with the pain of bone on bone in their joints. They end up giving [football] away because of that. I don't want injury to finish my career. I realized that very quickly after I've done this knee. It sort of changed my mind-set [to] not do more damage to it.

Ethan seemed to recognize the severity of his injury, but he also appeared desperate to play finals football, and I wondered how far he would go to become a premiership player. I asked Ethan if he felt any pressure from the club to rehabilitate quickly.

E: There is a little bit [of pressure from the coach]. It's in the back of my mind. I know that the coach wants me out there. He's speaking to me every day and . . . *frustrated* is not really the word, but he was quite concerned that I had a bad day yesterday. He knows that we are racing against the clock. I suppose, yeah, there is a little bit of pressure to get out there. I'm not going to do anything silly. . . . I don't want to do any more damage than necessary. He's [the coach] very good with the guys. He'll push them to their limits.

Ethan held an important position in the team, which helped him feel secure at the club. I was not sure if Ethan would still feel as if he did not need to "do any more damage than necessary" if his position on the team had not been secure. He knew the team needed him, and it seemed that he was more aware of his need to recover rather than push through, but I was not sure if he would be able to maintain a healthy balance between training and recovery. The "little bit" (more minimization) of pressure from the coach, in conjunction with his internalized beliefs that more is better and that pushing through pain is expected, made Ethan seem vulnerable to return to OT. It appeared that Ethan was trying to diminish the pressure he felt about playing from the coach in a similar manner to the way he diminished injuries and damage to live up to the cultural expectations of a footballer.

Ethan had mentioned the following: "Two of the last . . . games [before his injury] I had down games a bit, not beating my opponent as much as [the coach] would have liked." I asked him if he thought fatigue might have contributed to his being injured.

> E: I know fatigue can affect, um, can cause muscle injuries, and if you are not careful it can cause joint injuries. . . . You can get hit from some angle and not be aware of it, because you are not concentrating or thinking properly at the time. . . . It can definitely have an effect. How much, I am not sure. There are ways and means of getting around those sorts of things if you are not feeling that well. There are certain things that can pick you up that the doctor can give you.
>
> S: Can you tell me a little more about the ways and means to help?
>
> E: Things like Sudafed, you are allowed to take them in certain doses. Yeah, just pills and things like that, caffeine supple-

ments that can boost you up. With heavy legs and feeling fatigued going into a game, that's going to happen at times during the season. You just have to screw your guts up at times and try and work, work through those things. They're long seasons, and you're going to be feeling tired . . . but you have to be stronger in the mind than to concede to that and push through it. That's the way I approach it.

Ethan was adamant that players would be successful in football only when they found ways to perform while managing fatigue and injuries. It seemed that the norm for footballers was to manage pain without complaining while performing well. Ethan seemed a bit uncomfortable talking about the pills and supplements that he could take, and quickly moved the conversation on to his injury and the recovery process:

> E: People are off their feet for 6 weeks [with this injury]. It makes you realize that we push our bodies to the absolute maximum . . . to get the most out of ourselves, and [that is] the price you pay for absolute success. Some guys say that they would give their right leg to win a premiership, and that's what I'm basically doing. (He laughs.)
>
> S: Is it worth that much?
>
> E: Yeah, it is. It is. That's what I play for, and I'd say probably 85% to 90% of guys play to play in premierships. If I never played another game again, I would be a wreck for quite some time, but I would be a premiership player. That's what you want at the end of your career. But, yeah, it's the price that I am willing to pay.
>
> S: Sounds like a big price.
>
> E: It's a cruel world sometimes. (He laughs.) Like I said before, it's just, just how much you love it. It's what you did

as a kid. You do anything you can to get out there and play. I would be very surprised whether there would be many guys that would come out of AFL without some sort of lingering injury later in their life, and I know I am going to be one of them, probably. You don't sort of think much about it at the time; you just do whatever you can to play. You will probably regret it a little bit later, but it's just the passion that you have to play. It's hard to put that fire out when you are playing, yeah.

During our catch-up, Ethan's need to recover and get back in the game was so strong that he seemed to lose sight of the stress/recovery balance that he had talked about in previous meetings. All Ethan seemed to think about was how he could get his body to a point where he could manage to play football. He knew that if he were cleared to play, no matter how much pain he was in, he would play. Within his club, this behavior was admired.

Ethan had mentioned that at the end of the season, the coach told him he needed to undergo reconstructions on both knees. The surgery would enhance the stability of his knees, which meant less likelihood of another knee injury the following season. Ethan thought additional surgery and chronic bulging discs was a worthwhile price to pay, if he became a premiership player. Unfortunately, for Ethan, this year his club had not been successful. At the end of the season, his club was eliminated one step away from the final premiership match. I met Ethan next during the off-season.

Off-Season Conversation

When Ethan and I met again, he was 5 weeks into the off-season. Again, he arrived on crutches, but looked less mobile than the last time we met. Ethan had undergone reconstructive surgery on both knees, with his first operation a few days after the club played their final match, and the second reconstruction 2 weeks later. The first surgery repaired the damage from his injury during the season, and the second surgery was a preventive measure on the other knee. He had spent the previous month mostly immobile on the couch.

Ethan began by talking about the end of his last season; he was proud of himself for missing only two games after sustaining his knee injury. Ethan had played AFL less than two weeks after our previous interview. "I really did work hard at trying to get back as quickly as I could. I am pretty proud of only missing two games with the injury that I had." Ethan had done everything in his power to rehabilitate. He had left "no stone unturned," and did not think he could have done anything more to get the all clear from the doctor to play those last few matches. I asked Ethan if the doctors had the final say on whether he could return to play or not.

E: The physios and the doctors have the final say [if he is fit enough to play]. If you put your hand up and say, "Yep, I think I'm right to play," if you're not physically passed by the medical staff then you won't play, um, the majority of the time. That's the thing; players will always put their hands up all the time to play. You just want to be out there. The coach will sometimes push you a bit. He'll want you to play.

S: Sounds like a delicate balance between player, coach, and doctor, but you were able to play. How was your knee feeling?

E: Before the first match back . . . it was still sore during the week. Training that week, I had to take . . . painkillers to get through training. I was getting through, and I was rapt [enraptured] to know that I was going to be playing. I suppose that took my mind off the pain a little bit.

S: So you didn't need any injections? (Ethan had previously mentioned using painkilling injections to help him play.)

E: They [physios and doctors] weren't going to play me if I needed an injection. I just took some oral painkillers, and that took the edge off a little bit. When your adrenalin and your blood start pumping, you sort of forget about it.

S: Did you have a bit of leeway from the coach because of your injury?

E: (He laughs.) Once you're out there [playing a match], there are no excuses for injury, and I knew that. That's why you sort of have to forget about any niggles that you've got. The coach doesn't care. He doesn't have sympathy for you. If you put your hand up to play and you're playing, [then] you need to go flat out 100%. As good as it is playing, I was pushing through a little bit.

"Pushing through a little bit" was Ethan's pattern. After his back injury, Ethan had talked about trying to listen to his body. When he injured his knee, he was worried about doing more damage, so he limited how much he pushed through, but it sounded like the lure of trying to become a premiership player had been too much temptation for Ethan, and he had gone back to pushing through. Ethan had become concerned that he might not have been performing well enough during those last matches:

E: Having missed the 2 weeks and not having the physical conditioning, that was probably the doubt, not doubt, but the worry that you have on your mind that you might be off a couple of yards, and you might let the team down a bit.

S: You were more worried about letting the team down?

E: The club is bigger than the individual. The club's success is the ultimate thing that you sort of worry about.

I asked Ethan what his family thought about how he prioritized the club's needs over his body's needs. He laughed and replied, "Mum and dad always understood that. It's one of the risks that come with playing professional sport. So many good things come from the sport, so they've [mum and dad] never once said to me to stop." Ethan's partner thought a bit differently and wanted him to be healthy after his football career.

E: She wants me to be able to take the kids down to the park . . . and not go down in a bloody wheelchair. It's just part of the game, I guess. It's just the passion you have for the game. No matter what anyone told me, unless it was life or death, I'd never stop playing. It's all I've done since I was a little kid, and so many great things have come from playing the sport. There is nothing anyone else can say to stop me, anyway.

Ethan had always known there was a cost to being successful in football, and, as he had previously said, he was willing to pay that price to keep playing the game he loved.

Ethan began to talk about his surgeries. Following the end of season, players could have some time to engage in activities that the club did not usually permit: socializing, eating regular food, having a few drinks, and generally letting off steam. This year, Ethan had been immobile on his couch immediately after the season ended. He talked about his struggle getting through his convalescence: "After the second one, I was going insane. I was on the couch. It's supposed to be your off-time, being able to go out and do things that you can't do during the year. It's awful." Ethan mentioned that he had not expected his teammates to offer support after the surgeries. "I heard from a couple of teammates, but they are off doing their own thing as well. I certainly didn't expect them to come around or anything." Ethan had his family and friends to help him deal with his recuperation. I wondered if Ethan's limited support from his teammates was because the other players thought he did not need support, given that he worked hard not to show any weakness when he was at the club, or because the club culture meant that footballers were not supposed to need emotional support.

Usually, at this time of year, Ethan would have started his off-season training. "At this stage, I would be running four or five times a week, and trying to get as fit as I can." This year, however, Ethan had managed to get off the couch only a few days prior to us catching up. I asked him how he felt being in this position, knowing that he could not start proper off-season training. It sounded like Ethan was trying to be positive about his situation:

> E: Having both my knees reconstructed, it's forced me to build up my season slowly. I am forced to build the chain of my body up properly instead of going slap bang into off-season and pre-season, and then hurting my back like I did last year. I guess being injured is forcing me to be smarter. Hopefully, I've learnt some good lessons.

Ethan was still trying to view his injuries as educational. He talked wistfully about training:

> E: I want to be out riding, and swimming, and running, and running, but I think there are other areas that I can improve on while I can't do that. . . . It's hard for me to control. I was told off the other day by the physio, "Don't do that. You are progressing yourself too fast." I have to listen to what they say. They have dealt with these sorts of injuries before, and even though it's feeling good, something might not be healed properly. I will listen to them, but you always want to do that little bit extra. The performance coach said we will be able to top up sessions and do little bits extra here and there, to get me back.

The performance coach seemed to be helping Ethan's worries regarding his fitness by promising Ethan that when he recovered he could do some extras. The reassurance was enough for Ethan to allow himself time to recover properly. It seemed that Ethan was getting back into maintaining his stress/recovery balance.

The Following Preseason

I met with Ethan in the middle of the following preseason training. He had completed his rehabilitation and was back to full training with the senior team. Ethan's rehabilitation had gone from strength to strength without a problem. Once Ethan had become mobile, he had gone on holiday with his partner. Ethan talked about how he managed to incorporate his rehabilitation into his vacation.

> E: We'd get up pretty early in the morning, 6:30 or 7:00, and do 2 hours in the gym before we would even do anything. To the normal person [that] sounds ridiculous, but I knew it was going to help me get back to training quicker. . . . I made the effort of getting up earlier and making sure I could get it [rehab training] done. The whole time I was over there, I started my own training. I started three or four weeks before I had even come back [to the club].

It sounded like Ethan had used every opportunity to complete his rehabilitation early. As usual, Ethan had returned to training faster than expected:

> E: I wasn't supposed to be playing until the following week, but I played a practice match last Saturday, so I am at least two weeks ahead of where we thought I would be. I'm not pushing. (He laughs.) They [physios] have cleared me to play these practice games, because I worked so hard at my rehab early on. I'm still not quite 100%. I'm sort of about 95% to 96%. Once I get all these practice matches out of the way, I think I'll be back to 100%.

Ethan sounded like he had done everything possible to recover quickly to complete the bulk of preseason training. Even though he was almost back to full fitness, instead of being ahead of all the other players in the training drills, he was in the middle of the group:

> E: It was sort of hard [not being at the front of the group], but I had some pretty serious work done, not just one, but two knees completely fixed. I'm not a bozo. I realize that I need time to heal. I was doing a lot of cross-training. I knew I wouldn't be a long way behind [the other players]. . . . I progressed very quick with

the running, a lot quicker than they thought. My knees were responding really well to the running, and the treatment [ice machine and Game Ready machine at home] I was getting afterwards was allowing me to back up session after session.

Ethan had decided to focus on enhancing his recovery rather than training at the upper limits of the program. By using this approach, he had returned to full training much faster than expected. His confidence was starting to build again—perhaps partly due to his quick recovery. He wanted to prove to his teammates that he was still at the top of his game:

> E: I wanted them [teammates] to think, "How is he 2 weeks ahead? He is back up with the main running group, leading runs, and doing all that sort of thing. How is he doing that?" That was sort of my goal over this preseason.
>
> S: Achieving your goal must have helped your confidence within the team.
>
> E: It's more for guys to realize that I've had two knee reconstructions, [and] if someone else has an injury, don't whinge and mope about it, get on with the job. Look how fast you can come back into the main group. I guess it sort of spurs me on to be an example to other guys.

Ethan seemed to be setting himself up as a model to emulate, but also to foster unrealistic expectations for the rest of the team. He felt he could motivate his teammates to rehabilitate quickly if he could demonstrate how fast he returned to training after the surgeries. I thought one of the reasons Ethan was able to concentrate fully on his rehabilitation was because of his external support network of people who rallied around him and facilitated him doing everything possible to rehabilitate. I did not think many of Ethan's teammates had this nonjudgmental support. I reflected on a conversation that I had with a young player. This player had explained that if another player had rehabilitated quickly without any issues, then every player should be able to do that within a similar period without complaining. If a player took longer to recover from an injury or illness than expected, he would face questions from the club about his ability and commitment. I asked Ethan if he felt his quick recovery put pressure on his teammates.

> E: It's more as a leader to set an example [for] other guys. Preseason is so important to a whole team's setup. I haven't missed this preseason, although I've had these two major operations. If I can do it, there's hope for guys who have surgeries at the end of next year, [and] that it's not going to ruin their seasons. We're all going to be one team together, and everyone is going to be fit and healthy, and have a great season.

Ethan thought he was an asset to the team by working as hard as he did. He felt he motivated the team and gained respect because of his hard work. I wondered how much of what Ethan was saying came from his true feelings and how much was what he thought he should say to be accepted and admired within the club. Ethan started to talk about the importance of respect in the team:

> E: To get respect, it's a hard thing to get, because you have to grind your body, push yourself, be strong in the mind, and get through every day. Then you have to do that year after year after year. Some guys can't do that and can't handle that. Some guys are just happy to float through and get by. It's probably a 50/50 split [in the club] with guys who are pushing for perfection and then guys who go in and out of the system; they get found out. I reckon there would be a lot of guys who would leave the game with many, many regrets. Those guys with the regrets I doubt would get the respect from the players they played with. So I think guys should push more.

When Ethan said that he thought "guys should push more," it sounded like he could see only one way to play football. A footballer could gain respect from other players only when he showed he could grind himself during training and sacrifice his body for the team. Ethan seemed to be an example of how cultural demands occasionally bring forth shining examples who are then held up for others to emulate even though, for many, such standards are unreasonable, and striving to reach such unrealistic outcomes may lead to illness, injury, and OT.

Our conversation moved to reflecting on the previous season, talking about what he had learned about himself over the last year. Ethan suggested that his injuries had taught him important lessons:

> E: I think the [knee] injury taught me a few things about myself. I allowed myself to, um, when I was sort of rushing to get back [to play the last few games of the season], I rushed back within the limits. I didn't go outside the boundaries or do anything that I wasn't supposed to do. I took that approach again [after his knee reconstructions]. With my back, I guess I've learned it's more important to look after it. Yeah there's a certain point, and I push it to that point, but I never sort of go over that now.

> S: Do you think your beliefs about recovery have changed since we first met?

> E: I have definitely changed in that [recovery] aspect, for sure. I have definitely learned from my experiences in sport with my body, and I am a lot smarter now.

Ethan thought he now could control the voice in his head that said "do more." He explained:

> E: You've only got one body to use. . . . You've really got to take good care and push it to that line, but sort of don't go over it. As a young fellow, you thrash your body to try to be the best that you can. As I am getting more experienced

and older . . . I realize that's [his body] what is out in the field, producing for you in the game.

We started to discuss other ways in which he thought he had changed from our first conversation. I reminded Ethan that he had suggested mental toughness was about being able to thrash his body and keep going regardless of how the training feels. I asked Ethan what he thought mental toughness was now.

> E: I guess the thinking of more is better [has changed]. You know, my mental toughness will always be there, but it's just sort of a different sort of toughness, I think.

> S: Can you tell me more about your different sort of toughness?

> E: Oh, it's just a smarter [mental] toughness. I'll never back down if someone tells me to do something. I'll do it and want to do it with gusto, but within certain parameters. If it is going to affect my body for the long haul, then [I] sort of have to work out what's the best way to go about it rather than just going straight into it full steam ahead. I guess with experience, you come to realize where that sort of line is. Sometimes you learn the hard way, and I've certainly done that. (He laughs.)

> S: So there is more emphasis on balance now?

> E: I certainly train as hard as I ever did, but . . . rather than spending the extra 5 or 10 minutes out on the track . . . I might jump in the ice bath, or do something so I can back up again for the next training session. You soon realize that the older you get, your body can't, um, your body starts to struggle a little bit. I'm only 27, but you certainly start to feel the effects of footy after 9 or 10 years. So that's what I am more of a perfectionist in now.

That supermotivation will always be there, but it's more realizing that it's game day that you worry about more.

The idea of taking care of himself extended to his understanding of mental toughness, but although his idea of mental toughness had changed a little, he still needed to feel that others thought of him as mentally tough:

> E: There are just a few little adjustments that I have made with myself to allow myself to produce, [and] to keep producing my best as the years go on. As a young fellow, it is all about pushing, but as you get older, your body cannot just keep doing it. So you have to draw a balance with things. I don't think that makes me any less mentally strong, or anything. It probably makes me even more mentally tough being able to find the new balance, and be what I can be. I mean, for me, it's just being mentally smarter more than anything.

During our first interview, Ethan had said being mentally tough helped him be successful in football. I asked him if he still thought that mental toughness had benefited him in his career or if it had ever hindered him.

> E: Mental toughness definitely helps in the long run, but . . . it's the smartness and the way you go about it [that] will define whether it's a hindrance or not. I think I've learned that. I don't reckon I would be where I am today if I didn't have that fanaticism that I have had over the years. Some guys will get through on their talent, and that's fine. Most guys, to get to the top, top level, have to have that mental toughness to get you there. I'm probably the perfect example of that. I wouldn't be here [without mental toughness]. I've learned that you can be mentally tough, but realize that your body is your tool. Your body is your tool of the trade, so make sure you look after it and don't abuse it. If you are feeling

great, go for it hammer and tongs, and don't let anybody hold you back. But, yeah, just be smart, I guess . . .

Ethan's Tale and Implications for Exercise Practitioners

By the end of our last conversation, it seemed like Ethan had learned some valuable lessons about taking care of himself, but his journey represented numerous occasions of ignoring injuries, pushing through pain, and silencing his emotions. Even now, as one of the senior players on the team with a solid understanding of what his body needed to perform, it was difficult for Ethan to overcome the imperatives and demands of the no-pain-no-gain, do-more culture. The situations represented in Ethan's case study have much to offer the exercise practitioner. Gaining recognition for never stopping, pushing through pain, and working excessively to impress coaches and personal trainers are common themes in exercise and sport environments. As Ethan's case study demonstrates, when these themes are normalized, in any environment, as the principal way to gain recognition, then the risk of OT increases.

Ethan consistently received the message that working excessively was the expectation; the reinforcement that he was valuable as long as he kept going was a motivating factor for him. Ethan knew that when his body stopped producing, he would not last long in the football system. Understanding that reinforcement for hard work may drive exercisers to the limit, and basing their worth on the contingent attention that comes with pushing hard may lead exercisers to overtrain. For exercise practitioners, reinforcing clients who do not complain or show weakness and push through injury could lead to more injury, illness, and, potentially, OTS. Many people, similar to Ethan, would probably not enlist the services of an exercise psychologist, but would likely employ other readers of this book, such as exercise physiologists, strength and conditioning professionals, physical therapists, or personal trainers. It might be helpful for many professionals to recognize both the intraindividual and cultural influences on exercise behavior, and how there may be powerful combinations of factors that lead to OT, illness, and injury.

Throughout my time with Ethan, I could not help drawing parallels between his football culture and some exercise environments. It seemed that it could be simple to fall into the trap of reinforcing hard work and giving contingent attention based on the effort a client makes. Exercise practitioners may exacerbate the culture of no pain, no gain by paying attention to individuals who do not stop when they are tired and then congratulating them for pushing through pain. Trainers can be part of the problem by placing unrealistic expectations and goals on their clients' shoulders with the hope that motivation will carry them through to positive outcomes.

Ethan appeared to feel confident when he was able to please his coaches and when he had their admiration for his tough football and excessive work ethic, but when he was aiming to include more recovery in his life than he had previously done, he seemed increasingly vulnerable to being pressured into OT. Some exercise environments (e.g., gyms) are (vague) cultures that are strange and unfamiliar to some individuals, which may lead to feelings of vulnerability. Gaining confidence in such environments may come about when the client impresses the practitioner (e.g., personal trainer), and what easier way to do so in an exercise environment than to work hard? Exercise practitioners need to be aware that they might inadvertently be part of the institutionalized problem (e.g., strength coaches, head coaches pushing more than just "a little bit") by reinforcing excessive exercise and tacitly encouraging silence about any pain or discomfort. Reviewing participants' needs and recognizing when a practitioner may be going down the path of applying "a little bit of pressure" may be the beginnings of setting up an exercise culture where displaying emotions takes strength and recovery is seen as where one actually does gain power and endurance.

References

Brustad, R.J., & Ritter-Taylor, M. (1997). Applying social psychological perspectives to the sport psychology consulting process. *The Sport Psychologist, 11,* 107–119.

Budgett, R. (1998). Fatigue and underperformance in athletes: The overtraining syndrome. *British Journal of Sports Medicine, 32,* 107–110.

Durand-Bush, N., & Salmela, J.H. (2002). The development and maintenance of expert athletic performance: Perceptions of world and Olympic champions. *Journal of Applied Sport Psychology, 14,* 154–171.

Flynn, M.G. (1998). Future research needs and directions. In R.B. Kreider, A.C. Fry, & M.L. O'Toole (Eds.), *Overtraining in sport* (pp. 373–383). Champaign, IL: Human Kinetics.

Fry, R.W., Morton, A.R., & Keast, D. (1991). Overtraining in athletes: An update. *Sports Medicine, 12,* 32–65.

Gould, D., Dieffenbach, K., & Moffett, A. (2002). Psychological characteristics and their development in Olympic champions. *Journal of Applied Sport Psychology, 14,* 172–204.

Gould, D., Guinan, D., Greenleaf, C.A., Medbery, R., & Peterson, K. (1999). Factors affecting Olympic performance: Perceptions of athletes and coaches from more or less successful teams. *The Sport Psychologist, 13,* 371–394.

Gould, D., Jackson, S.A., & Finch, L.M. (1993). Sources of stress in national champion figure skaters. *Journal of Sport & Exercise Psychology, 15,* 134–159.

Gould, D., Tuffey, S., Udry, E., & Loehr, J. (1996). Burnout in competitive junior tennis players II: A qualitative psychological assessment. *The Sport Psychologist, 10,* 341–366.

Greenleaf, C., Gould, D., & Dieffenbach, K. (2001). Factors influencing Olympic performance: Interviews with Atlanta and Nagano U.S. Olympians. *Journal of Applied Sport Psychology, 13,* 154–184.

Gucciardi, D.F., Gordon, S., & Dimmock, J.A. (2008). Towards an understanding of mental toughness in Australian football. *Journal of Applied Sport Psychology, 20,* 261–281.

Hanin, Y.L. (2002). Individual optimal recovery in sport: An application of the IZOF model. In M. Kellmann (Ed.), *Enhancing recovery: Preventing underperformance in athletes* (pp. 199–218). Champaign, IL: Human Kinetics.

Hedelin, R., Kenttä, G., Wiklund, U., Bjerle, P., & Henriksson-Larsén, K. (2000). Short term overtraining: Effects on performance, circulatory responses, and heart rate variability. *Medicine & Science in Sports & Exercise, 32,* 1480–1484.

Hooper, S.L., & MacKinnon, L.T. (1995). Monitoring overtraining in athletes. *Sports Medicine, 20,* 321–327.

Jeukendrup, A.E., & Hesselink, M.K.C. (1994). Overtraining—What do lactate curves tell us? *British Journal of Sports Medicine, 28,* 239–240.

Kellmann, M. (2002). *Enhancing recovery: Preventing underperformance in athletes*. Champaign, IL: Human Kinetics.

Kellmann, M. (2010a). Preventing overtraining in athletes in high-intensity sports and stress/recovery monitoring. *Scandinavian Journal of Medicine and Science in Sports, 2,* 95–102.

Kellmann, M. (2010b). Overtraining and recovery. In S.J. Hanrahan & M.B. Andersen (Eds.), *Routledge handbook of applied sport psychology: A comprehensive guide for students and practitioners* (pp. 292–302). London, England: Routledge.

Kellmann, M., & Kallus, K.W. (2001). *Recovery-Stress Questionnaire for Athletes: User manual*. Champaign, IL: Human Kinetics.

Kenttä, G., & Hassmén, P. (1998). Overtraining and recovery: A conceptual model. *Sports Medicine, 26,* 1–16.

Kenttä, G., & Hassmén, P. (2002). Underrecovery and overtraining: A conceptual model. In M. Kellmann (Ed.), *Enhancing recovery: Preventing underperformance in athletes* (pp. 57–80). Champaign, IL: Human Kinetics.

Kenttä, G., Hassmén, P., & Raglin, J.S. (2001). Training practices and overtraining syndrome in Swedish age-group athletes. *International Journal of Sports Medicine, 22,* 460–465.

Kibler, B.W., & Chandler, T.J. (1998). Musculoskeletal and orthopaedic considerations. In R.B. Kreifer, A.C. Fry, & M.L. O'Toole (Eds.), *Overtraining in Sport* (pp. 169–190). Champaign, IL: Human Kinetics.

Krane, V., Greenleaf, C.A., & Snow, J. (1997). Reaching for gold and the price of glory: A motivational case study of an elite gymnast. *The Sport Psychologist, 11,* 53–71.

Kreider, R.B., Fry, A.C., & O'Toole, M.L. (1998). Overtraining in sport: Terms, definitions, and prevalence. In R.B. Kreider, A.C. Fry, & M.L. O'Toole (Eds.), *Overtraining in sport* (vii–ix). Champaign, IL: Human Kinetics.

Lehmann, M., Foster, C., Gastmann, U., Keizer, H.A., & Steinacker, J.M. (1999). Definitions, types, symptoms, findings, underlying mechanisms, and frequency of overtraining and overtraining syndrome. In M. Lehmann, C. Foster, U. Gastmann, H. Keizer, & J.M. Steinacker (Eds.), *Overload, performance incompetence, and regeneration in sport* (pp. 1–6). New York, NY: Plenum.

Mackinnon, L.T. (2000). Overtraining effects on immunity and performance in athletes. *Immunology and Cell Biology, 78,* 502–509.

Mallett, C.J., & Hanrahan, S.J. (2004). Elite athletes: Why does the 'fire' burn so brightly? *Psychology of Sport and Exercise, 5,* 183–200.

Martin, D.T., Andersen, M.B., & Gates, W. (2000). Using profile of mood states (POMS) to monitor high-intensity training in cyclists: Group versus case studies. *The Sport Psychologist, 14,* 138–156.

Maslach, C. (1982). *Burnout: The cost of caring*. New York, NY: Prentice Hall.

Matos, N.F., Winsley, R.J., & Williams, C.A. (2011). Prevalence of non-functional overreaching/overtraining in young English athletes. *Medicine & Science in Sports & Exercise, 43,* 1287–1294.

McNair, D.M., Lorr, M., & Droppleman, L.F. (1992). *POMS manual: Profile of Mood States*. San Diego, CA: Educational and Industrial Testing Service.

Meeusen, R., Duclos, M., Gleeson, M., Rietjens, G., Steinacker, J., & Urhausen, A. (2006). Prevention, diagnosis and treatment of overtraining syndrome. *European Journal of Sport Science, 6,* 1–14.

Morgan, W.P., Brown, D.R., Raglin, J.S., O'Connor, P.J., & Ellickson, K.A. (1987). Psychological monitoring of overtraining and staleness. *British Journal of \tab\Sports Medicine, 21,* 107–114.

Morgan, W.P., Costill, D.L., Flynn, M.G, Raglin, J.S., & O'Connor, P.J. (1988). Mood disturbance following increased training in swimmers. *Medicine & Science in Sports & Exercise, 20,* 408–414.

Nederhof, E., Zwerver, J., Brink, M., Meeusen, R., & Lemmink, K. (2008). Different diagnostic tools in nonfunctional overreaching. *International Journal of Sports Medicine, 29,* 590–597.

Purvis, D., Gonsalves, S., & Deuster, P.A. (2010). Physiological and psychological fatigue in extreme conditions: Overtraining and elite athletes. *Physical Medicine and Rehabilitation, 2,* 442–450.

Richardson, S.O. (2005). *Overtraining phenomena: Expert and athlete perspectives on pathogenic sport involvement*. Unpublished doctoral dissertation, Victoria University, Melbourne, Australia.

Richardson, S.O., Andersen, M.B., & Morris, T. (2008). *Overtraining athletes: Personal journeys in sport*. Champaign, IL: Human Kinetics.

Scanlan, T.K., Stein, G.L., & Ravizza, K. (1991). An in-depth study of former elite figure skaters: III. Sources of stress. *Journal of Sport & Exercise Psychology, 13,* 103–120.

Silva, J.M., III. (1990). An analysis of the training stress syndrome in competitive athletes. *Journal of Applied Sport Psychology, 2,* 5–20.

Smith, R.E. (1986). Toward a cognitive-affective model of athletic burnout. *Journal of Sport Psychology, 8,* 36–50.

Uusitalo, A.L., Huttunen, P., Hanin, Y., Uusitalo, A.J., & Rusko, H.K. (1998). Hormonal responses to endurance training and overtraining in female athletes. *Clinical Journal of Sport Medicine, 8,* 178–186.

Wiese-Bjornstal, D.M. (2010). Psychology and socioculture affect injury risk, response, and recovery in high-intensity athletes: A consensus statement. *Scandinavian Journal of Medicine & Science in Sports, 20,* 103–111.

Wrisberg, C.A., & Johnson, M.S. (2002). Quality of life. In M. Kellmann (Ed.), *Enhancing recovery: Preventing underperformance in athletes* (pp. 253–268). Champaign, IL: Human Kinetics.

CHAPTER 16

The Relationship Between Exercise and Eating Disorders

A Double-Edged Sword

Justine J. Reel

Historically, it has been controversial to incorporate exercise into eating disorder treatments because of the fear that any moderate to vigorous physical activity would become part of the problem and aggravate already distorted and compulsive exercise-related thoughts. In early documented cases of eating disorders in the late 1800s and early 1900s, practitioners described overactivity and referred to *hyperactivity* among clients with anorexia nervosa as both excessive and obsessive (Beumont, Arthur, Russell, & Touyz, 1994). The concern that high-frequency exercise behaviors would contribute to unhealthily low body weights and undermine weight restoration during eating disorder treatment led many early treatment providers to prescribe bed rest for their clients. Clinicians recognized that exercise could serve as a compensatory purging method geared toward changing one's body shape or burning calories that is symptomatic of an individual's eating disorder. Therefore, many helping professionals have been reluctant to introduce exercise to clients with eating disorders, with a few exceptions (e.g., Calogero & Pedrotty, 2004). Despite these concerns about the relationship between exercise and eating disorders, exercise can provide both physical and psychological benefits to clients who do not overdo physical activity. For the general population, physical activity has been associated with managing stress and anxiety (see Hays, 2002). Certain types of exercise may even prove to be therapeutic for decreasing depression and improving mood, self-confidence, and body image among clinical populations (e.g., Calogero & Pedrotty-Stump, 2010). Furthermore, eating disorder clinicians and researchers have observed that exercise can lead to decreased anxiety around meals, improved program compliance, increased weight gain, and lowered relapse risk, along with improved psychological well-being (Thien, Thomas, Markin, & Birmingham, 2000).

Because exercise can play both harmful and helpful roles for clients with eating disorders, exercise behaviors should be addressed within a comprehensive eating disorder treatment program (Waldron & Hatch, 2009). In this chapter, I discuss how to identify and address dysfunctional exercise behaviors while promoting healthful and mindful exercise during treatment and recovery. I outline recommendations for introducing exercise within treatment at various levels of care, with attention to movement being supervised, prescribed, and individualized. Then I argue for the need for psychoeducational groups and hands-on practice of enjoyable physical activity to challenge distorted thoughts and feelings about exercise (Calogero & Pedrotty, 2004). Finally, I present a case illustrating how dysfunctional exercise can be addressed in an outpatient setting.

Characteristics of Dysfunctional Exercise and Eating Disorders

Researchers disagree on what to call unhealthy exercise, and numerous terms exist to represent pathological relationships with exercise (Calogero & Pedrotty-Stump, 2010). The harmful roles that exercise can play have been labeled as activity anorexia, overexercise, exercise addiction, excessive exercise, exercise dependence, exercise abuse, and obligatory exercise (Calogero & Pedrotty-Stump, 2010). Generally, *excessive exercise* has referred to having an extremely high amount of activity relative to frequency, intensity, and duration that can result in increased risk of physical injury. *Compulsive exercise* captures the obligatory or obsessive quality of physical activity and rigid exercise routines that can appear as dependencies accompanied by compensatory goals (e.g., exercise to "purge" caloric intake, exercise to change body weight or shape; Meyer & Taranis, 2011; also, see chapter 17 in this book). Although both quantity and quality of exercise patterns are important, many researchers and clinicians have argued that dysfunctional exercise is largely tied to the client's mind-set (quality) surrounding exercise rather than the actual amount of physical activity (e.g., Calogero & Pedrotty-Stump, 2010). For example, in a recent study, Taranis and Meyer (2011) found that there was no correlation between the quantity of exercise and the level of disordered eating, suggesting that compulsive and compensatory features of exercise that resemble dependencies and addictions are more salient than the amount of exercise for identifying dysfunctional physical activity patterns.

De Coverley Veale (1987) coined the term *exercise dependence* to characterize the addictive-like features of feeling compelled to exercise. As chapter 17 covers in more detail, the term *exercise dependence* captures the potentially compulsive quality of physical activity and describes a negative mood state experienced in the absence of exercise, unlike previous terms (e.g., *runner's high*) that focus on feelings of euphoria associated with exercise. Exercise dependence can occur in the absence of an eating disorder (i.e., primary exercise dependence) or can represent purging behavior symptomatic of an eating disorder (i.e., secondary dependence; de Coverley Veale, 1987).

Hausenblas and Downs (2002) characterized exercise dependence by symptoms similar to substance dependence, including increased tolerance (e.g., a need to increase exercise amount to avoid guilt), withdrawal effects (e.g., experiencing symptoms such as anxiety and fatigue when unable to exercise), intention effects (e.g., exercise is often in larger amounts or over a longer period than was planned), lack of control (i.e., a persistent desire or unsuccessful effort to decrease or control exercise), time (i.e., a great amount of time is spent exercising), reductions in other activities (e.g., exercise is prioritized over social activities), and continuance (e.g., exercising despite being injured). Furthermore, people who exhibit exercise dependence feel unable to incorporate rest days into their workout routines. Dysfunctional exercise is often represented by rigid routines that select narrow physical activities that tend to burn more calories (e.g., running) than others (e.g., weight training). Additional psychological features of dysfunctional exercise include rapid mood swings, irritability, fatigue, anxiety, impaired concentration, and sleep disturbances (Hausenblas & Downs, 2002). The common theme for dysfunctional exercise among eating-disordered individuals is that exercise tends to be detrimental for eating disorder treatment and recovery (Calogero & Pedrotty-Stump, 2010).

Prevalence of Dysfunctional Exercise and Clinical Eating Disorders

Different definitions and labels have been used to identify and assess maladaptive exercise, but the prevalence of excessive exercise has been shown to be significantly higher among clinical eating-disordered populations than in the general population. Approximately 18% of university students reported compulsive exercise, with almost 2% of undergraduate students reporting both compulsive eating and exercise (Guidi et al., 2009) compared to the prevalence of excessive exercise that is estimated to range from 30% to 70% across clinical samples (Mond & Calogero, 2009). Even higher estimates of maladaptive exercise (i.e., 33–100%) have been reported among inpatient clients with eating disorders (Kiezebrink, Campbell, Mann, & Blundell, 2009).

The American Psychiatric Association identified clinical eating disorder categories in the pre-

Table 16.1　Eating Disorders and Their Characteristics From the DSM-V

Eating disorder diagnosis	Description of diagnosis for DSM-V (APA, 2013)
Anorexia nervosa	Restrictive eating behavior, negative body image
Bulimia nervosa	Binge episode followed by purging, negative body image
Binge eating disorder	Binge episode, lack of control, and feelings of distress

vious version of the *Diagnostic Statistical Manual of Mental Disorders* (DSM-IV-TR) as anorexia nervosa, bulimia nervosa, and eating disorder not otherwise specified (EDNOS; American Psychiatric Association, 2000). Anorexia nervosa was classified in the DSM-IV-TR to represent individuals who were severely underweight (with females experiencing amenorrhea) and severely restricted their food intake. In the most recent edition of the *Diagnostic Statistical Manual of Mental Disorders* (DSM-V; American Psychiatric Association, 2013) the word *refusal* has been removed from the anorexia nervosa diagnosis due to difficulties related to assessment. Also, amenorrhea (i.e., absence of at least three menstrual cycles) has been deleted from current criteria so that anorexia nervosa can be more inclusive of broader age groups (e.g., postmenopausal women) and male clients.

Bulimia nervosa diagnosis is ascribed to people who experience binge episodes followed with purging methods (e.g., vomiting, laxatives, excessive exercise; APA, 2013). Generally, these purging methods are used as a means to compensate high food intake. The term *exercise bulimia* has been used to refer to individuals who compulsively exercise after overeating. For the DSM-V, the frequency of behaviors has been changed from twice weekly to once a week to meet the clinical criteria for bulimia nervosa. This type of eating disorder can represent a vicious cycle of restricting, engaging in a binge episode (often triggered by an emotional event), and experiencing a compulsive desire to exercise after binging to rid themselves of guilt.

Until recently, the EDNOS diagnosis had often been applied when individuals exhibited eating disorder symptoms but did not fit the full criteria for anorexia nervosa or bulimia nervosa. EDNOS had also been assigned to people with binge eating disorder behaviors (i.e., binge eating episodes with

no purging symptoms), which is now included as a separate eating disorder diagnosis in the DSM-V (APA, 2013; Reel, 2013). In 2013 the American Psychiatric Association released the DSM-V criteria (see table 16.1) with some important changes for eating disorders. For example, the catch-all category of EDNOS was eliminated entirely from the clinical criteria. Furthermore, binge eating was added as a separate disorder. Binge eating disorder has been defined as repeated episodes of eating large quantities of food associated with feeling a lack of control related to how much food is consumed. The binge episode is followed by experiencing strong negative emotions such as guilt or embarrassment. Individuals must engage in binge episodes at least once a week over 3 months to be considered to meet the clinical criteria for binge eating disorder (APA, 2013). It is important to note the categorization changes for clinical eating disorders because research studies generally have used older criteria (i.e., DSM-IV; APA, 2000).

For example, the type of eating disorder diagnosis (i.e., anorexia nervosa, bulimia nervosa, EDNOS; APA, 2000) has been relevant in determining exercise prevalence in earlier studies. Specifically, people who were diagnosed with anorexia nervosa were more likely to abuse exercise than their counterparts who had bulimia (Penas-Lledo, Vas Leal, & Waller, 2002). For example, Grave, Calugi, and Marchesini (2008) found that excessive exercise prevalence among clients with clinical eating disorders was 45%, with excessive exercise lowest among clients with EDNOS diagnoses (32%) and highest among people with restricting-type anorexia nervosa (80%). Approximately 39% of clients with bulimia nervosa and 43% with binge/purging anorexia nervosa presented with excessive exercise (Grave et al., 2008). New research is needed to measure prevalence rates of excessive exercise among individuals with binge eating disorder.

Dysfunctional Exercise and Relapse Prevention

Relapse for people with eating disorders ranges from 22% to 51% across studies (Keel, Dorer, Franko, Jackson, & Herzog, 2005), and excessive exercise during treatment has been identified as one of the strongest predictors of relapse for eating disorders. For example, Carter, Blackmore, Sutandar-Pinnock, and Woodside (2004) determined that high-level exercise (i.e., 6 hours or more of intense exercise for weight control per week) in the first several months upon discharge was associated with a high probability of eating disorder relapse for both anorexia and bulimia nervosa. Thus, it is important to provide exposure to healthy physical activity, along with increasing awareness about an individual's dysfunctional disposition toward exercise to prevent relapse among eating disordered clients (Steinglass et al., 2011).

Assessment of Dysfunctional Exercise

Identifying both an individual's psychological dispositions and reasons for exercise can help practitioners understand whether a client has a dysfunctional relationship with exercise. Although numerous questionnaires (e.g., *Obligatory Exercise Scale*; Pasman & Thompson, 1988) have been used in research to evaluate excessive exercise, many of these self-report measures have been unidimensional, and they have not been able to distinguish between at-risk populations, nor have the authors of these scales operationally defined exercise dependence or dysfunctional exercise in a comprehensive manner. In contrast to earlier scales, Hausenblas and Downs (2002) developed the *Exercise Dependence Scale* (EDS) based on the previous DSM criteria (i.e., DSM-IV-TR) for substance dependence (APA, 2000) and modified for exercise. The EDS, a 29-item measure for dysfunctional exercise, covers the following criteria for exercise dependence: (a) narrow, stereotyped patterns of regular exercise once or more daily, (b) increased priority of exercise routines over other activities, (c) increased tolerance to the amount of exercise performed over the years, (d) presence of withdrawal symptoms (e.g., depressed mood) when not exercising, (e) relief or avoidance of withdrawal symptoms by further exercise, (f) subjective awareness of feeling compelled to exercise, and

(g) rapid reinstatement of the previous pattern of exercise and withdrawal symptoms after a period of abstinence (Hausenblas & Downs, 2002).

Clinical interviews have provided a useful tool for exploring an individual's relationship with exercise, in terms of both quantity and quality of physical activity (Reel, 2013). Although excessive exercise implies an amount of physical activity that is potentially pathogenic, it is just as important to assess an individual's motivation to exercise. For example, a client may reveal that permission to eat is contingent upon exercising that day. Conversely, someone who feels she has eaten too much, or consumed a "non-safe" food, may report feeling obligated to exercise in response to high caloric intake. It is also helpful to assess whether individuals exercise to escape negative affect or to improve their appearance (Mond & Calogero, 2009). In addition to exploring the feelings surrounding exercise, gathering specific information related to actual exercise behaviors may lead to treatment adjustments. For example, assessing the types of exercise that "count" as exercise can determine whether a client has a narrow definition of acceptable physical activities. Such information can be used to help with treatment planning. Furthermore, clients should be asked how much they vary their routines (e.g., type, frequency, and intensity of exercise) and whether they are comfortable exercising with other people (Reel & Voelker, 2013).

Exercise and Eating Disorder Treatment

Historically, individuals with anorexia nervosa who entered treatment were placed on bed rest, with all unnecessary movement restricted during their treatment; this closely resembled hospitalization. Beumont et al. (1994) introduced the first structured exercise program into eating disorder treatment using anaerobic exercise (e.g., resistance training) to avoid undermining weight restoration goals. The rationale for the inclusion of exercise was that distorted beliefs surrounding exercise should be addressed and challenged within treatment. The importance of incorporating exercise into treatment was beginning to be recognized with the realization that the elimination of unnecessary activity had been largely ineffective and unrealistic (Beumont et al., 1994). Furthermore, the benefits of exercise in regulating mood, improving body image, and decreasing anxiety have been well documented (e.g., Hays, 2002).

To address exercise issues within a treatment setting, clients who are medically cleared to exercise should engage in physical activity that is prescribed, supervised (to the extent possible within one's level of care), and individualized to their needs and preferences (Calogero & Pedrotty, 2004). Exercise education about healthy, mindful exercise with the opportunity to discuss conflicting motivations related to exercise should be integrated into comprehensive eating disorder treatment regardless of the level of care (i.e., inpatient, residential, partial hospitalization, intensive outpatient, outpatient) and the medical status of the client (Calogero & Pedrotty-Stump, 2010). Mindful exercise has been defined as listening to the body for cues about responses to exercise, and it can incorporate the use of a variety of senses (e.g., auditory, visual, olfactory). For example, a meditative walk to teach mindful exercise may help clients notice how their bodies are feeling throughout the walk, as well as the external environment (e.g., colors, sounds, smells). Clients can also be encouraged to notice kinesthetic senses, such as the heel striking the ground when walking. This approach of bringing clients into the moment is a novel way of reintroducing exercise to people who tend to be somewhat mindless during their compulsory routines (Reel & Miyairi, 2012). Exercisers who are mindless versus mindful are described as being *tuned out* during exercise sessions, which can result in less attention to pain and an increased potential for injury. Exercisers who are mindless rather than mindful also tend to use external cues (e.g., calories burned on display screen on cardio equipment) to determine the length and pace of their workouts (Reel & Voelker, 2013). Clients who have opportunities to practice exercise within treatment settings (e.g., yoga class as part of a residential program) should be afforded the time to process their feelings following exercise sessions to maximize progress in changing exercise attitudes and beliefs (Calogero & Pedrotty, 2004).

Exercise is not safe or suitable for some individuals in treatment, and it should be restricted to those clients who are medically cleared by a physician to participate in an exercise program (Beumont et al., 1994). Exercise that is provided within an inpatient or residential setting should be deliberately prescribed with specific functions (Tokumura, Yoshiba, Tanaka, Nanri & Watnabe, 2003). For example, clients who have been sedentary throughout treatment may be prescribed stretching to prevent or reduce back pain. Light lifting or resistance training can be useful for improving bone health. Types of exercise (e.g., yoga) that can promote mindfulness, relaxation, and enjoyment, while being modified to fit the desired intensity, can be introduced into an exercise program (Boudette, 2006; Dittman & Freedman, 2009). As previously mentioned, mindful movement can be practiced in meditative walking classes using instructor cues to encourage attention to present internal feelings and outside environments. Running generally should be avoided during initial stages of treatment due to high caloric demands, difficulties with varying the intensity, and the potential for injury (e.g., stress fractures). Individuals with bulimia nervosa or binge eating disorder, who may not have the caloric expenditure concerns associated with anorexia nervosa, have frequently used running as a punishment (and a purge) for overeating. Furthermore, some people with binge eating disorder have been referred to "obesity treatment" or "fat camps" where they are encouraged to exercise (e.g., run wind sprints) to the point of exhaustion. Given the negative role that exercise has played for many individuals with eating disorders, it is important to hit the reset button. People with disordered eating across the spectrum can benefit from exposure to different types of movement and varied approaches to exercising as they work to change their mind-set related to exercise. Generally, a treatment program should expose clients to a wide variety of movement patterns and types of exercise to deliver the message that many forms of activities count as exercise. Although some residential centers continue to link a client's ability to participate in exercise to treatment progression (e.g., meeting weight-restoration goals), Calogero and Pedrotty (2004) have warned that exercise should not be used as a treatment reward because sometimes exercise behaviors have been closely tied to eating patterns and moods for individuals with eating disorders. Instead, clients who are cleared to exercise should receive exercise prescriptions based on what will be helpful for their stages of treatment and recovery without undermining nutrition and weight-restoration goals (Calogero & Pedrotty-Stump, 2010).

Thien et al. (2000) introduced a graded exercise protocol (i.e., 7 levels) for follow-up outpatient clients with anorexia nervosa. The first two levels allow clients who are at 75% of ideal body weight (IBW) to only stretch, sit, and lie down. Beginning in the third level, some low-impact cardiovascular movement is added for clients at 80% IBW. Resistance training to build strength is recommended at level 5, when clients reach 90% IBW. The final level prescribes stretching, resistance strength training, and low-impact cardiorespiratory exercise three times a week for clients at 100% IBW.

Outpatient settings afford clients more independence than inpatient situations in relation to executing meal and exercise plans on their own. To prescribe and support exercise in an outpatient setting, the treatment team can include an exercise specialist who is knowledgeable about the specific needs and challenges associated with treating eating disorders. This specialist should work with the physician on the treatment team to prescribe exercise routines that emphasize quality over quantity (Reel & Voelker, 2013). The client should be encouraged to begin exercise gradually and introduce a variety of types of movement. Generally, yoga classes, resistance training, and other forms of stretching have been recommended to encourage mindful movement with motivations beyond appearance and calorie burning (Calogero & Pedrotty-Stump, 2010).

Supervised physical activity can be structured within a residential or inpatient setting. Nonetheless, activity should be monitored throughout the day. Researchers have recommended that all exercise and activity be structured (planned) and supervised by staff with exercise qualifications who can gauge intensity of exercise (Beumont et al., 1994). During exercise classes, the instructor can observe facial expressions to determine whether any clients are abusing exercise or becoming overly intense during the session. The exercise instructor should be trained to modify verbal cues as needed to fit with a group conscious of body image. For example, rather than reinforcing weight-loss and calorie-burning motives for exercise, the instructor should focus on enjoyment or health benefits (Reel, 2013). Some yoga postures may need to be modified to avoid competition within the group. Generally, I discourage mirrors in a treatment setting, but, if used, mirrors should serve as a guide for technique and form rather than as a way for clients to obsessively monitor weight changes and appearance.

It is not feasible to monitor the exercise behaviors of eating-disordered clients in an outpatient setting. Family members and significant others, however, can help support exercise plans so that clients do not engage in additional activities that lead to too much energy expenditure. Family members and friends may need to receive education that the exercise prescribed is actually helpful to treatment. Some personal trainers can help monitor exercise routines for outpatient clients, but few of these practitioners receive training in the needs of clients with eating disorders. A client may be encouraged to exercise with a friend who can help model varying levels of exercise intensity. The exercise buddy is particularly helpful for clients who engage in rigid exercise routines at consistently vigorous intensity levels. The treatment team should consider whether the client is able to continue organized sports and other activities that may have contributed to exercise abuse prior to admission to treatment.

In addition to being supervised and prescribed, exercise incorporated into eating disorder treatment should be individualized, like any other type of prescribed medication (Calogero & Pedrotty, 2004). For example, there may be exercise differences for clients with bulimia nervosa and binge eating disorder who may be able to engage in aerobic exercise sooner than those with anorexia nervosa who are still working on weight restoration. Additionally, client preferences may allow for certain modifications in the types of activities performed. Some clients may feel triggered (e.g., experience negative body image) by participating in yoga and may choose Nia (a type of exercise that promotes playful and empowering movement while incorporating dance and martial-art-like moves) or Zumba (dance exercise) instead. Although individualizing exercise plans may be less feasible due to staffing needs within a residential setting, clients should be provided with personalized exercise plans as they transition to outpatient settings (Calogero & Pedrotty-Stump, 2010). It is realistic to individualize treatment for clients in an outpatient setting based on exercise preferences, medical status, and exercise history. Moreover, an exercise counselor can help clients process their feelings surrounding exercise in sessions.

Types of Exercise

When clients are admitted for treatment, they should be screened for dysfunctional exercise, and it should be determined which (if any) activities they abused before they sought treatment. Clients should initially be prescribed new activities that are relatively low in aerobic demands (Beumont et al., 1994). Throughout treatment, clients should have the opportunity to practice many different types of exercise. Some of the more common forms of exercise available at eating disorder treatment centers include yoga, Nia, horseback riding, and stretching. Exercise options are expanding; depending on the geographical location, clients may be able to engage in water aerobics, hiking, or ice skating. Zumba, which has recently gained in popularity across the United States and Australia, shows much promise for eating disorder clients. Similar to dance, Zumba participants have the opportunity to embrace the music and learn steps and routines while moving in a low-impact fashion (Reel, 2013). Most Zumba, however, has high aerobic demands, and modifications in duration and speed might be needed for some individuals with disordered eating.

Yoga has been a popular addition to many inpatient and residential eating disorder programs due to its potential for relaxation and its links to mindfulness (see chapter 1 in this book). Research has found that participating in yoga can lead to decreased anxiety and depression as well as increased self-care and sense of well-being (Boudette, 2006). Specifically, yoga postures may help shift clients' awareness away from negative thoughts to breathing and clearing their minds

while heightening their sense of body awareness (Dittmann & Freedman, 2009). Researchers agree that more outcome research is needed to show the positive effects of yoga. Furthermore, certain types of yoga (e.g., power yoga, Bikram yoga) may be counterproductive due to their potential to be used as a form of purging (Boudette, 2006). Qualitative research, however, has demonstrated that clients can experience improvements in body satisfaction and disordered eating through practicing yoga (e.g., Dittman & Freedman, 2009).

Processing Feelings Surrounding Exercise

Calogero and Pedrotty (2004) emphasized the need to allow individuals with eating disorders to process feelings before, during, and after exercise sessions. Clients will likely experience a full range of emotions (e.g., mad, sad, glad) as they begin to engage in exercise. For example, clients may experience frustration in that they feel they cannot achieve a "good workout" with more moderate, less intense, and shorter bouts of movement than their previous exercise routines. Clients may also express anxiety related to not doing enough exercise to offset calories consumed in their meal plans. I find it to be extremely powerful when individuals process thoughts that occur during physical activity such as feeling compulsive or detached from their bodies or feeling joy associated with exercise. This debriefing or processing time can allow clients to challenge eating-disordered motives for exercise so that they can develop new patterns of physical activity to bring into recovery (Calogero & Pedrotty-Stump, 2010). The following case example represents a client, Donna, with disordered eating who is struggling with a dysfunctional relationship with exercise. Although Donna most closely fits the criteria for anorexia nervosa, the same approach is useful for individuals across the spectrum of eating disorders.

The Meaning of Movement: Donna's Story

Donna, a 27-year-old woman with anorexia nervosa, was referred to me by her outpatient eating disorder treatment team for an exercise consultation. Donna's primary therapist, a psychologist who has worked with her for several years, revealed to me that "Donna seems stuck." I learned that Donna would like to become pregnant, which is her self-reported primary source of motivation for recovery. Unfortunately, she has experienced menstrual disturbances for the past 5 years, and she severely restricts food. Her treatment team members, including a medical doctor and clinical psychologist, have confronted the incongruence between her goal and her medical status. Donna, however, continued to seek alternative methods for fertility (e.g., hormone injections). Despite Donna's motivation to have a child, she continued to engage in compulsive exercise with a lower-than-necessary dietary intake.

It is important to secure release of information for the treatment team members in the first session or even before I meet with clients like Donna. In Donna's case, I was able to secure a release to speak with her primary therapist prior to our session. When I met with Donna, I received her signature to speak with the other treatment providers on her team. Communication with treatment members is critical for presenting a unified support for treatment and recovery. I wanted treatment members to understand what was covered in my sessions with Donna and any exercise prescriptions provided during exercise sessions.

Interestingly, in my conversations with the primary therapist, I discovered that Donna had stopped seeing her dietitian, which may also serve as a red flag for Donna's level of motivation to recover from her eating disorder. I also wanted to explore dietary intake and the relationship to energy expenditure associated with exercise while leaving the medical side (e.g., pregnancy and fertility issues) to the doctors. During the first session with Donna, I wanted to conduct a careful and in-depth assessment while establishing rapport and trust. Gaining the release of information from Donna's other treatment providers in this session allowed me to gather information about the severity of the eating disorder, medical concerns and injuries, and medical clearance to exercise.

My role as an exercise counselor is unique within this outpatient setting, and it is not uncommon for a therapist or dietitian to send a client to me for an exercise plan. Ultimately, my consultations provide an assessment of quantity and quality of exercise, counseling related to feelings surrounding exercise, and the development of strategies to engage in mindful and healthy exercise. I appreciate that I am able to help a client with the exercise component of treatment rather than serve as the primary therapist on the treatment team. When I agree to serve as the primary therapist for a client who has an eating disorder, I commit to long-term treatment and understand that the relationship will likely include the need to provide additional support when the client is feeling emotionally vulnerable as well as the need to participate in hospitalizations in emergency situations.

Typically, I meet with my clients (i.e., clients who see a different primary therapist for general mental health issues) in a standard-looking therapy office. I requested that Donna wear athletic shoes and comfortable clothing for our first session. Donna was punctual. She glanced inside my office, furtively looking (I thought) for exercise equipment. I invited her to sit down in a chair opposite mine.

Justine (J): Did you find my office okay?

Donna (D): Yes, it was easy to find. (She pauses.) I'm just kind of wondering what I'm doing here. I've never been to an exercise consultation before.

J: Well, that's okay, and I think you'll find that our sessions are similar to the other appointments you have except that we will focus on movement and specifically your relationship with exercise. As your therapist may have explained to you, I see some clients to help them develop a positive and balanced approach to exercise the way that they are trying to do with food. I'm wondering if your dietitian has mentioned the term *intuitive eating*?

D: Yes. It means to eat when you are hungry and to stop when you are full. I'm still working on it because I worry I'll binge. It is a great concept but hard for me to actually execute.

J: Your worry is understandable. It takes a lot of trust to allow yourself to eat intuitively and listen to your physical cues for hunger and fullness rather than rules related to one's eating disorder that have become comfortable.

D: Exactly! Well, what do we do in here?

J: (I briefly pause.) Well, in here we will be working toward intuitive exercise, which is the parallel to [intuitive] eating—listening to your body, but focusing on moving for enjoyment and stopping when you feel pain or discomfort. The idea will be to become more mindful while exercising rather than just going through the motions.

D: Intuitive exercise sounds cool.

J: Yes, and do you remember hearing within the intuitive eating philosophy that there are no "good" and "bad" foods? Well, the same concept applies to exercise. All types of exercise count.

D: I'm pretty sure I don't do that. I have a certain set of exercises I do each day.

J: Tell me a little more about your daily exercises . . .

D: Basically, every morning I get up, go to the gym, lift weights, and run on the treadmill.

J: So, your exercise includes lifting and running?

D: Well, that and yoga. My therapist told me that I should vary it up a bit.

J: How often do you take yoga?

D: I go to a couple of classes a week. I don't really count that as part of my exercise, though, since it is not cardio.

J: Would you say that yoga gives you any other benefits?

D: I mean, yes. Yoga helps a lot with my flexibility. My hips get really tight, and I never stretch. I've been lucky to not experience a lot of injuries over the years. Yoga does also help with stress relief.

J: Yoga is a great relaxation strategy with flexibility benefits. I agree. And the intuitive exercise philosophy would support the idea that all exercise is good, but that different types of exercise have different positive qualities. What would you think of that concept?

D: I can see that for sure. That would be incredible and makes sense, but what will we *do* exactly in our sessions?

J: Today I'd like to get a chance to get to know you and better understand the meaning exercise has played for you throughout childhood, adolescence, and adult years. A goal would be to begin to develop a picture that represents what exercise means to you and how it relates to other areas of your life. Are there other goals we should add to the agenda for today?

D: My therapist suggested that I see you a year ago, but I wasn't ready to give up my exercise routine. I feel like the types of weightlifting sets I do really build my muscles and that if I stop doing as much that I will lose everything I have accomplished. Well, I thought I was improving for a while, but recently I lost 10 pounds without trying, and I have not had a period for several years. Everyone on my treatment team says I'm exercising too much. (She pauses.) I mean, if that's the case, I'll change it and do something different. But what I'm hoping is that you can give me an exercise plan so that I know exactly what to do and feel confident that I can still get the benefits I'm looking for. I should mention that exercise is therapy for me. I get really anxious, and exercising every morning helps me reduce my stress. I just want to be able to continue to exercise without jeopardizing my health or my baby's health when I get pregnant eventually.

This conversation with Donna reveals some common patterns related to exercise among eating-disordered clients. First, clients are often unsure about the purpose of the exercise consultation and many express concern that exercise will be taken away from them. To this end, many clients actively advocate the therapeutic effects of exercise (e.g., stress management, anxiety reduction, mood regulation) without discussing any drawbacks to their current exercise behaviors. Exercise consultations are not covered by insurance companies in my country (they are covered in other countries such as Australia through both national and private insurance plans), and they are different from personal training sessions at the gym. Although I am a licensed professional counselor who sees clients for eating disorder issues, in this role I focus primarily on helping to change the dysfunctional mind-set toward exercise, increase the diversity of movements, and modify rigid and ritualistic patterns around exercise. In the initial sessions, I typically confirm the positive psychological and physical benefits exercise can provide and try to alleviate concerns that I am anti-exercise.

Because it is common for clients to express skepticism about changing exercise behaviors and to indicate that they are visiting me because of concerned individuals (e.g., treatment team members, family members), I have to actively work to illuminate the damaging role that exercise is playing in their lives. For example, Donna clearly states having a paradoxical relationship with exercise. She recognizes that being unable to get pregnant is closely tied to her eating disorder and limited energy availability. Despite her desire to become pregnant, she feels compelled to exercise every morning, which leads to an increased caloric requirement. Exercise in Donna's case serves as both a powerful barrier to recovery from her eating disorder and a way to optimize her health. Therefore, it becomes important for me to

gently nudge Donna to see other options or exercise realities for her to be motivated for behavior change.

During my meeting with Donna, I conducted a clinical interview about eating disorder and exercise history. It is important to understand current and prior injuries as well as menstrual disturbances. My exercise assessments delved deeper into the quality and quantity of physical activity than a typical psychosocial assessment would so that I could identify Donna's self-reported strengths and challenges. I also wanted to explore Donna's support systems so that I could better understand if there are people who can help her break her rigid patterns of exercise. I learned that her husband goes to the gym with her early in the morning and does his own routine, but he can "eat whatever he wants and skip a workout if he chooses."

Usually, my exercise assessment in the outpatient setting relies entirely on self-reported responses from the client and on corroborative data from treatment providers and family members (with client consent). Therefore, I will sometimes do additional assessments, including fitness testing or objective measures of movement. Fitness testing can include flexibility (e.g., sit and reach test) and strength (e.g., push-ups) measurements. I usually am more interested in observing the *standard pace* for a client who abuses walking or running. Rather than relying on self-reported intensity, I will walk with clients around my building and ask them to set the pace. I will also observe body posture and study my client's focus. For example, while walking with Donna I will note if she is relaxed and conversational or if she is focused and zoned out in what I call *exercise abuse mode*.

If I still want more data, I can assign my clients to wear a pedometer or accelerometer, but I have to be cautious about the potential of such a device to trigger disordered thoughts and become another mechanism for tracking compulsive behaviors. Therefore, I use movement-monitoring devices judiciously and opt for accelerometers so that clients cannot see numbers (e.g., mileage, number of steps, estimated calories burned) or use pedometers that report only number of steps and mileage. Some researchers have attempted to seal the pedometer using tape or stickers, but doing so may be a problem for curious clients who want to gauge their progress.

Once I got a general idea of Donna's exercise history and current types of physical activities, I assigned her homework to maintain an exercise log for the week before our next session. I encouraged Donna to record all of her movement (including dog walks that Donna has dismissed as "necessary for my dog to get exercise, but not real exercise"). I also asked Donna to provide details about the types of weightlifting exercises, number of sets, and repetitions so that I can better conceptualize her strength-training regimen.

When Donna arrived to her second session, she indicated that she had e-mailed me her exercise log and stated, "Hopefully, you have had a chance to review it." I had read it, but I encouraged Donna to tell me in her own words about her week's exercise and to walk me through each day. Without being asked, Donna had also recorded her meals and accompanying caloric estimates. I learned about her weightlifting routine for Monday, which includes three to five sets of cable fly, tricep pull-downs, bench press, tricep extensions, decline fly, and a number of other exercises. I was struck by the similarity of Donna's routine to that of competitive bodybuilders.

J: Your workout routine shows expertise and weightlifting knowledge. As I reviewed your exercise log I wondered whether you are training for or have ever competed in any bodybuilding competitions?

D: In the past I thought about competing in bodybuilding competitions but I never have. I just got these exercises out of the Oxygen magazine.

J: What was it about these exercises that made you want to include them in your routine?

D: I really admire the way those women look. (She pulls out a photo of a female bodybuilder.) I want her arms.

J: What do her arms represent for you?

D: Strength and beauty. I think this image is healthier than anorexic models because it is not so thin.

J: So this picture is empowering for you?

D: Yes, absolutely. In the past, I only saw extremely skinny women as pretty.

J: So, it sounds like this image represents something beyond just "great arms." Is there any relationship to seeing these pictures as beautiful and your recovery?

D: Maybe so. I think so, actually. As I mentioned, I always thought thin was the only route to beauty and happiness. I see muscle as a way that women can actually have curves and not be skin and bones. I love that I see women in Oxygen magazine as gorgeous rather than the typical Cosmopolitan models.

J: Sounds like a victory. So, there is a part of being physical that represents a recovery voice for you. That is exciting. I'm trying to better understand what motivates you to exercise in addition to these photos. What would you say is your primary motivation for doing these routines?

D: The main reason I exercise is to look a particular way. I want to be muscular looking but lean too. I like how the models in Oxygen are not skinny but they look strong and beautiful.

J: Are there other motivations?

D: I exercise to reduce my anxiety. If I didn't exercise I think I'd be a lot more stressed out.

J: I'm interested to hear more about how exercise reduces your anxiety.

D: If I exercise in the morning I feel like I've accomplished something that day. The problem is that I have to get up at 5 a.m. to do my workout. I wish I could be more efficient with my workouts.

J: Ouch, that is early . . . What happens when you don't get up or get that workout in?

D: That has never happened. I force myself to get up no matter how tired I am.

J: You force yourself. That doesn't sound like it is always pleasant.

D: I'd say! It is early, but I know if I don't get the workout in I'll be stressed throughout the rest of the day.

J: Let me ask you this hypothetical question. If you could get the same benefits to reduce anxiety, what time would you want to get up?

D: No earlier than 8 a.m. for sure. In fact, I'd love to be able to say, "I'm going to sleep in today!" But I worry I would lose all of the benefits I've worked so hard for. (She goes silent.)

J: I hear you on sleeping in! But it sounds like you are also worried that a different routine may not do the trick! I wonder if you are expressing some fear in changing your routine despite a desire to be more efficient.

D: Yes, I feel like I have to get up and do it or else the whole day will fall apart.

J: What will happen?

D: Well, again I don't know because I've never slept in, but I think everything would just be thrown off. I told you about my anxiety, and I feel like my exercise keeps it in check. Knowing that I've done my routine allows me to have that assurance throughout the day.

J: I see. So, it sounds like this exercise is your "stress relief safety net," if you will?

D: Exactly.

J: Why don't you walk me through the rest of the day? It looks like you have more lines on your log.

D: Well, I included the dog walk like you told me to do, and on Monday we did our regular loop.

J: What did you think about writing down your walk?

D: Well, I never would have done this before. I thought it was exercise for Samuel, not me.

J: Well, sounds like you practiced some intuitive exercise concepts this week! How long does your loop take you and Samuel?

D: About 40 minutes.

J: Why do you think I encouraged you to include it in your log?

D: If I really admit it to myself, I know I am getting exercise when I walk Samuel even though I count it that these dog walks are for him.

J: Tell me more.

D: Samuel wouldn't mind if we went on a shorter walk and didn't go 40 minutes. That is me driving it.

J: What does that mean?

D: I would not feel comfortable giving up the dog walks.

J: Well, this sounds like some great insight. Even activities that are not part of your exercise routine are important to you.

Within the second session, I continued to focus on getting Donna to understand how all of these activities count toward her overall energy expenditure. Although I did not request that she track her caloric intake, Donna indicated that she was surprised at how tracking her exercise and food made her realize she was probably not getting nearly as much food as she needed. This realization offered me the opening to encourage Donna to see her dietician for some nutrition support and to coordinate her meal plan in accordance to her energy expenditure. At the end of the session, Donna expressed an impatience associated with not receiving a clear, tangible exercise plan from me. I supported her feelings of frustration in the moment. Given my desire to empower Donna in her exercise plan, I gently asked Donna to review her log and tell me what she thought the exercise plan should be, given her energy intake and treatment goals. She looked me straight in the eyes and said, "If it was someone else who was only eating 1,400 calories, I would tell them 'nothing.' They would not get any exercise. Of course, that is not an option for me." Donna's statement showed her strong insight and awareness of her own contradictions.

Because Donna was able to articulate her low dietary intake on her own, it opened the door to discussing her nutrition treatment. Donna admitted that she had not been attending nutrition sessions, and was not following her meal plan. Specifically, she showed me that she was particularly low on grains. When she asked me if I had any sport nutrition suggestions, I recommended that she see her dietitian. We agreed that we would revisit an exercise plan once she met with her dietitian.

Exercise consultations like this one with Donna can serve the purpose of getting a better handle on the amount of exercise and the feelings surrounding exercise. As indicated, exercise consultations can help with treatment compliance. Donna reinstated her weekly dietician sessions. Furthermore, exercise consultations offer the chance to educate eating-disordered clients about mindful exercise and intuitive exercise. In later sessions, I encouraged Donna to vary her exercise routines (e.g., types of movement, duration) and to be mindful about her emotions and how her body felt before, during, and after activities. Donna did show some difficulty identifying specific emotions because her exercise sessions prior to meeting with me were "mechanical," and often involved her denying any emotions or pain. However, with practice, Donna will become more attuned to her feelings associated with exercise.

After having Donna track her physical activity patterns and then recommending that she see her dietitian, I did not know when Donna would schedule to meet with me again. In 2 weeks, Donna booked an appointment and came back to see me. She was eating more than 1,400 calories, and she had introduced more grains into her diet. She informed me that she was also trying to be more efficient with her workouts.

D: I've cut my workout routine down to 45 minutes.

J: Wow, that is a drastic change from the last time I saw you.

D: Yes, I'm saving so much time that I can sleep in an extra hour.

J: That's a nice reward. What's the difference? How do you do it?

D: Well, basically I am combining some exercises and thinking about what I really need to do. I am reminded by your comment about my routine resembling a competitive bodybuilder. That made me think about what I am doing. I mean, yes, I want to look like a bodybuilder, but I can probably get some of the benefits without doing every little exercise.

When I work with clients who are struggling from dysfunctional exercise issues, we definitely focus on motivations for exercise. Learning that Donna still wants to look like a bodybuilder and that she is motivated by a certain aesthetic, remained in the back of my head as I worked with her. My philosophy is that I want to add to appearance as a motivation. I try to be realistic that appearance will likely serve as a form of motivation. It is my hope that when clients finish their treatment with me, they will have a much longer list of reasons why they exercise than they had previously. I also hope that the appearance motive for exercise will become much less important as clients are able to experience the other benefits (e.g., increased strength and coordination, decreased anxiety, improved mood) associated with exercise.

Conclusion

Exercise and eating disorders can present a double-edged sword. Although dysfunctional exercise has been associated with eating-disordered behaviors (e.g., purging), it is important to address distorted thoughts, feelings, desires, and unhelpful behaviors surrounding exercise while the client is in treatment to prevent relapse. Once a client is medically cleared to participate, exercise that is prescribed, supervised, individualized, and mindful should be encouraged as part of a comprehensive eating disorder treatment plan. It is important to include an exercise specialist in the multidisciplinary treatment team to help address exercise issues and to teach mindful movement.

References

American Psychiatric Association. (2000). *Diagnostic and statistical manual of mental disorders* (4th ed., Text Rev.). Washington, DC: Author.

American Psychiatric Association. (2013). *Diagnostic and statistical manual of mental disorders* (5th ed.). Washington, DC: Author.

Beumont, P.J.V., Arthur, B., Russell, J.D., & Touyz, S.W. (1994). Excessive physical activity in dieting disorder patients: Proposals for a supervised exercise program. *International Journal of Eating Disorders, 15,* 21–36.

Boudette, R. (2006). How can the practice of yoga be helpful in recovery from an eating disorder? *Eating Disorders, 14,* 167–170.

Calogero, R.M., & Pedrotty, K.N. (2004). The practice and process of healthy exercise: An investigation of the treatment of exercise abuse in women with eating disorders. *Eating Disorders, 12,* 273–291.

Calogero, R.M., & Pedrotty-Stump, K.N. (2010). Incorporating exercise into eating disorder treatment and recovery. In M. Maine, B.H. McGilley, & D. Bunnell (Eds.), *Treatment of eating disorders: Bridging the research to practice gap* (pp. 425–443). London, England: Elsevier.

Carter, J.C., Blackmore, E., Sutandar-Pinnock, K., & Woodside, D.B. (2004). Relapse in anorexia nervosa: A survival analysis. *Psychological Medicine, 34,* 671–679.

de Coverley Veale, D.M.W. (1987). Exercise dependence. *Addiction, 82,* 735–740.

Dittman, K.A., & Freedman, M.R. (2009). Body awareness, eating attitudes, and spiritual beliefs of women practicing yoga. *Eating Disorders, 17,* 273–292.

Grave, R.D., Calugi, S., & Marchesini, G. (2008). Compulsive exercise to control shape or weight in eating disorders: Prevalence, associated features, and treatment outcome. *Comprehensive Psychiatry, 49,* 346–352.

Guidi, J., Pender, M., Hollon, S.D., Zisook, S., Schwartz, F.H., Pedrelli, P., . . . Petersen, T.J. (2009). The prevalence of compulsive eating and exercise among college students: An exploratory study. *Psychiatry Research, 165,* 154–162.

Hausenblas, H.A., & Downs, D.S. (2002). How much is too much? The development and validation of the Exercise Dependence Scale. *Psychology and Health, 17,* 387–404.

Hays, K.F. (2002). *Move your body, tone your mood.* Oakland, CA: New Harbinger.

Keel, P.K., Dorer, D.J., Franko, D.L., Jackson, S.C., & Herzog, D.B. (2005). Postremission predictors of relapse in women with eating disorders. *American Journal of Psychiatry, 162,* 2263–2268.

Kiezebrink, K., Campbell, D., Mann, E., & Blundell, J. (2009). Similarities and differences between excessive exercising anorexia nervosa patients compared with DSM-IV defined anorexia nervosa subtypes. *Eating and Weight Disorders, 14,* e199–e204.

Meyer, C., & Taranis, L. (2011). Exercise in the eating disorders: Terms and definitions. *European Eating Disorders Review, 19,* 169–173.

Mond, J.M., & Calogero, R.M. (2009). Excessive exercise in eating disorder patients and in healthy women. *Australian and New Zealand Journal of Psychiatry, 43,* 227–234.

Pasman, L., & Thompson, J.K. (1988). Body image and eating disturbance in obligatory runners, obligatory weightlifters and sedentary individuals. *International Journal of Eating Disorders, 7,* 759–769.

Penas-Lledo, E., Vaz Leal, F.J., & Waller, G. (2002). Excessive exercise in anorexia nervosa and bulimia nervosa: Relation to eating characteristics and general psychopathology. *International Journal of Eating Disorders, 31,* 370–375.

Reel, J.J. (Ed.). (2013). *Eating disorders: An encyclopedia of causes, treatment, and prevention.* Santa Barbara, CA: ABC-CLIO Greenwood.

Reel, J.J., & Miyairi, M. (2012). The right 'dose' of activity: Health educators should promote mindful and intuitive exercise. *Journal of Community Medicine & Health Education, 2*(9), 1–2.

Reel, J.J., & Voelker, D. (2013). Exercise to the extreme? Identifying and addressing unhealthy exercise behaviors. *Athletic Insight, 15,* 301–314.

Steinglass, J.E., Sysko, R., Glasofer, D., Albano, A.M., Simpson, H.B., & Walsh, B.T. (2011). Rationale for the application of exposure and response prevention to the treatment of anorexia nervosa. *International Journal of Eating Disorders, 44,* 134–141.

Taranis, L., & Meyer, C. (2011). Associations between specific components of compulsive exercise and eating-disordered cognitions and behaviors among young women. *International Journal of Eating Disorders, 44,* 452–456.

Thien, V., Thomas, A., Markin, D., & Birmingham, C.L. (2000). Pilot study of a graded exercise program for the treatment of anorexia nervosa. *International Journal of Eating Disorders, 28,* 101–106.

Tokumura, M., Yoshiba, S., Tanaka, T., Nanri, S., & Watanabe, H. (2003). Prescribed exercise training improves exercise capacity of convalescent children and adolescents with anorexia nervosa. *European Journal of Pediatrics, 162,* 430–431.

Waldron, J.J., & Hatch, S.J. (2009). "I have to exercise to eat!" Body image and eating disorders in exercisers. In J.J Reel & K.A. Beals (Eds.), *The hidden faces of eating disorders and body image* (pp. 159–176). Reston, VA: AAHPERD/NAGWS.

CHAPTER 17

Exercise Dependence
Too Much of a Good Thing

Albert J. Petitpas, Britton W. Brewer, and Judy L. Van Raalte

The beneficial effects of regular physical activity on physical and psychological health are well documented (Herring, Puetz, O'Connor, & Dishman, 2012; Knöchel et al., 2012; Rimer et al., 2012; U.S. Department of Health and Human Services, 1996; Vogel et al., 2009). Despite these benefits, many individuals in industrialized societies lead sedentary lives and do not engage in physical activity sufficient for receiving its salubrious effects (e.g., Huy, Steindorf, Litaker, Thiel, & Diehm, 2011; Pleis, Lucas, & Ward, 2009). Some people, however, develop a strong exercise habit and partake in physical activity with such frequency and fervor that the dose–response curve turns downward. That is, increasing amounts of physical activity produce diminishing returns in terms of health. Physical activity that was once beneficial becomes detrimental. Such circumstances are within the realm of exercise dependence, a phenomenon in which people remain intensively involved in physical activity past the point at which benefits are obtained (de Coverley Veale, 1987).

Exercise Dependence

Known by terms such as *compulsive exercise, exercise addiction, negative addiction*, and *obligatory exercise*, exercise dependence has been observed for more than four decades (de Coverley Veale, 1987). In a groundbreaking study, Baekeland (1970) found that runners who regularly ran four or five days per week reported experiencing reduced psychological well-being (in the form of increased anxiety, nocturnal waking, and sexual tension) when deprived of exercise for a month. Notably, runners who habitually ran five or

six days per week elected not to participate in Baekeland's study in the first place!

Like the related, but conceptually distinct, phenomenon of overtraining (Kellman, 2010; Richardson, Andersen, & Morris, 2008), the number of terms used to refer to exercise dependence reflects the lack of definitional clarity on the topic. A key distinction has been made between individuals who are *committed* to exercise and those who are *dependent* on or *addicted* to exercise (Sachs, 1981; Szabo, 1995). Committed exercisers are motivated to exercise by extrinsic factors, view exercise as an important (but not the most important) activity in their lives, and experience only minor consequences when unable to exercise. Dependent or addicted exercisers, on the other hand, are motivated to exercise for intrinsic reasons; they consider exercise to be the most important thing in their lives and experience serious physical or emotional symptoms when unable to exercise (Sachs, 1981). Both groups might be expected to exercise excessively, but the persistence of the behavior and the adverse effects would be anticipated to be longer and more detrimental, respectively, among those classified as dependent or addicted (Szabo, 1995) than for individuals who are committed to exercise. Szabo, Frenkl, and Caputo (1997) and Warner and Griffiths (2006) provided evidence in support of the independence of the committed and dependent, or addicted, constructs.

Features

In an attempt to distinguish commitment to exercise from dependence on or addiction to exercise, researchers have drawn parallels between the characteristics of exercise dependence and the features of dependence and addiction. De Coverley Veale (1987) proposed diagnostic criteria for exercise dependence that mirrored those for psychoactive substance dependence in the then-forthcoming edition of the *Diagnostic and Statistical Manual of Mental Disorders* (3rd ed.; American Psychiatric Association, 1987). The principal criteria consisted of (a) a narrow, stereotyped pattern of regular, daily, scheduled exercise, (b) prioritization of exercise over other activities in one's life, (c) tolerance of exercise such that increasing amounts are required to achieve the same effects on the person, (d) emotional withdrawal symptoms if prevented from exercising, (e) relief of withdrawal symptoms upon resumption of exercise, (f) awareness or acknowledgement of a compulsive tendency toward exercise, and (g) rapid return to previous problematic behavior patterns if able to resume exercise. Griffiths (1996) identified similar features as applying not only to exercise, but to a variety of other behaviors as well (e.g., engaging in sexual activities, gambling, playing video games, using the Internet). Of particular note, features of exercise dependence identified consistently across the empirical literature include placing greater priority on exercise than on other important relationships and activities, continuing to exercise despite experiencing serious exercise-related physical health problems (e.g., injury, pain), and experiencing withdrawal symptoms (e.g., mood disturbance) when restricted from participation in physical activity (Hausenblas & Symons Downs, 2002a). Although frequently unheeded in research on exercise dependence, de Coverley Veale (1987) recommended that a distinction be made between primary exercise dependence, in which compulsive exercise and its effects are the central areas of concern, and secondary exercise dependence, in which the exercise issues are connected to a primary issue such as an eating disorder (e.g., anorexia nervosa, bulimia nervosa; see chapter 16 in this book).

Measurement

Reflecting the various conceptualizations of exercise dependence, several self-report inventories have been developed to assess the construct, including the Obligatory Exercise Questionnaire (Pasman & Thompson, 1988; Steffen & Brehm, 1999), the Exercise Dependence Questionnaire (Ogden, de Coverley Veale, & Summers, 1997), the Exercise Addiction Inventory (Terry, Szabo, & Griffiths, 2004), and the Exercise Dependence Scale (Hausenblas & Symons Downs, 2002b; Symons Downs, Hausenblas, & Nigg, 2004). Consistent with claims that the prevalence of exercise dependence in its primary form is rare (de Coverley Veale, 1987; Szabo, 2000), preliminary prevalence estimates in the 2% to 4% range among physically active college students have been obtained (Hausenblas & Symons Downs, 2002b; Terry et al., 2004).

Etiology

Although definitional and measurement issues have hampered investigations of the etiology of exercise dependence, several potential explanations for the phenomenon have been advanced. The personality traits explanation (Carron, Hausenblas, & Estabrooks, 2003) holds that exercise dependence is a behavioral manifestation of dysfunctional personality traits such as obsessive-compulsive tendencies, perfectionism, trait anxiety, and low self-esteem. In accordance with general addiction models, physiological explanations for exercise dependence have focused on pathways involving endogenous opioids (e.g., endorphins), catecholamines, and dopamine (Adams & Kirkby, 2002). A psychophysiologically based affect regulation explanation includes the hypothesis that people with exercise dependence become excessively drawn to exercise in an attempt to stave off the negative emotions they tend to experience due to frontal brain asymmetry (Gapin, Etnier, & Tucker, 2009). Definitive evidence has not been obtained for any of the explanations, and it is possible that multiple etiological factors contribute to the development of exercise dependence.

Recognizing the wide range of variables that could potentially predispose (or precipitate and perpetuate) athletes to exercise dependence, McNamara and McCabe (2012) proposed a biopsychosocial model to facilitate understanding of the condition. Long a staple framework for understanding phenomena in health psychology and psychopathology (Engel, 1977; 1980), a biopsychosocial approach to exercise dependence involves considering biological, psychological, and social contributions to the onset and maintenance of excessive exercise behaviors. Biopsychosocial models have been applied to several exercise-related issues such as injury (Brewer, Andersen, & Van Raalte, 2002), eating disorders, and the pursuit of muscularity (Ricciardelli & McCabe, 2004).

In their initial evaluation of the biopsychosocial model of exercise dependence, McNamara and McCabe (2012) examined one biological factor (i.e., body mass index [BMI]), two psychological factors (i.e., exercise beliefs and self-esteem), and three social factors (i.e., social support, coach and teammate pressures, and sociocultural influences) as predictors of exercise dependence in a sample of elite Australian athletes. Compared to the athletes categorized as not at risk for exercise dependence, the athletes identified as at risk reported lower levels of social support, greater BMI, and higher levels of maladaptive exercise beliefs and pressure from coaches, teammates, and other external agents to train hard, change their body shapes and sizes, improve their sport performances, and succeed in sport. McNamara and McCabe documented multiple mediational effects in the relationships between the biopsychosocial predictors and exercise dependence, suggesting that the predictors do not act independently on exercise dependence, but instead interact with each other in complex ways to influence risks for developing dependence. For example, the positive association between BMI and exercise dependence was strongly mediated by psychological and social factors.

Although McNamara and McCabe (2012) focused on a select group of predictor variables with a particular sample of athletes as participants, the implications of their research go beyond sport populations. Predictors of exercise dependence identified through the personality traits (Carron et al., 2003), addictions (Adams & Kirkby, 2002), and affect regulation (Gapin et al., 2009) approaches discussed previously can readily be integrated into the biopsychosocial model to facilitate understanding of the rich tapestry of influences underlying exercise dependence.

Treatment

Despite the substantial collection of empirical studies that have accumulated on exercise dependence over the past four decades, little research has focused on the treatment of the condition. Perhaps the earliest systematic treatment program for exercise dependence was the work of Morrow (1988), in which cognitive-behavioral interventions, along with positive reinforcements, were used to increase clients' coping skills as they gradually relinquished exercise time to other activities. Several self-help volumes are available (e.g., Kaminker, 1999; Powers & Thompson, 2007), but the treatment plans they contain are closely linked to eating disorder prevention efforts, and have not been evaluated empirically. Overall, guidance for intervening with people with exercise dependence is sorely limited, and it is clearly a topic that requires scientific attention.

In the absence of an existing framework for guiding treatment of individuals with exercise dependence, the biopsychosocial model McNamara and McCabe (2012) proposed for research purposes can serve an applied function as well. Considering exercise dependence to be the potential product of multiple interacting biological, psychological, and social factors offers an abundance of opportunities for assessments and interventions. A thorough evaluation of prospective etiological factors for particular clients may suggest specific courses of treatment. For example, the salience of biological influences may indicate the need for a treatment that produces biochemical changes similar to exercise, and can regularly be substituted for physical activity (e.g., massage). Or, when the exercise dependence seems driven by obsessive-compulsive personality characteristics, clients can be assisted to develop constructive exercise routines with the ritualistic properties they crave but without damaging features (e.g., doing a certain number of low-impact exercises in a particular order). Similarly, when the dependence seems tied more to reinforcement received for the social role of exerciser than to the exercise itself (Groves, Biscomb, Nevill, & Matheson, 2008), treatment can involve (a) ways of continuing to receive reinforcement for the exerciser role without engaging excessively in exercise or (b) development and valuation of other identities outside of being an exerciser.

The following case study highlights some issues that may arise when working with individuals showing exercise dependence. The practitioner (first author) uses a relationship-focused cognitive-behavioral approach to help the athlete gain insight into the advantages and disadvantages of his exercise behavior. A relationship-focused approach places particular emphasis on building rapport and creating a therapeutic alliance before addressing typical cognitive-behavioral issues such as self-defeating thinking patterns and avoidance behaviors. The practitioner endeavors to create an environment based on equality of power, and clients are viewed as the experts on themselves. Once this type of relationship is established, the practitioner assumes a collaborative rather than an instructive role typical of traditional cognitive-behavioral approaches. Stress inoculation training (Meichenbaum, 1985) was used as the cognitive-behavioral approach in the following case. This approach espouses the virtues of what Meichenbaum termed *learned resourcefulness*. In this approach, instead of providing clients with a set of strategies to help them avoid stressful situations, they learn skills that desensitize them to stressors and enable them to cope with stressful events directly.

The Case of Richard

Richard is a 40-year-old regional sales manager for a large North American company. In high school he was an outstanding basketball player, and he continued in the sport until 8 years ago. At that time, the "roughness of the city-league games" and his limited playing time led him to seek an alternative activity. Richard always had run to stay in shape for basketball, so it was not surprising when he decided to take running more seriously. Richard quickly progressed from 2 to 6 miles per run. He entered local road races. Eventually, basketball became no match for running competitions, trophies, positive feelings, and the "cardiovascular rush and endorphin highs" that running provided. He increased his training to 85 to 95 miles a week, often running twice a day. Richard also purchased a treadmill and an exercise bike for home. He said he had "never felt better."

At work, Richard was extremely successful. He became the youngest regional sales manager in the company's history. He said his social life "could be a little better," since he had broken up with his longtime girlfriend about a year ago, but his pattern had been long-term relationships (2–4 years) with highly successful women. "Unfortunately, things never seemed to work out," he commented.

Although Richard reported that his life was going well, he had become increasingly frustrated with the nagging foot, ankle, and back problems that he had experienced over the last 3 years. He often found himself struggling to run through the pain, only to find it worse the next day. On the advice of a friend, Richard decided that he could manage the injuries by cross-training for triathlons. He enrolled in an individualized fitness program, purchased an expensive racing bike, and took advanced swimming lessons. The resulting 3.5 to 5 hours of exercise per day put Richard in "the best shape of [his] life."

Unfortunately, the increased time commitment to working out began to affect Richard's work productivity, and his social life was "at an all-time low." On the advice of his fitness instructor, Richard decided to consult a sport psychologist at a sports medicine clinic for some life–work planning so he could "fit in everything."

AP: Hi, Richard. I'm Al Petitpas. Dave [fitness instructor] said you might be stopping in.

R: Yeah, I feel like I'm a little ADD.

AP: What do you mean?

R: I've got so much going on, I can't fit everything in.

AP: So you feel like you are always on the go.

R: Well, kind of.

AP: So help me understand what you mean.

R: Well, I'm managing the entire Northeast region sales force for Lone Star Enterprises [fictitious company name], 44 sales reps in all. On top of that, I'm a triathlete and I have to put in the training time, if I'm going to be able to compete.

AP: Sure sounds like that would keep you busy. What about family and social life?

R: Well, I'm single and there is nobody in my life right now. Family? (He takes a long pause.) I'm an only child, and my folks are out on the West coast. It's good that they're healthy because I don't get to see them except for maybe once or twice a year.

AP: So it sounds like work and being a triathlete are taking up all of your time.

R: Yeah.

AP: When you thought about coming in today, what were you hoping would happen?

R: I don't know. (He takes a long pause.) I thought you might be able to help me fit everything in so I don't feel so over-whelmed all the time.

AP: What's that like?

R: You know, sometimes it feels like I have so much on my plate that I am just spinning my wheels and don't seem to get anything done.

AP: Are you getting everything done?

R: Yeah . . . for the most part.

AP: You don't seem so sure.

R: Well, with everything going on, I don't feel on top of things like I used to.

AP: Where? At work, home, working out?

R: Mostly at work.

AP: What's going on?

R: I don't know. I used to get so pumped up watching our numbers go through the roof. Now, there are days when I would rather be working out than trying to mo-tivate my team or crunch all those sales figures.

AP: What do you think has happened?

R: Don't know.

AP: Any guesses?

R: (He takes a long pause.) Work just isn't as much fun.

AP: Is any place fun?

R: Working out.

AP: It almost sounds like work has become boring or unfulfilling.

R: Maybe so. (He pauses for about 45 seconds.)

Richard looked down and seemed to be thinking about my statement, so I remained silent and waited for him to look at me or give me a sign that he was ready to move forward with the discussion. During the silence, I sensed that Richard was ex-periencing some internal conflict, but he looked up at me and changed the subject. Although I be-lieved that he was experiencing a lot of stress at work, I thought it would be premature to confront him about his work situation at this point, and I chose to follow his lead. If rapport had been clearly established at this point in our interaction, I would have confronted Richard about his work sit-uation.

R: At least I have my workouts to keep me going.

AP: Dave mentioned that you have been fighting through some nagging injuries, but you are still hanging in there. You must really love it.

R: Yeah, I used to read about the runner's high. I get a lot of pleasure from a good workout or competition.

Unlike Richard, who stated he still enjoyed exercise, some individuals who are exercise dependent lose their enjoyment of working out. Similar to an alcoholic who needs to drink daily to maintain normal functioning, some people with exercise dependence may work out daily because it enables them to avoid anxiety or some other form of discomfort. "I work out because I need to, not because I want to" is how one exercise dependent person described his experience.

AP: So working through all the injuries is worth it.

R: Sure is.

AP: How do you do it?

R: What do you mean?

AP: Manage the pain and frustration.

R: Just keep gutting it out. (He smiles widely.)

AP: It almost looks like working through the pain is like a badge of courage for you. (I pause.) Has it ever been too bad?

R: Yes and no. A couple of years ago, I was logging 80 miles a week, but I think the constant pounding took its toll on my legs. So, I've switched to doing triathlons. The biking and swimming seem a little easier on my legs, and they keep me really fit.

AP: Just so I can get a sense of what it is like for you, what does a typical day look like?

R: Let's see. I get up early and go out for a quick run, 4 or 5 miles, take a shower, eat breakfast, and get to work by 7:30 or so. At noon, I head over to the Y and swim laps for an hour or so, sometimes more depending on the day. After work, I will go for a good bike ride, get some dinner, and finish up with some paperwork and then go to bed.

AP: Doesn't seem to leave you much time for anything else.

R: Guess not.

AP: You said you wanted to learn how to fit everything in. Besides work and working out, what else should we consider?

R: At this point, that's about all I can manage.

AP: Okay, then let's see if we can come up with some goals for our work together. You said you were having trouble fitting everything in. What is getting shortchanged?

R: Nothing.

AP: I'm confused, or maybe I just misunderstood your situation. So if you have enough time for working out and for work, what needs to be fit in?

R: (He pauses.) I don't know. Maybe it is just a feeling.

AP: Maybe, but when I hear you say that all you do is work and exercise, I wonder what you are doing for you.

R: Exercise! I love it and I can't imagine my life without working out.

AP: And is this why all the little injuries are so frustrating, because they can keep you from doing what you love?

R: I never thought of it that way, but maybe.

Listening to Richard, it seemed to be that working out served many positive functions for him. It gave him a source of competence and feelings of fitness, and it helped him avoid dealing directly with his frustrations at work and with his slumping social life. On the other hand, it appeared that Richard had increased his workouts to a point where overuse injuries and work decrements began to take a toll. At this point in our interaction, I feared that working out had become an avoidance behavior for Richard, allowing him to figuratively run away from his personal and work-related problems.

AP: I wonder what would happen if you were not able to work out.

R: That will never happen.

AP: I hope not, but I know of a couple of other athletes who thought the same way and then had a career-ending injury.

R: (He remains silent.)

AP: Maybe it would be helpful to get Dave involved so we can determine how much exercise would keep you in great shape without risking as many of those nagging injuries. As a sales guy, you are probably familiar with the business term *point of diminishing returns*. Well, the same principle applies in exercise; more is not always better. If you and Dave can work on an exercise plan, we can focus on balancing the other parts of your life so that you can fit everything in. What do you think?

R: It sounds okay.

AP: You don't seem too sure.

R: I want to do several triathlons a year and I know I have to push myself or I won't be competitive.

AP: Exactly. That's why I want you to work with Dave to come up with a plan to do the physical workouts smarter, not longer. I'll try to help you with some mental skills that can help you to perform at peak levels in competition. (I pause slightly.) What if you could get the same benefits without putting as much strain on your body?

R: That sounds great. (His nonverbal behavior suggests that he is skeptical.)

AP: It seems like there is a "but."

R: Well, yeah, what if it is not enough?

AP: If you want to work together, we can meet weekly to monitor how you feel about your workouts and competition performance. That way, if you are not getting the results you want, we can adjust your training. If you get injured again, or still feel you can't fit everything in, we will work on that. Does that sound like a plan?

R: Okay.

Although Richard seemed a little reluctant, he agreed to meet and work out a new exercise plan with Dave. My goal was to establish a working relationship with Richard and get his agreement on a plan of action. I was careful not to challenge the efficacy of exercise or directly confront his work decrements or interpersonal issues because I sensed that our working alliance was still fragile at this point. Over the next several weeks, we developed our working relationship and created a goal ladder to measure his progress toward his fitness goals and talked about how he might use the same strategy at work. During this process, Richard shared more information about his work and social situations.

Richard complied with the new exercise prescription for the first few weeks, but a decline in sales and several employee issues at work seemed to prompt him to avoid some of the stress by doing additional daily workouts. Eventually, the added exercise resulted in severe shin splints. At this point, I believed that our working relationship had developed to a point where I could be more direct.

AP: I hear that you are on the shelf for a while.

R: Yeah, shin splints, but I have increased my work at the pool. It takes longer than running, but it takes some of the pressure off my legs.

AP: One thing I noticed since we have been working together is that when stuff hits the fan at work, you up your workouts.

R: That's what I do.

AP: I know, but I have always believed that the more you avoid something, the more anxiety-provoking the situation becomes. Part of me is afraid that while the added workouts are giving you temporary relief from your work stress, the problems are not going away.

R: Maybe.

AP: Remember our agreement to find a point of diminishing returns. I know that working out feels good, but maybe too much leads to injury and keeps you from dealing with other stuff in your life.

R: (He takes a long pause.)

AP: So what do you think?

R: Maybe, but working out helps me get through all the crap.

AP: I know. (I pause.) Let's go back to the plan. Dave will help you come up with a new workout plan to take the pressure off your legs and I'll try to help you manage the work stuff.

R: Okay.

Richard and I continued to meet for several months. I introduced a stress-inoculation training (Meichenbaum, 1985) strategy to help him become more aware of the stress in his life and learn how to prepare for and address stressful situations more productively. Although I believe that he acquired some awareness of how exercise could be used as an avoidance behavior, he would still revert back to his old ways when pressure increased at work. During a subsequent meeting, I decided to confront Richard on this issue directly.

AP: Richard, you seem to be falling back to a pattern of increasing your workout time whenever stuff gets bad at work. I am afraid that if you keep avoiding work problems, things will only get worse.

R: I can handle it.

AP: How? By running away?

R: What do you want from me?

AP: I just want you to have enough time to be successful at work, at home, exercising, family, everything. (I pause.) I want you to listen to your body. Your body is telling you when you are doing too much. Listen to your mind when you want to avoid the pressure at work. Listen to your heart when it comes to family and relationships. (I pause.) Richard, I will support you in any way I can, but you have to do your part.

R: What if I don't?

AP: That's your decision, but I get a sense that things are closing in on you and you only feel safe when you are running or in the pool. Let me help you.

Richard and I continued to meet weekly for 3 months. During this time, our focus was primarily on work interactions. Richard was able to describe how he could manage various work situations during our sessions. However, when at the office, he would find excuses to avoid addressing personal and work-related problems with his sales team. As time went on, upper management placed more demands on Richard. Although he was doing a better job balancing the various parts of his life and devoting more time to his work responsibilities, he eventually lost his job. I continued to work with Richard during this transition. The suddenness of his work termination hit him by surprise and caused considerable anxiety and self-doubt to re-emerge. I was fearful that he would revert back to excessive exercise as a means to avoid situations, so I attempted to reframe the situation by suggesting that finding a new job was a job in itself and he would have to dedicate time and effort into the process of landing a new position. Over the next several months, I provided Richard with emotional support while following his progress with the outplacement counseling that his former company had provided. After about a year, Richard landed a job as a wilderness guide and moved to the Northwest.

During our last few sessions together, we spent considerable time discussing how our relationship had evolved and how he now viewed me as part of his support team. We talked about how he might need to develop a support team in his new location. Much to my surprise, he said he had already made contact with several old friends who had relocated to his new job location. We also reviewed the skills he had acquired and talked about how he might use them in some of the situations he was likely to face.

Overall, I believe that Richard had benefitted from our interactions. He attended every scheduled meeting. He understood that stress often resulted from a number of smaller incidents rather than a major issue. He could recognize the first physiological signs that stress was building within his body and he was able to use several techniques (e.g., diaphragmatic breathing) to cope with stressful situations. In the end, I was pleased that Richard found employment, but I worried that the new job might feed into his dependence and make it easier for him to avoid relationships. Richard had gained self-awareness and acquired several mental skills over the course of our interactions, but I believed he was still quite vulnerable and I recommended that he seek out the support and counsel of a professional in his new location. I provided Richard with names of several sport and clinical psychology practitioners whom I knew in his area, but learned that he had not contacted any of them. Exercise dependence, like any form of addiction, can become a lifelong struggle filled with occasional relapses. Individuals like Richard often benefit from ongoing counseling relationships that consist of periodic check-ins or booster sessions that extend the practitioner–client contact over a number of years. These sessions help to keep exercise-dependent individuals' awareness of how stress affects them on the front burner and remind them to use the mental skills they have acquired to face anxiety-provoking situations directly.

Conclusions

Scientific research on exercise dependence has been hampered by unclear definitions of the phenomenon. Nevertheless, there is some agreement that people who are exercise dependent are intensely involved in physical activity up to and then past the point at which benefits from exercise are obtained. Further, exercise-dependent people are likely to experience serious physical and emotional symptoms when they are unable to exercise. It has been hypothesized that exercise dependence is a result of personality factors, the psychophysiological (dis)regulation of affect, a combination of these, or other factors. Sociocultural factors (e.g., gender, nationality, race and ethnicity, socioeconomic status) may also influence how (and whether) exercise dependence is experienced and expressed. Treatment for exercise dependence has not been well studied, but therapeutic approaches from various theoretical backgrounds have been implemented. We presented a case study with a relationship-focused cognitive-behavioral approach to highlight the complexities of work with exercise-dependent clients. Familiarity with exercise dependence and treatment may help exercise and sport psychologists better serve the needs of the athletes and exercisers with whom they work.

References

Adams, J., & Kirkby, R.J. (2002). Excessive exercise as an addiction: A review. *Addiction Research and Theory, 10,* 415–437.

American Psychiatric Association. (1987). *Diagnostic and statistical manual of mental disorders* (3rd ed., Rev.). Washington, DC: Author.

Baekeland, F. (1970). Exercise deprivation: Sleep and psychological reactions. *Archives of General Psychiatry, 22,* 365–369.

Brewer, B.W., Andersen, M.B., & Van Raalte, J.L. (2002). Psychological aspects of sport injury rehabilitation: Toward a biopsychosocial approach. In D.L. Mostofsky & L.D. Zaichkowsky (Eds.), *Medical and psychological aspects of sport and exercise* (pp. 41–54). Morgantown, WV: Fitness Information Technology.

Carron, A.V., Hausenblas, A.H., & Estabrooks, P.A. (2003). *The psychology of physical activity.* New York, NY: McGraw-Hill.

de Coverley Veale, D.M.W. (1987). Exercise dependence. *British Journal of Addiction, 82,* 735–740.

Engel, G.L. (1977). The need for a new medical model: A challenge for biomedicine. *Science, 196,* 129–136.

Engel, G.L. (1980). The clinical application of the biopsychosocial model. *American Journal of Psychiatry, 137,* 535–544.

Gapin, J., Etnier, J.L., & Tucker, D. (2009). The relationship between frontal brain asymmetry and exercise addiction. *Journal of Psychophysiology, 23,* 135–142.

Griffiths, M.D. (1996). Behavioural addiction: An issue for everybody? *Journal of Workplace Learning, 8*(3), 19–25.

Groves, M., Biscomb, K., Nevill, A., & Matheson, H. (2008). Exercise dependence, self-esteem and identity reinforcement: A comparison of three universities in the United Kingdom. *Sport in Society, 11,* 59–73.

Hausenblas, H.A., & Symons Downs, D.S. (2002a). Exercise dependence: A systematic review. *Psychology of Sport and Exercise, 3,* 89–123.

Hausenblas, H.A., & Symons Downs, D. (2002b). How much is too much? The development and validation of the Exercise Dependence Scale. *Psychology & Health, 17,* 387–404.

Herring, M.P., Puetz, T.W., O'Connor, P.J., & Dishman, R.K. (2012). Effect of exercise training on depressive symptoms among patients with a chronic illness: A systematic review and meta-analysis of randomized controlled trials. *Archives of Internal Medicine, 172,* 101–111.

Huy, C.S., Steindorf, K., Litaker, D., Thiel, A., & Diehm, C. (2011). Physical activity in German adults: Types, settings and patterns of association by cardiovascular risk status. *European Journal of Sport Science, 11,* 375–385.

Kaminker, L. (1999). *Exercise addiction: When fitness becomes an obsession.* Center City, MN: Hazelden.

Kellmann, M. (2010). Overtraining and recovery. In S.J. Hanrahan & M.B. Andersen (Eds.), *Routledge handbook of applied sport psychology: A comprehensive guide for students and practitioners* (pp. 292–302). New York, NY: Routledge.

Knöchel, C., Oertel-Knöchel, V., O'Dwyer, L., Prvulovic, D., Alves, G., Kollmann, B., & Hampel, H. (2012). Cognitive and behavioural effects of physical exercise in psychiatric patients. *Progress in Neurobiology, 96,* 46–68.

McNamara, J., & McCabe, P. (2012). Striving for success or addiction? Exercise dependence among elite Australian athletes. *Journal of Sports Sciences, 30,* 755–766.

Meichenbaum, D. (1985). *Stress inoculation training.* Elmford, NY: Pergamon Press.

Morrow, J. (1988, October). *A cognitive-behavioral interaction for reducing exercise addiction.* Paper presented at the annual meeting of the Association for the Advancement of Applied Sport Psychology, Nashua, NH.

Ogden, J., de Coverley Veale, D., & Summers, Z. (1997). The development and validation of the Exercise Dependence Questionnaire. *Addiction Research, 5,* 343–356.

Pasman, L., & Thomson, J.K. (1988). Body image and eating disturbance in obligatory runners, obligatory weightlifters, and sedentary individuals. *International Journal of Eating Disorders, 7,* 759–769.

Pleis, J.R., Lucas, J.W., & Ward, B.W. (2009). Summary health statistics for U.S. adults: National Health Interview Survey, 2008. *Vital Health Statistics, 242,* 1–157.

Powers, P., & Thompson, R. (2007). *The exercise balance: What's too much, what's too little, and what's just right for you!* Carlsbad, CA: *Gürze.*

Ricciardelli, L.A., & McCabe, M.P. (2004). A biopsychosocial model of disordered eating and the pursuit of muscularity in adolescent boys. *Psychological Bulletin, 130,* 179–205.

Richardson, S.O., Andersen, M.B., & Morris, T. (2008). *Overtraining athletes: Personal journeys in sport.* Champaign, IL: Human Kinetics.

Rimer, J., Dwan, K., Lawlor, D.A., Greig, C.A., McMurdo, M., Morley, W., & Mead, G.E. (2012). Exercise for depression. *Cochrane Database of Systematic Reviews, 2012*(7). Available from http://onlinelibrary.wiley.com/store/10.1002/14651858.CD004366.pub5/asset/CD004366.pdf?v=1&t=hk37it9m

&s=8b56d5a4e18795371ed818ad0c061b5a76fcf4e
2

Sachs, M.L. (1981). Running addiction. In M. Sacks & M. Sachs (Eds.), *Psychology of running* (pp. 116–126). Champaign, IL: Human Kinetics.

Steffen, J.J., & Brehm, B.J. (1999). The dimensions of obligatory exercise. *Eating Disorders, 7,* 219–226.

Symons Downs, D., Hausenblas, H.A., & Nigg, C.R. (2004). Factorial validity and psychometric examination of the Exercise Dependence Scale-Revised. *Measurement in Physical Education and Exercise Science, 8,* 183–201.

Szabo, A. (1995). The impact of exercise deprivation on well-being of habitual exercisers. *Australian Journal of Science and Medicine in Sport, 27,* 68–75.

Szabo, A. (2000). Physical activity and psychological dysfunction. In S. Biddle, K. Fox, & S. Boutcher (Eds.), *Physical activity and psychological well-being* (pp. 130–153). London, England: Routledge.

Szabo, A., Frenkl, R., & Caputo, A. (1997). Relationships between addiction to running, commitment to running, and deprivation from running: A study on the internet. *European Yearbook of Sport Psychology, 1,* 130–147.

Terry, A., Szabo, A., & Griffiths, M. (2004). The Exercise Addiction Inventory: A new brief screening tool. *Addiction Research and Theory, 12,* 489–499.

U.S. Department of Health and Human Services. (1996). *Physical activity and health: A report of the Surgeon-General.* Atlanta, GA: U.S. Department of Health and Human Services, Centers for Disease Control and Prevention, National Center for Chronic Disease Prevention and Health Promotion.

Vogel, T., Brechat, P.H., Leprêtre, P.M., Kaltenbach, G., Berthel, M., & Lonsdorfer, J. (2009). Health benefits of physical activity in older patients: The evidence. *International Journal of Clinical Practice, 63,* 303–320.

Warner, R., & Griffiths, M.D. (2006). A qualitative thematic analysis of exercise addiction: An exploratory study. *International Journal of Mental Health and Addictions, 4,* 13–26.

Afterword

It is a pleasure to write this afterword for a sorely needed book in our field. *Doing Exercise Psychology* takes us beyond the content of traditional sport psychology books and into the realm of exercise and physical activity, areas where more people choose to engage in a variety of active behaviors than they do in sport. I use the word *choose* advisedly, because one of our main challenges as exercise psychologists is to get individuals to choose to participate in exercise or physical activity (or sport or other forms of human movement).

We are in the beginning of a great public health challenge—the sedentariness epidemic. Many would suggest we are dealing with an obesity epidemic. One look at people in the mall or on the beach indicates clearly that people are gaining weight and becoming overweight and obese at rates never seen before. Take a look at maps of obesity that the Centers for Disease Control has kept for the past 20 years or so. Scary stuff! But exercise epidemiologists would suggest that the increase in caloric intake doesn't explain the dramatic rise in overweight and obesity; there is more to the story.

That *more* is sedentariness. We are becoming more sedentary by the day because of two main factors. Our work lives, for many of us, have grown increasingly sedentary. The percentage of jobs requiring moderate to vigorous physical activity has decreased, and the percentage requiring work at a desk, perhaps on the computer or telephone, has increased. We have not done enough to inject physical activity into these more sedentary occupations (there are strategies that can be implemented, such as walking desks).

Our leisure lives have grown increasingly sedentary as well. Whereas before we might go outside and play, now many of us sit at our computers or televisions and use social media, play video games, or watch movies and television. This fairly dramatic decrease in activity leads directly to increasing weight.

The combination of increased caloric intake and decreased caloric expenditure leads directly to the "expansion" of America and the rest of the world in the dramatic increases in the past 20 years or so in overweight and obesity. Do we really need to give the Centers for Disease Control more to do in tracking weight across the nation (and perhaps the United Nations more globally)?

These issues are great public health challenges for us. How do we get people motivated to engage in physical activity and stick with it? I would like to think a Nobel Prize would await the person who unlocks the door of adherence so that we would live in a healthy world. Increasing exercise and physical activity will decrease our weight (assuming caloric intake is maintained at current levels) and, more important, will reduce the likelihood of various diseases such as cardiovascular problems and high blood pressure. These diseases are within our control, and we are called to action!

Doing Exercise Psychology will help in this quest. We start in the beginning: In chapter 1, Mannion and Andersen address exercise as well as therapeutic relationships. Many of our successful encounters with clients depend on the therapeutic relationship and the faith our clients have that adopting and maintaining exercise will help them physically and psychologically (the research is clear that it will). The authors start with mindfulness, a current buzzword for a concept psychologists have been using for decades that is now all the rage. That is good—living mindfully and behaving mindfully are to be desired. Martin and Peterson then talk about relationships in chapter 2. As David Yukelson of Penn State repeatedly says, "It's all about relationships." Sport and exercise scientists have a critical role in helping coaches and athletes succeed. The various parameters of how to be successful in this realm are explored insightfully in this chapter. Although it focuses on sport coaches, there are implications that can be taken for those working with exercise participants.

Hanrahan delves into cross-cultural issues within exercise psychology in chapter 3. This area is often neglected, yet critically important, in our field. We do not live within a United States or North American bubble; we have less than 10% of the world's population. Cultural implications of participation in exercise, especially for women, are vital to consider. One of my African-American female students raised a question in one of my classes the other day about African-American women and hair, and the challenges of maintaining hair the way many would like while still participating (or, alas, deciding not to) in exercise. The participation of Muslim women in physical activity is a challenge, especially in Muslim countries. To the degree that we work with individuals of other ethnicities, developing cultural competence is imperative.

Tony Morris, in chapter 4, eloquently discusses one of the great fears of regular exercisers—the possibility of physical inactivity. Although this anxiety would never cross the minds of most of us, it can (and does) sometimes happen. For exercise psychologists, inactivity seems especially incongruous and threatening to our identities. I am sure that many of us can relate to the concept of academic overtraining, and Tony's candor and self-disclosure are greatly appreciated. Having said that, the idea of practicing what you preach should be paramount for those of us within exercise psychology, not only in terms of self-care (as Morris discusses) but also in terms of being a role model for others. Some interesting theoretical approaches such as Anshel's (2008) disconnected values model might also aid in considering this personal perspective for each of us.

Dance is the subject of Hanrahan's chapter 5. We often forget how important dance is for many individuals, especially young women (starting in childhood and continuing through adolescence and adulthood). Men participate as well, but not to the same extent as women. And we also forget how vigorous dance can be in terms of physical activity. We should keep in mind that when we think of exercise and sport, we do really mean physical activity in its broadest sense. Unfortunately, *exercise* and *sport* are seen by some as negative terms. ("Exercise? You mean like running a marathon?") We just want people to be more physically active, whether it is sport, exercise, physical activity, or whatever you want to call it. Dance has all the wonderful physical and psychological benefits that can come from physical activity, but some dancers also face the challenges of such ac-

tivities, including eating disorders and overinvolvement (dependency).

Part II addresses the great challenge for us: changing behavior (from sedentariness to exercise and physical activity). Breckon provides some excellent insights in chapter 6 using the particularly effective intervention strategy of motivational interviewing (MI). He does a nice job of reviewing the basics of MI and the potential of MI as a helpful strategy for working with our clients. Carole's case study is helpful in identifying issues around both exercise and nutrition and the importance of using a decisional balance approach to address desires for behavior change in the first place. The Readiness Ruler tops out at a score of 10 with *trying*. Although this scaling seems suitable at initial stages of behavior change, we soon must think back to Yoda in *Star Wars*: "Do or do not. There is no try." As the case study indicates, we need to get to the doing—the action and adherence. We need to affirm the title of this book, *Doing Exercise Psychology*.

Taylor and Thompson address the challenges in changing multiple behaviors in chapter 7, focusing specifically on exercise adoption and smoking cessation. They identify some interesting connections and dynamics in the use of physical activity with smokers. As a strong antismoking advocate, I applaud this work and encourage any such approaches.

Chapter 8 provides a related multiple behavior connection as Martens and Smith examine exercise therapy and alcohol use. Alcohol has long had integral connections with sport, with professional sport especially used as a vehicle for advertising alcohol. Also, alcohol use and abuse is part of the culture of many sporting activities. There is a wide variety of approaches for addressing alcohol use and abuse. Alas, exercise is not often one of these approaches. The authors, however, make it clear that exercise should be considered as a possibility in the future, both in research and clinical practice.

Exercise for people with chronic conditions is explored in part III. Motl, Learmonth, and Klaren begin in chapter 9 with exercise and multiple sclerosis (MS). MS is an especially challenging neurological disorder, and most individuals with MS exercise little, if at all. This limited activity may be due to symptoms that create barriers to exercise, as well as in response to recommendations and feedback from others with MS or from those involved in treating MS. Research, however, has shown that exercise can be beneficial for many people with MS, and our challenge is to convey this message to both individuals with MS and to practitioners. Effective interventions will require knowledgeable practitioners in the exercise sciences, as well as exercise psychologists who can work effectively with this population.

Rogerson and Andersen in chapter 10 address the area of cardiovascular disease (CVD); exercise would logically be the primary intervention for preventing CVD in the first place and rehabilitating CVD in those who have developed it. If everyone behaved logically, we almost wouldn't need this book. People would adhere to programs of vigorous physical activity. Unfortunately, people don't always behave logically, but considering issues such as depression, self-efficacy, social support, perceptions, and knowledge may help us understand why individuals with CVD don't exercise more regularly. The authors identify many key negative perceptions about exercise, explore low motivation and depression, and offer suggestions for addressing these issues. Focusing on the facilitators of physical activity, as the authors note, is the path to travel.

Cancer presents a broad array of challenges, but patients can also benefit from the use of exercise, as Mustian, Sprod, Treviño, and Kamen point out in chapter 11. The authors use a key term—*biopsychosocial*—to emphasize the barriers to and benefits of exercise from biological, psychological, and social perspectives. I hope that someday we will have definitive evidence that exercise delays the onset of cancer or even prevents cancer from developing in the first place. For the moment, work on facilitating effective exercise interventions for individuals with cancer should play a central role in recovery.

Cameron and White address physical activity for individuals with chronic pain in chapter 12. As the authors note, pain plus exercise can be a catch-22; it is painful to engage in physical activity, yet physical activity may help alleviate chronic pain. Interventions must consider all three aspects: physiological aspects, the patients' psychological responses, and social factors.

Gaskin and Hanrahan examine exercise for individuals with disabilities in chapter 13. The psychosocial issues in exercise environments are critical in considering this population, and examining such issues through childhood, adolescence, young adulthood, middle adulthood, and older adulthood is helpful. People with disabilities often want to be as physically active as persons without disabilities (a case can be made that we are all temporarily able, just one misstep or injury from being temporarily, or even permanently, disabled). People with disabilities sometimes call those without disabilities TABs (temporarily able bodied) because people without disabilities at present are likely to experience some degree of disability at some point in their lives. Examining these parameters in people with both physical and mental disabilities is important. We must consider those with physical disabilities experienced later in life (perhaps as a result of accidents), wherein the individuals were sport and exercise participants before and wish to continue. Adaptive sport opportunities may be perfect for them. The greater challenge is to convince those who had no real-life experience with exercise and physical activity before acquiring a disability of the benefits that will come from participation.

Hays addresses, in chapter 14, the connections among exercise, depression, and anxiety. Although there is clearly a variety of treatment options for depression and anxiety, the literature, both research and applied, is clear that exercise can at the very least serve as an adjunct in such therapies. Some practitioners would advocate for a substantial role for exercise, but it is unlikely that exercise could really serve as the sole therapeutic intervention for someone with depression or anxiety. There may be a few individuals out there who are what we call *exercise evangelists*, who see exercise as the cure for all that ails us. Exercise and physical activity are not magic elixirs, but they are certainly key parts of holistic approaches to health and well-being. We can say that once individuals with depression or anxiety are in remission, a strong case can be made that exercise and physical activity can serve central roles in the management of affective states and prevent relapse. Hays also points out the importance of exercise for the therapist. One must be particularly cautious in engaging in exercise or physical activity with one's clients. The importance of self-care by therapists, however, almost demands exercise or physical activity as part of this self-care.

The final section of *Doing Exercise Psychology* is part IV, which examines the dark side of exercise. I see no chapters by Darth Vader, nor any about APEDS (appearance and performance enhancing drugs). Perhaps those will appear in *Doing Exercise Psychology: The Sequel*, but there is still enough here that is scary. Tibbert and Andersen's chapter 15 addresses overtraining in professional sport. The nuances of overreaching, overtraining, and overtraining syndrome (including staleness and burnout) are explored, with thoughtful commentary on the shades of gray among these various stages within training. This chapter seems more focused on sport than exercise per se, but, as the authors point out, there are lessons to be learned that one can apply within exercise. There are also connections to be made with chapter 17 on exercise dependence. The authors touch on the area of mental toughness, and this will be an area that experiences tremendous growth in the future. This concept and the related ones of resilience and grit (Duckworth & Quinn, 2009) are salient not only for athletes but also for exercisers. Anna-Marie Jaeschke has published some exciting work on mental toughness in ultra-distance runners (Jaeschke & Sachs, 2012), and work in this and related areas will help inform strategies for applying exercise psychology with endurance participants.

Reel examines eating disorders and exercise and chapter 16. The term *dysfunctional exercise* is helpful in considering ways in which individuals with eating disorders maladaptively use exercise. Reel also notes work by some professionals in the field, such as in Philadelphia at the Renfrew Center, in using exercise with inpatients (many with anorexia). Although seemingly counterintuitive, especially if one thinks only of persons with anorexia engaging in excessive exercise, the idea is to teach such individuals to use exercise in a healthy manner. Ideally, once these individuals return to the outside world, they will continue to exercise, but in a healthy (functional) manner. The

concept of mindful exercise (as opposed to mindless exercise) connects nicely with the current interest in mindfulness within psychology in general and in exercise and sport psychology in particular.

Last, but certainly not least, one of my favorite topics, exercise dependence, is the topic of the Petitpas, Brewer, and Van Raalte chapter. The authors provide a brief but helpful overview of various aspects of exercise dependence, as well as an insightful case study with Richard. Readers may be interested in pursuing connections between exercise dependence and athletic or exerciser identity, as well as connecting with work on exercise schemata by Deborah Kendzierski (1994). The potentially fine line between adherence to a regular program of vigorous exercise or physical activity and exercise dependence is one that bears examining in further detail. William Glasser (1976) talked about the concept of positive addiction, with exercise and meditation being positive even if one becomes "addicted" to them. One can suggest that, by definition, something cannot be both positive and addicting, but the key is finding that line for each individual where exercise remains an important but considered aspect of one's existence, as opposed to a controlling factor in one's life, depriving one of the ability to make other choices.

I enjoyed reading *Doing Exercise Psychology*. It is filled with insightful information, engaging case studies, and critical areas to review and consider. I am sure you, the reader, will find this excellent volume enjoyable as well. There is always nitpicking that one can do, but I have avoided doing so; picking nits is a fruitless exercise, and readers can find their own nits if they wish. The gestalt of *Doing Exercise Psychology* is worth the perusal, and this book also serves as a fine starting (or continuing) point for research and application. There is a great challenge ahead of us. As Buzz Lightyear from the *Toy Story* films would say, exercise and sport psychologists must go to infinity and beyond!

Michael L. Sachs

References

Anshel, M. (2008). The disconnected values model: Intervention strategies for health behavior change. *Journal of Clinical Sport Psychology, 2,* 357–380.

Duckworth, A.L., & Quinn, P.D. (2009). Development and validation of the Short Grit Scale (Grit-S). *Journal of Personality Assessment, 91,* 166–174.

Glasser, W. (1976). *Positive addiction.* New York, NY: Harper & Row.

Jaeschke, A-M., & Sachs, M.L. (2012). 100,000 miles closer to a definition of mental toughness. *Marathon & Beyond, 16*(5), 44–67.

Kendzierski, D. (1994). Schema theory: An information processing focus. In R.K. Dishman (Ed.), *Advances in exercise adherence* (pp. 137–159). Champaign, IL: Human Kinetics.

Index

Note: The italicized *f* and *t* following page numbers refer to figures and tables, respectively.

About the Editors

Mark B. Andersen, PhD, is an adjunct professor at Halmstad University in Sweden. He lives in Australia and collaborates intercontinentally with his Swedish colleagues in the areas of research, training, and supervision in applied sport and exercise psychology.

Andersen is a registered psychologist in Australia and is licensed to practice psychology in the United States. He is the former editor of the Professional Practice section of the international journal *The Sport Psychologist*. He has published seven books, two monographs, and more than 170 refereed journal articles and book chapters. He has made more than 100 national and international conference presentations, including 15 invited keynote addresses on four continents. He received his doctorate from the University of Arizona in 1988 and immigrated to Australia in 1994.

Stephanie J. Hanrahan, PhD, is an associate professor holding a joint appointment with the Schools of Human Movement Studies and Psychology at The University of Queensland, where she has worked since 1990. She was a UQ Teaching Excellence Award winner in 1997 and is the co-author or co-editor of nine books, including *Biophysical Foundations of Human Movement* published in 2013. Her work also appears in articles, book chapters, and conference papers. She is a registered psychologist in Australia and a certified consultant with the Association for Applied Sport Psychology. She has run applied workshops in more than 10 countries. She completed her doctorate at the University of Western Australia in the area of attributional style in sport.

About the Contributors

Jeff Breckon, PhD, is a reader in exercise psychology at the Centre for Sport and Exercise Science at Sheffield Hallam University in England and is a chartered sport and exercise psychologist with the British Psychological Society (BPS). His research interests include the use of motivational interviewing (MI) to promote behavior change as a preventative and rehabilitative approach, and he also does research into treatment fidelity and methods of assessing practitioner competence. In recent years, he has developed interventions applying MI and cognitive-behavioral approaches (as integrative therapies) to promote the initiation and maintenance of health behavior change. He has worked with clinical populations since 1993, when he learned that many interventions are limited at engaging patients in their own behavior change. From this point, he trained in MI; he became a member of the Motivational Interviewing Network of Trainers (MINT) in 2000, and he was trained by Professor Bill Miller and Professor Steve Rollnick. He delivered the international Training New Trainers program in Barcelona (June 2009) and Krakow (October 2013), and he chaired the trainers conference in Sheffield (2011). He has published and presented extensively on the use of MI in physical activity settings, and has been a reviewer for over 20 journals and three funding councils.

Britton W. Brewer, PhD, is a professor of psychology at Springfield College in Springfield, Massachusetts, where he teaches undergraduate and graduate psychology courses and conducts research on psychological aspects of sport injury and self-identity in sport. He is a certified consultant, Association for Applied Sport Psychology, and is a fellow of the American Psychological Association and the Association for Applied Sport Psychology. He currently serves on the editorial boards of the *Applied Research in Coaching and Athletics Annual*, the *International Journal of Sports Science and Coaching*, the *Journal of Sport & Exercise Psychology*, *Physical Therapy in Sport*, *The* *Open Journal of Rehabilitation*, and *The Sport Psychologist*.

Melainie (Lainie) Cameron, PhD, is an exercise physiologist and osteopath living in Brisbane. Her current appointment is as associate professor in clinical exercise physiology at the University of the Sunshine Coast in Queensland, Australia. She is passionate about the authentic integration of scientific evidence into clinical practice, and enjoys guiding students in refining the art of combined application of research data, clients' preferences, and practitioners' experience to serving clients' needs. In particular, she values case studies and clinical tales as educational tools. Rheumatology (arthritis care) is her prime area of clinical interest, although she works with clients across the range of musculoskeletal and chronic, complex health conditions. Her research covers two main areas: systematic reviews of non-drug (complementary medicines, manual therapies, exercise) interventions in rheumatology, and the professional development and clinical supervision of allied health practitioners.

Cadeyrn J. Gaskin, PhD, is the principal researcher at Gaskin Research, a Melbourne-based business providing research services to the government, health care, university, and sport sectors across Australia. With a strong human rights focus underpinning much of his work, his main areas of research interest are: (a) physical activity, social inclusion, and chronic health conditions, and (b) reducing and eliminating the use of restrictive practices (restraint, seclusion) within health care organizations and disability services. He also teaches in the postgraduate exercise rehabilitation programs of two universities. Away from his job, he practices what he preaches and works out at the gym several times per week. He also sails competitively in the Hansa Class, and has won titles at state and national levels.

Kate F. Hays, PhD, CPsych, offers sport, performance, and clinical psychology in Toronto,

Canada, through her consulting practice, The Performing Edge, as well as in a sports medicine clinic. Prior to her work in Canada, she practiced in New Hampshire for 25 years. Dr. Hays has authored five books on sport psychology, the mental benefits of physical activity, and performance psychology, as well as numerous articles and book chapters on these subjects. She has taught courses and workshops on these topics as well, internationally, to aspiring colleagues and the general public. Active in psychology and sport psychology governance, Dr. Hays is a fellow of the American Psychological Association (APA) and a fellow and certified consultant of the Association for Applied Sport Psychology (AASP). She is a past president of APA's Division of Exercise & Sport Psychology.

Charles Kamen, PhD, is an assistant professor (research) in the Department of Surgery at the University of Rochester Medical Center in Rochester, New York. His training background is in clinical psychology. His program of research focuses on behavioral interventions aimed at reducing psychological distress, improving quality of life, and addressing health disparities in diverse groups of cancer patients and survivors. Specifically, he is examining disparities affecting lesbian, gay, bisexual, and transgender (LGBT) cancer survivors and their care partners, and is delivering a tailored exercise intervention to this underserved group to address their psychological needs. His research on health disparities and interventions has led to over 25 peer-reviewed publications and book chapters and over a dozen national awards.

Robert M. Kaplan, PhD, joined the National Institutes of Health (NIH) as associate director for behavioral and social sciences and director of the Office of Behavioral and Social Sciences Research (OBSSR) in February of 2011. Prior to working for government, Kaplan was distinguished professor of health services at UCLA and distinguished professor of medicine at the UCLA David Geffen School of Medicine, where he was PI of the California Comparative Effectiveness and Outcomes Improvement Center. He led the UCLA/RAND health services training program and the UCLA/RAND CDC Prevention Research Center.

He was chair of the Department of Health Services from 2004 to 2009. From 1997 to 2004, he was professor and chair of the Department of Family and Preventive Medicine at the University of California, San Diego. He is a past president of several organizations, including the American Psychological Association Division of Health Psychology, Section J of the American Association for the Advancement of Science (Pacific), the International Society for Quality of Life Research, the Society for Behavioral Medicine, and the Academy of Behavioral Medicine Research. He is a past chair of the Behavioral Science Council of the American Thoracic Society. Dr. Kaplan is a former editor in chief of two academic journals: *Health Psychology* and the *Annals of Behavioral Medicine*. He is the author, co-author, or editor of more than 18 books and over 500 articles and book chapters. His work has been cited in more than 25,000 papers, and the ISI includes him in the listing of the most cited authors in his field (defined as above the 99.5th percentile). In 2005, he was elected to the Institute of Medicine of the National Academies of Sciences.

Rachel E. Klaren, BS, is a graduate student and research assistant in the Department of Kinesiology and Community Health at the University of Illinois at Urbana-Champaign. She received her bachelor's of science degree in integrative physiology from the University of Iowa. Rachel has been involved in multiple sclerosis (MS) research for two years, and has published and presented in the areas of physical activity and exercise in persons with MS. Her research areas of interest include physical activity interventions and exercise programs for the MS population and the specific biochemical mechanisms by which physical activity and exercise affect the central nervous system in persons with MS and other neurodegenerative diseases.

Yvonne C. Learmonth, PhD, is a postdoctoral research associate in the Department of Kinesiology and Community Health at the University of Illinois at Urbana-Champaign. She is a licensed physiotherapist (Health and Care Professions Council), and has previously held appointments in the Scottish National Health Service and in competitive sport. She obtained her doctorate in rehabilitation from the University of Glasgow, and she has been involved in MS research for over five years. She has published and presented internationally in the areas of physical activity and exercise for individuals with MS. Dr. Learmonth is passionate about understanding rehabilitation strategies to improve the health and quality of life of individuals with MS. To that end, her current research interests include physical activity and exercise strategies for those with disabilities and accurate measurement in rehabilitation practice, as well as establishing the impact of exercise on MS disease progression and encouraging physical activity and exercise prescription and education in health care.

Joe Mannion, MS, is grateful to make contributions to the performances and lives of clients of diverse backgrounds, from athletes to entrepreneurs, in his consulting practice, AllWorld Performance, LLC. He strives to embrace a scientist–practitioner model, and has published and presented at international conferences on a variety of topics, including mindfulness, neuroscience, Iraqi sport, professional practice, and pedagogy. He is currently a doctoral student in the clinical psychology program at Pepperdine University in Los Angeles, California. He was previously an adjunct instructor at Fontbonne University and Logan College in St. Louis, Missouri. Joe received his master's degree in sport psychology from Georgia Southern University and spent an additional year of graduate training, supervision, and surfing at Victoria University in Melbourne, Australia. He still struggles with separation anxiety from the Land Down Under. In his athletic past, he was competitive at the national level in Olympic-style tae kwon do and has participated in marathons and triathlons. He is keen to connect and may be found on LinkedIn, Twitter, and other platforms.

Matthew P. Martens, PhD, is a professor in the Department of Educational, School, and Counseling Psychology, and he is the division executive director in the College of Education at the University of Missouri–Columbia. He received his master's degree in sport psychology from the University of North Carolina and his doctoral degree in counseling psychology from the University of Missouri. His primary research interests are in the area of health psychology. In his most recent work, he has examined brief interventions for alcohol or other drug use, gambling, and the usefulness of physical activity in addressing such problems. He has been the principal or co-investigator on several federally and foundation-funded grants addressing these issues. When not focusing on his academic interests or administrative responsibilities, Dr. Martens enjoys trying to keep up with his two young daughters, seeking out delicious craft beer (not with his daughters), and golfing (sometimes all at the same time).

David T. Martin, PhD, received his BS degree in zoology from the College of Idaho, his MS degree in exercise physiology from Northern Michigan University, and his PhD in physiology from the University of Wyoming. Prior to his doctoral studies, David worked as a research assistant at the United States Olympic Training Center in Colorado Springs, Colorado. His master's research focused on stability of the "anaerobic threshold" training intensity, and his doctoral research centered on better understanding peaking, tapering, and overtraining in cyclists. David is currently a senior sports scientist working within the Department of Physiology at the Australian Institute of Sport in Canberra, and he is also the national sport science coordinator for Cycling Australia. As a sport scientist, David has provided support for Australian cycling teams in the lead-ups to the 1996, 2000, 2004, 2008, and 2012 Olympic Games. David has written more than 90 peer-reviewed publications and 8 book chapters, and he contributes articles to popular cycling magazines. As an advisor to Olympic coaches and athletes, David is interested in training environments that inspire excellence and in methodologies that reveal human potential.

Tony Morris, PhD, is a professor of sport, exercise, and health psychology at the Institute of Sport, Exercise, and Active Living (ISEAL), College of Sport and Exercise Science, at Victoria University in Melbourne, Australia. He has published 13 books, 45 book chapters, and around 200 refereed papers; has been associated with more than 150 research projects; and has graduated 37 PhD students. Tony has been a registered psychologist in the UK and Australia for nearly 40 years. He was inaugural chair of the College of Sport Psychologists in the Australian Psychological Society (APS), the first sport psychologist to be awarded fellowship of the APS, and the first to be given the APS Award of Distinction. He has been treasurer of the International Society of Sport Psychology (ISSP), and chair of the organizing committee for the 11th ISSP World Congress of Sport Psychology. He was president of the Asian South Pacific Association of Sport Psychology (ASPASP) for 14 years.

Robert W. Motl, PhD, is an associate professor in the Department of Kinesiology and Community Health at the University of Illinois at Urbana-Champaign. Professor Motl has systematically developed a research agenda over the past decade that focuses on physical activity and its measurement, predictors, and consequences in persons with neurological diseases, particularly multiple sclerosis (MS). For example, Professor Motl has generated a body of research on the validity of common physical activity measures in persons with MS. He has also conducted foundational research on quantifying differences in physical activity, particularly rates of moderate to vigorous physical activity, in MS versus nondiseased controls. These two lines of research have provided the basis for examining the outcomes of physical activity in individuals with MS, resulting in prominent papers on beneficial changes in cognition, depression, fatigue, walking disability, and quality of life. Professor Motl has undertaken research on social-cognitive predictors of physical activity that has informed the design and delivery of behavioral interventions for increasing physical activity in individuals with MS. This research has been supported by grants from the National Institutes of Health, National MS Society, and industry sponsors.

Karen M. Mustian, PhD, is an associate professor of surgery, radiation oncology, and public health sciences at the University of Rochester Medical Center in Rochester, New York. She is director of the PEAK Human Performance Clinical Research Laboratory and deputy director of the University of Rochester Cancer Center, National Cancer Institute Community Clinical Oncology Program Research Base. She is an international leader in the fields of cancer control and survivorship, exercise oncology, behavioral oncology, exercise physiology, exercise psychology, and integrative medicine. Dr. Mustian's research focuses on developing novel treatments for mitigating the toxicities and side effects stemming from cancer and its treatments, and her work is frequently featured in major lay press media including ABC, CBS, NBC, the Associated Press, and the *New York Times*. Dr. Mustian has been awarded $27 million dollars in grant funding, and has authored over 80 articles and book chapters. Her work has been honored with more than 37 distinguished research awards from groups such as the American Society of Clinical Oncology, the Multinational Society of Supportive Care in Cancer, the American Society of Preventive Oncology, and the Society of Behavioral Medicine.

Kirsten Peterson, PhD, works for the Australian Institute of Sport (AIS) as head of the AIS Performance Psychology Discipline. In this role, she oversees a team of five psychologists and coordinates sport psychology service provision for national sport teams across Australia. She also delivers direct psychological service to selected national squads. She previously worked as a member of the United States Olympic Committee's sport psychology staff in Colorado Springs, providing counseling and performance enhancement services to Olympic and Paralympic athletes and coaches. Dr. Peterson has been part of the American and Australian team staff, providing services for seven Olympic Games. She is a licensed (United States) and registered (Australia) psychologist, a former president of the American Psychological Association (APA) Division 47 (Sport and Exercise Psychology), a certified consultant through the Association of Applied Sport Psychology (AASP), as well as an APA Division 47 and AASP fellow.

Albert J. Petitpas, EdD, is a professor in the Psychology Department at Springfield College, Massachusetts, where he directs the college's Center for Youth Development and Research. The primary mission of the Center is to provide consulting services to organizations that use sport and physical activity as vehicles to help young people acquire important life skills and prepare for the future. He is a fellow and certified consultant of the Association of Applied Sport Psychology and a fellow of the American Psychological Association's Division of Exercise and Sport Psychology. He has provided consulting services to a wide range of sport organizations, including the Ladies Professional Golf Association, the U.S. Ski Jumping and Nordic Combined Teams, the United States Olympic Committee, the New England Blizzard of the American Basketball Association, the National Basketball Association, and the Montreal Alouettes.

Justine J. Reel, PhD, LCMHC, CC-AASP, is the author of *Eating Disorders: An Encyclopedia of Causes, Treatment, and Prevention* and *The Hidden Faces of Eating Disorders and Body Image*. Her third book, *Working Out? The Psychology of Sport and Exercise*, will be released in 2015. She is the associate dean of research and innovation and professor in the College of Health and Human Services at the University of North Carolina at Wilmington. She was previously on faculty for 13 years at the University of Utah. She completed her doctoral work at the University of North Carolina at Greensboro. She is currently a licensed professional counselor and an Association of Applied Sport Psychology certified consultant. She has treated clients with disordered eating in outpatient, partial hospitalization, inpatient, and residential levels of care and has provided sport psychology services to collegiate, Olympic, and youth athletes. She was named a fellow for the research consortium of the former American Alliance for Health, Physical Education, Recreation, and Dance (AAHPERD), now SHAPE America. She is a founding board member of the Utah chapter of the International Association of Eating Disorders Professionals Foundation (IAEDP) and the founder and director of SPEAK (Students Promoting Eating Disorder Awareness and Knowledge). For her community contributions related to eating disorder outreach, she was honored with the Beacons of Excellence Award. She has published over 65 articles in peer-reviewed journals, and she serves on editorial boards for the *Journal of Clinical Sport Psychology; Sport, Exercise, and Performance Psychology; Eating Disorders: Prevention and Treatment*; and *Women in Sport and Physical Activity Journal.*

Michelle Rogerson, PhD, is a research fellow and exercise psychologist who has been working at the Heart Research Centre in Melbourne for the past 6 years. Her research interests include physical activity, sedentary behavior, and mental health for people with chronic illness, as well as upskilling health professionals working in these areas with people with chronic illness. As a registered psychologist, she has worked in private practice, particularly with clients with chronic illness who wish to enhance their health through increased physical activity. Michelle has previously taught undergraduate and postgraduate students in exercise psychology, and she runs various workshops for clients and health professionals in maintaining physical activity. She has published and presented in the areas of exercise psychology, behavior change, and chronic illness. She is very passionate about physical activity and exercise and likes to practice what she preaches by keeping fit herself, walking regularly, playing tennis, going to the gym, and attending Pilates and yoga classes. She is also a proud mother, and enjoys keeping fit with her children.

Michael L. Sachs, PhD, is a professor in the Department of Kinesiology at Temple University in Philadelphia, Pennsylvania. He received his doctoral degree in sport psychology from Florida State University, a master's degree in general-experimental psychology from Hollins College (Virginia), a second master's degree in counseling psychology from Loyola University (Maryland), and his bachelor's degree in psychology from Union College (New York). Dr. Sachs is associate editor of *Psychology of Running* (Sacks & Sachs, 1981), and co-editor of *Running as Therapy: An Integrated Approach* (Sachs & Buffone, 1984). He also co-wrote *The Total Sports Experience for Kids: A Parents' Guide to Success in Youth Sports* (Fine & Sachs, 1987). His research interests focus on exercise psychology, particularly motivation and adherence, excusercise, exercise addiction, and the psychology of running. Dr. Sachs is a charter member and fellow of the Association for Applied Sport Psychology (AASP) and a certified consultant for the AASP. He also served as AASP's president (1991–1992). He is a past president of Division 47 (Exercise and Sport Psychology) of the American Psychological Association. He enjoys exercising, particularly running, swimming, shoveling snow, and reading (i.e., brain exercise).

Ashley E. Smith, PhD, is a postdoctoral fellow at the Harry S. Truman Memorial Veterans' Hospital in Columbia, Missouri. She received her doctoral degree in counseling psychology from the University of Missouri–Columbia. She has worked with Dr. Matthew Martens on several grant-funded research projects and has published and presented in the areas of substance abuse, behavioral economics, and health psychology. Clinically, Dr. Smith has worked with several populations, and she is currently conducting trauma-focused treatment with U.S. veterans.

Lisa K. Sprod, PhD, MPH, is an assistant professor in the School of Health and Applied Human Sciences within the College of Health and Human Services at the University of North Carolina at Wilmington. She received her PhD in exercise science from the University of Northern Colorado and completed her MPH and postdoctoral fellowship at the University of Rochester Medical School. She is a certified cancer exercise trainer through the American College of Sports Medicine, and her research focuses on reducing the side effects of cancer treatment through exercise interventions. Her passion for exercise began as a competitive basketball player, but she has since competed in long-distance and more recently ultradistance events with the hope of inspiring others to push themselves beyond their self-imposed limits.

Adrian H. Taylor, PhD, is a professor in health service research at Plymouth University Peninsula Schools of Medicine and Dentistry. He worked in the field of exercise and health psychology at three UK universities from 1989 to 2013, after completing his PhD at the University of Toronto. From 2003 to 2006, he was co-editor in chief of the journal *Psychology of Sport & Exercise,* and then became the founding co-editor in chief (with Professor Guy Faulkner) of the interdisciplinary journal *Mental Health and Physical Activity,* now in its 7th year. For over 10 years, he has contributed to an evidence base for how single sessions of physical activity (compared with sedentary behavior) influence affect and mood, and self-regulation of smoking, snacking, and alcohol use, based on self-reported urges, fMRI and cue reactivity, and eye-tracking and dot-probe tasks (to assess attentional bias). This experimental work has been used to inform novel behavior-change interventions (evaluated within randomized controlled trials, using mixed methods) to facilitate the treatment of depression, support disadvantaged smokers to reduce and quit smoking, and tackle simultaneous multiple-behavior change. He is also co-author of a Cochrane Review and several other systematic reviews. He has received over £3.5 million as principal investigator or coprincipal investigator for related work and has authored over 100 journal articles and book chapters. In his spare time, he runs about 15 miles a week as a competitor in orienteering and socializing with hash house harriers, and cycles 20 to 30 miles a week.

Stephanie J. Tibbert, PhD, is a recent sport psychology graduate of the College of Sport and Exercise Science and the Institute of Sport, Exercise, and Active Living at Victoria University, Melbourne. Previously, she completed an exercise psychology master's degree at the University of Glasgow. She currently lectures in sport, exercise, and rehabilitation psychology at Victoria University and Australian Catholic University in Melbourne. Her current research interests include understanding the mental toughness culture in elite sport, overtraining, relationships in sport, and examining strategies to enhance sport cultures to improve young athletes' experiences in elite sport. Her work on the cultural foundations of mental toughness has helped move this area of research into new territories. Previous research interests include investigating the psychological outcomes of exercise, specifically reviewing optimal modalities and dosages. Dr. Tibbert has two young boys who encourage her research interests in stress reduction and relaxation techniques.

Tom P. Thompson, MSc, is a research fellow within the health service research group at Plymouth University Peninsula Schools of Medicine and Dentistry, UK. After graduating from Loughborough University, he spent several years as a youth and social worker before returning to further study at the University of Exeter, where he is now finishing his PhD. Having worked on several large research trials investigating the effects of physical activity and lifestyle on mental health and addictions (both in intervention delivery and clinical trial management), he continues his primary interest in working with socially disadvantaged and low socioeconomic status groups in continuing efforts to address health inequalities in the UK. He has published and presented nationally and internationally in domains covering intervention and trial design for disadvantaged groups; process evaluation of interventions; the psychology of behavior change; and the roles of physical activity in addressing addiction (specifically nicotine addiction) and supporting mental health. If he can find time in between trying to better his golf handicap or fishing the coasts of southwest England, he will continue his mixed-methods research on physical activity and mental health among disadvantaged and marginalized groups well in to the future.

Lara A. Treviño, PhD, MPH, earned her doctoral degree in experimental and health psychology from the University of Texas at Arlington in 2011. Following her doctoral education, Dr. Treviño accepted an R25 National Cancer Institute postdoctoral fellowship at the University of Rochester Medical Center in Rochester, New York. During her time there, she developed a multisite pilot study to evaluate the effects of a multimodality intervention to promote smoking cessation in cancer survivors who had completed treatment at the University of Rochester or the Roswell Park Cancer Institute in Buffalo, New York. As part of her fellowship, she also completed her master of public

health degree. She is currently a clinical guidance metrician with Humana Insurance, and identifies members who would most benefit from health behavior change programs.

Judy L. Van Raalte, PhD, is a professor of psychology and director of the athletic counseling master's program at Springfield College in Springfield, Massachusetts. Dr. Van Raalte's research interests include self-talk, the professional practice of sport psychology, body issues, and athletic injury. She is co-editor of *Exploring Sport and Exercise Psychology* (now in its third edition), and is executive producer of 18 sport psychology videos. She is listed in the United States Olympic Committee Sport Psychology Registry and is a certified consultant with the Association of Applied Sport Psychology.

Janelle White is based in Sydney and is passionate about life in general. She had the privilege of being a torchbearer for the Beijing Olympics (2008) for her accomplishments in Ironman, ultra-marathons, and endurance events and for using her passion for these events to inspire others to achieve previously inconceivable goals. This energy, of course, naturally extends to her career, where she holds qualifications in education, science, and paramedicine. She is currently a PhD candidate at the University of the Sunshine Coast in Queensland, Australia. Her research focus for her PhD is chronic pain and its management in the community, in particular using the multiple perspectives of three key stakeholders, the person with chronic pain, the paramedic, and the general practitioner. She is a senior lecturer at the University of Tasmania, School of Medicine (Sydney campus), and she works on-road with the New South Wales (NSW) Ambulance Service as a paramedic specialist in extended care. Janelle is also the director of projects for the Australian Resuscitation Council (NSW), and she extends her research interests into the area of resuscitation. This allows her the incredible opportunity to explore two very different ends of the spectrum of health care.

You'll find
other outstanding
exercise psychology resources at

www.HumanKinetics.com

In the U.S. call

1-800-747-4457

Australia	08 8372 0999
Canada	1-800-465-7301
Europe	+44 (0) 113 255 5665
New Zealand	0800 222 062

HUMAN KINETICS
The Information Leader in Physical Activity & Health
P.O. Box 5076 • Champaign, IL 61825-5076 USA